Keys to Teaching Grammar to English Language Learners

A Practical Handbook

KEITH S. FOLSE, Ph.D.
University of Central Florida

Foreword by BETTY S. AZAR

Ann Arbor
University of Michigan Press

DEDICATION

This book is dedicated to the memory of Dr. Olga Pustovalova, who was a visiting Fulbright Scholar in our MATESOL program at the University of Central Florida in spring 2007. Her home campus was Metropolitan Institute for the Humanities in Moscow, where she was Professor of Linguistics.

I had the great pleasure of working with Olga during her time at UCF. Olga was a very vibrant and intelligent person, a very good scholar, and a fellow linguist. Her main research area was cross-cultural issues, and her main motive in coming to our university and area was to gather data for a book on American culture that she could then use with her students in Russia. I still remember a Saturday in February when my partner and I drove Olga around all day to see American garage sales, a drive-thru car wash, a Sonic® burger restaurant, and even a trailer park. All of these pieces of Americana fascinated her, and she took numerous photos and talked non-stop about her book project.

In March 2007, Olga and I flew to Seattle to attend the International TESOL conference. Instead of just attending a few sessions, Olga—ever enthusiastic—signed up for multiple certificate courses and spent her time attending workshops every day. It was on the return flight from Seattle that she first felt ill. Shortly thereafter, medical tests indicated cancer. She remained in Orlando for a few more months before returning to Russia in September 2007. Unfortunately, she passed away shortly afterward at the much too young age of 34. She was buried near Sochi, her hometown on the Black Sea, which she talked about so much while she was here in the U.S.

Although it was not part of her Fulbright duties, Olga attended my graduate TEFL class every Monday night without fail. She gave numerous presentations about Russian culture to groups in our area.

Because of the obvious love and dedication that Olga had for her English education, she reminded me of many of the students who come through our own MATESOL program, brimming with excitement about teaching either here or in a foreign country. For this reason, I dedicate this book to the memory of Dr. Olga Pustovalova. I also pledge to use portions of the royalties from this book to finance an annual fellowship in her honor for a TESOL student at the University of Central Florida.

Copyright © by the University of Michigan 2009
All rights reserved
Published in the United States of America
The University of Michigan Press
Manufactured in the United States of America

♾ Printed on acid-free paper

ISBN-13: 978-0-472-03220-4

2015   2014   6   5

FOREWORD

Were you surprised one day to find yourself teaching ESL? I think that happens to many of us. Certainly I got into ESL by pure serendipity. It was 1965, and I was in my first year of teaching freshman composition in the English Department at Iowa State University. One morning between classes, I was with a colleague who taught the only ESL course offered at the university at that time. As she and I were walking down the hall of the classroom building, we ran into the head of the English Department. My fellow teacher said to him, "My English for Foreign Students class has too many students. We need to open another section." The department chair said, "Okay. But who can we get to teach it?" There were only three of us in the hallway. So he turned to me and said, "How about you, Betty?" And I said, "Sure." I had no idea what it was all about, but as a young instructor, I knew not to refuse a request from my department chair!

That very afternoon at 1:10 PM, I walked into my first ESL class. I returned compositions that the other instructor had corrected before the sections were divided and walked around the class answering questions. One student, a Spanish speaker, showed me an error the previous teacher had marked. He had written *waters* (as in *I was thirsty, so I drank some waters*) and wanted to know why that was incorrect. I stared at his paper and gulped. I had no idea—absolutely no idea—but I said to myself, "Wow, what an interesting question!" and told him I would find the answer and tell him tomorrow. That was my introduction to ESL and the grammar questions that our English language learners (ELLs) ask us.

After some scrambling, I came back to class the next day with a handout of explanations and exercises on **count nouns** vs. **mass nouns,** two terms I had never even heard of before. I had never noticed that some nouns can be counted in English (*one chair, two sofas, three tables,* etc.), and others can't (*some furniture*). From that day to this, I have been fascinated by the workings of English grammar and especially fascinated by how the patterns of meaning in English are seen from a second language learner's perspective.

If you're like other teachers of ELLs, at one point or another you have found yourself standing momentarily wide-eyed in front of your class as your brain feverishly tries to puzzle through an answer to an unanticipated student question about an ESL grammar point, perhaps about comparative adjectives ("Why do we say *more expensive* but not *more cheap?*) or verb tenses ("What's the difference between *I've known him for years* and *I knew him for years?*"). What can you the teacher do to prepare yourself for this predictable hot seat?

As Keith Folse points out in Chapters 1 and 2 of this useful work, English grammar for ELLs is different from the grammar that native speakers learn in school, so native speakers need to learn to see English from their ELLs' point of view. In Chapter 3, Keith goes on to explain 15 important ELL grammar issues in clear, accessible language that teachers can relate to and offers relevant information on the grammar topic as well as how it is treated in certain foreign languages. More concrete help comes in the unique Chapter 4, which offers 20 Hot Seat Questions that prepare teachers for some of the most commonly asked ELL grammar questions, including some really tough ones, before their class has even begun.

As a teacher, from my very first day in an ESL class, I put my students' needs first, finding out what they wanted from their English class, and then provided materials and activities to meet these expressed needs as best I could. I was constantly inventing materials, like so many other ESL teachers. Knowing ELL grammar in more detail will enable you to prepare more effective materials specifically focused on the needs of your particular students. To be certain, this suggestion applies to all teachers—ESL or EFL, K–12 or adult, whether the focus is on conversation or academic usage.

Our field has seen tremendous changes since 1965, when language teaching was shifting away from grammar. Fortunately, we have shifted back (though some of us never stopped teaching grammar, much to our students' benefit and delight). With both research and teaching outcomes on its side, grammar is now recognized by most in the field as an essential component in balanced programs of second language instruction.

Keys to Teaching Grammar to English Language Learners: A Practical Handbook is not meant to be an exhaustive grammar reference book or summary of research studies. The biggest strength of this book is in fact the author's emphasis on teaching techniques. For example, each of the 15 grammar points in Chapter 3 ends with ideas for teaching the grammar. Further concrete teaching ideas can be found in Chapter 5, with techniques ranging from basic language drills to visual grammar presentations to more complex and fun games.

Using his lengthy background as a foreign language teacher and learner, Keith Folse has succeeded in creating a practical guide for teachers who want to learn more about grammar so that they can help their ELLs. To this end, the book avoids the heavy academic tone commonly found in some teacher development books. Teachers will also appreciate the lack of excessive grammar terminology. Like me, Folse advocates using only as much grammar terminology as needed to teach the material, advice that he himself adheres to in his own writing. Folse underscores that in teaching grammar, a teacher's goal is to show students how English works, not "teach grammar rules." Finally, as I have seen Keith demonstrate in many conference workshops and presentations, this book clearly focuses on practical application of grammar information in effective language teaching.

The whole purpose of teaching grammar to ELLs is to help our students gain language skills that will help them achieve their real-life goals. *Keys to Teaching Grammar to English Language Learners: A Practical Handbook* offers a wide array of ideas for teaching and practicing grammar with their learners. This invaluable work will benefit both teachers and their ELLs alike.

Betty S. Azar
Whidbey Island, Washington
September 2008

PREFACE

Interest in learning English as a foreign language is high in countries all over the world, including English-speaking countries with large numbers of non-native immigrants. Today's teachers of English language learners (ELLs) work with students who have a unique, diverse set of language needs. While some teachers deal exclusively with the teaching of English as a second language (ESL) or English as a foreign language (EFL), there are thousands of other teachers in English-speaking countries who suddenly find that their elementary school math classes or high school history classes, for example, have many ELLs who must learn the subject matter of math or history and at the same time somehow acquire English. Both of these groups of teachers—those who are obviously responsible for ELL instruction and those who teach subjects in K–12 settings—need to know about ELL grammar. The problem is that these teachers are often apprehensive of grammar and cannot understand its value in the teaching of ELLs.

In teaching graduate TESOL courses on grammar, I have worked with both novice and experienced ESL/EFL teachers as they attempt to understand ELL grammar. These teachers want to know how to explain why we use *–ing* in a certain sentence or why we use *the* instead of *a* with a certain noun. In these same courses and in numerous workshops, I have also worked with content teachers who have ELLs in their math, history, and science classes. Though well-trained in their subject matter, these teachers have no idea why their ELLs omit *–ing* endings or do not use the verb tenses that their native-speaking classmates do. Knowledge of ELL grammar can answer these questions.

Because of previous experiences with grammar, both of these groups of teachers tend to dislike—or at least have a negative mindset toward—grammar. Talking about grammar involves knowing some terminology, but teachers mistakenly tend to equate grammar knowledge with knowledge of grammatical labels such as *present perfect tense* or *dependent clauses*.

Grammar is the set of patterns that holds a language together. If vocabulary items such as words and idioms are the building blocks of a language, then grammar is the systematic glue that holds everything within a language together. Simply put, grammar is **the** foundation of a language, yet teachers often have trouble grasping the extent to which knowledge of ELL grammar will actually help them teach their students.

After one of many workshops that I had conducted on ELL grammar at a national conference, a teacher asked me about some of the grammar points that I had just introduced that day. "I understand count and non-count now," she said, "so now I understand why my ELLs make those mistakes on their papers, but are these rules written anywhere? Do you have a list of ELL grammar points? And do you have more ideas about how to teach these grammar points?" I could tell that this teacher—like almost all the teachers that I work with—really wanted to help her ELLs, but she had little knowledge about ELL grammar and very few ideas about how this information might inform her teaching.

The solution for these teachers and these questions is this book—*Keys to Teaching Grammar to English Language Learners: A Practical Handbook*. To meet the needs of all ELL teachers, I have written a book that presents grammar in a user-friendly way and assumes no prior grammar study. Because the teachers that I work with are first and foremost **teachers**, I provide information on our ELLs' problems with grammar points, their first language interference issues, and numerous examples and explanations of actual teaching techniques that all teachers can use in their classrooms.

Keys to Teaching Grammar to English Language Learners: A Practical Handbook is not meant to be an exhaustive reference book for ELL grammar. This book focuses on teaching teachers about some of the most common ELL grammar points that will enable them to help their English language learners achieve their language goals.

Over the years, grammar in foreign language education has occupied both extremes of the pedagogical continuum—from being the main component of language study in the grammar-translation method to being downplayed and even intentionally omitted during the peak of the naturalist/communicative methods that focused exclusively on communication. Regardless of the assigned role of grammar in the second language teaching method that happens to be in vogue at any given time, two things are clear: Grammar is an immensely important component of learning a second language, and all teachers of ELLs need to know about ELL grammar.

Why is knowledge of grammar so important for teachers? Instructors who are teaching an ELL course in which grammar is featured in any way obviously need to know about ELL grammar, but knowledge of ELL grammar is important for all teachers, including teachers of conversation courses, composition courses, and reading courses, as well as K–12 teachers who have ELLs in their classes. In a conversation class, lessons are often organized around specific tasks such as ordering food in a restaurant, and these tasks might require practice with **modals** (*May I take your order? What should I order?*). In trying to compose longer sentences in composition class, ELLs may make errors with **gerunds and infinitives** (*To solve this problem efficiently, I believe that we must try to avoid using fossil-based fuels in future vehicles.*). In the reading course, the teacher may want to check the number of **adjective clauses** (*O. Henry, who was arrested and sent to prison for embezzlement, is the most famous U.S. short story writer*) as well as **reduced adjective clauses** (*O. Henry, arrested and sent to prison for embezzlement, is the most famous U.S. short story writer*) in a reading passage to determine readability of the passage and to see the kinds of clauses to which ELLs are being exposed. Being able to explain their ELLs' errors is a high priority for many teachers, and K–12 teachers in particular might want to know why the ELLs say they have *many homeworks* and *much problem* with math or *I like the math. *Is easy for me.* (The use of asterisks indicate ungrammatical English. See page 2.) Because of the importance of an ELL's first language in learning English, all teachers should be familiar with those ELL grammar points that may be particularly problematic because of the ELL's native language.

To facilitate your learning about ELL grammar, this book will help you: (1) identify ELL grammar points; (2) understand the details associated with each one; (3) anticipate common ELL errors by grammar point, by first language, and/or by proficiency level; and (4) learn specific techniques to make teaching more effective. These objectives are for all teachers regardless of where you are teaching or who your students are.

Book Organization

This book is divided into five chapters and includes three appendices. A companion workbook is available for those who want additional guided written practice and ideas for further teacher research on ELL grammar.

In Chapter 1, you will examine the differences between ELL grammar and traditional grammar taught to native speakers in middle and high school. Chapter 1 includes four pre-tests that readers should answer before finishing the chapter. Chapter 1 explains what ELL grammar is and examines the role that ELL grammar can play in eight different teaching situations.

In Chapter 2, you will review (or learn!) basic grammar terminology. Section 1 focuses on twenty common native speaker errors in English. Section 2 presents the eight parts of speech from an ELL viewpoint. Building on the eight parts of speech, Section 3 looks at basic grammar functions such as subject and direct object. Section 3 also includes information on types of sentences. Because of the major role that verbs play in ELL grammar, Section 4 is dedicated entirely to the twelve English verb tenses.

Chapter 3 explains 15 key ELL grammar points. There are many grammar points that could have been included here, but these fifteen are the minimum that any ELL teacher should be aware of before working with ELLs. Four of the fifteen focus on verbs, with Key 1 being the verb *to be*, and Keys 2, 3, and 4 focusing on verb tenses used to express present, past, and future times, respectively. Keys 5 through 15 cover a diverse set of ELL grammar issues, such as count and non-count nouns, prepositions, articles, pronunciation of *–s* and *–ed*, adjective clauses, infinitives/gerunds, phrasal verbs, modals, word forms, passive voice, and conditional sentences. Each of these fifteen keys is organized around four topics: typical ELL errors, grammar explanation, native language information, and ideas for teaching.

In Chapter 4, teachers have an opportunity to prepare for the unexpected through Hot Seat Questions that students ask. Why do we spell *opening* with one *n* before the *–ing* but we spell *beginning* with two? What does *had had* mean? Why do we say *taller* and *windier*, but we do not say *comfortabler* or *recenter*? Teachers cannot know the answer to every student question, but this chapter includes 20 questions that ELLs frequently ask their teachers.

Finally, Chapter 5 offers 25 concrete "been there, done that" techniques on different aspects of carrying out your lesson plans with grammar. It is important to read all of the techniques in Chapter 5 because of a technique may be applicable to many different grammar points even though it is illustrated in this chapter with only one grammar point.

There is intentional overlap of information in this book, and you should take that into consideration when you research a certain grammar point. For example, Chapter 2 features terminology regarding count and non-count nouns on page 46. Chapter 3 provides specific information about count and non-count nouns, including the rules and common ELL errors, on pages 152–60. Chapter 5 offers several techniques that could relate to count and non-count nouns, including pages 290–92, 294–95, 300–1, 303, 308, and 309.

The three appendixes located at the back of the book include a mini-lesson on twenty common native speaker errors, a list of irregular past and past participles of verbs, and a glossary of grammar terms useful in reading this book.

How to Use This Book

There are as many different ways to use any book as there are different teachers, and each class or workshop group that I work with is somewhat different.

Chapter 1 is an overview of the differences between native speaker grammar and ELL grammar. In addition, Chapter 1 includes several pre-tests to help direct your learning toward areas that may need further information.

Of the four sections in Chapter 2, Section 1 can be completed individually or as a class, but the remaining sections (2, 3, 4) should be studied as a class since the grammar terminology may require deeper review. The 20 native speaker errors in Section 1 of Chapter 2 introduce the concepts of prescriptive versus descriptive grammar. A pre-test is provided to help individuals determine which of the 20 errors they need to study further.

Chapter 3 contains the core ELL grammar points, called Keys, and most of the course or workshop should deal with this chapter. Chapter 4 consists of 20 Hot Seat Questions, which may be viewed as an extension of some of the pre-tests in Chapter 1. Ideally, the teaching techniques in Chapter 5 should be covered whenever connections can be made with one of the 15 ELL grammar Keys. For example, Teaching Technique 1 (p. 288) mentions an option for starting a lesson on teaching *an* and *the* and is tied to Key 6, Articles. Teaching Technique 10 (p. 297) discusses using song lyrics as a vehicle for practicing verbs and modals (Key 12, Modals) or infinitives and gerunds (Key 10, Infinitives and Gerunds).

Finally, the goal of *Keys to Teaching Grammar to English Language Learners: A Practical Handbook* is for teachers to become not just better but the best teachers of ELL grammar possible. To accomplish this goal, teachers need to develop their own deeper understanding of the grammar of the 15 Keys in Chapter 3. To this end, each Key ends with a small action research question called *Find Out* that teachers should attempt to work through on their own. These questions allow teachers an opportunity to connect the material in the book with grammar issues that are meaningful to the individual teaching needs of teachers.

Acknowledgments

This grammar project has happened because of the generous help of many people. Without them, this, *Keys to Teaching Grammar to English Language Learners: A Practical Handbook* would not have happened. First and foremost, I am grateful to the University of Central Florida for the academic sabbatical that I received this past year that gave me the time to compile a work of this magnitude and to Dawn Trouard, who kept urging me to apply for a sabbatical in the first place.

Special thanks go to the many people who carefully read various versions of this manuscript and offered their ideas for improvements: Charlie Piper (University of Central Florida); Laura Villegas (Springdale Schools, Northwest Arkansas); Elena Vestri Solomon (University of Nevada—Reno and Emirates College for Advanced Education, United Arab Emirates); Ekaterina Goussakova (Seminole Community College); Robbie Bushong (U.S. Peace Corps); and Kate Brummett.

Many thanks go to colleagues near and far who offered samples of student work to serve as the basis for some of the example errors in this book: Barbara Smith-Palinkas; Virginia Lantry (Dixon High School, Dixon, California); Mark Richards (James Lyng Adult Education Centre, Montreal, Quebec); Sharon Yoder (Allegany College of Maryland); Jennie Farnell (American Language Program, University of Connecticut, Stamford); and Lynn Faught (Farmington School District, Arkansas).

Thanks also go to the professionals who provided information regarding native speaker errors: Dr. Alan Juffs (University of Pittsburgh), Chinese; Myrna Creasman (Center for Multilingual and Multicultural Studies, University of Central Florida), Tagalog; Bryan Stoakley (University of South Korea) and In-Kyung Breana Stoakley (National Language School), Korean; Dr. Martha Garcia, Ali Korosy, Dr. Lisa Nalbone (Department of Modern Languages, University of Central Florida), and Dr. Edwin Lamboy (City College of New York), Spanish; Dr. Alla Kourova (University of Central Florida) and Ekaternia Goussakova (Seminole Community College), Russian.

I very much appreciate the help that the following people offered on individual grammar issues: Theresa Pruett-Said (Macomb Community College, Michigan); Christine Tierney (Houston Community College); Karen Stanley (Central Piedmont Community College, Charlotte, North Carolina); Margi Wald (College Writing Programs, University of California, Berkeley), Carol Bandar (California Unified Schools); Aaron Lingenfelter (California State University, Sacramento); Joel Bloch (Ohio State University); Judy Hobson (University of Arkansas); Kathy Schmitz (Temple University, Tokyo); Jan Oppie (Rainbow Language House, Urasa, Japan); and Dr. Lynn Jensen (Lynn's School of English, California). I am particularly indebted to Rachel Koch, who helped me out with numerous grammar quandaries.

I also thank the numerous teachers who emailed items for the Hot Seat Questions in Chapter 4: Melanie Gonzalez (Seminole Middle School); Jill Blanc (Orlando Language School); Alison Youngblood (Samsung Corporation, Korea); Cynthia Jankovic (Defense Language Institute, San Antonio, Texas); Lindi Kourtellis (EAP Lab, Valencia Community College, Florida); Aneta Braczyk (New Jersey Adult Education Program); Chrissy Della Corte (University of Central Florida); Marcelle Cohen (Seminole Community College, Florida); Kevin Smith (Seminole Community College); Catherine Flores (Orlando Language School); Susan Reynolds (Seminole Community College);

Gena Kost (Pennyslvania State University); R. Kirk Moore (UAB Idiomes, Barcelona, Spain); David Tillyer (Westchester Community College); and Maria Spelleri (Manatee Community College).

Special thanks go to Betty Azar and Michael Swan for their generous and constant information about grammar. Betty's *Understanding and Using English Grammar* and Michael's *Practical English Usage* remain as iconic works in our field and serve to inspire all ELL materials writers and teachers.

I am especially indebted to Kelly Sippell, my editor at the University of Michigan Press, who has worked with me so diligently as this book endeavor went from an idea to a proposal to a chapter to some Word files. This book is a huge project, and Kelly was instrumental in making sure that this book happened.

Finally, I thank my partner Jim for his patience and support. A year is a long time to listen to someone talk incessantly about grammar.

Keith Folse
University of Central Florida
2009

CONTENTS

Appendixes

1

An Introduction to Grammar for English Language Learners (ELLs)

Section 1 What Do You Already Know about ELL Grammar? (Pre-Tests)

Section 2 Approaches to Teaching ELL Grammar: The Role of the Student, Setting, Course, and Teaching Situation

Grammar has been at the heart of learning languages for centuries. In almost all language teaching methods—from grammar-translation to more recent communicative methods—grammar has played a role to one degree or another. In this chapter of *Keys to Teaching Grammar to English Language Learners: A Practical Handbook*, you will consider the differences between grammar points for native speakers and those for ELLs. In a pre-test, you will have an opportunity to measure how much you already know about ELL grammar points. Reflecting the incredible variety of teaching settings worldwide, approaches to the teaching of grammar will be considered based on the student, the setting, the course, and other factors. Finally, suggestions will be made for using this book to maximize what you learn about teaching ELL grammar.

SECTION 1
What Do You Already Know about ESL Grammar? (Pre-Tests)

Example A: *I want to go there tomorrow.*
Example B: *I plan to go there tomorrow.*
Example C: **I can to go there tomorrow.*

*An asterisk: In ELL grammar and linguistics books, an asterisk * is placed before examples that are not grammatical in English and not usually made by native speakers. In contrast, a double dagger ‡ before an example indicates non-standard English used by native speakers.

Native speakers of English would never say **I can to go there tomorrow.* Those same native speakers, however, would probably not be able to explain why A and B are correct and C is wrong, nor would they normally have a need to know. (See Key 12 for the answer.)

For teachers of ELLs, however, the situation is quite different. Our ELLs do make errors such as **I can to go,* and they do want to know why one sentence is possible while another one is not. *Keys to Teaching Grammar to English Language Learners* provides information to help you identify and address ELL grammar issues and offers effective strategies and practical ideas to teach ELL grammar in your classes.

Grammar for ELLs is simply not the same as the grammar that native speakers usually study in middle school, high school, or college. Native speakers study the formal rules of a language that they already speak. Sometimes the focus is on ways of saying something better. In other cases, grammar teaching to native speakers focuses on avoiding common native errors such as double negatives (*We don't have no reason to go there* instead of *We don't have any reason to go there*) or using an unnecessary preposition (*Where are you going to?* instead of *Where are you going?*). (For more information on double negatives, see p. 324; for information on ending sentences with unnecessary prepositions, see pp. 313–15.)

ELLs are not only learning new words and idioms in English, but also how to put this new vocabulary together into phrases or sentences. ***Grammar for ELLs should then focus on how to correctly construct phrases and sentences that best express the ELLs' intended messages.*** ELLs need to learn, for example, that the simple present tense is for repeated actions (*I play tennis every day*) but that present progressive (also called present continuous in British English) is often for current actions (*I am playing tennis now*). Grammar instruction intended for ELLs would therefore focus on avoiding common ELL errors with simple present tense such as **Every day I am play tennis* (*am play* should be *play* because it refers to a daily action) or *Sorry, Maria is not here right now. *She plays tennis at the high school* (*plays* should be *is playing* because it refers to an event in progress at the time of the conversation). (For more information, see pp. 76 and 77.)

Teaching English to ELLs requires special training in key areas of the English language, including ESL grammar. Unfortunately, it is sometimes assumed that any English speaker can teach English, but this belief is incorrect.

Untrained native speakers are not in any way prepared to teach their language to a non-native speaker. The fact that you may be a native speaker of English does not automatically or remotely qualify you to be a good ESL teacher. I sometimes hear teachers with little experience working with ELLs say that teaching ESL is just good teaching and that no special teacher training is involved. In fact, being able to teach ELLs and monitor their language development most certainly is much more than just "good teaching." It requires detailed knowledge of ESL grammar, vocabulary, pronunciation, and cross-cultural issues.

In terms of ESL grammar, native speakers tend to have little knowledge of the particular issues that ELLs face, but this lack of knowledge is normal. Native speakers are not trained to know the second language aspects of their own first language because they are native speakers. The instinctual knowledge of grammar that comes with acquiring a language natively does not transfer to the understanding of the structure of another language. As a result, untrained ESL instructors are often unable to highlight these differences adequately to their students.

When asked about grammar, most native speakers fall back on their sometimes painful memories of grammar lessons from junior high and high school. They remember conjugating verbs for no apparent reason—*I went, you went, he went, she went, it went, we went, you went, they went*. Think about it. Why did we native speakers have to write out conjugations of the verb *to go* in the past tense when in fact the form is exactly the same for each subject—*I/you/he/she/it/we/you/they went*? Was this really productive?

Native speakers might remember diagramming sentences, which was supposed to help us learn the part of speech of words in a sentence. For example, if you diagram the sentence *The lazy brown fox jumped very quickly over the river*, your diagram would look like this:

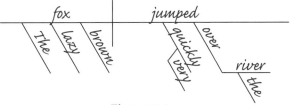

Figure 1.1

While I enjoyed diagramming sentences, I do not know if it really helped me to identify parts of speech. The irony of diagramming is that in order to diagram a sentence correctly, I had to already know the part of speech of each word; thus, it was not the diagramming but more likely the analyzing that was the real practice. In order to diagram the word *lazy* in the example sentence, I had to know first that it is an adjective, and then I had to remember what kind of line adjectives occupy when diagramming. The actual act of diagramming is not what taught me that *lazy* is an adjective.

When native speakers—even those with years of teaching experience—are asked to explain why we can say *I want to go* and *I plan to go* but not **I can to go*, they often give unhelpful and uninformative answers that do not at all resemble good teaching, such as, "We don't say that" (Yes, but why not?) or "You can't put *to* there" (Why not?) or "You need the infinitive in the first two sentences" (What does that mean anyway? What is an infinitive? Why do you need an infinitive?). Native speakers also try to explain ELL grammar questions by saying, "It's an exception." No, it's <u>not</u> an exception. To be sure, there are exceptions to certain grammar patterns, but if any language consisted of a high number of exceptions, no one would ever be able to speak it well. All languages—including English—have patterns of usage, and those patterns are what make up the grammar of that language. ***In fact, that is what grammar is—the systematic patterns of any language.***

Pre-Tests: Assessing Your ELL Grammar Knowledge

Before you begin reading the chapters of this book, you should assess what you already know about ELL grammar. The following four quizzes can serve as both pre-tests of your knowledge of ELL grammar and as springboards for thought and discussion. The content of these tasks is similar to language issues that teachers encounter in ELLs' writing or speech. In addition, ELLs commonly ask direct questions such as, "Teacher, why does *listening* have one *n* in the middle but *beginning* has two?" or "Teacher, why do you say *the Philippines* and *the Soviet Union* but not **the Canada* or **the China?*"

Most native speakers have never thought about English from an ELL point of view, so many of the issues addressed here may be brand new. Oftentimes, native speakers initially respond to these types of questions by saying, "I've never thought about that before." Therefore, if you find that you have to leave some questions blank on the pre-test, do not be alarmed. Blank answers are normal at this stage of the course, and if they are blank for you, they are most likely blank for your ELLs.

Quiz 1. *Distinguishing Traditional Grammar and ELL Grammar*

Grammar for native speakers is not the same grammar that ELLs learn. For each of these ten sentences, underline the grammar errors and then circle NS or ELL to indicate whether you think the grammar error is more likely to be committed by native speakers or English language learners. (Answers with brief explanations are on p. 14.)

NS   ELL   1. My favorite color is the blue because it makes me feel relaxed.

NS   ELL   2. Alaska is a U.S. state since 1959.

NS   ELL   3. Where does the president live at?

NS   ELL   4. Congress should to make a new tax law.

NS   ELL   5. George Washington was born in February 22, 1732.

NS   ELL   6. More people should of voted in the last national election.

NS   ELL   7. The taxi driver said that he felt badly about the accident.

NS   ELL   8. Most citizens want to avoid to pay higher taxes.

NS   ELL   9. A knowledgeable gardener does not need many equipments.

NS   ELL   10. All the students answers should be completed in ink.

Your Score: _____ /10

Quiz 2. Testing Your ELL Grammar Knowledge

For each of these 20 multiple choice questions, choose the one answer that best answers or completes the item. Answering these 20 questions should not take more than ten minutes, which allows approximately 30 seconds per question. If you need more time than this, then you do not know this material well enough yet. (Answers are on p. 14. For detailed explanations, see the Keys or other text reference indicated in the margin next to each question in the quiz.)

1. Adding the letter *–s* to a word in English can be confusing to an ELL because the letter *–s* means

   A. plural for nouns but singular for adjectives

   B. plural for count nouns and singular for non-count nouns

   C. plural for nouns but singular for verbs

   D. plural for nouns but singular for possessives

   E. plural for nouns and singular for irregular verbs

2. In English, we use *a few* (instead of *a little*) with

   A. non-count nouns

   B. count nouns

   C. negative nouns

   D. certain adjective phrases

   E. certain adverb phrases

3. Which of these verbs is in the past perfect tense?

   A. *had eaten*

   B. *was eating*

   C. *was eaten*

   D. *had been eating*

   E. *would have eaten*

4. When adding a suffix such as *–ing* or *–ed* to a verb, we may double the last letter if

   A. the last three letters are Consonant + Vowel + Consonant

   B. the last three letters are Vowel + Vowel + Consonant

   C. the last three letters are Vowel + Consonant + Vowel

   D. the last three letters are Consonant + Consonant + Vowel

   E. the last three letters are Consonant + Vowel + Vowel

5. Why do we use these prepositions after these adjectives: *accustomed <u>to</u>, composed <u>of</u>, famous <u>for</u>, interested <u>in</u>,* and *responsible <u>for</u>*?

   A. It depends on the number of syllables in the adjective.

   B. It depends on the number of vowels in the adjective.

   C. It depends on the first letter of the adjective.

   D. It depends on the tense of the verb used in the sentence where the adjective occurs.

   E. There is no reason. ELLs must memorize these usages.

6. *Had better, will,* and *ought to* are

   A. infinitives

   B. modals

   C. gerunds

   D. phrasal verbs

   E. idioms

7. In general, *the* is not used with the names of countries, but an exception is

   A. Asian and European country names

   B. country names that begin with a vowel letter

   C. country names that begin with a vowel sound

   D. country names that seem plural

   E. country names with 1 to 4 syllables

8. Choose the underlined verb that is in a tense that does not match the time normally associated with that particular tense.

   I <u>got up</u> early, drove to the post office, and <u>mailed</u> that box to Sue this morning. When she <u>gets</u> it, I <u>am</u> sure that she <u>will call</u> me.

   A. *got up*

   B. *mailed*

   C. *gets*

   D. *am*

   E. *will call*

9. Choose the one sentence in which the capitalized word is **not** a pronoun.

   A. They have their check, but the waiter took OURS.

   B. YOU have seen that movie twice, haven't you?

   C. Does Jane have HER paper with her today?

   D. Excuse me. Is this phone card yours or MINE?

   E. I don't know HIM very well, but I have known his brother for ages.

See Chapter 2.

10. Which sentence has an intransitive verb?

    A. *In the storm, the small bird plunged from the tree.*

    B. *In spite of the rain, we enjoyed the party a lot.*

    C. *Every student in the class uses a number 2 pencil for the weekly tests.*

    D. *Upon hearing all of the evidence, the jury reached a unanimous verdict.*

    E. *Who murdered the robber?*

See Chapter 2.

11. Which of these animal names ends in the sound /s/?

    A. monkeys

    B. lions

    C. tigers

    D. hippos

    E. giraffes

Key 8

12. Which of these is the least useful grammar category for ELLs (and is therefore almost never covered in any ELL grammar book for students)?

    A. articles

    B. clauses

    C. adjectives

    D. conjunctions

    E. interjections

See Chapter 2.

13. *Stop* becomes *stopping*; *listen* becomes *listening*. The *p* in *stopping* is doubled, but the *n* in *listening* is not. Why is the *n* **not** doubled to *listenning*?

A. The last letter is *n*.

B. The last letter is a consonant.

C. The word *listening* is a gerund.

D. The word *listen* has two syllables.

E. The first syllable of *listen* is stressed.

14. In this sentence from an autobiography, *When I was a kid, I would play with my imaginary friends, would* is used because it refers to

A. permission to do an action

B. a desire to do the action

C. very polite language for the action

D. past repeated actions

E. conditional situations

15. When a verb form occurs after any preposition (except *to*), the verb form used is usually

A. an infinitive

B. a past participle

C. a gerund

D. a verb phrase

E. a present participle

16. In which sentence is *light* used as a non-count noun?

A. She put on her *light* green sweater because it was cold.

B. We need more *light* in this office.

C. Please turn off the *light* when you are done.

D. The fire began to *light* up the entire room.

E. Will Janet *light* the furnace before she leaves?

17. For ELLs, which of these pairs of words exemplifies a whole group of adjectives that are immensely problematic in mastering English?

    A. *chosen* vs. *selected*

    B. *economy* vs. *economical*

    C. *fried* vs. *baked*

    D. *annoyed* vs. *annoying*

    E. *English* vs. *greenish*

18. Which of these sentences has a phrasal verb?

    A. *On our way to work today, the traffic held us up.*

    B. *The cat may have been sleeping since noon.*

    C. *If Mark will work harder, together we can finish this job.*

    D. *Joe typed the memo, put it in an envelope, and mailed it.*

    E. *Joe typed the memo, Sue put it in an envelope, and I mailed it.*

19. When we talk about a contrary-to-fact condition for right now, what does the verb in the *if* clause look like?

    A. simple present tense

    B. simple past tense

    C. present progressive tense

    D. *would* + VERB

    E. *would have* + VERB

20. Which of these CAPITALIZED parts is an adjective clause?

    A. No one is certain of WHAT THE OUTCOME OF THAT MEETING WILL BE.

    B. WHAT THAT BANK FAILED TO DO was to inform the clients of the approaching deadline.

    C. In spite of the scientific knowledge clearly available at that time, THAT RATS AND OTHER RODENTS COULD SPREAD DISEASE was discounted.

    D. Geologists had warned for decades OF THE POSSIBILITY OF A CATASTROPHIC EARTHQUAKE IN THAT REGION.

    E. The mechanic did his best to save the parts of the car THAT WERE SALVAGEABLE, but in the end, little could be saved.

Your Score: _____/20_____

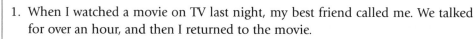

Quiz 3. Can You Explain ELL Grammar Errors?

The following errors are typical of ELLs. Circle and correct the errors. Then explain your corrections in the space provided. In other words, if you were the ELL teacher, how would you explain the error? (Answers are on p. 15. For detailed explanations, see the Key or other text reference indicated in the margin next to each question in the quiz.)

1. When I watched a movie on TV last night, my best friend called me. We talked for over an hour, and then I returned to the movie.

   _____

   _____

   _____

   _____

   _____

2. My parents visited Europe last year. They went to France, Belgium, and Netherlands.

   _____

   _____

   _____

   _____

   _____

*See pp.
278–79.*

3. Bolivia is a landlocked country. Other example is Paraguay.

   _____

   _____

   _____

   _____

   _____

*See pp.
277–78.*

4. I don't know where I left my watch, so I don't know what time is it.

   _____

   _____

   _____

   _____

   _____

5. The secretary is not from France, so she no speaks French well.

_____

_____

_____

_____

_____

Key 4

6. My sister won $1,000 in the lottery. She has lucky.

_____

_____

_____

_____

Key 1

7. I didn't know the words, so I looked up them in the dictionary.

_____

_____

_____

_____

Key 11

8. Maria was born in El Salvador, but she is a U.S. citizen. She lives in Dallas. She is in Dallas since 2007, and she loves the city.

_____

_____

_____

_____

_____

Key 2

Your Score: _____/8_____

Quiz 4. On the Hot Seat: Answering ELL Questions

ELLs ask many questions about English grammar. Sometimes their questions are about the lesson that you are teaching, but often their questions seem unrelated or only tangentially pertinent. How would you answer the following three typical ELL grammar questions? (Answers are on p. 15. For detailed explanations, see the Key or other text reference indicated in the margin next to each question in the quiz.)

1. I know the past tense ending is *–ed,* so I write *added, wanted, cleaned, hugged,* and *pushed.* I pronounce these words as two syllables, so I say *add•ed, want•ed, clean•ed, hug•ged,* and *push•ed.* Someone told me that *cleaned* and *hugged* are only one syllable and end in /d/ and that *pushed* is one syllable and ends in /t/. How can I know when to pronounce the ending as /d/ or /t/ or an extra syllable /əd/? Is there any rule?

   _____

   _____

   _____

   _____

   _____

   _____

2. I don't know when to use present perfect (*have worked*). I thought that present perfect tense is for actions that began in the past and still continue, so I say, *I've lived here for two years* because I still live here—so I can't say, *I live here for two years* even though that makes more sense to me because it's still a true, present action. However, I see sentences where the action is clearly finished, as in *Congress has decided to change the current laws regarding the federal income tax.* Congress's decision is finished. I don't know when to use present perfect tense. Is it for actions that are over or not?

   _____

   _____

   _____

   _____

   _____

   _____

3. If you want to compare two things in English, you can say that *A is bigger than B* and that *A is crazier than B*, but you also say *A is more interesting than B* (instead of *interestinger*). Can I say *A is comfortabler than B*? How about, *A is moderner than B*? When do you add *–er*, and when do you have to use *more*?

See pp. 283–84.

_____

_____

_____

_____

_____

_____

_____

Your Score: _____/3_____

Answers for Quizzes 1–4

Answers for Quiz 1, p. 4

Here are the answers with brief explanations. For detailed explanations, refer to the Keys or pages noted in the margin next to each question in the quiz.

1. ELL: *the blue* → *blue* (We do not use *the* with a noun when the noun refers to a general idea or thing.) (See Key 7.)

2. ELL: *is* → *has been* (We use present perfect for a past action that continues until now.) (See Keys 2, 3.)

3. NS: omit *at* (Including unnecessary prepositions, especially with questions that begin with *where*, is a common native error.) (See pp. 313–15.)

4. ELL: omit *to* (Modals are followed directly by the simple form of the verb, not the infinitive.) (See Key 12.)

5. ELL: *in* → *on* (We use *in* with months but *on* with days and dates.) (See Key 6.)

6. NS: *of* → *have* (In native English, *have* in past modal expressions sounds like *of*, so native speakers often write *of* instead of *have*.) (See pp. 326–27.)

7. NS: *badly* → *bad* (This is a hypercorrection. An adverb is used after action verbs—for example, *behave badly*, but *feel* is not usually an action verb and should be followed by an adjective form, not an adverb.) (See pp. 324–25.)

8. ELL: *to pay* → *paying* (When *avoid* is followed by an action, it must be a gerund—that is, an *–ing* form used as a noun.) (See Key 10.)

9. ELL: *many equipments* → *much equipment* (*Equipment* is a non-count noun, which means that it has no plural form. In addition, non-count nouns are preceded by *much*, not *many*.) (See Key 5.)

10. NS/ELL: *students* → *students'* (Native speakers frequently misuse possessive forms to the point where they cannot distinguish *students* from *student's* or *students'*. Though this error is possible by an ELL, a more common ELL error would be to confuse *student's* and *students'*. In other words, the ELL knows to use some form of a noun with an apostrophe, but a native speaker may not remember to use any apostrophe at all.) (See p. 330.)

Answers for Quiz 2, pp. 5–9

For detailed explanations, refer to the Keys indicated in the margin next to each question in the quiz.

1. C; 2. B; 3. A; 4. A; 5. E; 6. B; 7. D; 8. C; 9. C; 10. A; 11. E; 12. E; 13. E; 14. D; 15. C; 16. B; 17. D; 18. A; 19. B; 20. E

Answers for Quiz 3, pp. 10–11

For more detailed explanations, refer to the Keys indicated in the margin next to each question in the quiz.

1. Several corrections are possible. Change *When I watched* to *While/When I was watching*. The verb *watched* should be in past progressive tense *(was watching)* to indicate that this action was ongoing when it was interrupted by a telephone call.

2. The correct name of the country is *the Netherlands*. In general, *the* can be used only with country names that seem plural because of *–s, United, Union, Kingdom,* or *Republic*.

3. Change *other* to *another*. *Other* is used in the singular only when preceded by *the, my, this,* or a similar word. *Other* is used in the plural before a plural noun. Before a singular count noun, use *another*.

4. The stand-alone question is, "What time is it?" but when this is a noun clause, the correct word order is *wh-* word + SUBJECT + VERB. The correct answer is *what time it is*.

5. The correct way to negate a verb is to use a form of the auxiliary *do*. Here we use *does not speak*. Verbs that do not use the auxiliary *do* to negate are the verb *to be*, modals, and any verb that already has an auxiliary in it—for example, *has gone*.

6. Change *has* to *is*. Certain ideas that are expressed by *to be* + ADJECTIVE in English are expressed by *to have* + NOUN in other languages.

7. Change *looked up them* to *looked them up*. *Look up* is a phrasal verb. For phrasal verbs that contain the word *up*, a pronoun object must separate the verb and the word *up*.

8. Change *is* to *has been*. Actions that began in the past but are still true use present perfect tense *(has been)*, not simple present tense *(is)*.

Answers for Quiz 4, pp. 12–13

For more detailed explanations, refer to the Keys indicated in the margin next to each question in the quiz.

1. Yes, there is a rule, which is explained in depth on pp. 186–90. The last sound of the verb before you add the letters *–ed* or *–d* is what determines whether you pronounce the past tense ending as /d/, /t/, or an extra syllable /əd/. In brief, only verbs that end in the sound of /d/ or /t/ add an extra syllable. For example, *add, trade,* and *note* are one syllable, but in the past tense, they are pronounced with two syllables.

2. Present perfect tense is one of the most difficult tenses in English because it has multiple meanings. At one extreme, it is used for actions that began in the past but continue until now: *I have lived here for five years*. It is also used for actions that happened in the recent past but are important to a current situation. In your example of *Congress has decided to . . .* , the writer (or speaker) used present perfect to connect Congress's action with a current situation. Other uses for present perfect are discussed in greater detail on pp. 79, 104–5, 119–24, 281–82.

3. In general, adjectives and adverbs that are one syllable *(tall, hard)* or two syllables ending in *–y (heavy, crazy)* add *–er*. All others *(modern, comfortable)* use the word *more* instead. There are a few exceptions. More detailed information is on pp. 283–84.

SECTION 2
Approaches to Teaching ELL Grammar:
The Role of Student, Setting, Course, and Teaching Situation

Grammar for ELLs consists of a unique set of language issues. ELLs vary in many important ways, including setting (ESL or EFL), learner age (adults or children), curriculum (emphasis on grammar or emphasis on communication), and learner objective (academic preparation or survival skills). Because of these and other key factors, it is not surprising that ELL teachers approach the teaching of grammar in different ways.

A Direct Approach in Teaching Grammar

As students, many adult learners have **expectations** about what a teacher should do and what learners should do. These students may prefer the teacher to be in front of the room actively teaching. They may expect direct grammar instruction. Numerous surveys have shown that adults expect direct, explicit error correction. Adult learners come to class with "hot seat questions" (see Chapter 4) that may stump new teachers. No one knows your ELLs better than you, so it is up to you to gauge your ELLs' expectations early in the term.

Some teachers teach grammar directly. Teachers who use the direct approach include teachers of grammar classes, composition classes, and even test-preparation classes (e.g., TOEFL®). When teaching grammar, these teachers might write the name of the grammar point on the board, explain why the grammar point is important, and then proceed to give explanations with relevant examples. An essential element here is to relate the grammar to students' actual language needs. For example, if you are teaching present perfect tense, think of a real-world use for this grammar point. Perhaps your students will be completing applications in English for a job or for university admission. If so, then make sure that you include a task in which students work in pairs to interview each other with questions such as, "How long have you lived at your current address?" or "Have you ever worked in a similar job (to the one that you are applying for)?"

An Indirect Approach in Teaching Grammar

Other teachers rarely deal with grammar directly, but these instructors <u>are</u> aware of ELL grammar points and make sure that these grammar points are included or highlighted in class material whether or not the teacher actually points them out. These teachers are most likely not teaching ELL grammar or any ELL language class per se; instead, they are either ELL teachers teaching a special content course, often called English for Specific Purposes (or ESP), such as health, tourism, or business English, or they are K–12 teachers teaching math, reading, science, or social studies to mixed classes of both native speakers and ELLs. A good teacher is aware of what a real-world task would be for his or her own students, and that teacher has also thought about which ELL grammar issues could potentially be important in the students' writing (or speaking or reading or listening) task.

In an ESP course on Business English, for example, ELLs might be studying how to follow up on a business transaction by writing a thank-you email. Their grammar focus might be on infinitives and gerunds (see Key 10) as they write their messages:

> Thank you very much for *responding* to our query. We are interested in *receiving* more information about . . . . We plan *to use* your product provided that we do not need *to pay* additional taxes or other charges.

Based on the teacher's view of the role of grammar in overall instruction and the mindset of his or her students, the teacher might elect to tell students about infinitives and gerunds *before, during,* or *after* the task—or *even not at all.*

ELLs in a K–12 setting could be in any number of classes for different subjects. In a kindergarten class of native speakers and ELLs, the children might be learning the song "The Itsy Bitsy Spider." Songs naturally repeat certain lines, which makes their lyrics a perfect vehicle for learning language patterns. In this particular song, students learn three regular past tense forms (*climbed, washed, dried*) and two irregular forms (*came, went*).

In a fifth grade math class, students might be solving math problems that require knowledge of *many, much, a few,* and *a little,* or even *little* and *few.* These words are a core part of **count** and **non-count** nouns, as explained in Key 5. ELLs' ability to answer a math question correctly may well hinge on a thorough knowledge of these expressions. Obviously, the best teacher to help ELLs here is one who knows that terms such as *many* and *a little* are not simple words but rather part of a much more elaborate ELL grammar point. Whether or not the teacher explicitly teaches these expressions is his or her choice. At the very least, teachers with several ELLs in the class should have these words on wall posters (i.e., word walls) to help students become more familiar with the terms. A good fifth grade math teacher with several ELLs in his or her class recognizes that the ELLs are likely to have difficulty solving this math problem not because of any lack of math ability but rather because of English language issues, in this case count and non-count markers.

> In essence, **a song** is nothing more than a language drill set to music. See Technique 10, p. 297, for more information. One of the best books of songs as a vehicle to better English proficiency is *Jazz Chants* (Oxford University Press, 1978) by Carolyn Graham.

Learners' Objectives

Learners' objectives in studying English can range from improving conversation ability to passing a university entrance exam. Learner's objectives in studying English should dictate the amount and kind of grammar in their coursework.

In K–12 settings, many students' main objective is to master the material of third grade science or eighth grade math, but this material is being delivered in a foreign language, namely English. Knowing ESL grammar can certainly aid these ELLs in overall comprehension. Teachers of these students have two instructional responsibilities: the subject matter of the course, that is, third grade science, and, simultaneously, English as a second or foreign language.

At first glance, adult ELLs in a conversation class may not appear to need grammar, but a well-planned conversation lesson almost always has a grammar point as its basis. For example, a lesson on talking about occupations might practice the pattern *he/she + is* as well as using *a/an* with an occupation: *My brother is a doctor.* [Typical ELL errors here include: no verb (**My brother a doctor*), incorrect verb form (**My brother are a doctor*), or no article (**My brother is doctor*).]

ELLs in test-prep courses need grammar, too. Two examples of high-stakes tests are the Test of English as a Foreign Language (TOEFL®) and the *Ei-ken* in Japan. These tests are considered high-stakes because good results can lead to better educational opportunities or employment. To demonstrate a higher-proficiency level on these exams, students need to recognize and/or use certain grammatical structures such as present perfect tense. A test question might require students to distinguish a correct form from plausible distractors: *Most of the people in my class (live, are living, have lived, lived) in this same city for more than a decade.*

University-bound ELLs need to master writing essays in English, so a typical class could focus on grammatical structures for more advanced writing. An example of this kind of lesson would be to combine two or more shorter sentences into a longer sentence using an adjective clause (instead of using *and*):

- *The reason is valid.*
- *The reason is that they want to cancel the meeting.*
- → *The reason that they want to cancel the meeting is valid.*

ELLs in EFL settings as diverse as China or the United Arab Emirates may have different needs. EFL students do not interact much in English outside of class because people in their country do not speak English. EFL teachers appreciate the impact that their English teaching has on the development of student proficiency. In contrast, ESL teachers (e.g., those in the United States or another English-speaking country) sometimes mistakenly assume that simply because their students are in an English-speaking country, they will encounter English outside of class through TV or interactions with native speakers. In reality, however, many ELLs in this setting socialize primarily with other people who speak the same native language, making the learning environment more like that of an EFL, not ESL, setting.

Sometimes ESL teachers do not always recognize that they may well be the sole source of grammatically correct English input for their students. When half the class consists of ELLs from the same language background, the teacher is the students' only English input. The implication here is that the teacher's daily English input plays a much more important role in the English acquisition of ELLs than many teachers believe.

Teachers must be aware of ELL grammar problems. If not, ELLs' content work may be evaluated as unsatisfactory simply due to ELL errors even though these errors are a normal and natural part of the the English acquisition process. In order to be an effective content and ELL educator in this situation, teachers should focus on key ELL grammar structures that their ELLs need to acquire to improve their English. However, if teachers are not aware of what some of these key grammar issues are—and as we have seen, these grammar issues are not at all the same ones that native speakers have—then it is impossible for teachers to build a solid lesson plan throughout the school year that systematically addresses ELLs' grammar needs. (Yes, this means that even the science, mathematics, and physical education teachers are now responsible for their ELLs' English language needs and ultimately their language proficiency growth.)

Course Logistics

Course logistics have a major impact on how grammar is (or is not) covered in any English program. Perhaps the single most important issue is the amount of time available for instruction and study. How many times per week does the class meet? How

ELLs in an English-speaking country such as the U.S. or Canada study **ESL,** but ELLs in a non–English speaking country study EFL. For **EFL,** the teacher must create opportunities for ELLs to practice English because they don't hear English outside of class (and all speak the same native language). ESL learners can hear English in their environment and usually represent different native languages.

long is each class? Realistically speaking, how much time can the ELL devote to outside homework and out-of-class practice?

In an intensive program, which is usually for learners age 15 and up, ELLs have classes for four to five hours for five days a week. Each proficiency-level course often lasts eight to fifteen weeks, and if ELLs are starting from the beginning level, they may need a year or two to progress through all levels. In these intensive programs, the curriculum is often set up so that there are separate classes for the distinct language skills: grammar, reading, composition, listening, and speaking. In other programs, these same skill areas are integrated into one course, such as reading/writing or grammar/writing.

In programs with classes for each distinct skill, there is overlap and recycling of material, so a grammar point may be taught explicitly in the grammar class and then recycled in a composition or other class. Realistically, it is almost impossible to imagine a class that focuses purely on one discrete language skill to the exclusion of all others.

In these intensive programs, grammar is covered explicitly in a course called Grammar. Students have an ELL grammar textbook and often a workbook. In this class, students have an opportunity to ask questions that they have about ELL grammar. Their questions are not necessarily limited to the lesson; they may want an explanation of something that they heard at the store, from their child, or on television.

Adult learners have unique learning constraints. Many adult ELLs work all day and take English classes in the evening. These students' language objectives will vary considerably—from the desire to speak better English to secure a good job in their home country, to learning better English to improve their career chances here in the United States or another English-speaking country. Restrictive course logistics here include the limited class time, which is often a two-hour class meeting on two or three nights per week, and limited homework time due to students' work and family obligations.

ELLs in K–12 face very different course constraints depending on the state in which they go to school, a school district's resources, and even local attitudes toward immigrant acceptance. Ideally, an ELL in K–12 would have a teacher specialized in ELL issues, including ELL grammar and assessment. In the real world, however, even in cases where ELLs do have an ELL teacher, the teacher is sometimes a "roving" teacher who works with the ELLs only a few hours per week. As a default, the primary source of ELL instruction for our ELLs then falls on the content teachers, whose lesson plans are already filled with teaching objectives related to their particular K–12 subjects such as tenth grade geometry or seventh grade history.

In addition to these course constraints, there looms a larger issue. All K–12 students—including ELLs—and their teachers are often under time constraints imposed by large-scale tests such as the Florida Comprehensive Assessment Test (FCAT) in Florida, the California High School Exit Examination (CAHSE) in California, or the Texas Assessment of Knowledge and Skills (TAKS) or Reading Proficiency Tests in English (RPTE) in Texas. (Every U.S. state now has a similar examination that tests language arts and mathematics.) These test results are used by the respective state for a variety of purposes, such as determining whether a student is retained in a grade, whether a teacher's students have scored well enough for the teacher to receive a raise, or whether a school whose students have not performed well over several testing periods might lose valuable federal funding.

Given the importance of preparing students for these tests, it is easy to see how ELLs' language needs can be overlooked. At the same time, administrators know that if there are a number of ELLs taking the test in their school or district, the ELLs' scores will pull down the average. Non-native speakers may not be less knowledgeable in the content areas, but they often need more time to comprehend parts of these tests and sometimes cannot finish the work within the allowed time limits. The bottom line is that ELLs' lack of fluency impacts their subject examinations, which can have repercussions for ELLs, their teachers, and even their schools. To do their jobs well, teachers need to be able to distinguish between the content issues and the ELL issues—primarily grammar—in an ELL's paper or test regardless of the subject matter being addressed.

Course Location

In an EFL setting, ELLs speak a **common first language,** so your grammar teaching can focus on errors made by speakers of that specific language—for example, *I have hungry* by Spanish speakers or **I have car* by ELLs who speak Arabic, Japanese, Chinese, or Russian.

Course location usually refers to three categories: ESL, EFL, and K–12 ESL. ESL (English as a second language) refers to students who are learning English in an English-speaking country. Thus, ELLs in the United States, Canada, Great Britain, Australia, and other English-speaking countries are said to be studying ESL. ELLs who are learning English in a country where English is not spoken, such as Japan, Colombia, or the United Arab Emirates, are said to be studying English as a foreign language (EFL).

The reasons for making this distinction between ESL and EFL are many. In an ESL class, the students often speak different languages, so the primary language of communication in the classroom is English. In an EFL setting, getting students to interact in English can be more challenging since there is no real communicative need to use English (except that the teacher often requests that ELLs use English only).

In addition, ESL and EFL settings will require different resource materials for teaching grammar (or any other ELL skill such as reading or speaking). If you are teaching in Japan, a country where ELLs often have a much stronger ability on paper than in real-time conversations, you will probably need to have more speaking tasks than traditional fill-in-the-blank tasks to augment this deficit. To succeed in an EFL setting, teachers and materials should make use of locally known topics. For example, in an example that talks about food, food from the home country should be used. In Malaysia, you could mention *durians*; in Japan, *sushi*; and in Turkey, *kebabs*. In an ESL setting, resource materials can reflect the international nature of the students in the class. In all teaching settings, however, teaching should be geared to the learners' background and objectives for studying English.

The ESL-EFL dichotomy is very important in teaching grammar. In an ESL setting, it is important to know whether a grammar issue is problematic for many language groups in the class or only for some select groups. For example, almost all ELLs make errors with *many* and *much*. (The rule is that *many* is used with count nouns and *much* with non-count nouns: *many books, much information*. See page 155 for more information.) Because this grammar issue is a more universal problem, discussing it with the whole class makes sense.

In contrast, an error such as repeating an object pronoun in an adjective clause is usually made by speakers of Arabic or Persian (Farsi): *The woman that you met her is my aunt.* An EFL book written for the Middle East or Iran would most certainly include a lesson on this grammar point, and because it is problematic for speakers of these languages, all EFL teachers in these areas will cover this point. In an ESL class with speakers of several languages, including Spanish, Japanese, Korean, and Arabic, I would expect to cover this grammar point as a class (because it will be in the ESL books and is problematic for some of my students); however, I expect my Arabic and Persian speakers to have the biggest problem with this, not my Spanish, Japanese, or Korean speakers.

In an ESL class with no Arabic or Persian speakers—that is, with no students for whom this grammar point is a common error in English—I would skip this part of the lesson. Likewise, if I were teaching in Japan or Brazil with a book that had a lesson on pronoun repetition in adjective clauses, I would skip it because these ELLs would never make this mistake. I would exercise my professional judgment as a teacher to omit this portion of the lesson on adjective clauses. (I would cover adjective clauses, but I would skip this one aspect.)

In a K–12 setting, your approach depends on whether you are the ESL teacher or the content teacher. If you are the ESL teacher, much of the preceding information applies to you. If you are the content teacher, you will almost never be teaching ELL grammar explicitly. The material in your class textbook, however, and the language that you use in class in your teaching and even in your class worksheets play an extremely important role in the ultimate English proficiency that your ELLs will attain because you (and your textbook and your explanations and your worksheets) are quite possibly the primary or even the *only* source of English input for your ELLs. By default, you are your ELLs' link to English.

Consider this task from a fourth grade science class:

> *We learned that there is air in our atmosphere, but is there air in the ground? How can you find out whether your answer is correct? Work in small groups to come up with as many ways to prove your answer as possible.*

> **Phrasal verbs** are one of the most difficult of all ELL grammar points. You can *call off a meeting,* but you can't *call it on.* You can *come down with the flu,* but you *come up with an answer.* See Key 11 for more information.

To the average fourth grade science teacher, this task appears to be a normal part of the science curriculum. This task does not appear to have any ELL grammar issues. However, one important ELL grammar point that is covered here is phrasal verbs. Can you find the two phrasal verbs in this task? They are *find out* and *come up with.*

It is important to note here that textbook publishers might include key teaching points in the teacher's edition, so in the previous task, the words *atmosphere* and *prove* might be highlighted because the first word is a key science term and the second word is a key part of understanding how science works. These boldfaced words are the subject matter objectives for *all* students—both native and ELL alike—but for ELLs, this task also has ELL grammar examples in it that teachers should be ready to exploit for language development. However, no teacher can focus on something that he or she does not even recognize. As we have seen, native speakers often have no understanding of what ELL issues are since these speakers did not learn English as a second language. Therefore, it is imperative that teachers be able to recognize ELL grammar issues in their teaching materials quickly and accurately.

Once a non-ELL teacher can easily identify ELL grammar issues in the content subject material, what can the teacher do next? In this example task, at the very least, it is important for the teacher to know that phrasal verbs are not transparent to ELLs (and sometimes not even to native speakers). The teacher may write these phrasal verbs on a vocabulary word wall in the classroom. The teacher might make a special effort to use these phrases more often in the pre-task activities to make sure that everyone knows what they mean. The more you make your ELLs aware of these phrasal verbs (or any other ELL grammar issues), the more likely your ELLs are to acquire these structures.

What I would never do in a fourth grade science class is label these items as phrasal verbs. Grammar is not about labels; it is about helping ELLs acquire the grammatical patterns of English, a task that is impossible unless you first know what ELL grammar issues are. (In addition, science class should be first and foremost about science, not English.)

If you could hear a recording of yourself teaching several lessons over a few months, you might be quite surprised to discover that you tend to use many of the same words and expressions repeatedly. This repetition is actually a good teaching technique, which is why songs are often a good teaching vehicle. A simple example of this for kindergarten ELLs would be the song "Old MacDonald Had a Farm." The repetitive lyrics of "On his farm, he had a [duck, cow, etc.]" reinforce several ELL grammar issues, including: (1) *had* as past of *have*, (2) *on + farm* [NOTE: most ELLs will say *in a farm* instead of *on a farm*], (3) use of *a/an* with singular count nouns (e.g., a duck, a quack-quack, etc.), (4) *he* as subject and *his* as possessive adjective for a male, and (5) the basic sentence pattern of SUBJECT + VERB + OBJECT (S-V-O).

Grammar is really nothing more than language patterns. While songs with their repetitive lyrics might be an obvious example of the use of patterns, there are patterns in all types of English, including the English used in math, science, history, literature, and other subjects. Consider these three statements from the Florida Comprehensive Assessment Test (FCAT) 2007 Mathematics Released Test for fifth grade:

> 1. *Samantha baked a dessert for her class using the recipe shown below. She . . .*
> 5. *Mr. Henderson made the table below to show the number of pets owned by . . .*
> 6. *In art class, Rita drew the design below. For her second design, she . . .*

Look carefully at the word *below* in these three statements. A full version for all three of these sentences would include the words *that is,* so that #1 would read *the recipe that is shown below,* #2 would read *the table that is below,* and #3 would read *the design that is below.* Can you explain why the word *shown* is in #1 without any other verbs? The word *shown* is not the main verb. In ELL grammar, the words *shown below* in #1 and *below* in #5 and #6 are what we call reduced adjective clauses. (See Key 9 for more information on this ELL grammar point.)

As a native speaker, you realize that both forms are correct. In English, we can include *that + is* or we can omit it, but there are rules that allow this omission. As a native speaker, you are not conscious of the underlying grammar of when words may be omitted, but you do not make a mistake with this. This particular grammar point is extremely common in all levels of English, from informal conversation to very academic writing. To ELLs, however, it is sometimes incomprehensible because it appears that words and, quite possibly, ideas are missing. A content teacher who is aware of this ELL grammar issue is able to exploit it by focusing on the grammar point as it appears in the textbook.

The Importance of Grammar in Eight Teaching Situations

Grammar is the glue that holds a language together. Grammar affects all areas of English language learning, from writing to speaking to reading to listening. Grammar plays an obvious central role in grammar courses, but grammar is also important in ESP courses such as Business English and Tourism English as well as in K–12 or college content courses such as literature, science, and mathematics.

No one knows your subject matter and your ELLs better than you do. It is entirely up to you as their teacher to determine how much grammar instruction they need, which grammar points to teach, and what kinds of grammar activities are best for them. In the remainder of this chapter, we will look briefly at how grammar can impact different types of teachers in different teaching situations.

Situation 1. An ELL Grammar Teacher

If you are the grammar teacher, it is obvious that you need to know ELL grammar. The success of your class depends to a large extent on how well you know ELL grammar and how well you are able to develop that knowledge in your students. You should know ELL grammar points so well that you might be able to identify an ELL's first language by the types of grammatical errors that he or she makes in English. You should know that simple present tense and basic word order are grammar issues in beginning classes, present perfect tense and phrasal verbs are often in intermediate classes, and past perfect tense and gerunds are seen in higher-proficiency grammar classes.

Situation 2. The Composition Teacher

There are several types of teachers who teach composition, including a K–12 language arts teacher, a freshman composition instructor, a composition teacher in an intensive ESL or EFL program, or a composition teacher in an English for Academic Purposes (EAP) program in a university or community college. While the ESL, EFL, and EAP teachers work with ELLs enough to be familiar with ELL errors in writing, many K–12 and freshman composition teachers are not. The more familiar composition teachers are with ELL grammar issues, the better they can help their ELLs improve their English proficiency and writing skills.

When ELLs write in English, they make many types of errors. While ELLs may make just as many errors in their speaking, we tend not to pay as much attention to those errors. Because the act of speaking a message happens very quickly, once the words are spoken, they are gone. In contrast, a written message is a permanent record that everyone can see (and continue to see). The error is there and is a deeper, more visible "event." Therefore, our focus tends to linger on written errors more than spoken errors.

Consider this example of ELL student writing. In this fifth grade class, the assignment was to write a description of a painting.

> *Pablo Picasso's painting "Guernica" shows the 1937 bombing of Spain. One of the details of this gorgeos painting is a light bulb that could also stand for an eye. Another details are a very unforgetable bull. The people in the crowded room looks hurt almost dieing or an other words suffereing badly, other details are hapen all around the place and a sad horse. The "guernica" painting is a very interesting and unforgotable painting.*

It is obvious that the writing sample contains errors. As an ELL teacher, there are many factors to consider when providing feedback to the student writer. Of the errors that you see here, which ones would you mark? Would you mark all of the errors? How would you mark the errors? Would you just circle the errors? Should you write a correction there for the student?

Teachers who are not accustomed to ELL language problems usually correct the spelling errors first. Those errors are very clear in the native speaker's head; moreover, they are very easy to explain. However, what about errors that are only made by ELLs such as *another details* and *are hapen*? Of course you can correct the errors by writing *other details* and *happen*, but can you explain these errors? In doing so, can you avoid using grammatical jargon that will more likely confuse the student than help?

Teachers with English as their L1 frequently write the word *awkward* on their native student papers. To an ELL, this word is a general cop-out. Never use the word *awkward* on an ELL's paper (and probably not on any student's paper). Writing *awkward* on the paper acknowledges what ELLs already know—that their writing sounds "off." The word *awkward* is not helpful unless you really think that the student writer knows another way to word this and simply chose the current wording over the preferred wording, which is a completely different case of a writer having options and making a wrong choice. However, if you think that the ELL wrote this chunk this way because that is probably the only way that he or she can say this idea, then writing *awkward* is a vague and unhelpful teacher comment, so save your red ink! If the writer had known another way to express his or her ideas, the writer probably would not have written it that way in the first place.

The main point here is that a writing teacher needs to be aware of ELL grammar issues. In this student's paper, the subject-verb agreement error in "the people in the crowded room <u>looks</u> . . ." is applicable to all students, but other errors are unique to ELLs and are actually normal errors in the acquisition process of English. Learning about ELL grammar will help you differentiate ELL errors from those typically made by native speakers.

Situation 3. Judging the Readability of Texts

All teachers of all subjects worldwide have to look at a book or worksheet to determine if the level of the language or content is appropriate for their students. Teachers of ELLs need to be able to look over a reading passage to determine if it is within their students' English proficiency level. Whether the textbook in your class deals with ELL instruction, tourism English, or social studies, how do you know whether a passage is the right level for your ELLs? What kinds of grammar points might make a reading passage beginning, intermediate, or advanced? If you know ELL grammar well, then you can look at a passage and gauge the difficulty level for your learners.

Some ELL grammar points do not affect the comprehension of reading passages very much. For example, articles rarely change the meaning of a passage. In other words, their impact is relatively weak.

> *Example: I ate an apple* versus *I ate the apple.*

In the first sentence, it could be any apple, but in the second sentence, we know that this was a specific apple, one that had been mentioned somewhere earlier in the passage or one that we as the readers are supposed to know about already.

Different languages deal with articles in very different ways. Some languages have no articles (e.g., Japanese, Russian, Chinese); others have only definite articles (e.g., Turkish, Hebrew, Arabic); and still others have articles that look like those in English but sometimes function differently (e.g., Spanish, French). For example, Russian does not have any articles, so a Russian student who reads the sentence *George has a new car* may in fact read it and remember it as *George has new car* unless a knowledgeable teacher points out that we use *a* in English in this case. This does not mean that the teacher should label this inserted word as an indefinite article. Again, grammar teaching is not about students learning grammatical labels. A more effective approach might be to get students to notice the difference between what they have written and what is in their textbook. Your goal is to get students to notice this "gap" between their current English usage and what the target structure looks like in actual usage by native speakers.

Situation 4. K–12 and Other Non-ELL Content Teachers

You are quite possibly the main or even the sole source of English input for many of your ELLs, which means that you and your daily English input are what your ELLs will use to formulate and develop their English. If your English is not comprehensible or if ELLs have a hard time understanding your English, they are being denied an essential resource to further their English proficiency.

How can you make your language more comprehensible? Some helpful modifications include slowing down your rate of speech, pausing more after idea groups (i.e., chunks), raising your voice on key ideas, and writing (or pointing to) ideas on the board as you say them. However, what can you do to the actual language that you are speaking? For ELLs to acquire the language and not just the gist of your content, native speaker ELL instructors need to work on the language they speak, including not just the content but also the grammar in the language.

One way to simplify language for an ELL is to use easier grammar structures or vocabulary, but many native speakers do not readily understand which words or structures are difficult. For example, a native speaker will say, "The weather today is sort of humid" and upon seeing many blank faces in the class attempt a paraphrase by saying, "Yes, today's weather is kind of damp."

Using one idiom (*kind of*) to explain another idiom (*sort of*) is not very helpful. In analyzing spoken American English, Liu (2003) found that the most commonly used idiom in spoken American English is *sort of*. What does this idiom mean? Almost all native speakers will answer "kind of," which is ironically the second most commonly used idiom. In addition, many native speakers assume that word length indicates word difficulty and that *damp* (one syllable) would be easier than *humid* (two syllables), but that is not at all the case for ELLs. (An easier way to explain *kind of* or *sort of* is *a little*. Instead of *damp*, use *feels wet* because these words are used more frequently and are therefore more likely to be known already.)

Another technique to keep your teaching language more comprehensible is to break up longer sentences into more manageable chunks. Consider the two versions on page 27 of directions from a teacher in a social studies class:

Direct Explanation	Interactive Explanation
Class, today we're going to trace the route of Vasco da Gama across the Atlantic Ocean to India. (The teacher is pointing at a huge map of the world which is at the front of the class.) Vasco da Gama made several trips toward India, but basically all of his trips followed the route that I'm marking here on the board.	Class, does anyone know the name of the explorer who traveled across the Atlantic Ocean all the way around southern Africa and then on to India? (pause) Can anyone tell me the name of this man? (pause; some students guess incorrectly) Okay, I will give you a hint. (pause) He was from Portugal. (Some students say, "Vasco da Gama") Yes, that's right. It was Vasco da Gama.

Okay, here we have a map of the world. (teacher points to the map) Mark, can you come up here and show us where Portugal is? (Mark comes up) Thank you. Yes, this country right here (teacher points) is Portugal. That's where Vasco da Gama was from. Now what about the southern tip . . . the southern point . . . of Africa? Tanya, can you show us where the southern tip of Africa is? (Tanya comes up to show this) Okay, now everyone look at me. Watch me as I draw the route, the path, that Vasco da Gama took on his first trip. Okay, we start here at. . . . (teacher pauses and waits until someone says "Portugal")

. . . Yes, that's right. We start at Portugal, and then we go south around the west coast of Africa. (teacher draws the route) Yes, this is the route that Vasco da Gama took. Can everyone see this? What direction are we traveling here? (pause) Yes, we're going south. OK, when Vasco da Gama reached the southern tip of Africa, what did he do? (pause; Students offer answers) Did he go back to Portugal? (pause) Right, he did not go back to Portugal. He continued. He continued on to India. |

As you can see, the second teacher is much more interactive, which is a style that works well with second language learners because there is more repetition of key language and the teacher is actually engaging the ELLs in a sort of dialogue rather than a lecture. The pauses are important for learners who simply need some time to consolidate what they have heard. Many teachers, especially novice teachers, do not allow sufficient wait time for students to respond. In Western society, we tend to be uncomfortable with silence and often wish to fill this perceived void.

Situation 5. All Teachers—Observing the Growth of Students' Language

Regardless of your teaching situation, you want to monitor—directly or indirectly—the progress of your ELLs' English proficiency. One way to do this is to notice specific language structures that they are first attempting to use and then are actually producing correctly. For example, beginning ELLs tend to put a form of *be* in front of all verbs, so they say, **Every day I am go to school. *At school, I am study English.* Gradually, this *be* + VERB will give way to just VERB: *Every day I go to school. At school, I study English.*

All teachers need to learn to **wait for a response.** Many ELLs of all ages need and appreciate a teacher who can allow a few seconds between the teacher's words and the ELL's response. This reflective moment gives ELLs time to think about what they believe they have heard and to think of a possible English answer in their heads before they attempt to speak.

This does not mean that the incorrect form suddenly disappears. Actually, the structure will fluctuate, and a week later students might say, *Every day I am go to school. *At school, I am studying English.* A few weeks later, after the ELLs have studied about present progressive tense—*I am eating* or *I am studying*—they might "revert" to using the *be* + VERB + *–ing* pattern because many ELLs tend to overuse any structure that they have recently been taught and say, *Every day I am going to school. At school, I am studying English* when they should use only simple present tense.

This flowing in and out of the correct target structure is normal; in fact, it has a name, **interlanguage** (Selinker, 1972). Interlanguage refers to the way a structure is used by a language learner at any given point of time. For any target structure, interlanguage ranges from no ability to native ability with many points in between these two extremes. Interlanguage does not develop in a linear fashion; instead, progress can appear to be erratic, but this is normal. Your ability to recognize ELL grammar points in your ELLs' language output allows you to assess ELLs' language progress more accurately.

The errors that we see in an ELL's **interlanguage** reflect language growth and are a natural part of learning a language. For example, before ELLs say, *I go* or *I need*, they often say, *I am go* or *I am need*. This type of error is normal.

Situation 6. All Teachers—Answering ELL Questions

As teachers, we live for that "teachable moment," and there is no better teachable moment than one that actually comes from the student. If you have ELLs, you will be asked questions about English. If you are new to teaching ELLs, you will initially be stumped by many of these questions that you as a native speaker have never even thought about, much less heard or seen. Consider these three exchanges:

Exchange 1

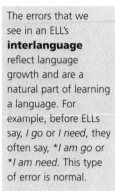

ELL:	Can I say <u>much people</u>?
Teacher:	No, you should say <u>many people</u>.
ELL:	Why?
Teacher:	Because . . . we don't say <u>much people</u>. We say <u>many people</u>.
ELL:	? (puzzled look)
Teacher:	Okay? (hoping that the ELL will say yes)

NOTE: The teacher has not explained anything.

Exchange 2

ELL:	Tomorrow I will to go to the movie with my friends.
Teacher:	That's great. Tomorrow you <u>will</u> go. (emphasizes *will* by saying it more loudly)
ELL:	Yes, to the movie.
Teacher:	Yes, I know, but you said you "will to go," but in English, we don't use *to* here.
ELL:	Really? Okay, thanks. Why not?
Teacher:	It doesn't sound right.
ELL:	What do you mean?
Teacher:	It's awkward.

NOTE: The teacher has not given an explanation at all.

Exchange 3

ELL: My mother is from Philippines.

Teacher: Your mother is from <u>the</u> Philippines. (emphasizes *the* by saying it more loudly)

ELL: The Philippines? I can't say just Philippines?

Teacher: No. You need to say <u>the</u> Philippines.

ELL: Why?

Teacher: Ummm . . . well . . . We use *the* with country names.

ELL: Like <u>the</u> United States?

Teacher: Yes, exactly.

ELL: Hmmm . . . So I need to say <u>the</u> Mexico and <u>the</u> Saudi Arabia?

Teacher: Well, no. We don't use *the* with those two countries.

ELL: Why?

Teacher: Because they're exceptions.

ELL: Which one is the exception—the Philippines or Mexico?

Teacher: Ummm . . . Well . . . .

NOTE: The teacher does not know the rule. The teacher has confused the student even more now.

Nothing is better for an ELL teacher than when a question comes from one of our students instead of our own mouth as we try to plant a question in the class. When ELLs ask questions about ELL grammar, a prepared ELL teacher is able to answer most of them. Yes, it is true that all of us get a question that we have not thought of before, but the examples here are ELL Grammar 101. (Chapter 4 in this book addresses 20 impromptu grammar questions, called Hot Seat Questions, to help you prepare for these questions.)

Situation 7. An Inquisitive Teacher: Action Research

When you first start teaching anywhere, you will be busy with the ins and outs of your new school, the students, the paperwork, the testing, school duties, and other daily tasks. As you gain experience, you will think about better ways to organize your class or better ways to teach a certain topic. As you experiment with different aspects of your teaching, you are engaging in what is referred to as **action research.** In action research, you, as the teacher and as informal researcher, have a purposeful question in mind—*if I teach these math procedures in a different order, will my students' scores on the state test be different?* You then make the change and thereby conduct an informal experiment with your new treatment.

If you are not an experienced ELL teacher, the first few times you teach ELLs, you will make some mistakes. As you gain teaching experience, you will develop better ways of teaching certain concepts. Because grammar is so important, teachers are always trying to come up with better ways to teach ELL grammar. To do this, teachers must first be familiar with basic ELL grammar points, which can be found in this book, particularly in Chapter 3.

Generation 1.5 refers to the growing number of U.S. high school ELLs who graduate from high school but enter college without a full command of English. Generation 1.5 students are similar to both first- and second-generation immigrants.

Situation 8. An ELL Teacher

Anyone who teaches ELLs—whether you are a high school science teacher with some ELLs in your class, a college instructor of Generation 1.5 students, or a conversation teacher in Greece—should be familiar with ELL grammar issues. Knowledge of these issues makes you better able to help students improve their speaking, writing, or reading proficiency in English.

2

Basic English Grammar:
Usage and Terminology

Section 1	Common Grammar Errors Made by Native Speakers
Section 2	Eight Parts of Speech
Section 3	Basic Grammar Labels for Sentence Structure
Section 4	Why the Twelve English Verb Tenses Matter

Before examining ELL grammar issues, it is important to have a solid understanding of grammar usage and key terminology. This chapter explores some of the most common errors made by native speakers of English as a way to help all teachers develop a solid understanding of their native language. As you speak to your ELLs, you must be able to easily differentiate Standard English from incorrect English. While regional variations of English do exist, learners hope to attain proficiency in Standard English. Section 1 includes a short pre-test of 20 common errors made by native speakers in spoken and/or written English. More information about each error can be found in Appendix 1.

Section 2 reviews the eight parts of speech, the basic building blocks of the English language. ELL grammar makes use of seven of the traditional eight parts of speech, but ELL grammar is not organized around the parts of speech in the same way that the grammar of native speakers is.

Because some grammar terms are applicable only to native English grammar while others are used primarily in ELL grammar, basic grammar terminology is reviewed in Section 3. Learning the labels for grammatical concepts, however, is not the same as understanding the underlying patterns within a language. Labels can be useful tools for teachers and students, but grammar is much more than labels. Therefore, you should exercise great care when using these labels in the classroom. Section 3 also contains a brief overview of sentence structure.

In observing grammar classes over the years, I have seen teachers confuse providing a grammar label with giving a good grammar explanation. They are not the same. In one class, a student asked the teacher a grammar question about a sentence that someone had told him was incorrect. Logically, he wanted to know why his sentence was incorrect.

> *Wish* has a special grammar for ELLs. See Key 15 for more information on the grammar of the verb *wish*.

Student: Why is it wrong to say, "I wish I studied more for today's test"? Why do I have to say, "I wish I *had studied* more for today's test"?

Teacher: Because *had studied* is past perfect tense.

Student: Excuse me? What?

Teacher: *Had* is the auxiliary verb, and *studied* is the past participle. When you use *had* as an auxiliary verb with the past participle, that's called past perfect tense.

Student: Okay. [clearly not understanding]

The label **past perfect** is in fact the correct label for the words *had studied*. However, the label **past perfect** is not the grammar explanation here. The correct explanation is that native speakers use past perfect tense of a verb after the word *wish* when we are wishing now about something in the past. Thus, the key component of the explanation is that the word *wish* triggers a mandatory verb form, which happens to be past perfect tense.

Because verbs occupy a special place in English grammar, Section 4 focuses on the twelve verb tenses in English. Just as native speakers of English often have bad memories of verb conjugations in the various tenses in Spanish, French, or other foreign language, ELLs find the many English verb tenses to be confusing and at times seemingly incomprehensible.

SECTION 1
Common Grammar Errors Made by Native Speakers

At one point or another, all of us make grammatical mistakes in our speech and writing. When we say or write something very quickly, our minds are so focused on the content of our message that we might pay less attention to our language and inadvertently make a grammatical error. A good example of this scenario occurs with email messages; we may have to answer so many messages daily that we aren't always as careful as we should be. However, in formal reports, academic writing, and public speeches, it is imperative that we use correct language so that our audiences pay attention to our message and are not distracted by our errors.

Teachers expect their ELL students to make mistakes with grammar. Students are in class to improve their language skills. As teachers, however, we are in a different category. What is the impression given when a teacher consistently makes a grammar mistake not because of time constraints but because of lack of knowledge about the language? When teachers make grammatical errors on a class handout, quiz, or note to a student, it does not reflect well on them or their credibility. (Like it or not, teachers are held to a high degree of language accountability.)

To assess your ability with 20 of the most common errors made by native speakers in spoken and written English, a pre-test follows. Use your results to review the detailed information on these grammar points, which can be found in Appendix 1.

Take the pre-test on pages 34–35 now, before reading on.

Why Grammar Matters

Many people have a negative image of grammar because they tend to associate grammar lessons with reprimands and warnings about not making certain kinds of errors. In fact, many of us associate the word *grammar* with the word *don't*. Don't say *me and my friend*. Don't use *ain't*. Don't misuse *broke* for *broken*.

"What's the big deal with grammar anyway?" some might ask. The style of language that you speak does matter in many situations, and grammar is a key component of that style. When we first meet people, we are already forming an opinion about them. Do they sound educated? Do they sound professional? Do they sound friendly? The list of questions goes on, and the answers to many of these questions are based on the kind of language being used, including the number and type of errors in a person's speech.

To be sure, some errors are judged—fairly or unfairly—as more serious than others. Language is spoken by humans, and human perceptions are very subjective. Society tells us that some errors are bad, but others are not so serious. For instance, most people would agree that hearing a person that we do not know say *ain't* or *it don't matter* lowers our perception of that speaker much more than adding the unnecessary (and incorrect) preposition *at* in *Where do you live at?* (Note that all three examples are incorrect.)

Pre-Test 1: Common Grammar Errors Made by Native Speakers

You will read 25 sentences that contain grammar points that are problematic for many native speakers. Five of these sentences are correct. For the 20 that have a grammatical error, circle the common error made by native speakers and write a correction above it. (NOTE: Individual stylistics vary considerably, so all 25 of these statements could be rewritten with different grammar and vocabulary. Your task, however, is to identify parts of the sentences that are obvious errors.) Suggested time limit: 15 minutes. (Answers are on pp. 86–87.)

1. It's essential to get the message out to parents that they have to know at all times exactly whom their loved ones associate with and where they are at.

2. I've encountered a problem when I'm trying to insert a record. Sometimes while I'm trying to build a menu list, I'll get an error message telling me something about too much recursion. What does this mean?

3. Between you and I, this situation is going to have a very unhappy ending.

4. My wife and I look forward to working more with the Matthew Community Program. Founded a decade ago by Theodore Jabil and myself, this organization serves children and families in the Brooklyn area.

5. I had went to different therapy services, but Pressure Point was the best ever.

6. The DC-10 jet cracked into two pieces and came to rest with the front section laying on its side.

7. The campus police department is proud to announce the publication of the long-awaited and revised Student Safety Guide. Note that the name has been changed to the Annual Report & Safety Guide to reflect its content more appropriately.

8. Team captains are receiving this article because they might want to pass it on to whomever would benefit from it the most.

9. What the boss don't know won't matter in the end.

10. If it wouldn't have been raining, the kids could have played in the backyard.

11. The jurisdiction that includes these seven heavily populated metropolitan areas should have its boundaries redrawn.

12. The school board's new plan will not hardly affect the students at this elementary school.

13. According to the author, when people feel stressed, angry, or ashamed, we give off negative energy. This is why viewing negative events causes us to feel badly. Similarly, witnessing acts of kindness causes us to feel good.

14. We cannot let them people vote. If we let them vote, they're not going to make the right decision.

15. My opinion is that the manager should of fired those employees on the spot.

16. Care should be taken when attempting to remove a tick from human skin. Cover the tick with this liquid for a few seconds. If you apply enough liquid, the tick will let go on it's own.

17. A clear advantage that this particular electronic dictionary software has over its competitors is the incredible number of words that can be quickly looked up.

18. If you want to play on the team, please send me an email letting me know that your interested. I need your response no later than Saturday.

19. Krashen came up with the concept of *i + 1* to help describe the distance between a persons language proficiency and the level of the language in the material.

20. If you are an employee who's contract expires annually and a renewal is done at the beginning of a semester, you may not be entered into the data system yet.

21. Yes, I'm looking for something that is more stable than my current job, but I haven't been going to job interviews to much.

22. Your place was terrific, but I want to say that your warm hospitality and great facilities are what we enjoyed the most and what made the trip so special to Kate and me.

23. Applicants may submit their paperwork either in person or via email. Note that the submission method will not effect the committee's decision regarding any application.

24. This plant can withstand temperatures to five degrees Fahrenheit, which is the point at which the plant may loose some or all of its leaves (but still not kill the plant).

25. In a recent ruling by five of the Supreme Court justices, there conclusion was that police should have more authority in some cases.

Your Score: _____/25_____

Language always involves people, so these judgments are based on the value that educated native speakers in our English-speaking society have assigned to certain errors. This does not suggest that anyone has actually made a list of the worst to not-so-bad errors, but English speakers as a group tend to recognize that certain errors seem to be made more often by uneducated speakers who are in a lower socio-economic group and that committing these errors tends to identify a speaker as a member of these groups—rightly or wrongly. (This judgment of a person's education or personality based on the language used is a universal; it is in no way confined to English with English speakers.) To be certain, ELLs need to learn standard English.

We also need to make a distinction between a true error and informal language. All speakers use different varieties, or levels, of a language when interacting with different people. The language that I use in telling a joke to a good friend has a different tone, vocabulary, and level of formality than when I am writing a document for publication. The key point is that I know the difference between these two extremes and have not only sufficient situational awareness but, more important, sufficient English proficiency to use one kind of language instead of the other. In sum, I can use both extremes when I wish because I know the difference. I know my options and have made an informed, conscious choice.

A good concrete example of this distinction is with the usage of *who* and *whom*. Grammatically, *who* is a subject and *whom* is an object. Therefore, we would ask, *Who helped you?* and *Whom did you help?* This grammatical difference between *who* and *whom* is clear. Current usage in the real world, however, is different.

First, no native speaker would ever misuse *whom* for *who*: **Whom helped you?* A native speaker would never say this, so the question is when to use *whom*, not when to use *who*.

Language is not spoken in a vacuum; we use it to interact with people in very different situations, ranging from the very formal to the very informal. In formal language, yes, we could ask, *Whom did you help?* However, in informal language, most of us rarely if ever use *whom*—even in a sentence like this one where *whom* is actually correct. For most of us, using *whom* sounds very formal, possibly even pretentious or "stuck up." In fact, I have never used (or heard) the word *whom* around my family or in my immediate circle of friends. In contrast, it is quite easy to imagine a switchboard operator at a large firm answering the phone by asking, *Good afternoon. Whom did you wish to speak with today?* If the operator used *who*, suddenly the initial greeting might not seem so formal.

Because it is natural to want to bond with other humans, we use certain levels of language to try to fit in. When applying for a job at a large company, we use the most formal language possible to sound educated and capable. However, if we stopped at a gas station to get our car repaired, we would probably ask, *Who do I talk to about getting my car repaired?* instead of *Whom do I speak with about having my car repaired?* Using *who* instead of *whom* is appropriate in informal situations; it is a way of establishing rapport in our conversations.

You may have noticed that although **whom** is often listed in grammar books and is something you might see in writing, you don't ever really hear it in spoken English. This is true because *whom* is almost exclusively used in formal language. Not using *whom* when speaking is NOT an error. The use of *who* instead of *whom* can be seen in songs because songs represent informal language. Thus, you've never heard a song title like, "Whom do you love?" even though that would be grammatically correct. People in love are not concerned with *who* vs. *whom*.

Prescriptive and Descriptive Grammar

The usage of *who/whom* illustrates **prescriptive grammar** vs. **descriptive grammar.** Prescriptive grammar prescribes, or dictates, exactly what should or should not be said or used. In contrast, descriptive grammar describes how the language is actually being used.

For instance, prescriptive grammar says to use *whom* for all object positions: *Whom would you like to speak with?* In contrast, descriptive grammar notes that in current usage, *Whom would you like to speak with?* is correct, formal language. Descriptive grammar would also note that in a very formal situation, we would probably begin the question with the preposition (*With whom would you like to speak?*) and that in more informal settings, people would use *who* (*Who would you like to speak with?*). Note the levels of formality in this series of questions posed by an operator at a business.

Most Formal   *With* **whom** *would you like to speak?*
       ↑   **Whom** *would you like to speak with?*
       | **Whom** *do you want to speak with?*
       | **Who** *would you like to speak with?*
       | **Who** *do you want to speak with?*
       | **Who** *do you want to speak to?*
       ↓   **Who** *do you want to talk with?*
Most informal **Who** *do you want to talk to?*

Table 2.1 shows how prescriptive grammarians and descriptive grammarians might treat three grammar topics.

Table 2.1 Examples of Prescriptive vs. Descriptive Grammar

Grammar Topic	**Prescriptive Grammar**	**Descriptive Grammar**
who / whom	Always use *who* as a subject and *whom* as an object.	1. We always use *who* as a subject. 2. In everyday language, people also use *who* as an object. In very formal language, we always use *whom* in the object position. 3. When directly preceded by a preposition, people usually use *whom*.
splitting an infinitive	Never split an infinitive. (Few people would dare to change the opening lines of the TV show "Star Trek" from *to boldly go* to *to go boldly*, but from a prescriptive viewpoint, only the second option is correct.)	1. People often split infinitives with adverbs of manner (*to quickly exit*) or adverbs of degree (*to almost double*).

Table 2.1 Examples of Prescriptive vs. Descriptive Grammar (continued)

Grammar Topic	Prescriptive Grammar	Descriptive Grammar
possessive adjective agreement with *everyone*	Indefinite pronouns such as *everyone* and *somebody* are always singular. When referring to indefinite pronouns, use *his*. (Many people find the use of *his* to be sexist. To sound less sexist, it is possible to use the phrase *his or her*.)	1. People often use *their* to refer to indefinite pronouns. 2. When trying to sound more correct—especially in formal writing, people often use the phrase *his or her* even though its repetitiveness can sound awkward.

Does this mean that if enough people say something, it will become part of descriptive grammar and acceptable to say? Every language has certain prescribed usage rules (hence the term *prescriptive grammar*). These rules are based on what is considered normal by educated speakers within that language group. Prescriptive grammar views language as finite; descriptive grammar accounts for current usage and consequently acknowledges that over time, language usage will change. Who knows? Maybe some day *whom* will disappear completely, and all speakers will ask, *Does everyone have their ID?* without any grammar guilt pangs.

Having discussed and acknowledged the two camps of prescriptivism and descriptivism, the bottom line is that in professional settings and, in particular, in the academic settings in which we teach, language accuracy does matter considerably. While spoken language allows more flexibility, written language does not. Mistakes made in writing are right there in front of our readers' eyes. Readers will judge us on our education, socio-economic status, professionalism, and even intelligence based on the types of errors we make in our writing.

The pre-test on pages 34–35 and Appendix 1 examine 20 typical errors made by native speakers. The errors are presented in two groups. The first group includes errors that appear in both spoken and written English, while the second group includes errors that appear more commonly in written English. The errors in the two groups occur for different reasons, but all are considered grammatical errors because they violate some aspect of grammar (as opposed to spelling or pronunciation errors).

20 Common Grammar Errors Made by Native Speakers	
Errors that Occur in Writing and Speaking	*Errors that Occur Predominantly in Writing*
1. unnecessary prepositions (e.g., *Where do you live at?‡*) 2. *I, me* 3. *myself* (reflexive pronouns) 4. past participles and past tense (e.g., *gone, went*) 5. *lie, lay* 6. *whoever, whomever* (or *who, whom*) 7. *he/she/it don't‡* 8. *if I would have known‡* 9. double negatives 10. *bad, badly* 11. *them, those*	12. *have, of* 13. *it's, its, its'‡* 14. *your, you're* 15. *'s* 16. *who's, whose* 17. *to, too, two* 18. *affect, effect* 19. *lose, loose* 20. *they're, there, their*
NOTE: More detailed information about these 20 language issues can be found in Appendix 1.	

While it is true that some of these errors are considered more egregious than others, no real effort has been made to rank these 20 topics in terms of severity. When you are applying for a teaching job, any error in your CV—**even just one**—will be glaring and will impact your chances of getting the job that you want.

Your goal is to recognize these usages as incorrect English. You are an extremely important source of English input for your ELLs. Because your students will look to you as a model of good language usage, your ultimate goal is to avoid making these common errors.

SECTION 2
Eight Parts of Speech

For many people, the eight parts of speech are the cornerstone of English grammar. Native speakers from elementary school to high school learn the definitions of the eight parts of speech along with numerous examples and usages. In this section, we will review the traditional eight parts of speech. To determine what you already know, two pre-tests follow to help you recognize where to concentrate your efforts.

Pre-Test 2: Eight Parts of Speech

Without looking ahead, list the eight parts of speech. Define each and give an example. Suggested time limit: 10 minutes. (Answers are on p. 87.)

1. _____

_____

2. _____

_____

3. _____

_____

4. _____

_____

5. _____

_____

6. _____

_____

7. _____

_____

8. _____

_____

Pre-Test 3: Eight Parts of Speech

Write the part of speech above each of the 25 underlined words in this book review. Suggested time limit: 15 minutes. (Answers are on p. 88.)

Formative Years:
Children's Health in the United States, 1880–2000
Alexandra Minna Stern and Howard Markel, Editors

Much has changed in ① the lives of children, and in the health
② care provided to them over the ③ past century. We like the book
Formative Years ④ because it explores how children's lives have become
⑤ increasingly medicalized, ⑥ traces the emergence of the fields of pediatrics, and offers ⑦ fascinating case studies of important and ⑧ timely
issues.

⑨ With contributions from historians and physicians, ⑩ this collection
illuminates some of the most important ⑪ transformations in ⑫ children's
health in the United States since the 1880s. Opening with a history of pediatrics as a ⑬ medical specialty, the book ⑭ addresses such topics as the formulation of normal growth curves, Better Babies contests ⑮ at county fairs,
the "discovery" of the sexual abuse of children, and the political radicalism
of the founder of pediatrics, Dr. Abraham Jacobi.

One of the first long-term historical and analytical ⑯ overviews of
pediatrics and child health in the twentieth century, *Formative Years* will be a
⑰ welcome addition to ⑱ several ⑲ fields, including the history of
medicine and technology, the history of childhood, modern U.S. history,
women's history, and American studies. ⑳ It ㉑ also has ramifications for
policymakers concerned with child welfare ㉒ and development and
㉓ poses important questions ㉔ about the direction of children's health
in the ㉕ twenty-first century.

Why the Parts of Speech Matter

The eight (traditional) parts of speech are **nouns, verbs, adjectives, adverbs, pronouns, conjunctions, prepositions,** and **interjections.** In reality, the English language can be divided into many more than eight parts of speech, but the approach in the past has almost always been to name only eight categories. Adjectives, for example, include articles (*a, an, the*), determiners (*some, any*), demonstrative adjectives (*this, that, these, those*), and possessive adjectives (*my, your, his, her, its, our, their*). Some grammar books for native speakers actually consider these groups to be separate categories. Because all of these categories modify a noun, which is a normal function of adjectives, these four categories are traditionally not considered separate parts of speech but rather types of adjectives in grammar books for native speakers. (For ELLs, these subcategories are important because their grammatical behaviors are different.)

Unlike other countries that rely on a central Ministry or Department of Education that is in charge of producing a national curriculum, the United States relegates most of its control of content to state and local school commissions. As a result, there is much more diversity in what is actually taught in U.S. schools nationwide. Despite this diversity, the eight parts of speech are taught pretty much the same from coast to coast, and the definitions that are taught—from a multitude of books provided by numerous publishers—tend to be very similar.

Before reading further, let's consider the example of just four of the eight parts of speech—namely nouns, verbs, adjectives, and adverbs. On Pre-Test 2 on page 40, what did you write for the definitions of a noun, a verb, an adjective, and an adverb?

Once you have done this, discuss your responses. If you are in a class, first find out the state, province, or country where everyone in class went to middle school. In most groups, you will be amazed at the geographical distribution. You will probably find that no matter whether you went to school in Colorado or Florida, your definitions tend to be fairly uniform.

What did you write for the meaning of a *noun?* Most people—regardless of where they studied this concept years ago—invariably say that a noun is "the name of a person, place, or thing." Some people may also add "or a feeling or idea." By contrast, how many people in your group said "a word that *names* something"? This definition is also possible, but hardly anyone says this.

What about a verb? How many people said, "a word that shows action"? Some people may say, "action, being, or state of being." No one says "movement" even though this definition is also possible.

In traditional grammar, an adjective is usually defined as "a word that describes a noun," but another good definition would be "a word that describes or limits a noun or pronoun."

Adverbs are extremely tricky. This category seems to be a dumping ground for a lot of very different kinds of words, and adverbs could in fact be six to eight different parts of speech! Did you say an adverb is "a word that modifies a verb, an adjective, or other adverb"? Why did you say *modify* instead of *describe?*

For whatever reason, no matter where we learned the eight parts of speech, we all tend to know a very similar wording of the definition. We say what a noun is (i.e., a noun *is the name of . . .*), but we tell what an adjective does (i.e., an adjective *describes, modifies, or limits a noun or pronoun . . .*). Similar patterns exist for all eight parts of speech.

Multiple Approaches to Explaining the Parts of Speech

As we have just seen (and have been taught all our school lives), the most common way to teach someone about a given part of speech is to give a definition. In addition to a traditional definition, teachers can also provide an example phrase or sentence where only one part of speech can be used. This kind of approach is called "slot and filler" grammar because we create a slot that could usually—if not (ideally) only—be filled with one part of speech. (Sometimes even just a portion of a word can be used in lieu of a phrase or full sentence to create the slot.)

We already said that a noun is the name of a person, place, thing, or feeling. What are some slots that would allow for nouns but not verbs or adjectives or another part of speech? What are some slots that will help ELLs visualize what a noun is? (In each slot, we assume we are putting only *one* word.)

1. I have a _____.
2. a _____
3. the _____
4. five _____
5. My favorite hobby is _____.

Sometimes what looks like a good slot for one part of speech is problematic for teaching because another part of speech can also fit. For example, a seemingly good slot of nouns is _____s because we can insert nouns such as *cat (→cats)*, *book (→books)*, and *car (→cars)*. However, we can also insert verbs such as *eat (→eats)* and *take (→takes)*. Since our goal is to help learners understand what makes each part of speech unique, we need slots that do not overlap or that have as little room for overlap as possible.

Sometimes slots that seem logical to you as a native speaker of English will not produce the same conceptualization in the mind of ELLs because that part of speech works differently in their languages. In Japanese, for example, adjectives have negative forms and past (tense) forms, which means that for Japanese speakers learning English, the line between verbs and adjectives may be obscured. A slot such as "Yesterday I _____ed" works in English for verbs only, but to a Japanese ELL, this slot could also hold an adjective. It is not essential that you know all of these linguistic nuances regarding how different languages treat the parts of speech. However, when you are coming up with slots that are appropriate for your learners, keep in mind that the confused faces of your ELLs might be due to interference between their native language and your particular example slot, so be prepared to present multiple example slots.

For each of the parts of speech, we will look at traditional definitions as well as common, productive slots to illustrate their usages. Skilled teachers are able to explain parts of speech (or any aspect of grammar) in multiple ways to accommodate ELLs' learning styles.

Nouns

Common ELL Errors	Examples
omission of plural –s	*five girl
unnecessary plural –s	*every girls
wrong noun ending	*enjoyation
plural of non-count nouns	*many equipments
no article with count nouns	*I have cat.
the with abstract nouns	Be brave. *You must have the patience and the hope.
not capitalizing proper nouns	I was born in guadalajara in mexico.

What is a noun?
A **noun** is the name of a person, place, thing, or quality.

person: a girl, a driver, Kevin

place: a park, a city, Boston

thing: tennis balls, milk, a Toyota

quality: friendship, joy, confidence

What questions does a noun answer?
A noun answers the questions *who* or *what*.

Question	Answer (= noun)
Who took the money?	John took the money.
What did you eat?	I ate salmon.

What are possible slots for a noun?

Slot	Examples
I see an _____	apple, igloo, Audi, ostrich
She is a _____	driver, grandmother, mechanic, swimmer
There are four _____	reasons, people, assignments, reports
the _____	title, money, equator, Philippines
_____ is important	oxygen, kindness, exercising, New York

Details of Nouns

- **What is the difference between common nouns and proper nouns?**
  Nouns can also be divided into common nouns and proper nouns. A **common noun** is the name of any person, place, or thing. A **proper noun** is the name of a specific person, place, or thing. A proper noun always begins with a capital letter, and a common noun begins with a lowercase letter.

Common Nouns	Proper Nouns
a princess	Princess Diana
a city	Los Angeles
a day	Friday
a product	a Toyota

A common ELL error is to use lowercase letters with proper nouns. ELLs write sentences such as *My parents grew up in miami* and *The most important document is the declaration of independence.*

- **What is the difference between concrete nouns and abstract nouns?**
  Nouns can be further divided into concrete and abstract nouns. A **concrete noun** is a noun that you can perceive with your five senses. That is, you can see it, hear it, smell it, taste it, or feel (physically touch) it. In contrast, an **abstract noun** names an emotion, idea, or quality. An abstract noun cannot be perceived with any of the five senses.

Concrete Nouns	Abstract Nouns
(I saw a) sunset.	patience
(I heard some) cats.	childhood
(I smelled your) cologne.	justice
(I tasted the) doughnut.	humor
(I felt a gentle) breeze.	success

A common ELL error is to use the definite article *the* with abstract nouns. ELLs write sentences such as, *You must have the patience* and *We really value the justice for everyone.*

- **What is the difference between count and non-count nouns?**
  Nouns can also be divided into count and non-count nouns. As its name implies, a **count noun** is a noun that you can count, which means that it has a singular form and a plural form. Count nouns include *cat* (*1 cat, 15 cats*) and *child* (*1 child, 15 children*). In contrast, a **non-count noun** is a noun that you cannot count. A non-count noun has only one form and cannot have a number in front of it. Non-count nouns include *homework, machinery, money, information,* and *traffic.* (NOTE: Non-count nouns are also called **mass nouns.**)

Count Nouns	Non-Count Nouns
assignment	homework
fact	information
machine	machinery

A common error occurs when ELLs assume that it is possible to count a noun that is actually a non-count noun. They write sentences such as, *We have many homeworks and *Thank you for the advices.

Verbs	
Common ELL Errors	*Examples*
misuse of *have* for *be*	*We have hungry now. Let's eat.
lack of verb endings for 3rd person singular	*The teacher drive a Toyota.
problems with **auxiliary verbs** in negating	*My sister no lives in Texas now.
problems with auxiliary verbs in questions	*Why you need more medicine?
wrong verb tense: present tense for present progressive	*She can't go now because she cooks the dinner.
wrong verb tense: present tense for present perfect	*How long do you live here?
verb tense switches	*In this story, the main character (Bill Newton) married his sweetheart (Carrie Sommers). Later, they have three children. Their oldest son became a famous doctor, but the youngest son decides to go to medical school, too.
lack of direct object for a **transitive verb**	The dinner was great. *We enjoyed very much.
use of infinitives after modals	*I believe that everyone should to learn a second language.

What is a verb?
A **verb** shows action or being (existence). A verb is the heart of any English sentence.

action: run, eat, prepare, destroy, ask

being (existence): be (am, is, are, was, were)

What question does a verb answer?
A verb answers the question, *What does/did [the subject] do?*

Question	Answer (= verb)
What does a dog do?	It <u>barks</u>.
What do you do?	I <u>teach</u>.
What did Jo and Bob do?	They <u>complained</u> to the manager.

What are possible slots for a verb?
You can conjugate a verb, so possible slots include:

Slot	Examples
I / you / we / they _____	work, worked, take, took
he / she / it _____ s	works, takes, needs, seems
Yesterday I _____ ed	worked, wanted, needed, seemed
I didn't _____ it	have, take, need, like

Details of Verbs

- **What are the principal parts of verbs?**
  Verbs have four principal parts: base form, past, past participle, and present participle. For regular verbs, the past and past participle forms use the suffix *–ed*. Irregular verbs use a variety of forms, including the suffixes *–en* and *–ne* as well as internal vowel changes or no change at all.

Regular Verbs	Base	Past	Past Participle	Present Participle
	work	worked	worked	working
	rob	robbed	robbed	robbing
	flash	flashed	flashed	flashing
	copy	copied	copied	copying
Irregular Verbs	Base	Past	Past Participle	Present Participle
	take	took	taken	taking
	go	went	gone	going
	sing	sang	sung	singing
	cut	cut	cut	cutting

- **What are verb tenses?**

  Verb tenses are verb structures that tell the time of the action expressed by the verb. There are twelve verb tenses in English: simple present tense, simple past tense, simple future tense, present progressive tense, past progressive tense, future progressive tense, present perfect tense, past perfect tense, future perfect tense, present perfect progressive tense, past perfect progressive tense, and future perfect progressive tense. (See pp. 74–83 for example.)

- **What is the difference between transitive and intransitive verbs?**

  Transitive verbs must have an object for their action, and intransitive verbs can never have an object for their action. For example, *like* is a transitive verb because you must put an object after it. You cannot say *I like* or *I didn't like at the restaurant.* You must say *I like the book* or *I didn't like the food at the restaurant.* Likewise, *consist* is an intransitive verb because you cannot put an object after it. You cannot say **The story consisted three parts* or **The exam consisted 20 questions.*

  In a dictionary, verbs that are only transitive are usually marked with the letters *vt*, verbs that are only intransitive by the letters *vi*, and a verb that can be both transitive and intransitive by the letter *v*. Consider these examples of the three categories:

  > transitive verbs (vt): *like, love, kill, take, make, furnish, persuade, put, sense*
  > intransitive verbs (vi): *die, occur, happen, arrive, thrive, travel*
  > both (v):   *read, move, study, watch, operate*

  There is a special category of intransitive verbs called **linking verbs.** Linking verbs do not express action. As their name implies, linking verbs connect the subject to additional information in another part of the sentence. (Linking verbs are followed by adjectives, not adverbs.)

  > Linking verbs: *appear, become, feel, get, go, grow, look, prove, remain, seem, smell, sound, stay, taste, turn,* and (any form of) *be*

- **What are auxiliary (or helping) verbs?**

  Most sentences have verbs that consist of one word, as seen in these two examples:

  > The earth **reveals** much about its past through natural records such as fossils.

  > Together with southern Mexico, Belize, Honduras, and Guatemala, the small Central American nation of El Salvador *is* home to some intriguing Mayan ruins.

  In other cases, the verb is actually a verb phrase consisting of more than one word, such as in *The cost of living* **has been rising** *sharply*. In these cases, there is a main verb *(rising)*, which is usually the word that carries the meaning of the verb phrase, and one or more helping or auxiliary verbs *(has been)*. We will study the most common helping verbs, which are forms of *be, have,* and *do,* as well as **modals**.

- **Examples of** *Be*

  There are eight forms of *be* that are possible as auxiliary verbs: *am, is, are, was, were, be, being,* and *been.* Remember that a form of *be* can also be the main verb in a sentence. (See pp. 77–78 and 81–83 for more information on progressive tenses.) Initially, ELLs have a problem remembering the different forms of *be.* Later, ELLs internalize the forms of *be* so well, especially *I am, you are, he is,* that they end up learning to use SUBJECT + *be* when in fact they really mean just subject. Therefore, it is common for ELLs at the intermediate level to say a sentence such as, **I am drive this kind of car because it is get really good mileage.*

  > The **verb** *be* has many different meanings: *She is a student* (be + noun); *He is hungry* (be + adjective); *It is in Oslo* (be + location); *She is working* (present progressive tense); *The class is at noon* (be + time).

Be as Auxiliary Verb	*Be* as Main Verb
(1a) Our fifth-graders *are studying* the chemical properties of water this week. (main verb = *studying,* from *study*)	(1b) For bulk buying at warehouse clubs, non-perishable items *are* often at unbeatable prices. (main verb = *are,* from *be*)
(2a) Medical scientists *have been working* on better ways to use ocean plant life to produce miracle drugs against cancer. (main verb = *working,* from *work*)	(2b) Oil *has been* the main export of Saudi Arabia for several decades now. (main verb = *been,* from *be*)
(3a) In the experiment, the water *is heated* in the dish for approximately twelve minutes. (main verb = *heated,* from *heat*)	(3b) Together with southern Mexico, Honduras and Guatemala, the small Central American nation of El Salvador *is* home to some intriguing Mayan ruins. (main verb = *is,* from *be*)
(4a) Arizona *was admitted* to the U.S. in 1912. (main verb = *admitted,* from *admit*)	(4b) Arizona *was* the 48th state to enter the U.S. (main verb = *was,* from *be*)

ELLs frequently confuse the **verbs do** and **make**: *We do the dishes* but *make the bed. A teacher makes a test,* but *the student does it.* These idiomatic usages are daunting (see Hot Seat Question 19, pp. 284–85.)

- **Examples of *Do***

There are three forms of *do* that are possible as auxiliary verbs: *do, does,* and *did.* A form of *do* is used as an auxiliary verb when the verb phrase is **interrogative** (a question), negative, negative **imperative** (command), or **emphatic** (for emphasis, as in *I do need more money*). Remember that a form of *do* can also be the main verb in a sentence. The use of the auxiliary *do* is very difficult for ELLs.

Do as Auxiliary Verb	*Do* as Main Verb
(1a) How many cups of sugar ***does*** the recipe ***call*** for? (main verb = *call,* from *call*) (interrogative)	(1b) According to my grandfather, he ***does*** gardening because it relaxes him. (main verb = *does,* from *do*)
(2a) We took the bus, but we ***did*** not ***save*** much money at all. (main verb = *save,* from *save*) (negative)	(2b) The taxi driver ***did*** us a favor by taking our bags to the lobby. (main verb = *did,* from *do*)
(3a) ***Don't do*** the dishes now! (main verb = the second *do,* from *do*) (negative imperative)	(3b) ***Do*** your work! (main verb = *do,* from *do*)
(4a) Yes, you ***do need*** a jacket today. Put it on! (main verb = *need,* from *need*) (emphatic)	(4b) Parents give sage advice, but some children ***do*** what they want. (main verb = *do,* from *do*)

The **verb *have*** usually means "possess" (*I have a car*), but it is used in many idioms (*have a baby* = give birth and *have a good time* = enjoy).

- **Examples of *Have***

There are three forms of *have* that are possible as auxiliary verbs: *have, has,* and *had.* (See pp. 79–80 for more information on perfect tenses.) Remember that *have* can be a main verb as well. ELLs are confused by the auxiliary *have.* ELLs have problems when *have* is used as both auxiliary and main verb, as in, *He has had several meetings today* or *If I had had a cell phone, I would have called you.*

Have as Auxiliary Verb	*Have* as Main Verb
(1a) Without a doubt, my parents ***have been*** the most important influence in my life. (main verb = *been,* from *be*)	(1b) My cats ***have*** several toys. (main verb = *have,* from *have*)
(2a) Nicole Kidman ***has devised*** a strategy to keep herself in the public eye. (main verb = *devised,* from *devise*)	(2b) Consisting of only crystals, a cirrus cloud ***has*** an altitude of approximately five miles above sea level. (main verb = *has,* from *have*)
(3) Scientists in Hawaii say that Mars ***has had*** at least 40 major ice ages during the past five million years. (auxiliary verb = *has;* main verb = *had,* from *have*)	

- **Examples of Modals**

  Modals are a special category of auxiliary verbs that express feelings, attitudes, or opinions in a verb phrase. Modal verbs include: *can, could, may, might, must, will, would, should,* and *shall.* Modal verbs are never main verbs; they are always used with a verb. (Modal verbs are difficult for ELLs and are covered extensively in Key 12.)

Modal	Examples
can	You *can do* anything if you try.
could	*Could* you *tell* me where the produce is?
may	You *may go* to see the park if you want.
might	It *might rain* tomorrow.
must	You *must have been joking* when you told him that.
should	*Should* we *eat* now or wait till later?
will	How *will* you *get* from the airport to your apartment?
would	I *would* not *eat* that if I were you.
shall	*Shall* we *sit* here for a while?

In modern North American English, **shall** is less common than other modals. *Shall* is usually restricted to (rare) questions about permission or plans, as in *Shall I sit here?* or *Shall we go now?* It also appears in legal documents (*the tenant shall pay . . .*).

Pronouns	
Common ELL Errors	*Examples*
omission of subject pronouns	My favorite city is Boston. *Is very special place to me.
confusion of *he* and *she*	Do you know my uncle? *I think that she is your neighbor.
pronoun reference	Cars are important. *People need it in today's world.
double subject pronoun	*My sister she is a good swimmer.
unnecessary object pronoun	*A computer is something that all students need it.
plural of indefinite pronouns	*Everyone were very happy.

What is a pronoun?
A **pronoun** is a word that can replace, or substitute for, a noun.

Oregon is on the western coast of the United States. It is in the Pacific Time Zone.
noun   pronoun

What questions does a pronoun answer?
A pronoun performs the same function as a noun, so a pronoun answers the same questions that a noun answers, namely *who* or *what*.

Question	Answer (= pronoun)
Who lives there?	They do.
What is the answer?	It is 42.

What are possible slots for a pronoun?
Pronouns occur in similar slots as nouns, so possible slots include:

Slot	Examples
(a person) am/is/are hungry. _____ want/wants to eat now.	I, You, He, She, We, They
Maria sees (a person). Can Maria see _____, too?	me, you, him, her, us, them
Dr. Smith is the professor _____ we like the most.	whom, that
Dr. Smith is the professor _____ helped us the most.	who, that
The flight arrived late, _____ caused us many problems.	which

Details of Pronouns

- **What are some of the different kinds of pronouns?**

  A **subject pronoun** is a pronoun that can be the subject of a sentence: *I, you, he, she, it, we,* or *they.* A common ELL error is to confuse *he* and *she,* as in, *Maria is from Morocco.* **He speaks French and Arabic.*

  An **object pronoun** is a pronoun that can be the direct object, indirect object, or object of a preposition: *me, you, him, her, it, us,* or *them.* A common ELL error is to use a subject pronoun in an object slot, as in, **These shirts are for they.*

  A **relative pronoun** is a pronoun that connects a clause to the rest of the sentence: *who, that, which,* and *whom.* A common ELL error is to use *what* instead of *that* in adjective clauses, as in, **I want to borrow the book what you bought last week.*

An **indefinite pronoun** does not refer to a specific person or thing: *anyone, anything, anybody, everyone, everything, everybody, someone, something, somebody, no one, nothing,* or *nobody*. A common ELL error is to confuse the various indefinite pronouns. An ELL might say, **I needed help, but anyone helped me* or **I read anything interesting in today's paper*. In addition, ELLs mistakenly assume that indefinite pronouns are plural, so they say **Everyone have a TV*.

A **reflexive pronoun** is used when a word refers to the same subject: *myself, yourself, himself, herself, itself, ourselves, yourselves,* and *themselves*.

A **demonstrative pronoun** stands in lieu of a specific thing (or person): *this, that, these,* or *those*. ELLs make mistakes with number such as *Here is your gift.*These is from Joshua.*

A **possessive pronoun** refers to a thing or person and its owner: *mine, yours, his, hers, ours,* and *theirs*. Sometimes ELLs use the definite article with possessive pronouns and say, **Your shirt is new, but the mine is really old*. Note that all possessive pronouns except *mine* end in *–s*, but one form is used for both singular and plural: *my book = mine, my books = mine; her book = hers, her books = hers*.

Two common **reciprocal pronouns** that cause problems for ELLs are *each other* and *one another*. ELLs may write **Romeo and Juliet loved themselves.*

> The word **her** is not a possessive pronoun. It is a possessive adjective: *I have my book, and she has her book.* The possessive word *her* must be used with a noun.

Adjectives	
Common ELL Errors	*Examples*
misplacement after nouns	*China is a country big.
making adjectives plural	*These books are very cheaps.
wrong comparative form	*China is more big than India.
lack of adjective ending	*In the summer, the weather here is very rain.

What is an adjective?
An **adjective** is a word that describes a noun or pronoun.

good, tallest, green, slow, Russian, delicious, problematic, national, expensive

What questions does an adjective answer?
An adjective answers the questions *which, how many, how much,* or *what kind*.

Question	Answer (= adjective)
Which?	The <u>green</u> book is mine.
How many?	There are <u>six</u> children in her family.
How much?	No one received <u>any</u> mail today.
What kind?	<u>Raw</u> milk can be dangerous.

What are possible slots for an adjective?

In English, adjectives have two general locations in a sentence. Adjectives precede nouns (*a difficult test*) or they come after *to be* (*the test is difficult*) or a linking verb (*the test seems difficult*).

Slot	Examples
a/an _____ person	happy, honest, short, smart
_____ book	a, the, my, this, thick, which
_____ books	some, the, my, these, French, purple
it is _____	awake, important, essential, blue
you look _____	tired, good, nervous, different

Details of Adjectives

- **What makes articles difficult for ELLs?**
  Articles are a difficult type of adjective. There are three kinds of **articles**, including **indefinite articles** *(a, an)*, the **definite article** *(the)*, and the **zero article**, which simply means no article is used, as in *I like tea* or *Tigers are wild animals.* Articles are very difficult for ELLs to acquire and are covered in greater depth on pp. 179–84.

- **What makes possessive adjectives difficult for ELLs?**
  Possessive adjectives include *my, your, his, her, its, our, their.* Sometimes ELLs confuse *his* and *her* or they attempt a plural form before a noun, such as **ours books.*

- **What makes demonstrative adjectives difficult for ELLs?**
  Demonstrative adjectives include *this, that, these, those.* Common ELL errors include using *this* or *that* with a plural noun (e.g., **that numbers*) or using *these* or using *those* with a singular noun (e.g., **these woman*) or a non-count noun (e.g., **those information*).

- **What makes quantity adjectives difficult for ELLs?**
  Quantity adjectives include numbers and words such as *many, much, a few, a little.* Common ELL errors include omission of a plural marker (e.g., **many animal*) or using the wrong quantity word for a count or non-count noun (e.g., **many money, *much ideas*).

- **What makes descriptive adjectives difficult for ELLs?**
  Examples of **descriptive adjectives** include *beautiful, stormy, green.* Common errors include using a noun as a descriptive adjective (**You have a beauty baby*) or using the wrong suffix to create an adjective (**stormed weather*). The most common error is placing descriptive adjectives after nouns (e.g., **a book interesting*).

Many ELL books have a lesson on how to **sequence three or four adjectives.** Skip this impractical lesson and focus on the more common problem of placing adjectives after nouns instead of before them, as in **a story sad.* In spoken English, we usually use only one adjective with a noun—if we use any at all. In contrast, the use of multiple adjectives before a noun is more common in written English.

- **What is the correct sequencing for multiple adjectives before a noun?**
  Which is correct: *the baby's small white socks* OR *the baby's white small socks?*
  Native speakers were never taught any rule for sequencing adjectives, but they
  rarely have a problem with this grammar. The general rule is that adjectives
  come in this order: (1) opinion, (2) size, (3) age, (4) shape, (5) color, (6) origin, (7) material. In actual English samples from native speakers, only one
  or two adjectives is used, so ELLs should generally be told to use no more than
  two adjectives in a row.

> When determining the **sequence of adjectives**, the more noun-like a word is, the closer it should be placed to the noun: *beautiful red shirts* is correct because *red* can be a noun (*Red is my favorite color*) and an adjective (*the shirts are red*), but *beautiful* is only an adjective (*the shirts are beautiful*).

Adverbs

Common ELL Errors	Examples
lack of adverb ending	*He plays the violin very beautiful.
misplacement of adverbs	*I like very much this food.
wrong adverb forms	*The professor explained the lesson detailly.
underuse of advanced adverbs of degree	not advanced: Gas prices have risen a lot. advanced: Gas prices have risen sharply.
use of *much* and *very much* in affirmative statements	not usual: I want to learn Spanish very much. more usual: I really want to learn Spanish.

What is an adverb?
An **adverb** is a word that modifies a verb, an adjective, or another adverb.

Modifying a verb:	Gas prices have risen <u>sharply</u>.
Modifying an adjective:	The company reported <u>sharply</u> lower profits.
Modifying an adverb:	Gas prices have risen <u>very</u> sharply.

> In grammar, **modify** is a synonym for describe or limit. We usually say that *adjectives describe* but *adverbs modify*. For ELLs, the word *describe* may be easier to understand than *modify*.

What questions does an adverb answer?
An adverb answers the questions *how* (manner), *when, where, how often,* and
how much (*to what degree*).

Question	Answer (= adverb)
How?	Evidence indicates that ocean levels are <u>slowly</u> rising.
When?	The news was announced <u>yesterday</u>.
Where?	The accident happened <u>downtown</u> at dusk.
How often?	The library <u>usually</u> has story hours for children at noon.
How much?	The exam was <u>extremely</u> difficult for the students.

What are possible slots for an adverb?
Adverbs can vary in location in a sentence.

Slot	Examples
She walked _____.	slowly, strangely, here, yesterday
The movie was _____ sad.	very, extremely, somewhat, so
We _____ drink coffee.	always, never, sometimes
_____, it began to rain.	Fortunately, Unexpectedly, Amazingly

Details of Adverbs

- **What are adverbs of manner?**
  Adverbs of manner tell how something happens. Examples include *quickly, skill-fully,* and *rudely.* They usually end in *-ly;* some common exceptions include *fast, slow,* and *hard.* Both *slow* and *slowly* are correct adverb forms, but only *slowly* may fit some situations, as in *People are slowly feeling the effects of the medicine.* ELLs may confuse the adverbs *hard* and *hardly,* which have very different meanings.

  A common ELL error involves placement of these adverbs in a sentence. In general, adverbs of manner occur after the main verb if there is no direct object but after the direct object if there is one. ELLs often mistakenly place the adverb of manner between the verb and the direct object and produce incorrect sentences such as, **You know very well Spanish* or **The students finished quickly the exam.*

- **What are adverbs of frequency?**
  Adverbs of frequency include *always, usually, often, sometimes, seldom, rarely,* and *never.* A common ELL error involves placement of these adverbs in a sentence. In general, adverbs of frequency come before main verbs (*Congress usually meets for several months in a row*) but after *be,* modals, and auxiliary verbs (*Our meetings are usually held in the morning*).

- **What are adverbs of degree?**
  Adverbs of degree include *almost, hardly, extremely,* and *very.* One common ELL problem is the overuse of *very* instead of other adverbs of degree. The most common error is with placement in a sentence. Adverbs of degree are usually placed before an adjective or adverb (*the plans are extremely complicated*) or before the main verb (*she almost spilled the soup*).

Conjunctions

Common ELL Errors	*Examples*
lack of conjunction	*The exam was difficult, I did not do well.
lack of punctuation	*The exam was difficult so I did not do well.
extra conjunction (double)	*Although I watched the movie, but I did not enjoy it.
fragment	Our flight to Bolivia was delayed. *Because the weather was really bad.

What is a conjunction?

A **conjunction** is a word that connects parts of a sentence together. Conjunctions link words, phrases, and clauses.

linking words: I see a cat and a dog.

linking phrases: The cat might be on the bed or under the sofa.

linking clauses: The cat couldn't walk because it had a broken leg.

What are possible slots for a conjunction?

Slot	Examples
We want a (noun) _____ a (noun)	and, or
The food was cheap _____ good.	and, but
I went inside _____ it began to rain.	because, when, as soon as, after, before
We want _____ tea _____ coffee.	both . . . and, either . . . or, neither . . . nor

Common conjunctions include:

coordinating conjunctions	and, but, for, nor, or, so, yet
subordinating conjunctions	after, although, before, because, even if, if, now that, since, though, unless, until, when, while
correlative conjunctions	Both . . . and . . ., either . . . or . . ., not only . . . but also . . .

In grammar, a **phrase** is a group of words with either a noun or a verb—but not both. Common examples include noun phrases (*a rare two-cent stamp*), verb phrases (*found a rare two-cent stamp under the table*), and prepositional phrases (*under the table*). A **clause,** in contrast, has both a subject and a verb. The sentence *Erica was excited because she found a rare two-cent stamp under the table* has two clauses: (1) *Erica was excited* and (2) *because she found a rare two-cent stamp under the table.* Note that each clause has a subject and a verb (*Erica was; she found*).

Details of Conjunctions

- **What are coordinating conjunctions?**

  A **coordinating conjunction** is a conjunction that joins words, phrases, or independent clauses: *for, and, nor, but, or, yet,* and *so.* (An easy way to remember these seven conjunctions is the mnemonic device FANBOYS.) One common error is to omit a comma between two independent clauses. An ELL might mistakenly write, **Mexicans use the word* tú *for* **you** *but Argentineans use the word* vos.

- **What are subordinating conjunctions?**

  A **subordinating conjunction** is a conjunction that introduces a dependent clause and explains its relationship to the main part of the sentence: *after, although, as, because, before, how, if, once, since, than, though, till, unless, until, when, where, whether,* or *while.* Some ELLs incorrectly attempt to use a subordinating conjunction and a coordinating conjunction in the same sentence: **Although the factory was profitable, but the company has decided to relocate it to another site.* A common ELL (and native speaker) writing error occurs when students have only one clause. A subordinating connector with a dependent clause only is called a **sentence fragment:** **‡Because the restaurant did not have any fresh vegetables.* (See p. 73 for more information on fragments.)

- **What are conjunctive adverbs?**

  Conjunctive adverbs are transitional devices that connect two main ideas: *consequently, however, likewise, moreover, nevertheless, nonetheless, otherwise, similarly,* or *therefore.* These adverbs are used in the second of the two ideas. Two of the correct punctuation options include

Punctuation Pattern	*Examples*
Sentence 1; conjunctive adverb, sentence 2.	Great minds devised the plan; however, it failed miserably.
Sentence 1. Conjunctive adverb, sentence 2.	Great minds devised the plan. However, it failed miserably.

- **What are correlative conjunctions?**

  Correlative conjunctions occur in pairs and connect equivalent sentence parts: *both . . . and, either . . . or, neither . . . nor, not only . . . but also, so . . . as,* or *whether . . . or.* ELLs make few errors with these conjunctions because ELLs do not make use of them enough.

Prepositions

Common ELL Errors	Examples
confusion of *at/on/in* with times	*in Monday, *on June, *at 1990
confusion of *at/on/in* with places	*in McDonald's, *in Main Street, *on her office
lack of preposition	*I am waiting the bus.
extra preposition	*How can we avoid for any problems?
wrong preposition	*The car is full from gasoline right now.

What is a preposition?

A **preposition** is a word that shows the relationship between a noun (or pronoun) and the rest of the sentence. A preposition is usually one short word (*at, on, with*), but some prepositions consist of two words (*according to*) or three words (*in spite of*). Many people mistakenly assume that prepositions are easy because prepositions are often one-syllable words that are very common. The truth is that prepositions are perhaps one of the most difficult grammatical points in English because they have multiple meanings that do not translate well from language to language.

The combination of a preposition with its object (and any modifiers or describing words) is called a **prepositional phrase** (*in the room, on my birthday, from the sixth floor*). Prepositions have many purposes, but they often give us information about place (*in Canada*), time (*at 9 PM*), and direction (*from the ocean*).

A longer list of prepositions can be found on pp. 164–67, but here is a list of some of the more common prepositions: *about, after, at, because of, before, between, by, except, for, from, in, in front of, in place of, in spite of, instead of, like, of, on, on top of, since, to,* and *with*.

What are the possible slots of a preposition?

Slot	Examples
The squirrel ran _____ the tree.	up, down, through
The ant is _____ the bottle.	under, by, before
The bird flew _____ the bushes.	around, over, under
What is the name _____ the book?	of, on, in

A good strategy in teaching **prepositions** is to use **animals.** Tell learners that a preposition is anything that a squirrel can do to a tree, an ant can be in relation to a bottle, or a bird can do to bushes. For example, a squirrel can run *up* a tree, *down* a tree, and *through* a (hollow) tree. An ant can be *under* a bottle, *by* a bottle, and *before* a bottle. A bird can fly *around* the bushes, *over* the bushes, and *between* the bushes. NOTE: Many prepositions can complete these visual learning aids, but some prepositions will not fit.

Details of Prepositions

- **Why are prepositions difficult for ELLs?**

  A simple explanation is that prepositions are notoriously polysemous, which simply means that a preposition can have numerous meanings—sometimes more than 30. Table 2.2 shows the eight most common English prepositions from the General Service List (West, 1953) along with their respective number of meanings from the unabridged dictionary.com reference tool. (No overt idiomatic meanings are included; thus, from an ELL's point of view, the actual number of meanings is certainly higher.)

Table 2.2 The Polysemy of the Most Frequent Prepositions

Rank	Preposition	Number of Meanings
1	of	16
2	in	8
3	to	22
4	for	32
5	with	17
6	on	30
7	at	10
8	by	24

To be certain, other parts of speech can also be polysemous. (For example, the noun *book* can be something to read, a written record at a business, or a set of items, such as stamps or matches). Consider these ten usages of *in*: *in the box, in the parking lot, in January, in time, in the hospital, in this report, in five minutes, in a hurry, in love,* and *in the universe.* From an ELL point of view, the differences in meaning here are more nebulous and therefore harder to grasp. In many cases, the "meaning" of a preposition is really based on its usage and must be seen in context.

Different languages handle prepositions differently. In some languages, they come after the noun, and are therefore postpositions, and in other languages, the meaning of the preposition may be expressed by a suffix rather than a separate word. Though these differences exist, what generally causes preposition problems for ELLs is usage, not location, of the preposition. For example, Japanese ELLs, whose native language uses postpositions [e.g., tsukue no ue ni = desk on = on (the) desk], rarely write *The book is the desk on.* Instead, like all ELLs, they are more likely to make a mistake in usage and write *The book is at the desk* or *The book is in the desk* (when the book is clearly on the desk).

Each of these "meanings," or usages, of prepositions requires a different word in another language. Therefore, when a teacher teaches a preposition to an ELL by giving one meaning or definition—"Class, *in* means the opposite of *out*—the ELL's job is hardly complete. The ELL and the ELL's teacher still have *at least* seven other meanings to cover—in addition to the numerous idiomatic usages that often include prepositions.

- **What are the different kinds of prepositions?**
There are many specific kinds of prepositions, including prepositions of location (*in the box*), prepositions of time (*at 10:30*), and prepositions of movement (*from the office*). The choice of preposition depends on the type of location, the type of time, or the type of movement. Other prepositions are determined by the adjective, noun, or verb that comes before them: the exact adjective (*interested in, fond of, perplexed by*), the exact noun (*the center of, the reason for, the rise of/in*), or the exact verb (*excel in, forget about, tire of*). However, a more helpful way for teachers (not students) to analyze prepositions is whether they indicate a concrete, lexical meaning or a more abstract, grammatical meaning.

    Lexical prepositions include *across, before, down, on top of, under,* and *with.* From a teacher's point of view, lexical prepositions are easy to explain or illustrate. Lexical prepositions pose few grammar problems. ELLs do not confuse *down* and *with* or *across* and *under.* If a mouse is in a tree and runs from the top of the tree to its base, we say, *The mouse ran down the tree.* We use *down*; ELLs can easily understand the meaning of *down* and produce original sentences mirroring this pattern.

    Grammatical prepositions include many usages of *at, in,* and *on.* The usage of grammatical prepositions is less predictable and therefore less teachable. For example, when talking about time, we say *at 1 PM, on Monday, in June, in the spring, in 1975, in this decade, in the 21st century.* There is a pattern in English that smaller points of time use *at,* "medium" points of time use *on,* and larger points of time use *in.* However, what is a "medium" point of time? In order to use *at* correctly with time, an ELL really has to know the various usages.

    When talking about places, *at, on,* and *in* can be both lexical usages and grammatical usages. We can clearly see lexical prepositions in the phrases *at Gate 7, on the table,* and *in the box* because, in these examples, *at* means "a very specific location," *on* means "touching the surface of," and *in* means "inside." However, the situation is less clear when we say *at McDonald's, on Green Street, on Park Lane, in my neighborhood, in London, in Canada,* or *in North America.* To be sure, there is a similar pattern of using *at* with smaller places, *on* with "medium" places, and *in* with larger places. Again, how can ELLs know what is a "medium" place? ELLs will definitely make seemingly logical and predictable mistakes such as **in McDonald's, *at Green Street,* and **on North America.*

Interjections

Common ELL Errors	*Examples*
For the most part, interjections are not a problem for ELLs (or native speakers), so ELL grammar books never cover this part of speech. (In fact, native speakers rarely study how to diagram an interjection.) An ELL teacher might need to discourage ELLs from repeating the informal interjections that they hear in the real world. ELLs may use interjections to fit in, not realizing that sometimes profanity is contained in a given interjection.	

What is an interjection?

An **interjection** is a word that expresses strong feeling or emotion. Interjections are more common in spoken language than in written language. Interjections often appear in fiction, especially when authors are trying to recreate natural dialogue. Examples include:

Wow! Great! Gosh! Ouch!

Interjections are perhaps the least important of the eight parts of speech, especially for teaching English language learners how to construct good sentences. Interjections are more of a vocabulary issue than a grammar issue.

Changeable Parts of Speech: Form vs. Function

This chapter has tried to classify words according to one part of speech, but in reality, a word can be more than one part of speech depending on how it is used in a sentence. This free variation primarily affects nouns, verbs, and adjectives, but to a lesser extent, adverbs and prepositions. Very few conjunctions can change parts of speech. Pronouns are usually pronouns. Interjections are not considered here.

Consider these usages of the word *book*:

She wanted to *book* a flight. (verb)

We had to read that *book* for class. (noun)

Our library has a *book* problem. (adjective)

Consider these usages of the word *well*:

Is there a lot of water in this *well?* (noun)

Tears began to *well* up in his eyes. (verb)

You play tennis very *well.* (adverb)

The doctor says that I will get *well* soon. (adjective)

Details of Changeable Parts of Speech

Focusing on the eight parts of speech individually may have given the impression that a given word form always belongs to only one part of speech. The part of speech of a word is more accurately determined by the function of that word in a sentence, not its form, although the ending (e.g., *-ly*) can be a clue.

For ELLs, the problem with word forms is that we have many ways of marking any given part of speech, yet that marking does not guarantee that the word will be used as that part of speech. For example, the suffix *-tion* generally forms a noun from a verb (*produce → production*), but a noun can also be formed from a verb with the suffix *-ment* (*enjoy → enjoyment*) or *-ing* (*clean → cleaning*). It is no wonder that ELLs invent words such as **enjoyation* or **cleanment*. However, even after the correct suffix has yielded a noun, that word with the supposedly distinct noun marker can sometimes serve as an adjective (*the production* vs. *the production problem*).

<u>Review of Parts of Speech</u>

Post-Test. In this excerpt about vocabulary, write the part of speech above each of the 40 underlined words. Suggested time limit: 15 minutes. (Answers are on p. 88.)

⑴ <u>Learning</u> vocabulary in a second language is ⑵ <u>always</u> a ⑶ <u>daunting</u> task because of the ⑷ <u>number</u> of ⑸ <u>single</u> words, phrases, idioms, collocations, ⑹ <u>and</u> other ⑺ <u>lexical</u> chunks that exist. In addition, learners must learn multiple aspects ⑻ <u>for</u> ⑼ <u>each</u> of these, including ⑽ <u>the</u> form of a word (e.g., its spelling), its pronunciation, its meaning(s), its connotations, its most common ⑾ <u>usages</u>, and ⑿ <u>its</u> register. All of this is ⒀ <u>even</u> ⒁ <u>more</u> ⒂ <u>complicated</u> for the skill of ⒃ <u>writing</u> in a second language. Writers often depend ⒄ <u>on</u> the nuance of a word, and nuances can ⒅ <u>only</u> be learned ⒆ <u>after</u> you ⒇ <u>have</u> learned the basic meaning(s) of a word. A ㉑ <u>piece</u> of writing often stands out ㉒ <u>because</u> the writer has used a ㉓ <u>few</u> ㉔ <u>key</u> vocabulary ㉕ <u>words</u> that are not ㉖ <u>so</u> common. At times, it is ㉗ <u>the</u> rarity of the words that makes ㉘ <u>them</u> effective ㉙ <u>communicators</u> for the writer. However, a rare word is usually learned after ㉚ <u>several</u> ㉛ <u>much</u> ㉜ <u>more</u> ㉝ <u>common</u> synonyms have been learned. In ㉞ <u>other</u> words, an ㉟ <u>advanced</u> writer needs a ㊱ <u>repertoire</u> of words for a ㊲ <u>given</u> concept. ㊳ <u>Clearly</u>, vocabulary with regard to second language writing, ㊴ <u>especially</u> at the upper proficiency levels, is a ㊵ <u>huge</u> task.

Source: Reid, J. (2008). *Writing myths: Applying second language research to classroom teaching.* Ann Arbor: University of Michigan Press.

SECTION 3
Basic Grammar Labels for Sentence Structure

This section contains ten key concepts regarding **sentence structure** in English. Key grammar terms relevant to sentence structure are explained.

1. In English, a **sentence** consists of a **subject** and a **predicate**. The **subject** is the person or thing that does the action of the verb. Simply put, the **predicate** is everything else, including the **verb** and all other sentence components.

   Sometimes we talk about the simple subject, the complete subject, the simple predicate, and the complete predicate. The simple subject is the main noun or pronoun, and the complete subject is the simple subject and all modifiers. The simple predicate is the verb (or verb phrase if there are several verb components, *have been eating*), and the complete predicate is the verb and all modifiers.

In an **imperative (command)** sentence, the subject is the person being commanded—**you**—and is usually omitted. In this case, the subject *you* is referred to as an **understood subject** because it is implied but rarely ever stated. Therefore, *Open the door* really means *(You) Open the door.* The subject of this clause is *you*. This subject is understood and not directly stated.

Sentence	Analysis	
*The brown <u>foxes</u> **jumped** quickly.*	complete subject simple subject	*the brown foxes* *foxes*
	complete predicate simple predicate	*jumped quickly* *jumped*
*The brown <u>foxes</u> **jumped** quickly over the lazy dog.*	complete subject simple subject	*the brown foxes* *foxes*
	complete predicate simple predicate	*jumped quickly over the lazy dog* *jumped*

Errors that ELLs Make with Subject-Verb Combinations	
Errors	**Examples**
Error 1. leaving out the subject completely, especially when the subject is a pronoun	I like tennis very much. **Is* my favorite sport. I like tennis very much. <u>It</u> *is* my favorite sport.
	The police arrested the man. *The police did this because *robbed* a store. *The police did this because <u>he</u> *robbed* a store.
Error 2. inverting the subject and verb (putting the verb before the subject)	*I am not sure where *is* <u>Calcutta</u>. I am not sure where <u>Calcutta</u> *is*.
	*Cairo is more populated than *thinks* <u>Joe</u>. Cairo is more populated than <u>Joe</u> *thinks*.

2. The verb may be followed by an **object.** The object may be a noun or a pronoun.

The <u>children</u> *played* a game .	<u>subject</u> + *verb* + object (noun)
The <u>children</u> *played* it .	<u>subject</u> + *verb* + object (pronoun)

3. When the object is the receiver of the action, it is called a **direct object.** When the object is the person (or thing) *to whom* or *for whom* the action was done, it is called an **indirect object.**

<u>John</u> *read* a story .	What did John read? a story = **direct object**
<u>John</u> *read* the <u>children</u> a story .	For whom or to whom did John read a story? the children = **indirect object**

4. A verb in English can be **transitive**, **intransitive**, or both.

    Some verbs must be followed by an object to be correct English. These verbs that have to have an object are called **transitive verbs.** Common transitive verbs are *bring, climb, contain, discuss, enjoy, like, prepare, put, rob, steal,* and *take.*

Errors that ELLs Make with Transitive Verbs	
Errors	**Examples**
Error 1. leaving out the direct object entirely	Tennis is my favorite sport. **I like* very much. Tennis is my favorite sport. I *like* it very much.
	*The police arrested the man because <u>he</u> *robbed*. The police arrested the man because <u>he</u> *robbed* the bank .
Error 2. inserting unnecessary prepositions (usually a result of translating or native language interference)	*In the meeting, <u>we</u> *discussed* about her ideas. In the meeting, <u>we</u> *discussed* her ideas .
	*Many <u>people</u> *enjoyed* of her innovative ideas. Many <u>people</u> *enjoyed* her innovative ideas .

    Some verbs can <u>never</u> be followed by an object in English. These verbs are called **intransitive verbs.** Common intransitive verbs are *complain, consist, die, emerge, happen, occur, resemble,* and *seem.* After an intransitive verb, you might find an adverb *(He died quickly),* or a prepositional phrase *(He died at home),* or nothing *(He died).*

Adverbs answer the questions *how, when, where,* and *to what degree.* Examples are *quickly, yesterday, there,* and *extremely.* Adverbs are discussed at length on pp. 55–56.

| Errors that ELLs Make with Intransitive Verbs ||
Errors	**Examples**
Error 1. treating the intransitive verb as if it were a transitive verb (by leaving out the required preposition, usually the result of translating or native language interference)	*<u>Water</u> *consists* hydrogen and oxygen. <u>Water</u> *consists* of hydrogen and oxygen.
	*At the finish line, the winner *emerged* the runners. At the finish line, the winner *emerged* from the runners.
Error 2. inserting incorrect prepositions (usually the result of translating or native language interference)	*In the meeting, <u>we</u> *complained* ~~for~~ the new rules. In the meeting, <u>we</u> *complained* about the new rules.
	*<u>What</u> *happened* ~~with~~ your car? <u>What</u> *happened* to your car?

A **prepositional phrase** is a preposition and a noun (or pronoun) that functions as the object of the preposition. Examples of prepositional phrases include *at the park, in the room, to the bank, with someone.* Prepositions are discussed in detail on pp. 59–61.

Finally, many verbs can be either transitive or intransitive, including *begin, change, close, drink, eat, end, finish, guess, leave, move, open, run, speak, start,* and *study.*

| Verbs with Both Transitive and Intransitive Usages |||
Verb	**Transitive Usage**	**Intransitive Usage**
begin	<u>We</u> *began* the meeting at noon.	The <u>meeting</u> *began* at noon.
move	The <u>wind</u> *moved* the boxes.	The <u>cat</u> *moved* slightly due to the noise.
speak	*Can <u>you</u> speak French well?*	*Can <u>you</u> speak at the meeting?*
study	<u>I</u> *am studying* business at college.	<u>I</u> *am studying* in the library these days.

5. Beyond a word, the next grammatical unit is called a **phrase**. A **phrase** is a group of words that does not contain both a subject and a verb. A phrase acts as one part of speech. The three most common types of phrases are **noun phrases, verb phrases,** and **prepositional phrases.**

The sentence *The red grammar book is lying on the coffee table* contains the following phrases: *the red grammar book* (noun phrase), *is lying on the coffee table* (verb phrase), *on the coffee table* (prepositional phrase), and *the coffee table* (noun phrase).

Part of Speech		Equivalent Type of Phrase	
Noun	*cats*	**Noun Phrase**	*four small cats*
	flowers		*tiny edible flowers*
Verb	*are eating*	**Verb Phrase**	*are eating some fish*
	arrived		*arrived late yesterday afternoon*
Preposition	*under*	**Prepositional Phrase**	*under the table*
	on		*on the table*

6. Beyond a phrase, the next grammatical unit is called a **clause**. A clause is a group of words with both a subject and a verb. There are two kinds of clauses: **independent** and **dependent**.

    An **independent clause** has a subject and a verb and expresses a complete thought and can therefore stand on its own. (An independent clause can be a sentence.)

    A **dependent clause** has a subject and a verb but does not express a complete thought and cannot stand on its own.

Independent Clause	Dependent Clause
*Many young <u>drivers</u> **avoid** driving in rainy weather*	*because <u>they</u> **do not have** enough experience driving under such conditions.*
*<u>One</u> of the first airlines in Asia **was** Air India,*	*<u>which</u> **began** as Tata Airlines in 1932.*
*<u>I</u> **want** to give you the book*	*that <u>I</u> **bought** at a garage sale yesterday.*

7. Dependent clauses can be **adverb clauses**, **adjective clauses**, or **noun clauses**.

    Adverb clauses answer questions such as *when, where, why, with what result,* and *under which condition(s)*. Adverb clauses usually modify the verb. Adverb clauses begin with **subordinating conjunctions**. Examples of subordinating conjunctions include *after, although, as soon as, because, before, if, when,* and *while*. Adverb clauses can come either before or after the main clause. However, adverb clauses that begin a sentence are always set off from the main clause by a comma.

Independent clause + adverb clause. (No comma)	*They **stopped** the game because the <u>rain</u> **started**.*
Adverb clause + , + independent clause.	*Because the <u>rain</u> **started**, <u>they</u> **stopped** the game.*

Some native speakers wrongly think that a sentence cannot begin with **because**. Yes, a sentence can begin with *because*, but it must have another clause. *Because it was raining* is not a sentence. It is a fragment. *Because it was raining, the coach canceled the game* is a correct English sentence. Don't forget to put a comma after the word *raining* to separate the initial dependent clause from the main clause.

Study these examples of sentences with **adverb clauses**:

a. *The term "staycation" became popular **after the price of gasoline skyrocketed**.*

b. ***Although the beginning of Cinderella is sad**, this fairy tale has a happy ending.*

c. *The soccer players walked back on the field **as soon as the lightning had stopped**.*

d. ***Because vitamins are so important**, many people take them every day.*

e. *It is important to finish the match **while the sun is shining**.*

Adjective clauses tell which one. Adjective clauses modify nouns (or pronouns). Adjective clauses begin with one of the five **relative pronouns** (*who, whom, whose, that,* and *which*) or one of two subordinating conjunctions (*when* and *where*). A special problem for ELLs occurs with *whom, that,* and *which* because they can be omitted in English at certain times. *Maria is the girl whom we saw* or *Maria is the girl* (– – –) *we saw.*

Original Sentences	Sentences with Adjective Clause
The <u>answer</u> *was* correct. <u>You</u> *gave* the answer.	The <u>answer</u> *that* <u>you</u> *gave* **was** correct. The <u>answer</u> (– – –) <u>you</u> *gave* **was** correct.
The <u>woman</u> *was* Dr. Stans. The <u>woman</u> *wrote* the speech.	The <u>woman</u> *who* **wrote** the speech **was** Dr. Stans. The <u>woman</u> *that* **wrote** the speech *was* Dr. Stans.

Study these examples of sentences with **adjectives clauses**:

f. *People **who live in glass houses** should not throw stones.*

g. *Consumers often prefer to watch movies of celebrities **whom they know something about**.*

h. *One of the main reasons **that the accident happened** was the weather.*

i. *No one wants to stay in a hotel room **where a murder has been committed**.*

j. *On September 11 of each year, there is a moment of silence in New York City at the exact minute **when a plane hit the first of the twin towers**.*

Noun clauses answer questions such as *who, whom,* or *what.* Some words that commonly introduce noun clauses include *that, what, who, why, when, where,* and *whether.* A special problem for ELLs is that sometimes these introductory words are optional: *I believe that she is in the office* OR *I believe she is in the office.*

Study these examples of sentences with **noun clauses**:

k. *It is better to keep **what you have** than to risk losing it by looking for something better.*

l. ***Why the accident happened** is still under investigation.*

m. *Do you really believe **that the price of gasoline might go down**?*

n. *I do not know **where Deanna lives**.*

o. *A true pessimist is never caught off guard by **what goes wrong**.*

Some of the same words can introduce both kinds of clauses: *who, whom, that, which.* If the clause can be changed to *it,* then it's probably a noun clause: *I believe <u>that taxes are necessary</u>. I believe <u>it</u>* (noun clause). Or, *The idea <u>that taxes are necessary</u> is sound. The idea <u>it</u> is sound.* (no).

8. There are four kinds of sentences: **simple sentences, compound sentences, complex sentences,** and **compound-complex sentences.** The type of sentence is determined by the number and type of clauses in the sentence.

A **simple sentence** has one independent clause. It is possible to have multiple subjects and multiple verbs, but there is still only one subject-verb relationship.

Simple Sentences
(a) <u>Washington</u> *was* the first U.S. president.   • subject: *Washington*   • verb: *was*
(b) <u>Washington and Lincoln</u> *were* U.S. presidents.   • subject: *Washington and Lincoln*   • verb: *were*
(c) <u>Washington</u> *was* president in 1789 and *served* for eight years.   • subject: *Washington*   • verb: *was* and *served*
(d) <u>Washington and Lincoln</u> *dedicated* their lives to the U.S. and *worked* hard to build a better country.   • subject: *Washington and Lincoln*   • verb: *dedicated* and *worked*

A **compound sentence** contains two independent clauses. (In other words, it contains two simple sentences.) The two independent clauses are connected by one of seven **coordinating conjunctions**: *for, and, nor, but, or, yet, so.* (A mnemonic device to remember these seven is FANBOYS.) A comma should always be inserted before coordinating conjunctions between two independent clauses.

The word *so* has at least four meanings in English: (1) result (*It was hot, so we went swimming*), (2) reason (*we went swimming so we could cool off*), (3) very (*it was so hot*), and (4) also (*I went swimming, and so did Tim*). When *so* means *result,* it is a coordinating conjunction and must be preceded by a comma.

Compound Sentences
(e) <u>Washington</u> *died* in 1799, and <u>Lincoln</u> *was* born in 1809.   • independent clause: *Washington died in 1799*   • independent clause: *Lincoln was born in 1809*
(f) <u>Washington</u> *died* in 1799 before Lincoln's birth, so these two famous <u>citizens</u> never *met* each other.   • independent clause: *Washington died in 1799 before Lincoln's birth*   • independent clause: *these two famous citizens never met each other*

A **complex sentence** has one independent clause and at least one dependent clause.

Complex Sentences
(g) The last <u>runner</u> *collapsed* at the finish line because <u>she</u> *had run* for more than two hours.   • independent clause: *The last runner collapsed at the finish line*   • dependent clause: *because she had run for more than two hours* (adverb clause)
(h) The <u>runner</u> <u>who</u> *crossed* the finish line last *had run* for more than two hours.   • independent clause: *the runner had run for more than two hours*   • dependent clause: *who crossed the finish line last* (adjective clause)

A **compound-complex sentence** contains two independent clauses and at least one dependent clause.

Compound-Complex Sentences
(i) The last <u>runner</u> *collapsed* at the finish line because <u>she</u> *had run* for more than two hours, so a medical <u>team</u> *examined* her.   • independent clause: *the last runner collapsed at the finish line*   • independent clause: *a medical team examined her*   • dependent clause: *because she had run for more than two hours* (adverb clause)
(j) <u>Washington</u> *died* in 1799 before Lincoln's birth, <u>which</u> *was* in 1809, so these two famous <u>citizens</u> never *met* each other.   • independent clause: *Washington died in 1799 before Lincoln's birth*   • dependent clause: *which was in 1809* (adjective clause)   • independent clause: *these two famous citizens never met each other*

9. In sentences, the subject must agree with the verb. **Subject-verb agreement** means that a singular subject needs a singular verb and a plural subject needs a plural verb. The most problematic point with subject-verb agreement is with 3rd person singular in simple present tense verbs, which must have an –*s* ending. ELLs have learned that –*s* makes nouns plural, so they are confused by adding –*s* to make some verbs singular.

Simple Present Tense of the Verb *to need*		
	singular	plural
1st person	*I need*	*we need*
2nd person	*you need*	*you need*
3rd person	*he needs*	*they need*
	she needs	*they need*
	it needs	*they need*

In grammar, we use the term ***person*** to indicate whether the subject of the sentence is the person speaking, the person being spoken to, or the person being spoken about. In English, there are three persons with a singular and plural forms for each: **1st person** refers to *I* or *we*; **2nd person** refers to *you*, and **3rd person** refers to *he, she, it*, or *they*.

One important rule for subject-verb agreement is that the object of a prepositional phrase can never be the subject of a sentence because it is already an object. The prepositional phrases are in boxes.

Sentence	Subject-Verb	Notes
(a) The <u>box</u> on the paper *is* green.	*box—is*	on the paper is irrelevant
(b) The <u>box</u> on the papers *is* green.	*box—is*	on the papers is irrelevant
(c) The <u>boxes</u> on the paper *are* green.	*boxes—are*	on the paper is irrelevant
(d) The <u>boxes</u> on the papers *are* green.	*boxes—are*	on the papers is irrelevant

10. Three common errors in writing involve incorrect sentence composition: **fragments**, **run-on sentences**, and **comma splices.**

A **run-on sentence** has two parts that the writer has pushed together without a proper conjunction or punctuation. For this reason, run-on sentences are also called **fused sentences.**

Correcting Run-On Sentences	
run-on sentence	*Each country desperately needed the other's natural resources a serious war broke out.
Correction 1: add a comma and a coordinating conjunction	Each country desperately needed the other's natural resources, **so** a serious war broke out.
Correction 2: add a subordinating conjunction (no punctuation)	A serious war broke out **because** each country desperately needed the other's natural resources.
Correction 3: add a semi-colon	Each country desperately needed the other's natural resources; a serious war broke out.
Correction 4: make two sentences	Each country desperately needed the other's natural resources. A serious war broke out.
Correction 5: add a transitional word or phrase; note the two punctuation options (; or .)	Each country desperately needed the other's natural resources; **thus,** a serious war broke out.
	Each country desperately needed the other's natural resources. **Thus,** a serious war broke out.

A **comma splice** has two parts, but the writer has put a comma in between them without any connector word.

Correcting Comma Splices	
comma splice sentence	*Each country desperately needed the other's natural resources, a serious war broke out.
Correction 1: add a coordinating conjunction (after the comma)	Each country desperately needed the other's natural resources, **so** a serious war broke out.
Correction 2: add a subordinating conjunction (no punctuation)	A serious war broke out **because** each country desperately needed the other's natural resources.
Correction 3: change the comma to a semi-colon	Each country desperately needed the other's natural resources; a serious war broke out.
Correction 4: make two sentences	Each country desperately needed the other's natural resources. A serious war broke out.
Correction 5: add a transitional word or phrase; note the two punctuation options (; or .)	Each country desperately needed the other's natural resources; **thus,** a serious war broke out.
	Each country desperately needed the other's natural resources. **Thus,** a serious war broke out.

A **fragment** is an incomplete sentence. In writing, a fragment is frequently a phrase or a dependent clause that is not properly connected to the main clause. There are several ways to correct a fragment. In many cases, however, fragments can be corrected by removing the period and connecting the fragment to the main clause properly.

| Correcting Fragments ||
Fragments	Possible Corrections
*Age discrimination is an important factor in today's society. *Because the number of senior citizens is increasing each year.*	*Age discrimination is an important factor in today's society because the number of senior citizens is increasing each year.*
*The man whose shirt was on fire ran out of the building into the street and began to jump up and down. *Which is one of the worst things that he could have done in this situation.*	*The man whose shirt was on fire ran out of the building into the street and began to jump up and down, which is one of the worst things that he could have done in this situation.*
*Without realizing it, the criminal entered the building through a door that had a very sensitive motion detector. *Setting off a silent alarm that alerted the police that there was a crime in progress.*	*Without realizing it, the criminal entered the building through a door that had a very sensitive motion detector, setting off a silent alarm that alerted the police that there was a crime in progress.*

SECTION 4
Why the Twelve English Verb Tenses Matter

The verb is arguably the central part of any English sentence. In English, there are twelve tenses that express different combinations of **time** (present, past, future) and **aspect** (simple, perfect, progressive). Verb tense errors are one of the most common errors in ELL writing and speaking. Errors occur in form (lack of *–ing:* *right now I am eat my lunch*) or usage (wrong tense, here simple present for present progressive: *right now I eat my lunch*).

Languages handle verb tenses differently. In languages such as Chinese, there are no verb tenses per se; instead, adverbs of time—*yesterday, before then*—indicate when actions happened. Other languages such as Spanish and German have verb tenses that look similar to those in English with some overlap in meaning with those in English, but the usages vary. For example, simple present tense (*I accompany*) in English is used for habitual actions. While this tense also has that usage in Spanish, this same tense is commonly used for future events. In Spanish, you can say, *Tomorrow I accompany you if you want,* but in English we need to use future tense to say, *Tomorrow I will accompany you if you want.*

In addition to the cross-linguistic interference, there are difficulties even within English because any given verb tense in English can have multiple usages. A common example is the use of **present progressive tense.** We primarily use it for actions that are happening at this moment (*Brian is driving to Vancouver*), but this same verb tense can also be used for a **future event** (*Brian is driving to Vancouver tomorrow*) and even as a **habitual action** (*Brian is always driving to Vancouver*). However, when we use present progressive for a habitual action, it often implies anger, disapproval, or annoyance.

Principal Parts of a Verb:
Base, Past, Past Participle, Present Participle

In English, verbs have four principal forms: the **base,** the **past,** the **past participle,** and the **present participle.** These four principal parts allow us to make all twelve verb tenses.

The verb *to grade* is a regular verb because both the past and past participle forms are formed with *–ed.* In contrast, the verb *to take* is an irregular verb because its past and past participle forms are not formed with *–ed.*

Verb	Base	Past	Past Participle	Present Participle
to grade	grade	graded	graded	grading
to take	take	took	taken	taking

Note that many grammar books do not include the present participle as one of the principal parts of a verb because it is always formed by adding *–ing* to all verbs, whether the verb is regular or irregular.

The **present participle** can be an *–ing* form (such as *going, eating, taking*) that is used as part of a verb. The present participle can be used in the six progressive tenses (*I am going, I was eating, I will be taking*) or as an adjective (*an exciting story, rising prices, the leading candidate*).

For regular verbs, the **past participle** of a verb ends in *–ed* and is therefore the same as the simple past tense. For irregular verbs, common endings include *–en* (*written*) and *–ne* (*gone*). The past participle can be used in the six perfect tenses (*I have fried, I have been frying*). It can also be used as an adjective (*fried shrimp, written communication*).

ELLs do not generally have problems with regular verb forms in English; their problems often occur with the irregular verbs because these forms must be memorized individually. Many languages have irregular verb forms, and many—but certainly not all—of the irregular verbs in English are also irregular in other languages. For example, *to be, to have, to go,* and *to do* are irregular in English, French, Spanish, Portuguese, and German. (I remember Mrs. de Montluzin telling us on the first day of French to memorize the forms of *être, avoir, aller,* and *faire,* which are *to be, to have, to go,* and *to do.* These four verbs, which are essential to conversation in any language, are irregular in French. From the first day, we knew that we had to memorize certain verb forms.)

Review these examples for regular and irregular verbs in all twelve tenses.

Regular verbs: the past tense and past participle forms end in *–ed (grade, graded, graded)*

Grade	**Simple**	**Progressive**	**Perfect**	**Perfect Progressive**
Present	*I grade*	*I am grading*	*I have graded*	*I have been grading*
Past	*I graded*	*I was grading*	*I had graded*	*I had been grading*
Future	*I will grade*	*I will be grading*	*I will have graded*	*I will have been grading*

Irregular verbs: the past tense and the past participle forms do not both end in *–ed (take, took, taken)*

Take	**Simple**	**Progressive**	**Perfect**	**Perfect Progressive**
present	*he takes*	*he is taking*	*he has taken*	*he has been taking*
past	*he took*	*he was taking*	*he had taken*	*he had been taking*
future	*he will take*	*he will be taking*	*he will have taken*	*he will have been taking*

Common irregular verbs include *be, begin, do, drink, eat, find, get, have, leave, make, run, send, speak, think,* and *wear.* A longer list can be found in Appendix 2.

Simple Tenses

Simple Present Tense		
Form	**Usages**	**Examples**
VERB or *VERB + –s* (for *he, she, it*)	(a) a fact that is true now	(1) The U.S. *has* 50 states. (2) Kaylin *speaks* six languages.
	(b) a recurring event	(3) The people *vote* for the president every four years.
	(c) state or condition	(4) He *seems* very angry.
	(d) a planned future action (with a future time word)	(5) The meeting *is* tomorrow. (6) This plane *leaves* in an hour.
Question *do/does* + subject + *VERB*	How many pens *does* **each person** *need?*	
Negative *do/does* + not + *VERB* (Contractions are possible.)	Houses *do not* always *have* a dining room. Houses *don't* always *have* a dining room.	
ELL Error	**ELL Issue**	
including *be*: **Every day I am work here.*	ELLs learn *I am, you are, he is,* etc., so well that they unconsciously include a form of *be* after the subject pronoun.	

Simple Past Tense		
Form	**Usages**	**Examples**
VERB + –ed (Irregular verbs use different patterns: *run—ran, go—went, break—broke*)	(a) a completed action	(1) I *lived* in Brownsville in 2000.
	(b) an activity that took place regularly in the past	(2) In the 1990s, I *took* the bus to work almost every day.
	(c) a completed condition	(3) The temperature *fell* ten degrees last night.
Question *did* + subject + *VERB*	When *did* **you** *arrive* at the meeting?	
Negative *did* + not + *VERB* (Contractions are possible.)	The committee *did not select* a winner. The committee *didn't select* a winner.	
ELL Error	**ELL Issue**	
including *be*: **Yesterday I was work here.*	ELLs learn *I was, you were, he was,* etc., so well that they unconsciously include a form of *be* after the subject pronoun.	

Simple Future Tense		
Form	**Usages**	**Examples**
will + VERB	(a) a prediction about a future event	(1) The price of gasoline *will go* up.
	(b) a decision at the time of speaking (not planned in advance)	(2) [The phone suddenly rings when you are visiting your friend's house.] *"I'll answer* it."
	(c) an agreement to do something	(3) If you *will go* to the store for me, I *will cook* dinner for us.
Question *will* + subject + VERB	*Will* **Flight** 62 *arrive* on time or not?	
Negative *will* + *not* + VERB (Contractions are possible.)	You *will not have* any gas left over. You *won't have* any gas left over.	
ELL Errors	**ELL Issues**	
using simple present tense for future time: *In five minutes, I return here. Please wait.	This is probably a case of native language interference. In Spanish, for example, simple present tense is routinely used for future actions.	
overusing *will* (instead of *be going to)*: *Jo: What are your plans for Friday?* *Ed: *I will have a party.*	ELLs have been taught that *will* means "future time," so they use *will* for every future action. For previously planned actions, we usually use *be going to*, however.	

Progressive Tenses

Present Progressive Tense		
Form	**Usages**	**Examples**
am/is/are + VERB + *–ing*	(a) an action happening now	(1) It's *raining* really hard.
	(b) an action *this* (*week, month,* etc.)	(2) I *am working* at the beach this week.
	(c) an action (with a future time word)	(3) They *are flying* to Texas tomorrow.
Question *am/is/are* + subject + VERB + *–ing*	*Is* the cost of a stamp *increasing* by 10%?	
Negative *am/is/are* + *not* + VERB (Contractions are possible.)	My cats *are not sleeping* right now. My cats *aren't sleeping* right now.	
ELL Error	**ELL Issue**	
putting non-action verbs in present progressive: *I am hearing you.	ELLs do not know that non-action verbs do not usually occur in the progressive, most likely from native language interference.	

Past Progressive Tense		
Form	**Usages**	**Examples**
was/were + VERB + *–ing*	(a) an action in the past that was interrupted in the past by another action	(1) I *was living* in Japan when my mom died.
	(b) a repeated past action (an activity that took place over a long time)	(2) We *were planning* our wedding for many months.
Question *was/were* + subject + VERB + *–ing*	Where *was* the thief *hiding?*	
Negative *was/were* + *not* + VERB (Contractions are possible.)	I *was not sleeping* when you called me. I *wasn't sleeping* when you called me.	
ELL Errors	**ELL Issues**	
omitting *–ing*: *When I was sleep, someone called me.*	ELLs forget the correct form.	
using simple past instead of past progressive: *When I slept, someone called me.*	ELLs may be concentrating on maintaining the same verb tense (per their teacher's proverbial direction to use only one verb tense).	

Future Progressive Tense		
Form	**Usages**	**Examples**
will + *be* + VERB + *–ing*	an action that begins before another action and will be happening at a point of time in the future	You *will be sleeping* when I get off work tonight, so I'm not going to call you.
Question *will* + subject + *be* + VERB + *–ing*	In ten years from now, where *will* we *be working?*	
Negative *will* + *not* + *be* + VERB + *–ing* (Contractions are possible.)	After this year, the city *will not be selling* any more annual bus passes. After this year, the city *won't be selling* any more annual bus passes.	
ELL Error	**ELL Issue**	
This tense is rarely used. Student and teacher time should be directed to more critical language issues.		

Perfect Tenses

Present Perfect Tense		
Form	**Usages**	**Examples**
have/has + *PAST PARTICIPLE*	(a) an action that happened at an unspecified time in the past	(1) *Jo:* I wonder what sushi is like. *Sue:* **I've eaten** it before. It's pretty good. (2) **Have** you ever **flown** on the Concorde?
	(b) a recent action that is important to the current situation or conversation	(3) *Ann:* Wow, it's hot in here. *Liz:* Well, **I've turned** on the air conditioner. Just wait a minute.
	(c) an action that began in the past but continues in the present	(4) We **have worked** here since noon.
	(d) repetition of an action before now	(5) **I've traveled** to Asia many times.
Question *have/has* + subject + *PAST PARTICIPLE*	Where **have** you **worked?**	
Negative *have/has* + *not* + PAST PARTICIPLE (Contractions are possible.)	He **has not flown** on a 747 jet. He **hasn't flown** on a 747 jet.	
ELL Error	**ELL Issue**	
using present tense for present perfect: *I live here since 1995.*	Some languages use present tense to express "still true" usages of present perfect, especially usages (c) and (d).	

Past Perfect Tense		
Form	**Usages**	**Examples**
had + PAST PARTICIPLE	(a) a past action that occurred before another past event, action, or time	(1) I *had eaten* dinner when my mom called. (2) By midnight, we *had watched* three movies.
Question *had* + **subject** + PAST PARTICIPLE	Where *had* **you** *seen* this movie before?	
Negative *had* + *not* + PAST PARTICIPLE (Contractions are possible.)	When the voting office closed promptly at 7 PM, many citizens *had not voted* yet. When the voting office closed promptly at 7 PM, many citizens *hadn't voted* yet.	
ELL Error	**ELL Issue**	
using past perfect for a single event: *Millions of years ago, dinosaurs had roamed on the planet.*	ELLs do not grasp that perfect tenses are in relation to other actions, not in relation to how long ago the action happened. ELLs often mistakenly believe that past perfect is simply much older than simple past. Thus, an example from "millions of years ago" might trigger an unnecessary use of past perfect.	

Future Perfect Tense		
Form	**Usages**	**Examples**
will have + PAST PARTICIPLE	(a) a future action that will occur before another particular future action (or time)	(1) By next Friday, we *will have finished* the first two units in this book. (2) When you reach home tomorrow night, I *will have spoken* to Jim about the problem.
Question *will* + **subject** + *have* + PAST PARTICIPLE	By the year 2050, *will* **the population of our nation** *have doubled?*	
Negative *will* + *not* + *have* + PAST PARTICIPLE (Contractions are possible.)	By the time you get to your office, your assistant *will not have finished* the reports. By the time you get to your office, your assistant *won't have finished* the reports.	
ELL Error	**ELL Issue**	
ELLs make few errors with this tense because they do not attempt it much. In reality, this tense is not used frequently in English.		

Perfect Progressive Tenses

Present Perfect Progressive Tense		
Form	**Usages**	**Examples**
have/has + *been* + *VERB* + *–ing*	(a) an action that began in the past, has continued into the present, and may continue into the future (when a speaker wants to emphasize the duration of an action)	(1) Why are you so late? I *have been waiting* here for almost an hour.
	(b) a general action in progress recently for which no specific time is mentioned	(2) *Ken:* Wow, your tennis game is really good now! *Kay:* I*'ve been practicing* a lot recently.
	(c) an action that began in the past and has just recently ended	(3) *Jim:* There's green stuff in your hair. *Dan:* Oh, don't worry. I*'ve been painting* my house. It will come out with a little soap and water.
Question *have/has* + **subject** + *been* + *VERB* + *–ing*	Why *has* it *been raining* so much lately?	
Negative *have/has* + *not* + *been* + *VERB* + *–ing* (Contractions are possible.)	Many of today's flights *have not been leaving* on time. Many of today's flights *haven't been leaving* on time.	
ELL Error	**ELL Issue**	
using present progressive tense for present perfect progressive: *I am living here since 1995.*	Some languages use present tense to express the "still true" usages of present perfect progressive.	

Past Perfect Progressive Tense		
Form	**Usages**	**Examples**
had + been + VERB + –ing	(a) an activity that occurred before another action in the past (when a speaker wants to emphasize the duration of an action)	(1) The pilot *had been flying* the plane for over an hour before he noticed that there was a problem with the engine.
	(b) a long action occurring recently before another action in the past	(2) *Greg:* Why didn't you go to the party last night? *Lisa:* I was too tired. I *had been working* all day long.
⬜Question⬜ *had + subject + been + VERB + –ing*	How long *had you been working* here when you were promoted to manager?	
⬜Negative⬜ *had + not + been + VERB + –ing* (Contractions are possible.)	The factory *had not been selling* many cars, so the company closed it down. The factory *hadn't been selling* many cars, so the company closed it down.	
ELL Error	**ELL Issue**	
This tense is rarely used. Student and teacher time should be directed to more pressing issues.		

Future Perfect Progressive Tense		
Form	**Usages**	**Examples**
will + have + been + VERB + –ing	(a) a long action that is taking place in relation to another future event (when a speaker wants to emphasize the duration of an action)	(1) By next Friday, we *will have been working* here five years.
	(b) a long action occurring before another action (or point of time) in the future	(2) *Wes:* Do you want to go out with us after the party tomorrow night? *Ben:* I don't know. By the time of the party, I *will have been standing* on my feet for eight hours, so I don't know if I'll feel like going to a party or not.
Question *will + subject + have + been + VERB + –ing*		How long *will* we *have been living* here when you retire?
Negative *will + not + have + been + VERB + –ing* (Contractions are possible.)		I'm not sure, but **we *will not have been living*** here for more than 20 years. I'm not sure, but **we *won't have been living*** here for more than 20 years.
ELL Error		**ELL Issue**
This tense is rarely used. Student and teacher time should be directed to more pressing issues.		

Activity 1. Verb Tenses in English

Write the examples of these verb tenses for the verbs *cook* and *write*. (Answers are on p. 88.)

Verb Tense	Cook	Write
simple present	1.	2.
simple past	3.	4.
simple future	5.	6.
present progressive	7.	8.
past progressive	9.	10.
future progressive	11.	12.
present perfect	13.	14.
past perfect	15.	16.
future perfect	17.	18.
present perfect progressive	19.	20.
past perfect progressive	21.	22.
future perfect progressive	23.	24.

Activity 2. Verb Tenses in English

Match the examples with their correct verb tense by writing the correct letter next to the corresponding example. Some tenses will be used more than once. (Answers are on p. 88.)

Example	Verb Tense
1. _____ I will work.	a. simple present
2. _____ I was working.	b. simple past
3. _____ I will have been working.	c. simple future
4. _____ I had worked.	d. present progressive
5. _____ I have been working.	e. past progressive
6. _____ I will be working.	f. future progressive
7. _____ I work.	g. present perfect
8. _____ I worked.	h. past perfect
9. _____ I had been working.	i. future perfect
10. _____ I have worked.	j. present perfect progressive
11. _____ I am working.	k. past perfect progressive
12. _____ I will have worked.	l. future perfect progressive
13. _____ I didn't work.	
14. _____ I wasn't working.	
15. _____ Have you worked?	
16. _____ She didn't work.	
17. _____ It doesn't work.	
18. _____ You haven't worked.	
19. _____ He hasn't been working.	
20. _____ Did you work?	

Answers to Pre-Test 1: Common Native Speaker Grammar Errors, pp. 34–35:

1. It's essential to get the message out to parents that they have to know at all times exactly whom their loved ones associate with and where they are (at) . (1) unnecessary preposition

2. I've encountered a problem when I'm trying to insert a record. Sometimes while I'm trying to build a menu list, I'll get an error message telling me something about too much recursion. What does this mean? Correct

3. Between you and ⓘ *me* this situation is going to have a very unhappy ending. (2) wrong pronoun

4. My wife and I look forward to working more with the Matthew Community Program. Founded a decade ago by Theodore Jabil and (myself) *me* this organization serves children and families in the Brooklyn area. (3) wrong pronoun

5. I had (went) *gone* to different therapy services, but Pressure Point was the best ever. (4) wrong verb form

6. The DC-10 jet cracked into two pieces and came to rest with the front section (laying) *lying* on its side. (5) wrong word

7. The campus police department is proud to announce the publication of the long-awaited and revised Student Safety Guide. Note that the name has been changed to the Annual Report & Safety Guide to reflect its content more appropriately. Correct

8. Team captains are receiving this article because they might want to pass it on to (whomever) *whoever* would benefit from it the most. (6) wrong word

9. What the boss (don't) *doesn't* know won't matter in the end. (7) 3ʳᵈ person singular in present tense requires –s in the verb

10. If it (wouldn't have) *hadn't* been raining, the kids could have played in the backyard. (8) wrong verb form in *if*-clause

11. The jurisdiction that includes these seven heavily populated metropolitan areas should have its boundaries redrawn. Correct

12. The school board's new plan will (not hardly) *hardly* affect the students at this elementary school. (9) double negative

13. According to the author, when people feel stressed, angry, or ashamed, we give off negative energy. This is why viewing negative events causes us to feel (badly) *bad*. Similarly, witnessing acts of kindness causes us to feel good. (10) wrong word

14. We cannot let (them) *those* people vote. If we let them vote, they're not going to make the right decision. (11) wrong word

15. My opinion is that the manager should (of) *have* fired those employees on the spot. (12) wrong word

16. Care should be taken when attempting to remove a tick from human skin. Cover the tick with the liquid for a few seconds. If you apply enough liquid, the tick will let go on *its* (it's) own. (13) wrong word

17. A clear advantage that this particular electronic dictionary software has over its competitors is the incredible number of words that it can be quickly looked up. Correct

18. If you want to play on the team, please send me an email letting me know that *you're* (your) interested. I need your response no later than Saturday. (14) wrong word

19. Krashen came up with the concept of *i + 1* to help describe the distance between a *person's* (persons) language proficiency and the level of the language in the material. (15) wrong word

20. If you are an employee *whose* (who's) contract expires annually and a renewal is done at the beginning of a semester, you may not be entered into the data system yet. (16) wrong word

21. Yes, I'm looking for something that is more stable than my current job, but I haven't been going to job interviews *too* (to) much. (17) wrong word

22. Your place was terrific, but I want to say that your warm hospitality and great facilities are what we enjoyed the most and what made the trip so special to Kate and me. Correct

23. Applicants may submit their paperwork either in person or via email. Note that the submission method will not *affect* (effect) the committee's decision regarding any application. (18) wrong word

24. This plant can withstand temperatures to five degrees Fahrenheit, which is the point at which the plant may *lose* (loose) some or all of its leaves (but still not kill the plant). (19) wrong word

25. In a recent ruling by five of the Supreme Court justices *their* (there) conclusion was that police should have more authority in some cases. (20) wrong word

Pre-Test 2: Eight Parts of Speech, p. 40

(Answers, especially examples, will vary. The order of the eight parts of speech is irrelevant.) 1. A noun is the name of a person, place, thing, or quality. (*cat*) 2. A verb is a word that shows action or state of being. (*wish*) 3. An adjective is a word that describes a noun or a pronoun. (*good*) 4. A pronoun is a word that can take the place of a noun. (*she*) 5. A preposition is a word that shows a relationship between one word and another word in the sentence. (*with*) 6. A conjunction is a word that connects words, phrases, or clauses. (*and*) 7. An adverb is a word that modifies verbs, adjectives, or another adverb. (*carefully*) 8. An interjection is a word that shows strong emotion. (*Ouch!*)

Pre-Test 3: Eight Parts of Speech, p. 41

1. adjective 2. noun 3. adjective 4. conjunction 5. adverb 6. verb 7. adjective 8. adjective 9. preposition 10. adjective 11. noun 12. adjective 13. adjective 14. verb 15. preposition 16. noun 17. adjective 18. adjective 19. noun 20. pronoun 21. adverb 22. conjunction 23. verb 24. preposition 25. adjective

Review of Parts of Speech, p. 63

1. noun 2. adverb 3. adjective 4. noun 5. adjective 6. conjunction 7. adjective 8 . preposition 9. pronoun 10. adjective 11. noun 12. adjective 13. adverb 14. adverb 15. adjective 16. noun 17. preposition 18. adverb 19. conjunction 20. verb 21. noun 22. conjunction 23. adjective 24. adjective 25. noun 26. adverb 27. adjective 28. pronoun 29. noun 30. adjective 31. adverb 32. adverb 33. adjective 34. adjective 35. adjective 36. noun 37. adjective 38. adverb 39. adverb 40. adjective

Activity 1. Verb Tenses in English, p. 84

Cook: I cook, I cooked, I will cook, I am cooking, I was cooking, I will be cooking, I have cooked, I had cooked, I will have cooked, I have been cooking, I had been cooking, I will have been cooking

Write: I write, I wrote, I will write, I am writing, I was writing, I will be writing, I have written, I had written, I will have written, I have been writing, I had been writing, I will have been writing

Activity 2. Verb Tenses in English, p. 85

1.c 2.e 3.l 4.h 5.j 6.f 7.a 8.b 9.k 10.g 11.d 12.i 13.b 14.e 15.g 16.b 17.a 18.g 19.j 20.b

3

15 Keys to ELL Grammar

This chapter covers 15 grammar issues that are key to teaching grammar to ELLs. These 15 issues, or Keys, can be found in the contents in most beginning to high- intermediate ELL books. The 15 Keys presented in this chapter present verb tenses, count and non-count nouns, prepositions, articles, pronunciation of –s and –ed, adjective clauses, infinitives and gerunds, phrasal verbs, modals, passive voice, and conditionals. Though there are certainly many other useful ELL grammar issues, a solid understanding of these 15 Keys will provide a sound basis for teachers as they plan and carry out their own ELL grammar lessons. (Additional ELL grammar points are addressed in Hot Seat Questions in Chapter 4.)

Each grammar Key opens with a brief explanation of the importance of this particular grammar point for ELLs and their teachers. The information for each grammar point consists of four parts, and for each subcategory of the grammar, teaching points to minimize ELL errors are offered:

- Part A shows five **examples of typical ELL errors** made with the grammar point.

- Part B includes **detailed grammar explanations** with useful charts and examples.

- Part C briefly highlights how this grammar point is handled in the **seven languages** most commonly spoken by today's ELLs—namely Arabic, Chinese, French, Japanese, Korean, Russian, and Spanish.

- Part D offers some **ideas on how to teach the grammar point.**

ELL Grammar Key 1:
to be

The verb *to be* is usually one of the first grammar points in any ESL book. If you studied a foreign language, *to be* was also the first verb in your French book (*être*), Spanish book (*ser* or *estar*), or even Japanese book (*desu* or *imasu* or *arimasu*).

In addition to being the most frequently used verb in English, *to be* appears early in many ESL books because it allows students and teachers to practice a lot of new vocabulary (primarily nouns and adjectives and then prepositional phrases of location) in simple sentences with the same verb (usually *is*, initially) used repeatedly: *My name is Susan. The book is green. I am here. Our test is today.* In other words, by using *to be*, we are able to keep the grammar of the sentences very easy for the students so that they can concentrate on understanding how the vocabulary in the sentences is arranged to produce the speaker's or writer's intended message.

In addition to the form *be*, this common verb has five basic forms in English: *am, is, are, was,* and *were.* There are also two other forms that are taught later: *being* and *been.* With a total of eight forms (including *be*), *to be* is the most inflected verb in English. (Other verbs can have far fewer forms; for example, the verb *to work* has only four different forms: *work, works, worked, working,* and the verb *to cut* has only three different forms: *cut, cuts, cutting.*)

1.A. Typical ELL Errors: Noticing the Gap

Can you identify and explain these five common ELL errors with this grammar point?

1. *I have hungry now.
2. *Joseph and Mark no are in the car.
3. *India and Pakistan two countries in Asia.
4. Mrs. Williams is a good store manager. *Is my friend.
5. *Does the weather is hot in your country?

> An **inflection** is a change in the form of a word that shows a grammatical change, such as *–ed* for past tense in *needed* or *–en* for plural in *oxen.* Some languages have few inflections; others have many. For example, nouns in Japanese do not have a plural inflection, so the same form is used for singular and plural. Nouns in German have several different plural inflections based on whether the noun is grammatically masculine, feminine, or neutral and whether the noun is the subject or object of the sentence. Nouns in English have only two forms, singular and plural, and by far the most common plural inflection is *–s.*

1.B. Grammar Explanation

1. B.1. Simple Present Tense of *Be*

Singular	Plural
I am	we are
you are	you are
he/she/it is	they are

In the simple present tense, *be* has three forms: *am, is, are.*
I, you, he, she, it, we, and *they* are called **subject pronouns.**

Common ELL Mistakes: What Your ELLs Should Know

1. Do not use **am, is,** or **are** with the wrong subject.

   wrong: Joseph and Mark is in the kitchen.

   correct: Joseph and Mark are in the kitchen.

2. Do not omit **am, is,** or **are** from the sentence.

   wrong: India and Pakistan two countries in Asia.

   correct: India and Pakistan are two countries in Asia.

3. Do not use **have** for **be** with these words: *hungry, thirsty, right, wrong, sleepy, tired, lucky, . . . years old.*

   wrong: The author of this book has 49 years old.

   correct: The author of this book is 49 years old.

4. Do not forget to include the subject.

   wrong: My brother's name is Kirk. Is 47 years old.

   correct: My brother's name is Kirk. He is 47 years old.

1.B.2. Simple Past Tense of *Be*

Singular	Plural
I was	we were
you were	you were
he/she/it was	they were

In the simple past tense, *be* has only two forms: **was** and **were.**

At first glance, perhaps *was* and *were* appear quite different from *am*, *is*, and *are*, but there are similarities. Notice that both *is* and *was* end in −*s* and that both *are* and *were* end in −*re*. Pointing out these similarities early in the learning process may be helpful to your ELLs.

i<u>s</u> ➔ wa<u>s</u>   a<u>re</u> ➔ we<u>re</u>

1.B.3. Negative Forms

Making the negative of *be* is easy: you put the word *not* after the form of *be*. (In other chapters, you will see that negating other verbs in English is more complicated. Students will soon confuse this negation pattern with other patterns, e.g., *do not go, might not go, have not gone,* so it is important to practice the negative of *be* well.)

Present	am not	is not	are not
Past	was not		were not

1.B.4. Contractions

Contractions of the verb *to be* are possible in both affirmative and negative in the present tense but only in negative in the past. Considered less formal, contractions occur much more in spoken language than in written language. Contractions are one feature of overall spoken language that can potentially make a speaker sound more friendly, so they are important.

Present				**Past**			
Affirmative		**Negative**		**Affirmative**		**Negative**	
I am	I'm	I am not	I'm not	I was	———	I was not	I wasn't
you are	you're	you are not	you aren't you're not	you were	———	you were not	you weren't
he is	he's	he is not	he isn't he's not	he was	———	he was not	he wasn't
she is	she's	she is not	she isn't she's not	she was	———	she was not	she wasn't
it is	it's	it is not	it isn't it's not	it was	———	it was not	it wasn't
we are	we're	we are not	we aren't we're not	we were	———	we were not	we weren't
they are	they're	they are not	they aren't they're not	they were	———	they were not	they weren't

1.B.5. Forming Questions

There are two types of questions in English, and both kinds, in the case of *to be*, are easy to learn. Questions that are answered either yes or no are called **yes-no questions**. Questions that are answered with other answers such as a person, a place, or a time are called *wh-* **questions** (or sometimes **information questions**) because the initial word often begins with a *wh-*, as in *who, whom, what, why, where, when,* or *which*. While some initial question words begin with *how* (*how, how many, how often*), they are still referred to as *wh-* questions.

To change an affirmative statement into a yes-no or *wh-* question, you simply move the form of *be* just in front of the subject—you invert the subject and the verb.

	yes-no	*wh-*
Statement	Ana is from Peru.	Ana is from Peru.
Question	Is Ana from Peru?	Where is Ana from?
Short Answer	Yes, she is. (OR: No, she is not.)	Peru. (OR: She is from Peru.)

Contractions are possible: *No, she's not* OR *No, she isn't* OR *She's from Peru*. However, no contractions are possible in affirmative short answers. We cannot answer **Yes, she's* or **Yes, I'm*.

Books for beginners, especially in EFL situations where ELLs have less contact with English daily, usually teach yes-no questions over the course of a few chapters before introducing *wh-* questions. A universally effective teaching technique is to build upon previous knowledge, so in this case, remind students of yes-no questions and then transition to *wh-* questions. Be sure to highlight the similarities. Many students know the *wh-* words of *what, when, where, who,* and *why*. While ELLs probably know the meaning of these words, at this point they probably have a rather vague understanding of the grammar of forming *wh-* questions. As a result, ELLs at this proficiency level often form questions like **Where you from?* or **Who do you are from?*

A good teacher will ask the students what is similar between the two questions rather than just giving out this information, as can be seen in the teacher's presentation that follows here:

> *T = teacher; S = one student; C = whole class; . . . = pause between sentences; / = short break between idea groups within a sentence*

Class Talk	Whiteboard
T: Can one of you tell me your birthday? . . . Can one of you / tell me / your birthday? . . . Yes, Lim.	
Lim: June 30.	
T: June 30th. Ok, June 30th.	[T. writes now]
T: Lim's birthday . . . anyone?	*Lim's birthday* . . .
C: Is June 30.	
T: Right. Lim's birthday is June 30th. OK? . . . Now if I am not sure about Lim's birthday? Maybe it's the 30th or maybe it's the 31st or maybe it's the 10th. If I want to know yes or no if Lim's birthday is June 30th, what is my question? . . . Right. The yes-no question is, "Is Lim's birthday June 30th?"	[T. circles *is* in the previous sentence and draws a line with an arrow to show how *is* moves in front of *Lim's birthday*.] *Lim's birthday (is) June 30th.* [T. writes as students tell her] *Is Lim's birthday June 30th?*
T: Ana, ask me this question now (points).	
Ana: Is Lim's birthday June 30th?	
T: Class, what are two possible answers?	
C: Yes, it is. No, it isn't.	[T. writes]
T: OK, but now we are going to see something new, something different, a new kind of question. What if I don't want to know yes or no? What if I don't know Lim's birthday? What if I have NO idea when Lim's birthday is. What is my question going to be?	*Yes, it is.* OR *No, it isn't.* [T. writes a big question mark] ?
C: Who . . .	
T: Who? Who is for people. Is birthday a person?	[T. writes] *who?*
C: No . . .	
T: OK, what is the best question word for birthday?	[T. crosses out *who* and then erases it.] ~~*who?*~~

C: When?

T: Yes, that's right: when. So what is the question?

C: When Lim's birthday?

T: Look at our original sentence.

T: You are 100% correct that we will use **when** as our question word. Who knows which words in this sentence are the same as, equal to, **when?**

S: June 30th?

T: Yes, that's right.

T: Question words like **when** or **who** always begin a question, so let's move this to the beginning, like this.

T: When we studied yes-no questions, what do you remember, what do you know about **is** in a yes-no question? Where does it go?

C: Before.

T: Yes, it goes before, just like this.

T: Yes, that's it. Now we have a correct question, so let's put a question mark.

T: Can everyone see how yes-no questions and wh- information questions are similar? Can you see this?

C: is Lim's birthday

T: Yes, that's right. Look how *is Lim's birthday* is the same in both questions.

[T. writes on board] *When?*

[T. points to]
Is Lim's birthday June 30th.

[T. circles June 30th, then crosses it out lightly, and writes *when?* across the top.]

When?
Is Lim's birthday ~~June 30th?~~
[Teacher draws an arched line with arrow from WHEN to the front of the sentence, then crosses out WHEN lightly, and writes it at the beginning of the question:]
When is Lim's birthday

[T. adds question mark:]
When is Lim's birthday?

[T. writes the yes-no question with the wh- question below so as to line up *is Lim's birthday*
Is Lim's birthday June 30th?
When is Lim's birthday?
[T. should now underline <u>is Lim's birthday</u> in both questions:]
<u>Is Lim's birthday</u> June 30th?
When <u>is Lim's birthday</u> ?

1.C. Native Language Interference: Compare English with Other Languages

Language	Notes on to be
Arabic	1. Arabic does not use *to be* in present time, but it does express it in past time. A typical error is **My house special for me.* 2. In past tense, verb forms change according to the subject.
Chinese	1. There is a verb *to be* in Chinese, but it is followed only by nouns, as in *Mary is a student.* 2. For location (*Mary is in the room*), a separate verb (other than *to be*) is used. 3. For adjectives, no verb is used, which explains why Chinese students may write **Mary very busy now.*
French	1. There is a verb that functions in a similar way to *to be* in English. 2. Some expressions that use *to be* in English—*hungry, thirsty, right, wrong, . . . years old, sleepy, lucky*—use *have* in French, so common errors include **I have hungry* and **She has 27 years old.* 3. Verb forms change according to the subject—much more than *to be* does in English. 4. French does not have any progressive/continuous tenses, so *je mange* can mean either *I eat* or *I am eating.* 5. The present perfect tense for most verbs is formed by the auxiliary *have* and the past participle, but verbs of motion use *be* + past participle instead, so French–speaking students may write **We are arrived* for *We have arrived.*
Japanese	1. Japanese has three different verbs that function as *to be* in English. 2. To express existence (*there is/are/was/were*), Japanese uses one *be* verb with animate subjects (*a person, a cat*) but a different *be* verb with inanimate subjects (*a cloud, a car*). 3. For adjectives, no verb is used, which explains why Japanese students may write **Mary very busy now.* 4. Verb forms do not change according to the subject. 5. Subject pronouns are often omitted. 6. A verb can be a complete sentence. In answering the question *Are your reports ready now?* a Japanese ELL may simply respond **Are* or **Ready.*

Korean	1. There is a verb *to be*. 2. In Korean, *to be* cannot be followed by a noun or an adjective, so Korean ELLs may write **My father a taxi driver* or **The weather tomorrow will hot.* 3. Verb forms do not change according to the subject.
Russian	1. Russian does not use *to be* in present tense, but it does express *to be* in past time. Thus, a common error is **Moscow a very big city in Russia.* 2. In past, verb forms change according to the subject.
Spanish	1. Spanish has two different verbs for *to be*, so Spanish-speaking ELLs may be confused by the lone *to be* in English. 2. Some expressions that use *to be* in English—*hungry, thirsty, right, wrong, . . . years old, sleepy, lucky*—use *have* in Spanish, so common errors include **I have hungry* and **She has 27 years old.* 3. Verb forms change according to the subject—much more than *to be* does in English. 4. Subject pronouns are usually omitted; the verb endings indicate the subject. A persistent error is *I like cats. *Are very good pets.*
All Languages	1. Different languages negate in different ways. French puts *ne* in front of the verb and *pas* after. Spanish puts *no* in front of the verb. Japanese changes the middle of the word. (This is called an **infix**—as opposed to a prefix or suffix.) Many ELLs incorrectly negate the verb *to be* by placing *no* before or after the verb: **I no am a teacher* or **I am no a teacher*. 2. Different languages form questions in different ways. Some languages invert the subject and verb; some languages use a special marker at the beginning of the question (Arabic) or end of the question (Japanese) that indicates a question. In contrast, English relies on word order. To form a question in English, the verb *to be* is moved before the subject. Many ELLs forget to make the inversion and write **You are a teacher?*

1.D. Ideas for Teaching

If you are teaching *to be*, you are probably teaching beginning-level students, so it is important to concentrate initially on one usage of *be* and keep the vocabulary level of your explanations low.

By controlling the vocabulary level, I mean that you should use simple vocabulary, including familiar words, **cognates,** and proper nouns when possible, and you should make an attempt to have those words appear multiple times. For example, if you are going to use color words to teach *be*, try to use four or five colors several times instead of using ten or twelve colors once. Use words like red, white, blue, and green, not colors like tan, beige, and fuschia.

The verb *to be* can be followed by several grammatical units, including nouns, adjectives, and prepositional phrases. For initial teaching, I strongly recommend choosing one of these three, not a combination. You need to think about examples that you can give that will be meaningful for your students.

If you opt to use examples with **nouns,** you can talk about famous people:

> (name of popular singer) is a singer.
>
> (name of president) is a president.
>
> (name of soccer player) is a soccer player.

If you opt to use examples with **adjectives,** you can talk about colors:

> The sky is blue.
>
> A dollar is green.
>
> The grammar book is red.

If you opt to use examples with **prepositional phrases,** you can talk about objects that are in your classroom:

> The clock is on the wall.
>
> (name of student) is by the door.
>
> The teacher is next to the board.

If your students are from different places, you can also use this information in **prepositional phrases.**

> Reiko is from Japan.
>
> Ahmed is from Kuwait.
>
> Carlos is from Colombia.

All of these examples so far use *is*, not *am* or *are*. If you are working with very low-level students who have little formal training and/or time for English study, which is more typical of EFL situations or some ESL refugee programs, I would recommend teaching *is, are,* and *am* one at a time. It is not necessary for students to know initially that these are three forms of the same verb *(to be)*. In contrast, for ELLs who have a good

For ELLs, **prepositions of location** (<u>on</u> the table; <u>in</u> the box) **are often easier to grasp than prepositions of time** (<u>on</u> Monday; <u>in</u> June). Why we say <u>on</u> in *on the table* seems more logical than why we say <u>on</u> in *on Monday*. Key 6 explains the nuances of prepositions in depth.

Cognates are words from different languages that look similar. Without knowing Spanish, for example, the average native speaker of English can recognize Spanish words such as *radio, tomate,* and *preparar* as radio, tomato, and to prepare. **False cognates** appear to be cognates, but they actually have different meanings—for example, Spanish *embarazada* means "pregnant" not "embarrassed" and *actualmente* means "currently," not "actually."

grasp of grammar (in their own or another language), you can start with a full set of examples with seven subject pronouns that refer to people:

I am from the United States. We are from Colombia.

You are from China. You are from Saudi Arabia.

He is from Dubai. They are from Mexico.

She is from Japan.

Again, notice that all of my examples follow one pattern. I chose origin: **subject** + *be* + *from* + country name. As I write these on the board, I would point to a specific student or students in the class that the sentence is about. I would look at Reiko when I write the example about Reiko, and I would look at Carlos, Maria, and Tomas when I write *They are from Mexico.* The lower the proficiency level of your students, the more you need to use concrete examples in the here and now.

I would start by writing one of your three examples on the board. Then write only the noun of the second sentence and have students complete the idea. Your board would look like this:

An apple is red.
A dollar is

Let them tell you the word *green*. If no one knows it, then provide the word. Keep your class interactive by having a student spell the word for you as you write it. Before you start writing the word *green*, say "green." Make the students repeat it. Then spell it as you write it slowly on the board: G (write *g*), R (write *r*), etc. Again, it is easy to keep students' attention if you require it by teaching interactively. Then go to your next example, the grammar book.

A simple way to practice this at this low level of proficiency is with scrambled sentences. Either on a worksheet or on the board (or overhead projector or newsprint), write some scrambled sentences:

apple red is an
dollar a green is

Students have to unscramble the sentences. You can also practice capitalizing the first word of a sentence and punctuating with a final period. You can make the activity more challenging but still within students' level as follows:

the the blue is on desk book
Canada white of flag is red the and

Notice how these examples still practice *is* and follow the pattern **subject** + *is* + color. It is a mistake to include patterns such as present progressive tense at this point (e.g., *The man is sleeping*). This kind of sentence is acceptable if your students are reviewing *be*, but for low-level students, this selection represents extremely poor planning on the teacher's part and is likely to cause confusion.

FIND OUT

Ask students of different first languages to translate these six sentences into their native languages:

❶ I am not from Canada.

❷ He is 40 years old.

❸ I am a teacher.

❹ He was a teacher.

❺ I am at the bank now.

❻ I am eating now.

Compare the forms of *be* for these six sentences. What differences are there with English in terms of the verb *to be?*

ELL Grammar Key 2:
Verb Tenses to Express Present Time

In grammar, we tend to think of present time as a very easy concept to express in English. We have a tense called simple present tense that is used to express actions that happen repeatedly, such as *I play tennis on Saturday mornings*. However, we need a different tense, present progressive tense, to express an action that is happening right now, as in *I am playing tennis now*. In addition, we need yet another tense, present perfect tense, to express an action that began in the past and is still true or happening now, such as *I have played tennis since 2005*. Clearly, expressing actions in the present time is not as "simple" as it might initially appear. As you can imagine, the situation for ELLs is even hazier.

2.A. Typical ELL Errors: Noticing the Gap

Can you identify and explain these five common ELL errors with this grammar point?

1. *I am in this city for all of my adult life.
2. *The solution to my problem isn't depend on another person.
3. *Is working your uncle at the bank now?
4. *Modern cars are having much better tires than in the past.
5. *Do you have worked at this bank since the last time I saw you?

Much of the time, the tense of a verb in English logically matches the time of the action. However, there is sometimes a difference between the time of an action and the verb tense that is used to express it. For example, present progressive tense (also called present continuous tense) is logically used for actions that are happening right now. As the name of the tense actually implies, the action is progressing or happening at the present moment. Thus, a student in this course might say, *Right now I am reading this book*. However, that same student can also use the same verb tense to indicate future time and say, *I am reading a different book tomorrow*. To be sure, this lack of exact match between the tense and its time is disconcerting to many ELLs and, as expected, leads to confusion.

There are four verb tenses that express some aspect of present time. These four verb tenses are shown here.

Verb Tense	Example	Meaning
Simple Present	*I study Chinese every day.*	a habitual or repeating action
Present Progressive	*I am studying Chinese today.*	a current action
Present Perfect	*I have studied Chinese since 2006.*	an action that began in the past but continues to be true
Present Perfect Progressive	*I have been studying Chinese all morning.*	an action that began in the past but is continuing now (with emphasis on the fact that it is still happening)

No ESL textbook and no teacher should ever try to teach all these verb tenses at the same time. Traditionally, these verb tenses would be interspersed with other tenses like the simple past and past progressive. However, a usual order of presentation within the twelve verb tenses in English is: simple present → present progressive → present perfect → present perfect progressive.

Some L2 researchers and materials writers, however, advocate teaching present progressive tense first because that tense is much more frequent in English usage than simple present tense. The counterargument for the more traditional order with simple present first is that ELLs can learn the base form of a verb first (e.g., *run, decide, cook*) before learning an expanded version (e.g., *running, deciding, cooking*). You should follow the curriculum that your school has established, but you should pay attention to the language in your ELLs' textbooks to see which of these four tenses is actually used more often.

2.B. Grammar Explanation

2.B.1. Simple Present Tense

We use simple present tense for habitual or repeated actions.

Example: Every day I *walk* from my house to the bus stop.

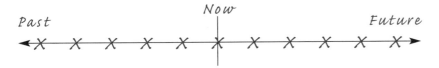

Singular	Plural
I walk	we walk
you walk	you walk
he/she/it walks	they walk

The simple present tense takes the form: VERB or VERB + –s. The –s for third person singular can be pronounced in three different ways: /s/ (*cooks*), /z/ (*lives*), /əz/ (*sneezes*). The reasons and rules for these pronunciations are explained in Key 8. (In this book, sounds are noted between slashes: /k/, /ə/, and /t/ are the three sounds in the word *cut*.)

Some verbs are irregular in spelling yet even so follow patterns: *study* → *studies* (not *studys*), *go* → *goes* (not *gos*), *do* → *does* (not *dos*), and *have* → *has* (not *haves*).

ELLs learn the simple present of *be* (*I am, you are, he/she/it is, we are, they are*), so well that they accidentally include a form of *be* when they really want to say only the subject pronoun. Therefore, an error such as ***I am walk*** (instead of the intended *I walk*) is a natural, expected error in English acquisition.

Common ELL Mistakes: What Your ELLs Should Know

1. Use VERB + –s only when the subject is **he, she,** or **it** (i.e., third person singular).

   wrong: Laura cook scrambled eggs for breakfast every day.

   correct: Laura cooks scrambled eggs for breakfast every day.

2. Remember to change **–y** to **–i** and add **–es.** (We do not change **–y** to **–i** if a vowel precedes : *stay* → *stays, enjoy* → *enjoys.*) Remember to add **–es** after **o, sh, ch,** and **s.**

   wrong: My baby sister crys when she is hungry.

   correct: My baby sister cries when she is hungry.

3. Do not use **be** with verbs in simple present tense.

   wrong: I am walk to school every day.

   correct: I walk to school every day.

2.B.2. Present Progressive Tense

We use present progressive tense for actions that are happening right now.

> *Example:* Right now I ***am walking*** from my car to my office.

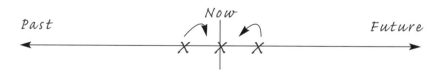

Singular	Plural
I am walking	we are walking
you are walking	you are walking
he/she/it is walking	they are walking

The present progressive tense takes the form: **am/is/are** + VERB + **–ing**. The **–ing** form is called the present participle. Use **am, is,** or **are** according to the subject; that is, the verb must agree with its subject.

Follow these spelling rules for the present participle:

1. Drop the final **–e** before adding **–ing**: *take* ➔ *taking, write* ➔ *writing.*
2. If the verb ends in consonant-vowel-consonant: double the final consonant: *hop* ➔ *hopping* (compare *keep* ➔ *keeping*).
3. For a two-syllable verb ending in consonant-vowel-consonant, double the final consonant if the stress is on the second syllable: *begin* ➔ *beginning* (compare *happen* ➔ *happening*).

Common ELL Mistakes: What Your ELLs Should Know

1. Don't use VERB or VERB + **–s** for actions that are happening just now or only once.

   wrong: We study very hard for tomorrow's test.

   correct: We are studying very hard for tomorrow's test.

2. Don't use **–ing** for actions that happen every day or all the time.

   wrong: The earth is going around the sun once a year.

   correct: The earth goes around the sun once a year.

3. Don't forget to use **be.**

   wrong: My baby brother crying now.

   correct: My baby brother is crying now.

4. Be careful with the spelling of the present participle.

   wrong: cuting, siting, planing, eatting, helpping, openning

   correct: cutting, sitting, planning, eating, helping, opening

5. Don't use present progressive if the verb does not show an action (as opposed to a state of being). Examples of verbs that are rarely in progressive tenses are: *own, possess, like, love, need, want, have, seem, feel, be, prefer, remember, forget, believe.*

   wrong: I am owning two cars.

   correct: I own two cars.

When **have** means "possess," it is not used in progressive tenses (**I **am having** a car*). When *have* expresses action as in *have a party, have a good time,* or *have a baby,* progressive tenses are possible. When *have* expresses *action,* we have two options: *I **am having** a good time now* and *I always **have** a good time at the beach.* When *have* expresses ownership, we have only one option: *I **have** a car.*

2.B.3. Present Perfect Tense

We can use present perfect tense for an action that began in the past but is still true now. It may or may not continue.

Example: I ***have walked*** in this park every Saturday for the past two years.

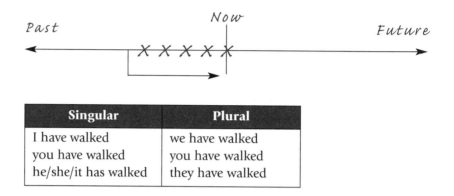

Singular	Plural
I have walked	we have walked
you have walked	you have walked
he/she/it has walked	they have walked

The present perfect tense takes the form: **have/has** + PAST PARTICIPLE. For the auxiliary (or helping) verb **have**, use **have** or **has** according to the subject.

Past Participle for Regular Verbs. The past participle of a regular verb is the same as its past tense. You add **–ed** to the base form of the verb. This **–ed** ending is pronounced in three different ways: /d/, /t/, /əd/. See Key 8 for more detailed information.

Follow these spelling rules:

1. For verbs that already end in –e, just add –d: *create* → *created, sneeze* → *sneezed.*
2. Double the final consonant if there is only one vowel before it: *step* → *stepped, rob* → *robbed.*
3. Do not double the final consonant if there is not one (and only one) vowel before it: *end* → *ended, ask* → *asked.*

Past Participle for Irregular Verbs. Common endings for the past participle forms of irregular verbs include **–en, –ne**, or **–n** as in *chosen, done,* and *torn,* but there are other possibilities. Some irregular forms are the same for present, past, and past participle as in *cut, cut, cut* or *put, put, put.* Another pattern is different vowels, especially *i→a→u* as in *sing, sang, sung* or *ring, rang, rung.* The good news for students is that only a small number of all the verbs in English are irregular. Students will need to memorize the irregular forms that are most commonly used. (See Teaching Technique 9 and Appendix 2.)

Common ELL Mistakes: What Your ELLs Should Know

1. Do not forget to use **have** or **has** with the past participle for an action that began in the past and still continues.

   wrong: I was born here and I will die here. I **lived** here my whole life.

   correct: I was born here and I will die here. I have lived here my whole life.

2. Do not use **have** or **has** with the wrong subject.

   wrong: Sarah have rented the same apartment since 2005.

   correct: Sarah has rented the same apartment since 2005.

3. Use the correct past participle with present perfect tense.

   wrong: Sarah has already complete all the homework.

   correct: Sarah has already completed all the homework.

2.B.4. Present Perfect Progressive Tense

We use present perfect progressive tense to express an action that began in the past but is continuing now with emphasis on the fact that it is still happening.

> *Example:* I **have been walking** in this park for almost an hour.

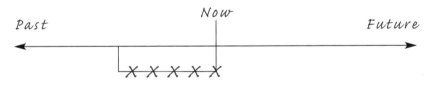

Singular	Plural
I have been walking	we have been walking
you have been walking	you have been walking
he/she/it has been walking	they have been walking

The present perfect progressive tense takes the form: **have/has + been + VERB + –ing.** For the auxiliary verb **have**, use **have** or **has** according to the subject. In this tense, **been** never changes.

Common ELL Mistakes: What Your ELLs Should Know

1. Do not forget to use **have** or **has** with **been** followed by the present participle.

   wrong: I been waiting for the bus for almost 45 minutes.

   correct: I have been waiting for the bus for almost 45 minutes.

2. Do not use present progressive tense for an ongoing action (even though it is happening in present time), especially when *for* or *since* is used.

   wrong: I am waiting for the bus for almost 45 minutes.

   correct: I have been waiting for the bus for almost 45 minutes.

2.B.5. Negative Forms

Tense	Negative Form
Simple Present	*I/you/we/they* + *do* + *not* + VERB *he/she/it* + *does* + *not* + VERB
Present Progressive	*I am* + *not* + VERB + *–ing* *you/we/they are* + *not* + VERB + *–ing* *he/she/it* + *is* + *not* + VERB + *–ing*
Present Perfect	*I/you/we/they* + *have* + *not* + PAST PARTICIPLE *he/she/it* + *has* + *not* + PAST PARTICIPLE
Present Perfect Progressive	*I/you/we/they* + *have* + *not* + *been* + VERB + *–ing* *he/she/it* + *has* + *not* + *been* + VERB + *–ing*

Of the four tenses for expressing present time, the most difficult to negate is simple present tense.

In simple present tense, a negative takes the form: **do/does + not + VERB**. **Do not** is used with **I, you, we,** or **they**; **does not** is used with **he, she,** or **it**. ELLs consistently and frequently make three mistakes: (1) omission of **do/does** (**I not understand*), (2) use of **be** (**I am not watch TV every morning*), and (3) including **–s** (**This supermarket does not sells fresh fish*).

In present progressive tense, negating is easy because you negate the auxiliary **be** as shown on page 92: **am not, is not, are not, was not, were not.**

Both present perfect and present perfect progressive tenses form their negative by adding **not** after the auxiliary verb: **have/has + not.**

To summarize, the difference between simple present and the other three tenses is that the last three tenses contain an auxiliary verb. In English, an auxiliary verb is negated by adding **not** after it. In contrast, simple present has only one word, which is the main verb. It is not possible to add **not** after a main verb. Instead, you must add the auxiliaries **do** or **does** (or **did** for past, as you will see on pp. 128–30) and the word **not.**

The usual way to negate the verb *go* is with **don't go**. In poetry, you may find lines such as "Go not into the night," but this is not usual negation. If you are teaching a literature lesson with such language, have your ELLs compare the text's language (*go not*) with current usage (*don't go*). Most ELLs have no need to know about *go not* and should be taught only *don't go*. Learner needs determine which language is taught.

Common ELL Mistakes: What Your ELLs Should Know

1. Do not forget to use **do not** or **does not** with questions and negative forms of the simple present tense.

   wrong: I no speak French well.

   correct: I do not speak French well.

2. Do not use **am, is not,** or **are not** with the base form of a verb. Use **do not** or **does not** only.

   wrong: The man is not like this food.

   correct: The man does not like this food.

3. With simple present tense, use **–s** for **he/she/it** only one time in the verb. If you have **does,** then the verb cannot have an **–s,** too.

   wrong: This soup doesn't smells good.

   correct: This soup doesn't smell good.

4. Do not use **don't, doesn't,** or **didn't** to negate verbs in present perfect or past perfect tenses. Don't confuse **don't have** with **haven't.** Don't confuse **doesn't have** with **hasn't.**

   wrong: We don't have eaten at that restaurant yet.

   correct: We have not eaten at that restaurant yet.

   wrong: I applied for a visa to visit Brazil, but the Brazilian embassy doesn't have returned my passport yet.

   correct: I applied for a visa to visit Brazil, but the Brazilian embassy hasn't returned my passport yet.

In North American English, we **negate the main verb *have*** with *do not have, does not have,* or *did not have.* When *have* is an auxiliary verb, we use only *not,* as in *have not eaten* (instead of *have no eaten or *no have eaten).

2.B.6. Contractions

Contractions for these verb tenses are not difficult. Several combinations are possible as seen in this chart. (Only those parts of the verbs that can be contracted are included here.)

If your students are exposed to the non–standard form **ain't** in songs or in conversation, they should be made aware of its meaning and non–standard status. If your ELLs will not be exposed to this word, there is no need to learn about it.

Verb Tense	Affirmative	Negative
Simple Present	– – –	do not → don't does not → doesn't
Present Progressive	I am → I'm	am + not → – – –
	he/she/it is → he's/she's/it's	is not → isn't
	you/we/they are → you're/we're/they're	are not → aren't
Present Perfect; Present Perfect Progressive	I/you/we/they + have → I've/you've/we've/they've	have not → haven't
	he/she/it + has → he's/she's/it's	has not → hasn't

NOTE: Another way to negate here is to use the affirmative contractions and add *not*. For example, *he is not* → *he isn't* OR *he's not; they are not* → *they aren't* OR *they're not*.

Explain to your ELLs that **Linda's** can mean three different things: Linda is (*Linda's here*), Linda has (*Linda's taken your keys*), or possessive (*Where is Linda's car?*). It is necessary to practice each of these three forms separately and then practice them all together. You should appreciate how hard it is for ELLs to know which form is being used in rapid conversation.

Common ELL Mistakes: What Your ELLs Should Know

1. There is no contraction for **am not**.

   wrong: I amn't from northern India.

   correct: I am not from northern India. OR I'm not from northern India.

2. Only use –'s for **has** when it is used as an auxiliary, not as the main verb.

   wrong: Linda's bought a new car. It's an amazing sound system.

   correct: Linda's bought a new car. It has an amazing sound system.

2.B.7. Forming Questions

Just as with negating, the only difficult tense here is simple present because it requires the addition of a form of the auxiliary **do**. In the other three tenses, you invert the auxiliary (**be** for present progressive and **have** for both present perfect and present perfect progressive).

Tense	Interrogative Form
Simple Present	*do + I/you/we/they* + VERB *does + he/she/it* + VERB
Present Progressive	*am I* + VERB + *–ing* *are + you/we/they* + VERB + *–ing* *is + he/she/it* + VERB + *–ing*
Present Perfect	*have + I/you/we/they* + PAST PARTICIPLE *has + he/she/it* + PAST PARTICIPLE
Present Perfect Progressive	*have + I/you/we/they + been* + VERB + *–ing* *has + he/she/it + been* + VERB + *–ing*

Common ELL Mistakes: What Your ELLs Should Know

1. For simple present tense, remember to use **does** with **he, she,** and **it.** Use **do** with other subjects.

   wrong: Do Luke like hockey?

   correct: Does Luke like hockey?

2. For simple present tense, do not put **–s** on the verb in yes-no questions. Use only the base (simple) form of the verb. For **he/she/it,** you need only one **–s** in the question.

   wrong: Does Valerie goes to class every day?

   correct: Does Valerie go to class every day?

3. Do not begin simple present tense verb questions with **am, is,** or **are** unless the main verb is **to be.**

   wrong: Is Mary own a sports car?

   correct: Does Mary own a sports car?

4. For questions using present progressive, begin with **am, is,** or **are,** not **do** or **does.**

   wrong: Do you wearing a new tie today?

   correct: Are you wearing a new tie today?

5. Do not use **do, does,** or **did** in the question form of the present perfect tense.

wrong: How many international trips did you have taken in your life?

correct: How many international trips have you taken in your life?

2.C. Native Language Interference: Compare English with Other Languages

Language	Notes on *Present Verbs*
Arabic	1. Arabic has a present tense form, which means that the action is not finished. 2. There is no progressive form. 3. English present perfect tense can be rendered in Arabic by the present form or the past form, depending on the exact meaning or context of the present perfect example in English. 4. The endings of the verbs change according to the subject. In fact, the verb in Arabic is much more inflected than in English, which has only two forms: VERB (*you like*) and VERB + –s (*she likes*). Arabic has 14 separate verb endings, including separate forms for *I,* (male) *you,* (female) *you, he, she, you* (two), (male) *they* (two), (female) *they* (two), *we* (two), *we* (more than two), (male) *you* (more than two), (female) *you* (more than two), (male) *they* (more than two), and (female) *they* (more than two).
Chinese	Chinese verbs do not have different forms to mark tense. Instead, time adverbials such as *every day* or *always* are used to convey the time meaning.
French	French has verb tenses that appear to mirror the English system, but there are important differences. 1. French has no progressive tenses, so French-speaking ELLs write *It rains now.* 2. English present perfect is rendered by present or past in French according to the specific kind of present perfect. Thus, *I have already eaten* would be past, but *I have lived here since 2004* would be present. In fact, a common error is *I live here since 2004.* 3. The endings of verbs change according to the subject.

Japanese	1. Japanese has distinct forms for simple present, present progressive, simple past, and past progressive.
	2. The different meanings of English present perfect can be expressed with special constructions, but these constructions do not overlap perfectly with English.
	3. There is no future marker; instead, present tense is used with appropriate time adverbs.
	4. Japanese has at least two conditional forms; one is very similar to English and the other is stronger and means *if and only if* or *provided that*. In either case, the word *if* (*moshi*) is not required because the special verb form indicates conditional.
	5. Subject pronouns are often omitted.
Korean	1. Like Japanese, basic Korean word order is subject-object-verb, so the verb is near the end of a sentence.
	2. Simple present and present progressive exist, but there is no perfect aspect.
	3. Verbs do not have endings for the various subjects.
Russian	1. Russian has simple present tense.
	2. Russian has no progressive tenses per se, but present progressive may be expressed by using the imperfect aspect with the present tense.
	3. When present perfect tense refers to a past action that is still true, such as *I have lived here since 2005*, Russian uses present tense. A common error is **I live here since 2005* or **I am living here since 2005*.
Spanish	Spanish has verb tenses that appear to mirror the English system, but there are many differences.
	1. English present perfect is rendered by present, past, or present perfect in Spanish according to the specific meaning of present perfect.
	2. Spanish has a future tense and can also use *be going to* as English does, but simple present tense is often used with an appropriate future time adverbial. As a result, Spanish speakers often say **In a little while, I cook dinner* or **If you need a ride to the store, I take you*.
	3. The endings of verbs change according to the subject.
	4. Subject pronouns are usually omitted; the verb endings indicate the subject.

All Languages	1. The use of the auxiliary verbs *do* and *does* plus *not* to negate verbs is unique to English. Many ELLs will form negatives by placing *no* before the verb: *I no like onions* or *she no work here*.
	2. ELLs have difficulty understanding the difference in negating the verb *have* (*I have a car* = *I don't have a car*) and the auxiliary verb *have* in present perfect tense (*I have studied* = *I haven't studied*). Be prepared for this question.
	3. The use of the auxiliary verbs *do* and *does* in questions is unique to English. Many ELLs will write questions with subject-verb inversion or regular statement word order: *Uses more fuel a car or a pick-up truck?* or *The trip takes six hours?*

FIND OUT

Consult a content textbook such as science, health, business, or mathematics. In any 1,000-word excerpt, underline all the verbs. In most content textbooks, we expect a high number of present tense verbs, but is this the case? Use a rubric with all twelve verb tenses to see which tenses are represented and to what extent. (Calculate percentages when you have finished labeling and tallying the verbs.)

2.D. Ideas for Teaching

This section presented four tenses that express some form of present time. Simple present tense is usually used for habitual actions. Present progressive is usually used for actions that are happening at this moment. Present perfect is a very difficult tense because it has at least four distinct meanings, some of which involve the present. Present perfect progressive tense is used for actions that began in the past and continue now, with emphasis on the duration of the action.

Simple present tense and present progressive are usually covered in a beginning class. Present perfect is covered at the intermediate or sometimes upper-intermediate levels. Present perfect progressive is covered after present perfect has had an opportunity to sink in. One phenomenon of ELL teaching that you will observe with these tenses is that ELLs seem to handle the first tense—no matter which one is taught first—just fine, but when they are introduced to a second and third tense, problems begin to occur because at that point, there are several forms (i.e., verb tenses) competing in the learners' heads. The more tenses that an ELL studies, the greater the mental battle as the ELL attempts to remember the form of the tenses and their correct uses.

Simple present is taught first even though we know that present progressive tends to occur much more frequently in spoken English than simple present. Simple present is covered first, I think, because of tradition and sequencing. If your students study simple present first, then it is easier to follow with present progressive next. Any time you teach something, you should always put yourself in your ELLs' shoes and ask yourself, "What have I learned already that is likely to be confused with what I am about to learn?" ELLs manage fine with simple present tense, which they incorrectly (over)use in lieu of other tenses. Beginning ELLs will say, *I wait here since 7 o'clock* or *I cannot talk any more now because my wife waits for me in the car.*

A simple follow-up activity for present progressive is charades. Write out actions on small slips of paper. Ask students to sit in a circle. One student comes to the front of the class, takes a strip of paper, and demonstrates the activity. Students must respond only with the pattern, *You are VERBing.* For example, they must say, *You're dancing. You're walking. You're jumping* as they try to guess the person's action. Only statements or questions that are worded in present progressive can win points.

Present perfect tense is perhaps the most difficult of all tenses because this tense has at least four very distinct uses (covered elsewhere in this book). I recommend teaching each of these uses separately. The easiest use, which should be taught first, is for an action that began in the past but continues until now: *I have worked at this company since 2000.* Ask ELLs to think of actual situations that began in the past and are still true. Ask them to arrange their sentence in this concrete format:

1. I work at this company.
2. I began this action in 2000.
3. I have worked at this company since 2000.

The most difficult use for ELLs to produce on their own is a past action that is relevant to the present: *I am shocked by the news today that the price of gasoline has risen again.* Bring in newspapers and ask your ELLs to search for present perfect in the opening paragraphs of five to ten articles. Because writers must quickly build background information for readers, they frequently use the present perfect tense in the first two or three sentences of their article.

Present perfect progressive is an upper-intermediate verb tense. Like present perfect, this tense is difficult for ELLs to produce on their own, but it is easier because it does not have the number of potential uses that present perfect does.

ELL Grammar Key 3:
Verb Tenses to Express Past Time

In Chinese, Malay, and other languages, there are no verb tenses as in English. The most common devices used to indicate sequencing of actions are time adverbials such as *yesterday* or *before I arrived*. In Spanish, Arabic, Japanese, and other languages, there are verb tenses like those in English, but the tenses have somewhat different uses. Consider the situation of an ELL who wants to tell a story in past tense. That ELL has seven choices, including: *I have eaten. I ate. I had eaten. I was eating. I had been eating. I used to eat. I would eat.*

First, the ELL has to learn how to make the seven forms. *Have eaten* or *have eating? Ate* or *eated? Had been eating* or *had been eaten?* In addition to having to learn these seven different options listed in the previous paragraph, the logical question for the ELL is when to use which form. Which past tense is the most appropriate to use in a given situation? As a teacher, can you explain the difference between the seven short sentences at the end of the last paragraph? If native speakers have a hard time distinguishing these, imagine how tough it is for an ELL to distinguish these forms.

3.A. Typical ELL Errors: Noticing the Gap

Can you identify and explain these five common ELL errors with this grammar point?

1. *According to the report, dozens of people did not received their tax information.
2. *When I ate dinner last night, my uncle called me.
3. *How many people did you talked to at the party?
4. *By the time I was old enough to vote, I participated in two local campaigns.
5. *Do you have ever flown on a 747 jumbo jet?

There are five verb tenses and two special verb expressions that express some aspect of past time.

Verb Tense / Expression	Example	Meaning
Simple Past	*I **ate** dinner at 8 PM.*	a single past event
Past Progressive (Continuous)	*I **was eating** dinner when you called.*	a past action that was happening (when it was interrupted by another)
Present Perfect	*I **have eaten** at that restaurant.*	a past action (indefinite time) that could happen again
Past Perfect	*I **had eaten** dinner before you called.*	a past action that was completed before a second past action
Past Perfect Progressive	*I **had been eating** dinner before you called.*	an action that began in the past before a second past action (with emphasis on the duration of the action)
Used to and *Would*	*When I was still single, I **used to** eat dinner in front of the TV. I **would** put my food on a plate, and then I **would** take it to the small table in front of the TV. Then I'd eat dinner while I was watching TV. Now that I'm married, things have changed, and we eat at the dining room table.*	*Used to*: an action that happened many times in the past but is no longer true; frequently opens a past narrative *Would*: refers to smaller actions that happened repeatedly in a past narrative but are no longer true (cannot be used with non-actions)

It would be very confusing to an ELL if these verb tenses were taught at the same time. Traditionally, these verb tenses would be interspersed with other tenses like the simple present and future. However, the traditional order of presentation of the tenses that express past time is: simple past → present perfect → past progressive → past perfect → past perfect progressive → *used to* → *would*. You should follow the curriculum that your school has established, but you should pay attention to the language in your ELLs' textbooks to see which of these tenses is actually used more often.

3.B. Grammar Explanation

3.B.1. Simple Past Tense

We use simple past tense for an action that was completed in the past.

Example: Yesterday I **walked** from my house to the bus stop.

Singular	Plural
I walked	we walked
you walked	you walked
he/she/it walked	they walked

The simple past tense usually takes the form: VERB + **–ed**. The **–ed** ending can be pronounced in three different ways: /t/ *missed*, /d/ *studied*, /ǝd/ *needed*. The reasons for these pronunciations are explained on pp. 189–90.

Spelling the past form is problematic. Some letters are dropped while others may be doubled. Study these spelling rules:

- For verbs that end in **–e** already, you add only **–d**: *live → lived*.
- Some verbs are irregular in spelling: *study → studied* (not *studyed*). For verbs that end in consonant + **–y**, you change the **–y** to **–i** and then add **–ed**: *study → studied*. For verbs that end in vowel + **–y**, just add **–ed**: *play → played*.
- The rules for whether or not to double the final consonant when adding **–ed** (*seemed* vs. **seemmed*) are easy. For verbs of

one syllable that end in consonant + vowel + consonant (C-V-C), double the last consonant and then add –**ed**: *slip* ➔ *slipped, hum* ➔ *hummed, rob* ➔ *robbed.* For verbs of two syllables that end in C-V-C, double the last consonant before adding –**ed** if the stress is on the second syllable: *commit* ➔ *committed, refer* ➔ *referred.* If the stress is on the first syllable, however, we do NOT double the final consonant : *open* ➔ *opened, happen* ➔ *happened, visit* ➔ *visited.* (See Teaching Technique 9.)

While it is possible to find lists of irregular verbs with more than 400 such verbs, perhaps 150 occur with any notable frequency and only 50 to 60 of those are truly useful in mastering basic English. These irregular patterns are varied: *do* ➔ *did, go* ➔ *went, cut* ➔ *cut.* See Appendix 2.

Longer lists of irregular verbs include rare words such as ***bid (bade)***, *partake (partook),* or *slay (slew).* Giving ELLs long lists of rare or useless verbs represents old-fashioned grammar teaching for grammar's sake and is wrong because it completely ignores learners' real English needs. When you teach irregular past tense verbs, teach the most useful ones for your ELLs. No one knows your learners and their needs better than you do.

Common ELL Mistakes: What Your ELLs Should Know

1. Don't use VERB or VERB + –**s** in the past tense. Don't forget to use –**ed.**

   wrong: Laura cooks scrambled eggs for breakfast yesterday.

   correct: Laura cooked scrambled eggs for breakfast yesterday.

2. Do not use **was/were** with verbs (other than **to be**) in simple past tense.

   wrong: I was walk to school yesterday.

   correct: I walked to school yesterday.

3. Don't forget to change –**y** to –**i** and add –**ed.**

   wrong: My baby sister cryed last night.

   correct: My baby sister cried last night.

4. If a verb ends in consonant-vowel-consonant (C-V-C) (in its stressed syllable), don't forget to double the consonant before adding –**ed.**

   wrong: She stoped the car to answer her cell phone.

   correct: She stopped the car to answer her cell phone.

ELLs first acquire *I was* or *we were,* so it is logical that ELLs often say ***I was walk*** instead of *I walked* for a past action. ELLs have learned—and teachers have taught—*I was* so well that ELLs have learned the whole chunk. This error is a natural part of acquiring past tense in English.

3.B.2. Past Progressive Tense

We use past progressive tense for an action that was happening when another action interrupted it. In other words, the first action began and was continuing when the second action occurred. We use past progressive for the first or longer action and use simple past for the second action (i.e., the one that interrupts the first).

> *Example:* The rain started while we *were walking* to the
> park.

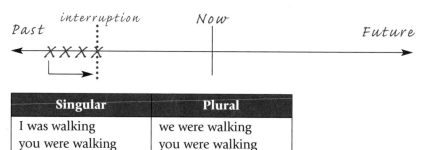

Singular	Plural
I was walking	we were walking
you were walking	you were walking
he/she/it was walking	they were walking

The past progressive tense takes the form: **was/were** + VERB + **–ing**. The **–ing** form is called the present participle. Use **was** or **were** according to the subject.

To create the present participle, add **–ing** to the base form of the verb. Follow the spelling rules outlined earlier on pages 103.

Common ELL Mistakes: What Your ELLs Should Know

1. Do not use **was/were** and a verb without **–ing** to indicate past progressive tense.

   wrong: When I got my first job, I was live in Los Angeles.

   correct: When I got my first job, I was living in Los Angeles.

2. Don't mix up past progressive tense and simple past tense.

   wrong: I cut the onions. Then I was putting them in the soup.

   correct: I cut the onions. Then I put them in the soup.

3. Be careful with the spelling of the present participle.

   wrong: cuting, siting, planing, eatting, helpping, openning

   correct: cutting, sitting, planning, eating, helping, opening

4. Don't use past progressive if the verb does not show an action (as opposed to a state of being). Examples of verbs that are rarely in progressive tenses are: *own, possess, like, love, need, want, have, seem, feel, be, prefer, remember, forget,* and *believe.*

   wrong: From 2000 to 2007, I was owning two cars.

   correct: From 2000 to 2007, I owned two cars.

3.B.3. Present Perfect Tense

We use present perfect tense to express several types of past actions. What these different usages have in common is that the past action is important to the present situation.

> *Example:* The company *has stated* its opposition to the
> workers' plan.

Singular	Plural
I have walked	we have walked
you have walked	you have walked
he/she/it has walked	they have walked

The present perfect tense takes the form: **have/has** + PAST PARTICIPLE. For the auxiliary verb **have,** use **have** or **has** according to the subject. The past participle is the third principal part of any verb.

Past Participle for Regular Verbs. The past participle of a regular verb is the same as its past tense form. You add **–ed** to the base form of the verb. Follow these spelling rules:

1. For verbs that already end in **–e**, just add **–d**: *create* → *created, sneeze* → *sneezed.*
2. Rules for when to double the final consonant are discussed on pp. 116–17.
3. Pronunciation rules for past participle **–ed** can be found on p. 189.

Past Participle for Irregular Verbs. Common endings for the past participle forms of irregular verbs include **–en, –ne,** or **–n** as in *chosen, done,* and *torn,* but there are other possibilities. Some irregular forms are the same for present, past, and past participle as in *cut* → *cut* → *cut* or *put* → *put* → *put.* Another pattern is different internal vowels, especially *i* → *a* → *u* as in *sing* → *sang* → *sung* or *ring* → *rang* → *rung.* The good news for students is that of all the thousands of verbs in English, only a relatively small number are irregular. The bottom line: Students must memorize the irregular forms that are most commonly used. (See Appendix 2 for a list of past participles.)

We can use present perfect tense for several different past times. Note these seven usages.

Usage No. 1: Past Action or Situation that Continues Now

Example	Key Words
José: How long **have** you **worked** at Carpet World?	*how long*
Sara: I**'ve been** there for 18 years. In fact, I**'ve worked** there longer than any of my supervisors!	*for* + time
José: What do you do there?	
Sara: I used to work on the assembly line, but since 1995, I**'ve been** with the sales force in the front office.	*since* + time

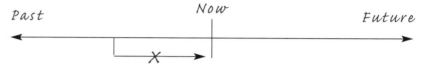

We can use present perfect to talk about a past action or situation that continues now. (It can be affirmative or negative; the important thing is that it still continues.) In this example, Sara tells José that she has been at this same company for 18 years. This means that the action began 18 years ago and still continues today.

Usage No. 2: Recent Past Action that Is Important to the Current Situation

Example	Key Words
Amber: It's hot in here. Why don't you turn on the air conditioner?	
James: Actually, I**'ve** just **turned** it on. We have to wait a few minutes to feel it. Can I help you with the reports?	*just*
Amber: Thanks, but I**'ve** already **finished** them. Here they are.	*already*

We can use present perfect to talk about a past action that happened a short time ago and that is still important to the current situation. In this example, Amber is complaining about the temperature in the room right now. James explains to Amber that he has turned on the air conditioner. When James says, *I've just turned it on*, this means that the action is finished but that it is still important to the current situation. In other words, there is a connection between his action and the current situation in the room. This kind of sentence often uses the word just to show that the action just happened in the here and now. (In North American English, Usage No. 2 can also use simple past tense.)

Usage No. 3: Past Experience, Indefinite Past Time

	Example	Key Words
Katie:	Susan's just gotten back from China. She told me she had a great time.	
Sean:	That's wonderful news. She must be tired. That was really a long trip.	
Katie:	I wonder how many hours it is from here to China. **Have** you ever **gone** there?	*ever* *never*
Sean:	No, I**'ve** never **gone** there, but my uncle **had traveled** there many times. In fact, he went there last month. He had to go there on business.	*many times* (others: *before, already*)

We can use present perfect to talk about a past experience. In this situation, one person wants to know if a second person has ever done a particular action. In this example, Katie is telling Sean that Susan has just returned from China. Katie wants to know if Sean has ever traveled to China. She uses the common question, *Have you ever . . . ?* Notice that **went** is in simple past tense because it refers to a specific past event. In other words, **went** refers to definite past time, not indefinite past time.

Usage No. 4: With *Yet* (indicates a past indefinite action)

	Example	Key Words
Mike:	We don't have much time. Are you almost ready?	
Kent:	Give me just a few more minutes, Mike.	
Mike:	What about the travel report and the salary sheets? **Have** you **finished** them yet?	*yet* (in a question)
Kent:	I've already finished the salary sheets, but I **haven't finished** the travel report yet. I only need a few more minutes, okay?	*yet* (in a negative)

We might use present perfect with **yet** in a question to show that we expect the action to be finished soon. We use present perfect with **yet** in a negative statement to show that the action is a little late or that it should be finished soon: *It hasn't rained yet.* (= *The sky is black.* OR *The weather report has predicted rain for today.*)

Usage No. 5: With a Superlative (Indicates a Past Indefinite Action)

	Example	**Key Words**
Saleh:	How was the movie that you went to see last night?	
Marcos:	Don't waste your money! That was the worst movie that I **have** ever **seen** in my life.	*the worst* *ever*
Saleh:	Wow, I'm surprised. You know it's the most expensive movie that anyone in Hollywood **has** ever **made**.	*the most* *expensive* *ever*

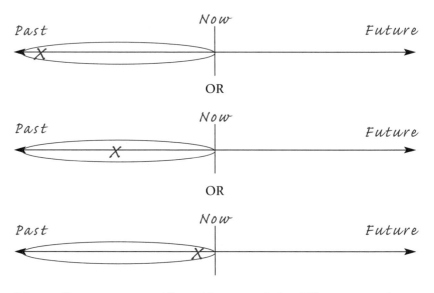

We usually use present perfect with a superlative. When we say that a movie is the best, we mean that it is the best that we have seen up to that point in time.

Usage No. 6: The First . . . , The Third . . . (Refers to a Past Indefinite Time)

	Example	**Key Words**
Mother:	Is that the third paper that you **have had** to write for that class this semester?	*the third . . .*
Bernadette:	Yes, but it's the first paper that the teacher **has asked** us to complete on the computer.	*the first . . .*
Mother:	So what are you worried about now?	
Bernadette:	I'm not good at using the computer.	
Mother:	You have to practice! This seems like the hundredth time that I**'ve told** you that you need to practice!	*the hundredth time*

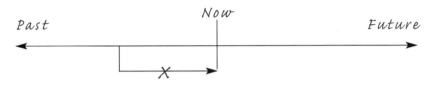

When we say, *It's the first paper that he's asked us to complete on the computer,* we are connecting all the past papers to the present paper, so we use present perfect because present perfect connects a past event and the present time or a present event.

Usage No. 7: Repetition of an Action before Now (Exact Time Is Not Important)

	Example	**Key Words**
Weiping:	Can you believe it? There's another test next Monday!	
Paolo:	Yeah, it's crazy. We**'ve had** six tests so far this month.	*six . . . so far*
Weiping:	You know, in my biology class, the teacher **has given** only one test this semester.	*one . . . this semester*
Paolo:	Well, that's not good either. If you did badly on that one test, then your grade for the course is in trouble.	
Weiping:	Maybe so, but I**'ve had** a lot of classes like that here.	*a lot*

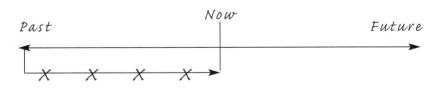

It is common to use present perfect to talk about the number of times that you have done something. In these sentences, the idea is that there is still a possibility that the action or event may happen again. We do not use this if the time period is finished. The three present perfect examples refer to this month, this semester, and Weiping's time as a student at this school. All three of these time periods are still continuing. We could not use present perfect if specific past time periods like *last month, last semester,* or *when Weiping was a student in high school* are used.

Common ELL Mistakes: What Your ELLs Should Know

1. Do not forget to use **have** or **has** with the past participle.

   wrong: I was born here and will die here. I been here my whole life.

   correct: I was born here and will die here. I have been here my whole life.

2. Do not use **have** or **has** with the wrong subject.

   wrong: Sarah have already completed all the homework.

   correct: Sarah has already completed all the homework.

3. Do not use *be* here with present perfect tense.

   wrong: Sarah is already completed all the homework.

   correct: Sarah has already completed all the homework.

4. Do not use present perfect with any specific past tense time words.

   wrong: I have gone to Mexico several times when I was in college.

   correct: I went to Mexico several times when I was in college.

5. Do not use simple past tense with actions that are still continuing.

   wrong: I lived in this same apartment since 1996.

   correct: I have lived in this same apartment since 1996.

3.B.4. Past Perfect Tense

We use past perfect tense to express past actions that occurred before another past event, action, or time.

Example: I **had walked** along the beach long before the sun set.

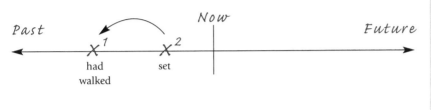

Singular	Plural
I had walked	we had walked
you had walked	you had walked
he/she/it had walked	they had walked

The past perfect tense takes the form: **had** + PAST PARTICIPLE.

<table>
<tr><td>

Common ELL Mistakes: What Your ELLs Should Know

1. Do not forget to use the past participle after **had**.

   wrong: I had work for the bus for almost 20 years.

   correct: I had worked for the bus for almost 20 years.

2. Do not use past tense when past perfect is required.

   wrong: When the company went bankrupt, I **worked** there for 20 years.

   correct: When the company went bankrupt, I had worked there for 20 years.

</td></tr>
</table>

In many cases, context makes clear which of the two actions happened first, so the **past perfect** verb may also be in simple past: *I **walked** along the beach before the sun went down.* Past perfect is often mandatory after *if* (*If I **had won,*** *I would have told you*) or *wish* (*I wish I **had won***). See Key 15 for more information.

3.B.5. Past Perfect Progressive Tense

We use past perfect progressive tense to express an action that began in the past and continued until another time in the past.

Example: I ***had been walking*** on the trail for almost an hour when the rain started.

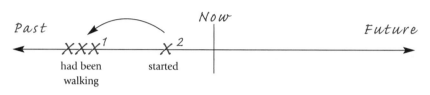

Singular	Plural
I had been walking	we had been walking
you had been walking	you had been walking
he/she/it had been walking	they had been walking

The past perfect progressive tense takes the form: **had** + **been** + VERB + **–ing**.

Common ELL Mistakes: What Your ELLs Should Know

1. Do not forget to use **had** with **been** followed by the present participle.

   wrong: I been waiting for the bus for almost 45 minutes when you arrived.

   correct: I had been waiting for the bus for almost 45 minutes when you arrived.

2. Do not use past progressive tense for an ongoing action.

   wrong: I was waiting for the bus for almost 45 minutes when you arrived.

   correct: I had been waiting for the bus for almost 45 minutes when you arrived.

3.B.6. *Used to* and *Would*

Both **used to** and **would** are used to express certain actions in the past. For many ELLs, active use of these expressions might be considered advanced proficiency, but all ELLs need to be able to recognize these expressions and what they mean in terms of past actions.

Used to		Would	
Singular	*Plural*	*Singular*	*Plural*
I used to walk	we used to walk	I would walk	we would walk
you used to walk	you used to walk	you would walk	you would walk
he/she/it used to walk	they used to walk	he/she/it would walk	they would walk

Used to expresses two ideas:

1. the idea that a past action happened repeatedly, but it is no longer (usually) done now

> When I was a teenager, my dad and I **used to** go fishing almost every weekend.

2. a past fact that is no longer true

> When I was a teenager, my family **used to** live in Mexico.

Would expresses only one idea (which it shares with *used to*):

1. the idea that a past action happened repeatedly, but it is no longer (usually) done now

> When I was a teenager, my dad and I **would** go fishing almost every weekend.

While *used to* + verb and *would* + verb describe actions with similar time frames (i.e., past actions that are no longer true), it is important to note that these two verb patterns are different in that **would** is not used to describe a fact. Consider this ESL practice activity where students underline one or both of the two forms as possible answers:

a. When we were younger, my family (<u>used to live</u>, would live) in Texas.
b. Centuries ago, people (<u>used to think</u>, would think) the world was flat.
c. My grandmother says that she (<u>used to walk</u>, <u>would walk</u>) to school even when the weather was extremely cold.
d. Before cell phones, people (<u>used to set</u>, <u>would set</u>) an alarm clock before going to bed at night.

Common ELL Mistakes: What Your ELLs Should Know

1. ELLs are unsure of these two structures, so they rarely use them, which in turn makes their papers and speech sound "off" to a native speaker. For past repeated actions in particular, English almost always requires *used to* and *would*.

   IMPORTANT: Notice that when native speakers recount a past narrative, we often utilize **used to** to set the scene and then **would** for all the internal details of the story.

   ELL: When I was a teenager, my dad and I went fishing every weekend. We got up early and drove to the lake. We stayed there all day. We took the fish home for dinner. Yes, my dad and I did that every weekend.

   Native speaker: When I was a teenager, my dad and I **used to** go fishing every weekend. We **would** get up early and drive to the lake. We'**d** stay there all day. We'**d** take the fish home for dinner. Yes, my dad and I **used to** do that every weekend.

2. Don't use **would** for non-actions.

   wrong: When I was a kid, I would hate onions.

   correct: When I was a kid, I used to hate onions.

3.B.7. Negative Forms

Tense	Negative Form
Simple Past	SUBJ + *did* + *not* + VERB
Present Perfect	*I/you/we/they* + *have* + *not* + PAST PARTICIPLE *he/she/it* + *has* + *not* + PAST PARTICIPLE
Past Progressive	*I/he/she/it* + *was* + *not* + VERB + *–ing* *you/we/they* + *were*+ *not* + VERB + *–ing*
Past Perfect	SUBJ + *had* + *not* + PAST PARTICIPLE
Past Perfect Progressive	SUBJ + *had* + *not* + *been* + VERB + *–ing*
Used to	SUBJ + *did* + *not* + *use to* + VERB
Would	SUBJ + *would* + *not* + VERB

Of the five tenses and two expressions for expressing past time, the most difficult to negate is simple past tense. (Note that *used to* follows the same rule as simple past tense.)

In simple past tense, a negative takes the form: **did + not + VERB.** ELLs routinely make three mistakes: (1) omission of **did** (**I not understood*), (2) use of **be** (**I was not watch TV last night*), and (3) including **–ed** (**The clerk did not charged me the correct price*).

In past progressive tense, negating is easy because you negate the auxiliary **be: was not, were not.**

Present perfect tense forms the negative by adding **not** after the auxiliary verb: **have/has not.**

Both past perfect and past perfect progressive tenses form the negative by adding **not** after the auxiliary verb: **had not.**

Used to forms the negative in the same manner as any other verb: **did not + use to.** Note that you must omit the **–d.** A common native error is to include it: ‡*I didn't used to like coffee, but now I do.*

Would is a modal, and the negative of all modals involves putting **not** afterward: **would not.**

To summarize, past expressions that involve an auxiliary verb are negated by adding **not** after them. In contrast, simple past and **used to** are main verbs, and it is not possible to add **not** after a main verb. Instead, you must add the auxiliary **did.**

Common ELL Mistakes: What Your ELLs Should Know

1. Do not forget to use **did not** with simple past tense.

   wrong:　I not understood the directions well.

   correct:　I did not understand the directions well.

2. For simple past tense, do not use **was not** or **were not.** Use **did not** only.

   wrong:　The man was not like the food because it was too salty.

   correct:　The man did not like the food because it was too salty.

3. With negative simple past tense, do not use **–d** with the verb. The auxiliary **did** means past, so you don't need another **–d** to indicate past (again).

wrong: The man did not liked the food because it was too salty.

correct: The man did not like the food because it was too salty.

4. For past progressive, do not forget to use **was** or **were**.

wrong: The passengers were very uncomfortable because the airplane's cooling system not working.

correct: The passengers were very uncomfortable because the airplane's cooling system was not working.

5. Do not use **don't** or **doesn't** to negate verbs in present perfect tense. Don't confuse **don't have** with **haven't**. Don't confuse **doesn't have** with **hasn't**.

wrong: We don't have eaten at that restaurant yet.

correct: We haven't eaten at that restaurant yet.

6. Do not use **didn't** to negate verbs in past perfect tense. Don't confuse **didn't have** with **hadn't**.

wrong: When we met you, we didn't have lived in this house for very long.

correct: When we met you, we hadn't lived in this house for very long.

7. The negative of **used to** is **did + not + use to +** VERB. Do not write **used**.

wrong: I didn't used to like animals, so my parents did not get any pets for me.

correct: I didn't use to like animals, so my parents did not get any pets for me.

3.B.8. Contractions

Contractions here are not difficult. Several combinations are possible as seen in this chart. (Only those parts of the verbs that can be contracted are included here.)

Verb Tense	Affirmative	Negative
Simple Past	– – –	*did not* → *didn't*
Present Perfect	*I/you/we/they + have* → *I've/you've/we've/they've*	*have not* → *haven't*
	he/she/it + has → *he's/she's/it's*	*has not* → *hasn't*
Past Perfect; Past Perfect Progressive	*I/you/he/she/it/we/they + had* → *I'd/you'd/he'd/it'd/we'd/they'd*	*had not* → *hadn't*
Used to	– – –	*did not* → *didn't*
Would	*I/you/he/she/it/we/they + would* → *I'd/you'd/he'd/it'd/we'd/they'd*	*would not* → *wouldn't*

> The contraction **'d** can be confusing to ELLs because it can mean *had (I'd taken)* or *would (I'd take)*, depending on the verb form that follows.

Another option for negative contractions is to use the existing affirmative contractions and add **not**. For example, *I have not* → *I haven't* OR *I've not; we had not* → *we hadn't* OR *we'd not.*

3.B.9. Forming Questions

Just as with negating, the only problematic tense is simple past and the expression **used to** because they require the addition of the auxiliary **did.** In the other tenses, you simply invert the auxiliary (**was/were** for past progressive, **have** for present perfect, **had** for past perfect and past perfect progressive, and the modal **would**).

Tense	Interrogative Form
Simple Past	*did* + SUBJ + VERB
Past Progressive	*was* + *I/he/she/it* + VERB + *–ing* *were* + *you/we/they* + VERB + *–ing*
Present Perfect	*have* + *I/you/we/they* + PAST PARTICIPLE *has* + *he/she/it* + PAST PARTICIPLE
Past Perfect	*had* + SUBJ + PAST PARTICIPLE
Past Perfect Progressive	*had* + SUBJ + *been* + VERB + *–ing*
Used to	*did* + SUBJ + *use to* + VERB
Would	*would* + SUBJ + VERB

The structure **have + NOUN/PRONOUN + PAST PARTICIPLE** (as in *Did you have your work done when you went to class?*) is a very complex structure that very few ELLs know about, let alone actually use. An ELL who asks *Did you have done your work . . . ?* is probably not attempting this advanced structure. Instead, the ELL has most likely confused **Did you have done* with *Have you done?*

Common ELL Mistakes: What Your ELLs Should Know

1. For simple past tense, use only the base (simple) form of the verb when asking questions.

   wrong: Did Valerie attended class yesterday?

   correct: Did Valerie attend class yesterday?

2. Do not begin simple past tense verb questions with **was** or **were.**

   wrong: Was Mary own a sports car?

   correct: Did Mary own a sports car?

3. For questions with past progressive, begin with **was** or **were,** not **did.**

   wrong: Did you wearing a new tie when you met your new boss yesterday?

   correct: Were you wearing a new tie when you met your new boss yesterday?

4. Do not use **did** in the question form of the present perfect tense.

   wrong: How many international trips did you have taken in your life?

   correct: How many international trips have you taken in your life?

5. Do not use **did** in the question form of the past perfect tense.

   wrong: Did you have finished the project before your boss called?

   correct: Had you finished the project before your boss called?

6. In questions with **used to,** be sure to drop the **–d** in **used.**

   wrong: How many children did families used to have a century ago?

   correct: How many children did families use to have a century ago?

3.C. Native Language Interference: Compare English with Other Languages

Language	Notes on *Past Verbs*
Arabic	1. Arabic has a past form that means that the action is finished. 2. There is no progressive form. 3. English present perfect can be rendered in Arabic by the present form or the past form, depending on the exact meaning of the present perfect in English. 4. The endings of the verbs change according to the subject.
Chinese	1. Chinese verbs do not have different forms to mark tense. Instead, time adverbials such as *yesterday* or *before the war* are used. 2. Verbs do not change form according to the subject.
French	French has verb tenses that appear to mirror the English system, but there are differences. 1. French has no progressive tenses. Thus, a French–speaking ELL may say **John called when I ate dinner* (instead of *when I was eating dinner*). 2. English present perfect is rendered by present or past in French according to the specific kind of present perfect. 3. The most common way to express simple past tense in French is with a tense whose form is similar to present perfect in English. Thus, *Marie a fini son travail* (literally "Marie has finished her work") can be translated as either *Marie finished her work* or *Marie has finished her work*, depending on the context. 4. The endings of verbs change according to the subject.
Japanese	1. Japanese has distinct forms for simple past and past progressive, but there are no separate perfect tenses. 2. The different meanings of English present perfect can be expressed with special constructions. A sentence in the recent past such as *I've just eaten* is rendered by a special construction consisting of past tense with an equivalent word for *just*. However, a present perfect verb whose action is still true such as *I've lived here since 2000* would use a form of present tense because the action of the verb is still true. 3. Japanese has a special structure to express the *have you ever* meaning of present perfect, as in *Have you ever flown on a 747 jet?* (This is rendered literally as **747 jet in flew-event made is there?* or **Is there the*

	the experience of flying on a 747 jet? or more naturally *Have you ever flown on a 747 jet?*) Japanese ELLs may produce errors such as **I just eaten lunch* or **Since 2000, I live here.* 4. Japanese ELLs have a difficult time with past perfect tense.
Korean	1. Korean has distinct forms for simple past and past progressive, but there are no perfect tenses per se. 2. The different meanings of English present perfect can be expressed with special constructions. A recent past sentence such as *I've just eaten* is rendered as past tense with an equivalent for *just*. However, a still true present perfect sentence such as *I've lived here since 2000* would use a form of present tense because the action of the verb is still true. 3. Korean ELLs have a difficult time with past perfect tense.
Russian	1. Russian has simple past tense. 2. Russian has no progressive tenses per se, but past progressive may be expressed by using the imperfect aspect with the past tense. 3. When present perfect tense refers to a past action that is finished, such as *I have just eaten dinner*, Russian uses past tense. 4. Russian ELLs find past perfect and past perfect progressive tenses challenging.
Spanish	1. Spanish has verb tenses that appear to mirror the English system, but there are many differences. 2. English present perfect is rendered by present, past, or present perfect in Spanish according to the specific kind of present perfect, that is, whether it refers to a current situation or a completed one. 3. The endings of verbs change according to the subject. 4. Subject pronouns are usually omitted; the verb endings indicate the subject. A typical error is **Has rained a lot recently.*
All Languages	1. The use of the auxiliary verb *did* plus *not* to negate verbs is unique to English. Many ELLs will form negatives by placing *no* before the verb: **The workers no saved any money.* 2. ELLs have difficulty understanding the difference in negating the verb *have* in simple past tense (*I had a car* → *I didn't have a car*) and a verb in past perfect tense (*I had studied = I hadn't studied*). Be prepared for this question.

3. The use of the auxiliary verb *did* in questions is unique to English. Many ELLs will write questions with subject-verb inversion or regular statement word order: *How much fuel used this car?* or *The war ended in 1918?*

3.D. Ideas for Teaching

To express past time in English, ELLs have at their disposal at least five tenses and two expressions (*used to* and *would*). Beginning students usually study only simple past tense. At the intermediate level, ELLs study past progressive and present perfect. At the upper-intermediate or low-advanced levels, ELLs study past perfect and past perfect progressive. At the advanced level, ELLs learn about the nuances that **used to** and **would** can give to a story being told in the past.

Learning to add –**ed** to base verbs to create simple past tense is not difficult. The hard part for many ELLs is mastering how to negate and how to ask questions. Teaching simple past tense involves four stages: affirmative, pronunciation of –**ed**, negative, and question.

To teach the **affirmative** form, show students how it is related to simple present tense. On the board, draw two columns. Write *every day* and *yesterday* at the top of each. Begin with three regular verbs. Write the verb with the word *I* in each column.

every day	yesterday
I _____	I _____
I need	I needed
I want	I wanted
I grade	I graded

> **FIND OUT**
>
> Find a 1,000-word excerpt of a transcript of a live conversation. Look for all occurrences of past tense verbs. Categorize the usages. Does any one tense dominate?

Notice how all these three example verbs end in the sound of either /d/ or /t/. I intentionally use only /d/ or /t/ verbs because I know that these verbs will add /əd/ as an extra syllable. I am not going to teach the pronunciation of –**ed** yet, but we want to start with the least confusing verbs first. Use verbs that have a strong extra syllable pronunciation because this matches what the students expect to see. (If you use *watch* or *raise*, then students will ask you why you don't say *watch•ed* or *raise•ed* as two syllables. While this is a valid question, you should avoid the scenario that creates this question—at least on day one.)

Now you write the simple present column for other verbs that end in /d/ or /t/ and let students tell you the past tense form. To keep the class interactive, have students spell the past tense form for you as you write. If your class is quiet, lead the spelling for them.

After students have learned that **–ed** is for past tense, work on the pronunciation of **–ed**. Ask students to tell you any verb that adds **–ed**. They will tell you some irregular verbs that they know at this point, such as *went* or *did*, but just say that those verbs are special and will be studied later. Your board should have four columns in it. Put the past tense above Column 1, but do not put any header on the other columns for now.

Past Tense			

The three columns will be for verbs that end in /t/, verbs that end in /d/, and verbs that add an extra syllable /əd/. At this point, this information is not on the board. As students tell you a verb, write it in the first column and then write it in the appropriate column. For example, when someone says *work*, write *worked* in the first column and in the third column because *worked* ends in /t/. If the next verb is *want*, write *wanted* in the first column and the fourth column. At this point, students will be curious why you are not writing anything in the other columns. Offer no explanation. If students ask, tell them that you want them to tell you what the system is. After eight verbs, your board would look like this:

Past Tense			
worked		worked	
wanted			wanted
needed			needed
closed	closed		
prepared	prepared		
liked		liked	
watched		watched	
played	played		

At this point, ask the class if anyone knows why you have these verbs in three columns. (Probably no one does.) Ask what *worked, liked,* and *watched* have in common. If you want to give them a hint (NOTE: write *hint* on the board as a new vocabulary word), tell them it is something about the pronunciation of the three words. Ask the students to analyze *closed, prepared,* and *played.* Then ask the same about *wanted* and *needed.* If no one has any idea, let the students call out five more verbs. Write the past tense form in the correct column. If no one is able to guess that it is the final sound of the –**ed** form, tell them that there are three ways to pronounce the –**ed.** If they cannot hear the ending, put the word in a phrase so that the –**ed** is followed by a vowel sound. This combination usually helps ELLs hear the /t/ or /d/. For *worked,* use the phrase *She worked all morning.* Say it three times. Make the students say it with you. Ask students what word they hear in the middle. Many will say that they hear the word *tall!* By the end of this activity, the headers /t/, /d/, and /əd/ should be over the three columns.

For the negative and question form, help students visualize the –**ed** being cut and then traveling to the auxiliary *did.* For negatives, your board could look like this:

Write example in past; leave space in between.	*Mary* *called the bank.*
Ask students what tense it is and how they know; circle the –**ed.**	*Mary* *call(ed) the bank.*
Draw an X over the –**ed** and then an arrow to just after Mary.	*Mary* *call⊠ the bank.*
Now just below the arrow pointing to the space next to Mary, write *did.*	*Mary did* *call⊠ the bank.*
Add *not.*	*Mary did not call⊠ the bank.*
Ask students what the pattern is; write SUBJ + under *Mary, did not* + under *did not,* and VERB under *call.*	*Mary did not call* *the bank.* SUBJ + did not + VERB

When teaching the pattern for questions, do something similar by showing that the –**ed** is cut and transformed into *did.* Then show that *did* travels all the way to the beginning of the question.

ELL Grammar Key 4:
Verb Tenses to Express Future Time

The ultimate irony of the English verb tenses to express future time is that we have a future tense that uses **will** + VERB (*We will travel*), but we rarely use this future tense. Instead, it is much more common to use **be going to** (*We are going to travel*) or even just present progressive tense (*We are traveling*) for future actions. We also have two other future tenses that are rarely ever used: future perfect tense (*We will have traveled*) and future perfect progressive tense (*We will have been traveling*). In addition to having to learn these various tenses and their uses, ELLs need to figure out which tenses are more critical to them and their language needs.

4.A. Typical ELL Errors: Noticing the Gap

Can you identify and explain these five common ELL errors with this grammar point?

1. Pam: Why do you want this stamp?
Tom: *I will write a letter to my grandparents, and I want to mail it right away.
2. Pam: What plans do you and Tom have for tomorrow?
John: *We go to the beach with some friends who are visiting from California.
3. *I'm leaving now, but I promise to call you just as soon as I will get home tonight.
4. *Several of my friends going to help me when I move out of my apartment.
5. *If you don't have received an e-mail from my boss by tomorrow afternoon, call me and I will talk to him personally.

There are six verb tenses and one special verb expression that can express some aspect of future time.

Verb Tense / Expression	Example	Meaning
Be going to	We **are going to fly** to New York tomorrow.	an event in the future, especially one already planned
Simple Future	If the weather clears up soon, Flight 87 for Paris **will depart** from this gate about an hour from now.	an event in the future, especially one that is scheduled or expresses strong desire to do something
Present Progressive	We **are flying** to New York tomorrow.	an event in the future
Simple Present	1. Flight 87 for Paris **departs** from this gate about an hour from now. 2. If the weather **clears** up soon, we will be able to play tennis.	1. a future action marked by a specific future adverb 2. a future action in a dependent clause (no future tense permitted in a dependent clause)
Future Progressive	If you call at 8 PM, I **will be eating** dinner, so please call before then.	an action that will be taking place at some point in the future
Future Perfect	By the time that you are 50 years old, you **will have visited** 50 countries.	an action that will be finished by a specified time in the future
Future Perfect Progressive	By the time I see you again, I **will have been working** at this company for 30 years.	how long an action has been happening at a future point; focus is on the duration

Obviously, we do not teach all these verb tenses at the same time. Traditionally, these verb tenses would be interspersed with other tenses, but future tenses usually come after some of the various present and past tenses. It is important to note that although the word *will* is the traditional way to mark future time, there are many other ways that are actually more common, including the use of *be going to* and present progressive tense.

4.B. Grammar Explanation

4.B.1. *be going to*

We use **be going to** for an action in the future. We particularly use this expression to talk about future actions or events that we have already planned. (Sometimes the meanings of **be going to** and **will** overlap, but sometimes they do not. For a comparison, see p. 77.)

> *Example:* In an hour, I *am going to walk* from my house to the bus stop.

Singular	Plural
I am going to walk	we are going to walk
you are going to walk	you are going to walk
he/she/it is going to walk	they are going to walk

A verb with *be going to* usually takes the form: **be going to** + VERB.

Common ELL Mistakes: What Your ELLs Should Know

1. Don't forget to use **be**.

   wrong: Laura going to cook scrambled eggs for breakfast tomorrow.

   correct: Laura is going to cook scrambled eggs for breakfast tomorrow.

2. Don't forget the word **to**. It is a small but very important word.

   wrong: Our boss is going miss work tomorrow.

   correct: Our boss is going to miss work tomorrow.

3. Don't use **–s** or **–ed** or **–ing** with the verb after **to**.

   wrong: I believe that Olga's going to studies with me.

   correct: I believe that Olga's going to study with me.

4.B.2. Simple Future Tense

We use simple future tense for an action in the future. We especially use **will** to talk about future actions that we did not have a prior plan to do. In addition, we use **will** to ask someone to do something: *Will you help me with this work?* (Sometimes the meanings of **be going to** and **will** overlap, but sometimes they do not. For a comparison, see p. 77.)

> *Example: Jim:* I'm so tired. I don't know if I can stay awake to finish this report.
>
> *Ken:* Okay, I ***will get*** you a cup of strong coffee.

Singular	Plural
I will walk	we will walk
you will walk	you will walk
he/she/it will walk	they will walk

The simple future tense takes the form: **will + VERB.**

Common ELL Mistakes: What Your ELLs Should Know

1. Do not use **to** after **will.**

   wrong: Andrea will to study more if she has more free time.

   correct: Andrea will study more if she has more free time.

2. Do not add any endings (**–s, –ed,** or **–ing**) to verbs after **will.**

   wrong: Shawn will helps Jim with the work.

   correct: Shawn will help Jim with the work.

3. Use **be going to** (not **will**) to talk about a future event that you have already planned.

   > *A:* I need someone to help me with this homework tomorrow. Can you help me?

   wrong: *B:* Sorry, but I can't help you. I will visit my aunt. She's in the hospital.

   correct: *B:* Sorry, but I can't help you. I'm going to visit my aunt. She's in the hospital.

4.6.3. Present Progressive Tense

We can use present progressive tense to express a future action.

Example: Tomorrow I *am walking* from my house to my office.

Past   *Now*   *Future*

X X X

Singular	Plural
I am walking	we are walking
you are walking	you are walking
he/she/it is walking	they are walking

The present progressive tense takes the form: **am/is/are** + VERB + **–ing.** The **–ing** form is called the present participle. Use **am, is,** or **are** according to the subject.

Rules for creating the present participle are on p. 103.

Common ELL Mistakes: What Your ELLs Should Know

1. Don't forget to use **be.**

   wrong: Tomorrow we cooking red beans and rice.

   correct: Tomorrow we are cooking red beans and rice.

2. There must be a clear future time established in the conversation, either by the speaker or by the previous speaker.

   unclear time: We are cooking red beans and rice. (When? Now? Tomorrow?)

   correct: Tomorrow we are cooking red beans and rice.

4.B.4. Simple Present Tense

We use simple present tense to express future actions in two ways.

Usage No. 1: With a Future Time Adverb

> *Example:* I **leave** for Miami tomorrow.

This usage usually occurs in only a few sentences in a conversation or paragraph. It is rare to have multiple examples.

Usage No. 2: In a Time Clause

> *Example:* When I **arrive** (OR *have arrived*) in Los Angeles
> tomorrow night, I will call you.

It is not acceptable to use **will** (or **be going to**) in a time clause. You may, however, see **will** in a dependent clause, but the meaning is different, that is, it is not a time clause. The meaning of **will** in a dependent clause is "if you agree to do something." For example, *If you will call me tonight, I will tell you everything about John* means "if you agree or promise to call me tonight, then and only then will I tell you the information about John."

Present perfect can be used in a time clause talking about the future when the speaker wants to emphasize the completion of the action. This usage is especially common with these connectors: *when, after, as soon as, by the time. When you finish work, you can call me. When you have finished work, you can call me.*

Singular	Plural
I walk	we walk
you walk	you walk
he/she/it walks	they walk

Common ELL Mistakes: What Your ELLs Should Know

1. Do not use simple present tense for a future action without a future time marker.

   wrong: I leave for Miami.

   correct: I leave for Miami around noon tomorrow.

2. Do not use **will** or **be going to** in a future time clause. Use simple present tense.

   wrong: As soon as your plane will arrive, please call me and I'll pick you up.

   correct: As soon as your plane arrives, please call me and I'll pick you up.

4.B.5. Future Progressive Tense

We use future progressive tense to express a longer action in relation to a specific future time or a longer action that will be interrupted by a shorter action.

Example: I ***will be walking*** from my house to the office around noon tomorrow.

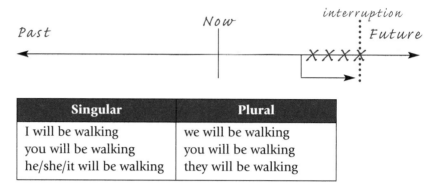

Singular	Plural
I will be walking	we will be walking
you will be walking	you will be walking
he/she/it will be walking	they will be walking

The future progressive tense takes the form: **will** + **be** + VERB + *–ing*.

Common ELL Mistakes: What Your ELLs Should Know

1. Do not forget to use **be** and a present participle for future progressive tense.

   wrong: When you call tomorrow, I will studying for my big test on Monday.

   correct: When you call tomorrow, I will be studying for my big test on Monday.

2. Do not use future progressive tense for a short action even though it is happening in future time.

   wrong: If you need help tomorrow, I will be assisting you.

   correct: If you need help tomorrow, I will assist you.

4.B.6. Future Perfect Tense

We use future perfect tense to express an action that will be completed before another future action or future event.

> *Example:* I ***will have walked*** from my house to the office
> before you leave your place.

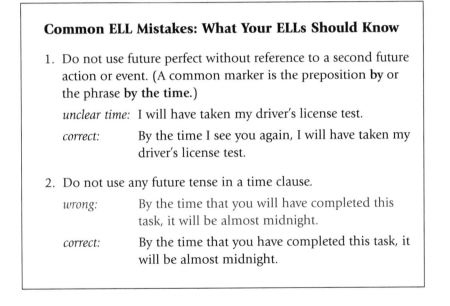

Singular	Plural
I will have walked	we will have walked
you will have walked	you will have walked
he/she/it will have walked	they will have walked

The future perfect tense takes the form: **will** + **have** + PAST PARTICIPLE.

Common ELL Mistakes: What Your ELLs Should Know

1. Do not use future perfect without reference to a second future action or event. (A common marker is the preposition **by** or the phrase **by the time.**)

   unclear time: I will have taken my driver's license test.

   correct: By the time I see you again, I will have taken my driver's license test.

2. Do not use any future tense in a time clause.

   wrong: By the time that you will have completed this task, it will be almost midnight.

   correct: By the time that you have completed this task, it will be almost midnight.

4.B.7. Future Perfect Progressive Tense

We use future perfect progressive tense to express how long an action has been happening at a future point. The focus is on the duration of the action.

Example: I ***will have been walking*** for about an hour by
the time you leave your place.

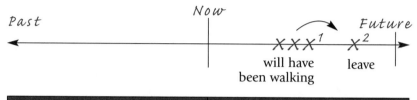

Singular	Plural
I will have been walking	we will have been walking
you will have been walking	you will have been walking
he/she/it will have been walking	they will have been walking

The future perfect progressive tense takes the form: **will + have + been** + VERB + *–ing*.

Common ELL Mistakes: What Your ELLs Should Know

1. In future perfect progressive tense, do not forget to use **been** and the present participle.

   wrong: As of next Friday, I will be working here for 20 years.

   correct: As of next Friday, I will have been working here for 20 years.

2. Do not use future perfect progressive without reference to a second future action or event. (A common marker is the preposition **by** or the phrase **by the time**.)

   unclear time: I will have been working here for 20 years.

   correct: By next Friday, I will have been working here for 20 years.

4.B.8. Negative Forms

Tense	Negative Forms
Be going to; **Present Progressive**	*I am + not +* VERB *+ –ing* *you/we/they are + not +* VERB *+ –ing* *he/she/it + is + not +* VERB *+ –ing*
Simple Present	*I/you/we/they + do + not +* VERB *he/she/it + does + not +* VERB
Simple Future	SUBJ *+ will + not +* VERB
Future Progressive	SUBJ *+ will + not + be +* VERB *+ –ing*
Future Perfect	SUBJ *+ will + not + have +* PAST PARTICIPLE
Future Perfect Progressive	SUBJ *+ will + not + have + been +* VERB *+ –ing*

Of the six tenses and one expression for expressing future time, the most difficult to negate is simple present tense, which was discussed on p. 106.

In **be going to** and present progressive tense, negating is easy because you negate the auxiliary **be: am not, is not, are not**.

Negating is also easy for simple future, future progressive, future perfect, and future perfect progressive because you negate **will: will not**.

To summarize, all of these future expressions except simple present tense involve an auxiliary verb, and an auxiliary verb is negated by adding **not** after it. In contrast, simple present has a main verb, and it is not possible to add **not** after a main verb. Instead, you must add the auxiliaries **do** or **does**.

Common ELL Mistakes: What Your ELLs Should Know

1. With **be going to,** don't forget to use the correct form of **be**.

   wrong: The bus driver not going to drive fast today.

   correct: The bus driver is not going to drive fast today.

2. Do not use **don't**, **doesn't**, or **didn't** to make negative of **will**.

   wrong: Kathy doesn't will attend the meeting tomorrow.

   correct: Kathy will not attend the meeting tomorrow.

4.B.9. Contractions

Contractions here are easy because you are only contracting the subject and auxiliary verbs. Possible combinations can be seen in this chart.

Verb Tense	Affirmative	Negative
Be going to; **Present Progressive**	*I am → I'm*	*am + not → – – –*
	he/she/it is → he's/she's/it's	*is not → isn't*
	you/we/they are → you're/we're/they're	*are not → aren't*
Simple Future; Future Progressive; Future Perfect; Future Perfect Progressive	SUBJ + *will → I'll/you'll/he'll/ she'll/it'll/we'll/they'll*	*will + not → won't*
Simple Present	– – –	*do not → don't* *does not → doesn't*
NOTE: Contractions can also be formed by adding *not* after the affirmative contractions: *I'm not, you're not, he's not,* etc.		

4.B.10. Forming Questions

Just as with negating, the only problematic tense is simple present because it requires the addition of the auxiliaries **do** or **does.** In the other tenses, you simply invert the auxiliary (**am/is/are** for **be going to** and present progressive and the modal **will**).

Tense	Interrogative Form
Simple Present	*do + I/you/we/they* + VERB *does + he/she/it* + VERB
Be going to; **Present Progressive**	*am + I* + VERB + *–ing* *are + you/we/they* + VERB + *–ing* *is + he/she/it* + VERB + *–ing*
Simple Future	*will* + SUBJ + VERB
Future Progressive	*will* + SUBJ + *be* + VERB + *–ing*
Future Perfect	*will* + SUBJ + *have* + PAST PARTICIPLE
Future Perfect Progressive	*will* + SUBJ + *have* + *been* + VERB + *–ing*

Common ELL Mistakes: What Your ELLs Should Know

1. Do not use **do, does**, or **did** in a question with **will**.

   wrong: Do you will help me with this homework?

   correct: Will you help me with this homework?

2. The subject comes just after the auxiliary verb in questions using **be going to,** present progressive, simple future, future progressive, future perfect, and future perfect progressive.

   wrong: When will have you finished?

   correct: When will you have finished?

4.C. Native Language Interference: Compare English with Other Languages

Language	Notes on *Future Verbs*
Arabic	Arabic often uses present tense with future time markers to indicate future time for an action.
Chinese	Verbs do not have different forms to mark tense. Instead, Chinese relies on time adverbials such as *tomorrow* or *by 2025.*
French	1. French has a future tense. However, there is no single word for *will*. Instead, word endings on the verbs indicate future tense. French–speaking ELLs may write *The president will arrives tomorrow.* 2. These verb endings change according to the subject. 3. French can also use *be going to* as English does, but French has no progressive and instead uses only *go*, so French speakers may write *Tomorrow I go to play tennis with Marie.* 4. Simple present tense is often used with an appropriate future time adverbial. 5. French requires future tense in adverbial time clauses that refer to the future, but English requires simple present (or present perfect). French-speaking ELLs may default incorrectly to future tense: *When I will arrive in Chicago, I will call you.*

Japanese	1. Japanese has no future marker; instead, present tense is used with appropriate time adverbs. 2. Subject pronouns are often omitted.
Korean	1. Korean has a future tense marker for *will*. 2. Like many languages, Korean allows the use of simple present tense with a future adverbial of time, so Korean ELLs may produce **Tomorrow I call you if I need your help.*
Russian	1. Russian has simple future tense. 2. Russian has no progressive tenses per se, but future progressive may be expressed by using the imperfect aspect with the future tense. 3. Russian has a special structure that makes use of *plan + verb* that is often used to talk about future actions. 4. Simple present is often used for future actions. 5. Verb endings vary according to the subject.
Spanish	1. Spanish has a future tense. However, there is no single word for *will*. Instead, word endings on the verbs indicate future tense. 2. These endings vary according to the subject. 3. Spanish can also use *be going to* for future as English does, but Spanish uses present tense of *go*. So, Spanish speakers may incorrectly say **I go mail these letters later* or **I go to mail these letters later.* 4. Simple present tense is often used with an appropriate future time adverbial. 5. Spanish uses a subjunctive form in adverbial time clauses that refer to the future, so Spanish-speaking ELLs may inadvertently use a wrong verb form, including the use of *will*: **When I will arrive in Chicago, I will call you.* 6. Subject pronouns are usually omitted; the verb endings indicate the subject.
All Languages	1. Negating the auxiliary verb *will* or *to be* in *be going to* is unique to English. Many ELLs will form negatives by placing *no* before the verb: **The workers no will save enough money.* 2. ELLs often confuse when to invert the subject and the auxiliary verb (*will, has/have, am/is/are*) and when to use the auxiliary verb *do, does,* or *did*. Many ELLs will incorrectly form questions with a form of *do* or regular statement word order: **How many people do you will invite to the meeting?*

4.D. Ideas for Teaching

Many beginning students learn the word **will** before their course, so in theory they know how to express future time. The unfortunate thing is that **will** is not the main way in English to talk about the future. Yes, **will** means future, but it is not nearly as common as the expression **be going to,** so you should start with **be going to.**

On the board, create three columns labeled *yesterday, every day,* and *tomorrow* with the subject *I* and a blank written under each. Your goal is to take verbs that students in the class shout out and write them, with class help, in all three time slots.

yesterday	every day	tomorrow
I _____	*I* _____	*I* _____

FIND OUT

How do spoken language and written language differ on how they treat future verbs? Analyze 500-word excerpts of spoken language and written language on the same topic. Find out how often any verbs discuss a future action and which verb tenses are used for those discussions. Are there any differences in how future time actions are expressed in these two genres?

Ask the class for any verb. A student says *work.* Ask for the past tense of *work.* When someone says *worked,* say, *Yes, but say it with I.* When someone says *I worked,* then write *I worked* in Column 1. Move to Column 2. Get someone to say, *I work.* Write that. Then for the last column, ask about tomorrow. Some students might say, *will,* but tell them that *will* is possible for future, but this is not the number one way to express future. Don't write the answer yet. Ask, *Does anyone know* gonna *or* going to? Most likely, at least one student does. Then you should write *I am going to work.* Your board should now look like this:

yesterday	every day	tomorrow
I _____	*I* _____	*I* _____
I worked.	*I work.*	*I am going to work.*

Try to elicit one more regular verb before doing an irregular verb. Working with your class, you should try to put seven to ten examples on the board.

In another class meeting, you should work on differentiating when **will** is used and when **be going to** is used. You should teach your students that **be going to** should be their default way of expressing future.

At the intermediate level, students learn that present progressive can be used for future time: *I'm working tomorrow.* This structure should not be taught to beginning students as it will only cause confusion. Beginning students have just learned that present progressive is for current actions and **be going to** is for future. To tell them otherwise is too much for the average beginning student.

Future perfect tense and its progressive tense are for advanced students. These two tenses are used so infrequently that I recommend skipping them if possible. If you must cover them, I would dedicate the minimum time possible.

ELL Grammar Key 5:
Count and Non-Count Nouns

Most native speakers have not heard of the terms **count** and **non-count** for grammar and do not know what they mean. (Non-count nouns are also called **mass nouns.**) As native speakers, we have not needed to know why we can say *three assignments* but not **three homeworks* even though *homework* and *assignments* are synonymous. We might find it difficult to explain why a large house can have *many chairs* and *much furniture* but never **much chairs* and **many furnitures*. Finally, even the most sociable of us has rarely if ever thought about the difference between *I have a few good friends* and *I have few good friends*. Understanding the role of count and non-count nouns can help you answer these questions and avoid **much problems* and **many turmoils* in your ESL classroom.

5.A. Typical ELL Errors: Noticing the Gap

Can you identify and explain these five common ELL errors with this grammar point?

1. **If I could have any pet in the world, I would prefer to have cat because it is very clean and friendly animal.*

2. **I like how Mr. Johnson teaches, but one thing that I don't like about his class is that he gives us so many homeworks every night.*

3. **My mother was elementary school teacher from 1992 to 2007, and she taught hundreds of student during this time.*

4. *Mike: Do you know exactly how many people attended the party?*

   Noah: *No, I don't know, but there were a lot of.

5. *I was thinking of dropping out of school, but I talked it over with my uncle. *He gave me a really good advice about my future, and I decided to stay in school. I have never regretted this decision.*

5.B. Grammar Explanation

5.B.1. Count Nouns

Nouns that name things you can count are called **count nouns.** Count nouns can be singular or plural.

Singular	a house	a book	my cousin	one reason
Plural	some houses	ten books	my cousins	reasons

> **Determiner** is a large grammatical category that includes (1) articles (*a, an, the*), (2) demonstrative adjectives (*this, that, these, those*), (3) numbers (*one, two, ten*), (4) possessive adjectives (*my, your, his, her, its, our, their*), and (5) quantifiers (*many, each, several*).

All singular count nouns must have an article (**indefinite:** *a, an;* **definite:** *the*) or some other **determiner** before them.

Some ELLs whose first language does not have indefinite articles (e.g., Arabic, Chinese, Hmong, Malay, Japanese, Korean, Russian, Vietnamese) routinely omit **a** and **an**. In addition, many ELLs—even those whose native languages have **a** and **an**—mistakenly omit the indefinite article when descriptive adjectives come between the determiner and the noun, so be sure to demonstrate some examples of this combination.

Determiner	Determiner + Noun	Determiner + Descriptive Adjective + Noun
Articles	a cat	a black cat
Demonstrative	that book	that interesting book
Number	one reason	one specific reason
Possessive	my class	my worst class
Quantifier	each problem	each serious problem

There are a few idiomatic expressions where singular count nouns are used with no article: *have dinner, in school, on vacation, at home, at work, by phone.* See Key 6.

5.B.2. Non-Count Nouns

Nouns that cannot be counted are called **non-count nouns.**

Foods	sugar	rice	flour	salt	mustard
Liquids	milk	water	juice	coffee	oil
Ideas	honesty	importance	intelligence	peace	wisdom
Nature	snow	scenery	thunder	sunlight	hail
Collective Words	luggage clothing	furniture fruit	advice vocabulary	research makeup	homework money

> The word *fruit* is generally non-count, but the word *vegetable* is count. *Homework* is non-count, but *assignment* is count. There seems to be no way to predict **whether a given word is count or non-count.**

Native speakers sometimes use non-count foods and liquids in a countable sense, but they are referring to containers or servings, not the thing. For example, *two coffees* means *two cups of coffee* and *two sugars* means *two packets of sugar*. This information should not be included in a beginning lesson about non-count nouns. Likewise, *I like chickens* refers to a count noun (i.e., the animal), but *I like chicken* refers to a non-count noun (i.e., the meat).

Many non-count nouns may be used in a countable sense, but the meaning changes to **type of.** For example, the word *cheese* is a non-count noun. You may sometimes see the word *cheeses* used in a countable sense, but here cheeses means types of cheese, as in *France produces more than sixty cheeses.* The use of non-count nouns in a countable sense is not so common and should be taught only to ELLs with advanced proficiency (if at all).

3. Words to Count Non-Count Nouns

It is not possible to count non-count nouns, but sometimes we do need to quantify a non-count noun. Notice the quantifying phrases such as *two pounds of, three or four pieces,* and *a glass of* in the following examples:

a. What did you buy? I bought *two pounds of* ground beef.
b. How much of the furniture is new? Not much—just *three or four pieces.*
c. Are you thirsty? Yes, give me *a glass of* chocolate milk.

Quantifying phrases:

Easy for ELLs	More Difficult for ELLs
The quantifying words for foods and liquids are the easiest because they are concrete nouns: *cup, bowl, slice.* <ul><li>*a cup of sugar*</li><li>*a bowl of rice*</li><li>*a bag of flour*</li><li>*a teaspoon of salt*</li><li>*a glass of milk*</li><li>*a can of juice*</li><li>*a loaf of bread*</li><li>*a slice of cake*</li><li>*a piece of chocolate*</li></ul>	ELLs have trouble with the quantifying word *piece*, which they associate with something that is broken: <ul><li>*a piece of luggage*</li><li>*a piece of furniture*</li><li>*a piece of advice*</li><li>*a piece of research*</li><li>*a piece of my (your, his, etc.) mind*</li><li>*a piece of wisdom*</li></ul>

5.B.3. *How Many?* vs. *How Much?*

To ask about the quantity of a noun, English uses two question phrases: *how many?* and *how much?* We use *how many* to ask about count nouns (e.g., *How many people are there? How many hours did you work?*), and we use *how much* to ask about non-count nouns (e.g., *How much money did you spend? How much information did they give you?*).

English is one of the few languages that uses two different words to ask about quantity. In many languages, there is only one word you can use when you want to ask about the quantity of a noun. In French, there is only *combien*, and in Malay, only *berapa*. The distinction between *how many* and *how much* is relatively easy for all ELLs to learn, but keep in mind that, at least initially, your ELLs may be confused by the mere idea of having two expressions that match one mental slot in their native language.

5.B.4. *Many* vs. *Much*

We use *many* with plural count nouns. We use *much* with non-count nouns. When in doubt, it is always correct to use *a lot of* with both count and non-count nouns.

	many	*much*	*a lot of*
Count	many books	——	a lot of books
Non-Count	——	much money	a lot of money

Note that we omit the preposition *of* if the noun is not used:

Sharon: How many people attended the meeting?

Gail: I don't know. *A lot.* (NOT: *A lot of.*) I think about thirty people were there.

One teaching point for advanced ELLs concerns the word *much*. We use *much* with non-count nouns, like *much money, much time,* or *much information*. We can use *much* in negative statements (*I don't have much money left*) and in questions (*Does a lawyer make much money?*). However, we don't usually use *much* in affirmative statements. Read these sentences, which are grammatically correct, and you'll see that something sounds a little strange to a native speaker:

1. I have much money. **Better:** I have a lot of money.
2. Much equipment is needed. **Better:** A lot of equipment is needed.
3. To make a great cake, you should use much butter. **Better:** To make a great cake, you should use a lot of butter.

When we use **a little** with a non-count noun, it refers to the quantity of the non-count noun. Thus, *a little sugar* refers to the quantity of sugar and means that you don't have a lot of sugar. However, when we use *a little* with a count noun such as *car*, it refers to the size of the car, not the quantity of cars. *A little car* means that the car is not big. It does not refer to the quantity or number of cars; there is only one car and it is little.

A common ELL error is the use of the word *only* with **few** or *little*, which is not possible. **A few** and *a little* have a positive meaning, but *few and little* have a negative meaning. We can say *only a few* or *only a little*. However, we cannot say **only few people* or **only little time* because *few* and *little* already have a negative meaning, so it would be like having a double negative (in theory).

5.B.5. *A Few / A Little*

We use *a few* with plural count nouns. We use *a little* with non-count nouns.

	a few	*a little*
Count	a few books	——
Non-Count	——	a little money

5.B.6. *A Few* vs. *Few; A Little* vs. *Little*

The distinction between *I have a few friends* and *I have few friends* is not one that should concern beginning or intermediate proficiency ELLs; in fact, this distinction is an advanced-level grammar point. When we say *a few*, we are being positive. We are saying that the person does indeed have some friends. In contrast, *few friends* has a negative connotation.

The same distinction exists for *a little* and *little*. A person who has *a little time* might be able to help you if you need his or her help, but a person with *little time* is too busy to help you.

5.B.7. Advanced Quantity Expressions

Once ELLs have mastered the use of *a few, a little, many,* and *much*, it is time to provide explicit instruction in variations of these quantifying terms. Using more explicit terms will improve ELLs' speech and writing. The terms listed are not synonyms and need to be considered in context multiple times to learn them well. NOTE: Words in red can be either count or non-count.

	Count	Non-Count
0% ↑	no, not any, a (complete) lack of	no, not any, a (complete) lack of
	few a lack of	little a lack of
	a few	a little, a bit of
	some	some
	several, a number of	
100% ↓	a great number of, a great many, a good number of, a lot of, lots of, plenty of	a great deal of, a large amount of, a substantial amount of, a lot of, lots of, plenty of

Common ELL Mistakes: What Your ELLs Should Know

1. Do not use a singular count noun without an article or other determiner.

   wrong: job   apple   reason   best choice
   delicious sandwich

   correct: a job   an apple   that reason   the best choice
   a delicious sandwich

2. Non-count nouns do not have a plural form, so do not add **–s.**

   wrong: homeworks   equipments   advices
   informations   clothings

   correct: homework   equipment   advice
   information   clothing

3. Do not use an article or other determiner before a non-count noun. With non-count nouns, you cannot use **a** or **an** for the same reason you cannot use one (or two or ten).

   wrong: a homework   an equipment   an advice
   an information   a clothing

   correct: homework   equipment   advice
   information   clothing

4. Use **many** and **a few** with count nouns. Use **much** and **a little** with non-count nouns.

   wrong: much problems   a few difficulty

   correct: many problems   a little difficulty

5. Avoid using **much** in affirmative statements. It is not necessarily wrong, but it can sound strange in some cases.

   unusual: She's rich. She has much money.

   better: She's rich. She has a lot of money.

6. Do not use **a lot of** without a noun after it. Add a noun or drop the preposition *of.*

   wrong: Do you have any good reasons for quitting your job?
   Yes, a lot of. I'm really ready for a change too.

   correct: Do you have any good reasons for quitting your job?
   Yes, a lot. I'm really ready for a change too.

5.C. Native Language Interference: Compare English with Other Languages

Language	Notes on *Count and Non-Count Nouns*
All Languages	1. Making such an important grammatical distinction between count and non-count nouns is unique to English, so many ELLs of various first language backgrounds experience difficulty with this language point. 2. None of the seven languages discussed here has separate words for *many* and *much*. For example, French has only *beaucoup* and Japanese has only *takusan*.
Arabic	1. Arabic nouns have singular, dual, and plural forms. (A dual form involves a suffix that means "two" much as *–s* in English means "two or more.") 2. Singular forms are not preceded by the word *one*; likewise, the dual form is not preceded by the word *two*. (In Arabic, *kitab* means "book" and *kitabain* means "two books." The word *ithnain* means "two," but you cannot say *ithnain kitbain*. This combination is redundant and translates as "two two books.") 3. Plural forms of nouns in Arabic often involve internal changes to a word; English usually adds the suffix *–s*. 4. The plural form is used with three to ten, but singular is used for eleven or more. In Arabic, *kitab* means "one book," *kitabain* means "two books," and *kutub* means "books." For three to ten books, *kutub* is used; for eleven or more, the singular form *kitab* is used.
Chinese	1. Most nouns have only one form (i.e., there is no plural form). (There is a suffix for plural, but it is used for human nouns only, e.g., women, children). 2. Indefinite and definite articles do not exist, but there is a word to express *this* and *that*.
French	1. French nouns are similar to English nouns in that nouns have singular and plural forms. 2. Some nouns (e.g., abstract nouns) do not have a plural form. 3. Some nouns that are non-count in English are count in French and therefore have plural forms. Common errors include *informations* and *homeworks*.
Japanese	1. Nouns have only one form; there is no difference between singular and plural. 2. An elaborate system of counter words is used with nouns, similar to *two cups of coffee* or *two sheets of paper* in English. However, almost all Japanese nouns require a counter, which is not the case in English.

Korean	1. Nouns have both a singular and a plural form. For plural meaning, however, sometimes the singular form suffices. 2. An elaborate system of counter words is used with nouns, similar to *two cups of coffee* or *two sheets of paper* in English.
Russian	1. Russian nouns have a singular and a plural form. 2. Some nouns that are non-count nouns in English are plural count nouns in Russian (**She has a lot of moneys*).
Spanish	1. Spanish nouns are similar to English nouns in that nouns have singular and plural forms. 2. Some nouns (e.g., abstract nouns) do not have a plural form. 3. Some nouns that are non-count in English are count in Spanish and therefore have plural forms, so common errors include **informations* and **homeworks*.

5.D. Ideas for Teaching

The general concept of count and non-count is usually taught in a beginning-level class. Thus, when teaching this, you should limit your language to easy vocabulary. Finer points such as not using *much* in affirmative statements are taught at higher levels.

If we consider frequency of the words involved in count and non-count, **many** and **much** occur more often than **a few** and **a little,** so it makes sense to focus on **many** and **much** initially. If we examine **many** and **much** further, we find that the phrases **how many** and **how much** are more frequent than the single words **many** and **much,** so I would start with these two common phrases: **how many** and **how much.**

It is almost always a good idea to involve the students in your teaching. One way to present this grammar point is to write these six questions on the board:

_____ students are in this room? (answer = 12)

_____ letters does the word *classroom* have? (answer = 9)

_____ time do you spend in this class every week?
(answer = 3 hours)

_____ money do you have with you right now?
(answer = 40 dollars)

_____ gasoline can I buy with $4? (answer = about 1 gallon)

_____ watches do you own? (answer = 2)

Make sure that the answers are true for your class of students. Tell students you want to ask a question that matches the answers on the board. Some students will know *how many* and others may know only *how much*. Teach these one by one. (You can let students work alone or in pairs for a minute or less.) As you go over these, write whatever the students tell you. If there is disagreement, ask them to tell what they know about *how many* or *how much*.

When all six answers are on the board, if they are correct, then as a group, talk about the difference in usage between **how many** and **how much**. If two answers are wrong, then say, "Two of these are wrong. Who knows which two are wrong?" If no one can guess which, then correct the two that are wrong. Then ask the class again to figure out what the pattern is. After the pattern has been discussed, ask students to generate four more examples. Write those examples on the board (or ask students to come to the board to write out their examples or ask four students to come up to the board to write out four examples from classmates).

If no one gets the answer, just tell students the pattern. After you tell them the pattern, explain it again. Then go over the examples one by one. (Your board should have only six to ten examples at this point.) Now give more examples with blanks and let them fill them in. After some students get the pattern, have those students come up with more examples that you will write on the board. At all times, involve your students.

Follow this with a short pattern drill in which you rapidly call out a noun and students have to say the question, *How many _____ do you have?*

T:	cats
Class:	How many cats do you have?
T:	money
Class:	How much money do you have?

Do this for about one minute. Follow this pattern drill with a communicative drill, that is, one in which students' answers are unknown to the rest of the class and therefore matter. Do drill as before, but now one student will ask another student as a follow-up.

T:	cats
Class:	How many cats do you have?
T:	Maria, ask Paula.
Maria:	Paula, how many cats do you have?
Paula:	I don't have any cats.
T:	sugar

(The drill continues.)

ELL Grammar Key 6:
Prepositions

Prepositions are small words, but they are perhaps the most difficult words to use correctly in another language. Common English prepositions include **at, for, from, in, of, on, to**. Why do we say <u>on</u> *Monday* but <u>in</u> *June*? Why do we say *fall in love <u>with</u> someone* and *be married <u>to</u> someone* but *get divorced <u>from</u> someone*? There are no logical explanations, which means that ELLs must learn the usage of a grammar area that has relatively vague rules—especially from an ELL's point of view.

6.A. Typical ELL Errors: Noticing the Gap

Can you identify and explain these five common ELL errors with this grammar point?

1. If you want to travel to Brazil, you must have a visa. You can find the visa application with all the directions on the Brazilian Embassy's website. Mail your passport, the application, a small photo, and a money order for $100 to the address listed on the website. *After that, all you have to do is wait your passport to come back with a Brazilian tourist visa in it.
2. *I want to thank you so much for to call me while I was in the hospital. Your call meant a lot to me.
3. I was planning to call you last Sunday to ask you whether you would be free on Tuesday to meet or not. *However, I was involved an accident last Sunday, and I couldn't call you. I hope you understand.
4. I was happy to get your email, and I was especially glad to hear your news. *I know you are very busy now, so thanks for wrote an email at this time. If you give me your phone number, I can call you so we can talk more.
5. *My friend and I bought an apartment in Argentina, so I'm pretty sure that I'll go there on August. That's when I have my next vacation. In fact, I'm trying to find a cheap flight now.

6.B. Grammar Explanation

6.B.1. Why Prepositions Are So Difficult

As all ELLs and their teachers know, prepositions are one of the most difficult areas of English for ELLs to master. Even after years of study, advanced proficiency ELLs will still make errors with prepositions.

One difficulty may be that individual prepositions do not translate well from one language to another. In English, you say, *I am married <u>to</u> Jim*, but in Spanish and French, you say *I am married with Jim*. Consider the English word *on* in these five common examples: <u>on</u> *the wall*, <u>on</u> *the table*, <u>on</u> *Friday*, <u>on</u> *Main Street*, <u>on</u> *second thought*. These are all very different meanings of *on*, and a second language would be unlikely to have one word that would work equally well for these same five examples.

A second reason may be that one language requires a preposition after a certain word but another language does not. For example, in Japanese, you say, *I walk the park*, but in English you say, *I walk through the park*. In French, you say, *I entered in the room*, but in English, you say, *I entered the room*.

A third reason may be that one language does not use prepositions in the same way that we do in English. In English, prepositions come before the noun, so they are called PRE-positions, with *pre* meaning "before." In Japanese, prepositions come after nouns, sometimes with a possessive marker in between, so our English sentence, *I go to the post office for stamps* is rendered *stamps'* (yes, possessive!) *[purpose] post office to I go.* Thus, Japanese has postpositions. In other languages, such as Hungarian, there are no separate words that equal English prepositions. Instead, inflections (prefixes, infixes, and suffixes) are made to the noun to indicate the preposition. In Hungarian, *with my cat* is rendered as *cat/my/with*, but it is one word instead of three.

Fourth, prepositions are used in many idioms, and an idiom defies translation. An idiom is by definition a group of words in which the meanings of the individual words do not add up to the meaning of the whole group of words. For example, when you say, *the bottom line* and *a piece of cake*, there is no line and there is no cake. Many idioms make use of common prepositions, as in these ten examples: <u>in</u> *love* <u>with</u> *someone*, *(it's) up* <u>to</u> *you*, <u>at</u> *odds* <u>with</u> *someone*, <u>in</u> *and* <u>out</u> (not *out and in*), <u>off</u> *and* <u>on</u> (OR: <u>on</u> *and* <u>off</u>), <u>down</u> *the road*, <u>with</u> *a grain* <u>of</u> *salt*, <u>of</u> *course*, *sort* <u>of</u>, *kind* <u>of</u>.

Finally, given that there are so many commonly used prepositions and that each one can have several meanings and then multiple usages, it is logical that it takes a long time to master prepositions.

6.B.2. Prepositions and Prepositional Phrases

A **preposition** is a word that shows the relationship between a noun (or pronoun) and the rest of the words in the sentence. Prepositions have many purposes, but they often give us information about place, time, and direction.

place	**at** *the bank,* **in** *my car,* **near** *the store,* **on** *Main Street,* **under** *the sofa*
time	**at** *10:10,* **before** *noon,* **for** *a few hours,* **on** *Friday,* **in** *2009*
direction	**from** *the post office,* **to** *the post office*

The combination of a preposition and its object (noun or pronoun and any modifiers such as articles or adjectives) is called a **prepositional phrase**.

on Tuesday   in the middle   at a secret location

PREP + N   PREP + ARTICLE + N   PREP + ARTICLE + ADJECTIVE + N

One area of prepositions that confuses ELLs is the location of prepositional phrases within a sentence. A prepositional phrase can come at the beginning, middle, or end of a sentence.

beginning	**In northern China,** the weather can be very cold.
middle	Zina worked **in northern China** for several years.
end	Dr. Kevin Ford teaches at a college **in northern China.**

When a sentence has both a prepositional phrase of place and of time, we generally put the **place phrase** before the **time phrase**. (HINT: Alphabetically, **P** comes before **T**, so remember **place** before **time**.)

                          time   place

not usual: Engineers discovered oil in 1901 in Texas .

                          place   time

usual: Engineers discovered oil in Texas in 1901 .

When we have two prepositional phrases of place or two of time in the same sentence, we generally arrange them from smaller to larger, as seen in these examples:

place: Your bilingual dictionary is in the box on the table in the kitchen .

time: Our meeting was at 3 PM on Monday .

In northern China, the winters can be very harsh. We usually use a **comma after a prepositional phrase** that begins a sentence. However, no comma is used when the prepositional phrase occurs at the end of the sentence: *The winters can be very harsh in northern China.*

6.B.3. 70 Common Prepositions

Some lists have more than 150 prepositions, but they contain rare prepositions such as *abaft* and *amid*. ELLs are already worried enough about prepositions; teachers should not compound this situation by introducing prepositions that students will never need. This list contains 70 common prepositions and example sentences. The alphabetical list is arranged in three groups: one-word prepositions (*about*), two-word prepositions (*due to*), and three-word prepositions (*on top of*).

One-word prepositions:

1. about	This book is **about** a family who gets lost in the mountains.
2. above	I have a small reading lamp **above** my bed.
3. across	The Washington Bridge is the best way to go **across** the river.
4. after	I hope to have more free time **after** June 1st.
5. against	Why are you **against** the President's plan?
6. along	In the early morning, people run **along** the east bank of the river.
7. among	Laura Vinson is **among** the best tennis players in the world.
8. around	Two squirrels were running **around** the oak tree.
9. as	For Halloween, I'm dressing up **as** Dracula.
10. at (+ place) (+ time)	When I travel, I prefer to stay **at** that hotel. The flight arrived promptly **at** 11:37.
11. before	The flights that leave **before** 9 AM are not full.
12. behind	The little girl is hiding **behind** that tree.
13. below	If your final score is **below** 70, you will not pass the course.
14. beneath	**Beneath** these rocks, you might find a spider or a snake.
15. beside	My cat usually sleeps **beside** my bed.
16. between	**Between** you and me, I don't think he is a good leader.
17. beyond	People who can't swim well shouldn't go **beyond** those rocks.
18. but	Most restaurants in this area are open every day **but** Monday.

19. by	
(+ time)	**By** noon, most of the seats had been taken.
(+ *-self*)	Of course it is more expensive if you live **by** yourself.
(+ place)	My car is parked **by** the train station.

20. despite	**Despite** my money problems, I am thinking about buying a car.

21. down	The rat ran **down** the tree.

22. during	**During** my last vacation, I spent two weeks in Mexico.

23. except	You can call me any day **except** Thursday.

24. for	
(+ person)	I believe that this gift is **for** you. Happy birthday!
(+ period)	My husband and I lived in Montreal **for** five years.

25. from	This gift is **from** my wife and me.

26. in	
(+ period)	The price of oil may double **in** the next five years.
(+ place)	Was George Washington born **in** Virginia?
(+ time)	My sister got married **in** 2005.

27. inside	If you look **inside** the refrigerator, you'll find some soft drinks.

28. into	Please put your coins **into** the machine if you want a sandwich.

29. like	I prefer subtle colors **like** tan and gray.

30. near	San Diego is not **near** Sacramento.

31. of	What is the title **of** your favorite book?

32. off	The little boy fell **off** the bed, but he was not hurt.

33. on	
(+ street)	Our house is **on** Jasmine Avenue.
(+ surface)	There is a map **on** the back wall in my classroom.
(+ day)	The store is closed **on** Sunday.

34. onto	The cat jumped **onto** the table where the meat was.

35. opposite	There are some apartments that are **opposite** the park.

36. over	The small plane had difficulty flying **over** the mountain.

37. past	If you walk **past** the lake, you will see dozens of ducks.

38. since	I have worked here **since** 1999.

Remember that **an infinitive** consists of **to** and a **verb:** *to go, to exist, to delay.* Remember that *to* is part of an infinitive and is not a preposition here.

39.	than	Mexico City is larger **than** Toronto.
40.	through	At dusk, hundreds of birds were flying **through** the trees.
41.	throughout	**Throughout** her lifetime, my grandmother saw some huge changes in our society.
42.	till	As a farmer, he worked from dawn **till** dusk.
43.	to	Driving from here **to** Miami takes about six hours.
44.	toward	We walked **toward** the park, but then we decided not to go there.
45.	under	Your socks are **under** the bed.
46.	until	To finish the project, we worked **until** 11 PM.
47.	up	We watched a squirrel run **up** the tree.
48.	upon	The cat was sleeping **upon** the sofa.
49.	with	The director asked me to go **with** him to the meeting.
50.	within	Everyone must finish the test **within** the announced time limit.
51.	without	**Without** any extra help, Josh managed to get an A in math.

> Remember that an **infinitive** consists of *to* and a verb: *to go, to exist, to delay*. *To* is a part of an infinitive and is NOT a preposition.

Two-word prepositions

52.	according to	**According to** this dictionary, this word has multiple meanings.
53.	ahead of	If you need to hurry, you can get in line **ahead of** me.
54.	as for	Bill liked the book. **As for** me, I wasn't able to finish it.
55.	because of	We started eating here **because of** your recommendation.
56.	close to	Do you live **close to** the bank on Smith Street?
57.	due to	The flight was cancelled **due to** the bad weather.
58.	far from	We walked an hour and were then **far from** our hotel.
59.	instead of	I'd like tea **instead of** coffee, please.
60.	next to	Who would like to live **next to** a cemetery?
61.	prior to	**Prior to** arrival, you should complete this tourist card.

Three-word prepositions

62. in addition to	**In addition to** Monday, I can meet on Tuesday or Friday.
63. in back of	There is a huge tree **in back of** our house.
64. in case of	**In case of** emergency, call 911.
65. in front of	Our house is the only one without a tree **in front of** it.
66. in lieu of	For his birthday, he requested that we donate money to a local charity **in lieu of** giving him a gift.
67. in place of	Would you mind giving me ten dimes **in place of** a dollar bill?
68. in spite of	**In spite of** the cooler temperatures, we went to the beach.
69. on behalf of	I'd like to thank you **on behalf of** my entire family.
70. on top of	Your briefcase is **on top of** the coffee table.

6.B.4. *at* / *on* / *in* for place and time

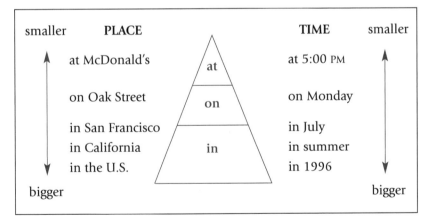

Learn these special idiomatic phrases:

- *in the morning*
- *in the afternoon*
- *in the evening*
- *at night*

Place. Use **at** with the name of a place or with an address with a number. (A) He studies **at** Boston University. (B) I live **at** 653 Maple Drive.	Time. Use **at** with clock times. (C) Please come **at** noon. (D) The class ends **at** 1:20.

1. Use **at** for very specific places or times.

We use **on** with names of **streets, roads,** avenues, lanes, drives, and highways, but we use **at** if the street address contains a specific number. We say *on Jasmine Avenue* but *at 330 Jasmine Avenue*.

Place. Use **on** for streets, roads, avenues, etc., when there is no number. (E) I live **on** Maple Drive. (F) There were many cars **on** the highway yesterday. (G) Los Angeles is **on** the Pacific Coast.	Time. Use **on** with days. (H) His birthday is **on** March 15. (I) What did you do **on** Saturday?

2. Use **on** for "medium"-sized places or times.

The use of the definite article **the** with names of seasons is optional. Both *the summer* and *summer* are correct.

Place. Use **in** for cities, states, and countries. (J) They live **in** Paris. (K) We grew up **in** Florida. (L) Florida is **in** the South. (M) Moscow is **in** Russia. (N) Bill is not here now. He's **in** the kitchen. (O) You can sleep **in** the front bedroom.	Time. Use **in** for months, seasons, and years. (P) The weather is hot **in** July. (Q) The weather is hot **in** the summer. (R) I was born **in** 1979.

3. Use **in** for large places or times.

Common ELL Mistakes: What Your ELLs Should Know

1. Do not use **in** with specific names of businesses or the like.

   wrong: I work in Burger King.

   correct: I work at Burger King.

2. Do not forget to use a preposition.

   wrong: My sister is England now.

   correct: My sister is in England now.

3. Do not use **at** with years or with cities or other geographical locations.

   wrong: I was born at 1967.

   correct: I was born in 1967.

   wrong: San Francisco is at California.

   correct: San Francisco is in California.

4. Don't use **in** for streets or days.

   wrong: He lives in Maple Street.

   correct: He lives on Maple Street.

   wrong: I called Sam in his birthday.

   correct: I called Sam on his birthday.

5. Be careful with prepositions for special idiomatic phrases with *morning, afternoon, evening,* and *night.*

   wrong: I watch TV in the night.

   correct: I watch TV at night.

Regardless of native language, ELLs tend to overuse ***in*** (instead of ***at***) **with names of businesses.** Big Macs are sold *at* McDonald's, not **in* McDonald's. Mickey Mouse lives *at* Disneyworld, not **in Disneyworld.*

6.B.5. Problem Prepositions

Certain pairs of prepositions and post-preposition words such as **ago** cause confusion for some groups of ELLs. Spanish speakers, for example, have a difficult time with **for** and **since** while Arabic speakers have trouble with **before** and **ago**.

a. **for** vs. **since**

for	We use **for** with a period of time. We use **for** to answer the question *How long?* With **for**, the answer is the period of time: *I've worked here for ten years.*
since	We use **since** with the name of the start of the time. We use **since** to answer the question *How long?* With since, the answer is the period of time but it is expressed by saying when the action began: *I've worked here since 2000.*
wrong:	They visited France since two weeks.
correct:	They visited France **for** two weeks.

b. **before** vs. **ago** (for past time)

before	We use **before** with the name of a specific point of time such as *before Monday, before June, before computers were invented.* We use **before** to answer the question, *When (did something happen)?*
ago	We use **ago** with the name of a period of time. We use **ago** to answer the question, *How long in the past (did something happen)?*
wrong:	My parents called me before two days.
correct:	My parents called me two days **ago**.

c. **in** vs. **after** (for future time)

in	When talking about the future, we use **in** with a general period of time. We use **in** to answer the question, *When will something happen?*
after	When talking about the future, we use **after** with the name of a period of time. We use **after** to answer the question, *When specifically will something happen?*
wrong:	The new cars will be available after two weeks.
correct:	The new cars will be available **in** two weeks.

d. **for** vs. **during**

for	We use **for** with a general period of time. We use **for** to answer the question *How long?*
during	We use **during** with the name of a period of time. We use **during** to answer the question *When?*
wrong:	They visited France during two weeks.
correct:	They visited France **for** two weeks.

e. verbs of motion: **enter, go, return**

enter + Ø	Generally, we do not use a preposition after **enter.**
go + to	Some ELLs use **go** with no preposition, but you must use **to** (or **in**).
return + to	Some ELLs use **return** with no preposition, but you must use **to.**
wrong:	The students entered ̶i̶n̶ the room between 8:30 and 8:45.
correct:	The students **entered the room** between 8:30 and 8:45.
wrong:	Some people went the party on Saturday night.
correct:	Some people **went to the party** on Saturday night.
wrong:	They will return their country in two more weeks.
correct:	They will **return to their country** in two more weeks.

> Sometimes **no preposition** is possible. In English, we *enter a room,* but many ELLs will incorrectly say **enter in a room.* For ELLs, these small prepositions "sandwiched" between two major concepts, the verb of motion and the place, are very hard to hear in rapid conversation.

> The word ***home*** does not use a preposition after verbs of motion. ELLs may mistakenly say **go to home* or **return to home,* but these combinations are incorrect.

6.B.6. Adjective/Noun/Verb + Preposition Combinations

For no apparent or logical reason, many adjectives, nouns, and verbs must be followed by a certain preposition.

ELLs can learn these preposition combinations in one of three ways: rote memorization, direct teacher instruction followed by practice, and/or massive exposure to them through extensive reading. All three of these techniques can work, but the first two are recommended for ELLs who are on a tight schedule. For very young ELLs who will have years of exposure to English, the third option is good, but exposure works especially well after direct teacher instruction because direct instruction increases the likelihood that learners will actually notice certain features in the language, in this case, preposition combinations. In singing (i.e., repeating) a seemingly simple song such as "Old MacDonald Had a Farm," learners are not just singing the line "and on his farm he had a (duck, cow, etc.)." They are in fact indirectly learning that we say <u>on</u> a farm in English, not **in* a farm.

For adjectives, we are **accustomed to** something, **happy about** something, and **proud of** something.

For nouns, we want to know the **answer to** something, the **cost of** something, and the **reason for** something.

For verbs, we **agree with** someone, we **count on** someone, and we **worry about** someone. Why we say **about** in one case and **for** or **with** in another is not rule-governed, so it is up to good teachers to help their students learn these combinations as quickly and easily as possible.

Alphabetical lists of 53 adjectives + preposition combinations, 80 noun + preposition combinations (including prepositions followed by nouns), and 30 verb + preposition combinations follow. These lists can serve as a source of reference information as well as springboards for making you more aware of the hundreds of other word combinations involving prepositions. These lists focus on commonly used preposition combinations.

> ELLs tend to use the base form of a verb after prepositions, but the correct form is a **gerund:** *afraid of flying, interested in going, sorry about leaving.* Use gerunds after prepositions.

6.B.6a. Adjectives + Prepositions

1. accustomed to	19. divorced from	38. married to
2. acquainted with	20. embarrassed by	39. necessary for
3. afraid of	21. excited about	40. okay with
4. all right with	22. familiar with	41. opposed to
5. angry about/at	23. famous for	42. proud of
6. annoyed by	24. far from	43. pleased with
7. bad at	25. frustrated with	44. ready for
8. bad for	26. full of	45. related to
9. bored with/by	27. good at	46. responsible for
10. certain about/of	28. good for	47. satisfied with
11. committed to	29. guilty of	48. sick of
12. composed of	30. happy about/with	49. similar to
13. concerned about	31. harmful to	50. sorry about
14. confused about	32. important for/to	51. successful in
15. confusing to	33. in favor of	52. sure about/of
16. dedicated to	34. innocent of	53. surprised at/by
17. different from	35. interested in	54. tired from/of
18. disappointed in/with	36. involved in/with	55. willing to
	37. known for	56. worried about

6.B.6b. Nouns + Prepositions; Prepositions + Nouns

Noun + Preposition	*Preposition + Noun*
1. advantage of	1. at church
2. advice on	2. at home
3. alternative to	3. at present
4. answer to	4. at war
5. application for	5. at work
6. benefit of	6. at your convenience
7. cause of	7. by car/bus/air mail
8. center of	8. by credit card
9. confusion about	9. by hand
10. cost of	10. by law
11. decision to	11. by mail
12. decrease by/in/of	12. by mistake
13. demand for	13. for lunch
14. difference between/in/of	14. for sale
15. example of	15. in advance
16. experience in/with	16. in a hurry
17. excuse for	17. in danger
18. fall in/of	18. in charge of
19. increase in/of	19. in debt
20. invitation to	20. in general
21. interest in	21. in love
22. lack of	22. in my opinion
23. matter with	23. in school
24. middle of	24. in shape
25. need for/of	25. in stock
26. opinion of	26. in the hospital
27. price of	27. in time
28. problem with	28. in trouble
29. question about	29. in writing
30. reason for	30. on a trip
31. reply to	31. on business
32. request for	32. on hold
33. rise in, of	33. on purpose
34. solution to	34. on sale
35. source of	35. on the phone/computer
36. tax on	36. on television
37. trouble with	37. on time
	38. on vacation
	39. on your mind
	40. out of date
	41. out of order
	42. under pressure
	43. with reference to

6.B.6c. Verbs + Prepositions

1. agree to/with	11. disagree about/with	21. look forward to
2. argue about/ with	12. dream about	22. pay attention to
3. ask about/for	13. explain (some- thing) to	23. speak about/to/with
4. apologize for	14. forget about	24. stare at
5. be accustomed to	15. give to	25. study for
6. be used to	16. introduce to	26. talk about
7. belong to	17. keep on	27. thank someone for
8. complain about	18. laugh at	28. think about/of
9. count on	19. listen to	29. work on
10. depend on	20. look at/for	30. worry about

Common ELL Mistakes: What Your ELLs Should Know

1. Be sure you use the correct preposition for the word combination that you are using.

   wrong: I complained the homework. (Mistake: no preposition)

   wrong: I complained ø̶f̶ the homework. (Mistake: wrong preposition)

   correct: I complained about the homework.

2. If you use a verb form after a preposition, the verb must end in **–ing.** (This form is called a gerund, which is a verb form used as a noun. Here it is as an object of the preposition.)

   wrong: I complained about do the homework. (Mistake: wrong verb form)

   correct: I complained about doing the homework.

3. With adjectives, one of the most common errors is using the preposition *for* too often.

   wrong: We are happy f̶o̶r̶ the professor's decision. (Mistake: wrong preposition)

   correct: We are happy about the professor's decision.

6.B.7. Common Idioms

Idioms are groups of words whose overall meaning is different from the meanings of the individual words. Prepositions are often polysemous, that is, having multiple meanings, so it comes as no surprise that this ambiguity affects the many idioms that use prepositions. Why do we say *once* **in** *a blue moon?* What about **on** *cloud nine* or *a horse* **of** *a different color?* A short list of some of the most common idioms in English follows; it is by no means complete. Study these prepositions and how they do or do not contribute toward the overall meaning of the idiom. Studying this list should help train your eye to recognize idioms, especially those with prepositions, in your students' reading and content material so that you can plan your teaching accordingly.

1. at the eleventh hour	21. jump to a conclusion
2. be a piece of cake	22. keep an eye on
3. be fed up with	23. keep an eye out for
4. be on the go	24. keep (stay) in touch
5. be on the road	25. live from hand to mouth
6. beat around the bush	26. lose track of
7. bent out of shape	27. make a mountain out of a mole hill
8. by the skin of one's teeth	28. Not on your life!
9. can't make heads or tails of something	29. on the cutting edge
10. down in the dumps	30. on the dot
11. for ages	31. on time
12. get a kick out of something	32. once in a while
13. get on one's nerves	33. over one's head
14. get out of hand	34. sleep on it
15. go with the flow	35. state of the art
16. in over one's head	36. step on it!
17. in the black	37. under the weather
18. in the red	38. until you're blue in the face
19. in time	39. wet behind the ears
20. jump all over someone	40. with bells on

6.C. Native Language Interference:
Compare English with Other Languages

Language	Notes on *Prepositions*
All Languages	1. Prepositions do not translate well from one language to another. No two languages have the same set of prepositions. 2. All ELLs—regardless of native language—may exhibit persistent errors with prepositions. (Articles and prepositions are two of the last grammatical areas that ELLs acquire.) Making errors with prepositions is a natural part of English acquisition. 3. Even when one preposition appears to be the same in both languages, actual usage may be different. The following example is from Spanish, but dozens of similar examples can be found between English and all languages. Spanish has the preposition *en*, which appears to equal English *in*. While there are many areas of overlap, there are many more examples where Spanish uses different prepositions and even no preposition for English *in*.

same usage	*en* la cocina = *in* the kitchen *en* mi opinion = *in* my opinion
different preposition	*vivo en la calle Orange =* *I live on Orange Street* *en este momento = at this moment/minute* *estoy pensando en un regalo =* *I'm thinking about a gift*
no preposition	*entramos en el hotel =* *we entered [Ø] the hotel*

4. Almost all ELLs have problems with *at, on,* and *in* because these three common English prepositions may be expressed by one, two, three, or more prepositions in different languages. For location, Arabic often uses *fi,* French uses *à, en,* and *dans,* Japanese uses *ni* and to a lesser extent *de,* and Spanish uses *en.* French has three prepositions, but each of them may at different times be translated as *at, on,* or *in.* No other languages uses these three prepositions in the same way as English does.

Almost All Languages	A surprising feature of English for most ELLs is that English allows prepositions to separate from the objects and occur at the end of an utterance. This is called **stranding** and usually happens with *wh-* questions and adjective and noun clauses. *What are you waiting for?* This is a normal question in English, but many languages would say *For what are you waiting?* *This is the book which I told you about.* This is a normal example of an adjective clause in English, but the word order in many languages is *This is the book about which I told you.* *I don't know which country they are fighting against.* This is a normal example of a noun clause in English, but the word order in many languages is *I don't know against which country they are fighting.* In English (and other Germanic languages, a few dialects of French, and some African languages), speakers have the option of **stranding** or not stranding, but in most languages, prepositions cannot be stranded to the end of a sentence. You can expect that your ELLs will almost never strand their prepositions. You should also expect that many of your ELLs will be confused by stranded sentences that they encounter in their reading or listening. They cannot grasp the sudden appearance of *with, about,* or another preposition at the end of a sentence with no apparent object.
Arabic	Arabic–speaking ELLs often misuse *in/after* for future and *ago/began* for past: **I'll see you after three days; *I did this work before two weeks.*
Chinese	Chinese has both prepositions and postpositions.
Japanese	Japanese has postpositions, not prepositions.
Spanish	The Spanish preposition *en* looks like our English *in,* so Spanish speakers tend to overuse *in*: **I work in Washington Bank, *I will see you in Monday, *The steak is in the plate.*

The word **than** can be a preposition (*Korea is bigger than Taiwan*), but the word **that** is never a preposition. Some languages such as French and Spanish may render *than* and *that* with the same word instead of two as in English, so speakers of these language may confuse *than* and *that*. A common error occurs when comparing two things: **Colombia is larger that Ecuador.*

6.D. Ideas for Teaching

I offer three suggestions for teaching prepositions to ELLs—regardless of their proficiency level. The first maxim in teaching prepositions to ELLs is that there are many possible lessons on prepositions. There are prepositions to indicate meaning such as place (*in Miami*) or time (*in June*), and there are prepositions that have more of a grammatical than semantic function such as *interested in a topic*. Second, mastering prepositions takes a great deal of time. In terms of time, I do not mean that you should necessarily spend more time on prepositions. Instead, I mean that ELL acquisition of prepositions requires a longer period of time than other grammar points do—even with instruction. After your instruction, you should expect mistakes to continue. Finally, this need for time to acquire prepositions requires that your lessons should provide opportunities for ELLs to practice and receive feedback on their preposition use. Prepositions are often unstressed in natural conversation, so ELLs can hardly hear, let alone actually notice and then learn correct preposition usage without a teacher or textbook pointing it out. ELLs need activities that allow them to see and hear the various ways in which prepositions are used.

Beginning students tend to focus on very common prepositions with concrete, non-idiomatic meanings. This would include **under** *the desk*, **on** *the desk*, and **in** *the desk*. To teach these, you can bring a ball (or any object) to class and move it from place to place, asking students about the location of the ball. Write the answers on the board so that students can hear and see the examples. Perhaps the hardest preposition information covered at the beginning level is clarification about *at, on*, and *in* with place and time.

Intermediate students must deal with confusing pairs (or trios) of prepositions and similar words. Examples would be *since* vs. *for, for* vs. *during, in* vs. *after* (for future), *than* vs. *that,* and *before* vs. *ago* in addition to the usual persistent problems of *at, on,* and *in.*

At the upper-intermediate and advanced levels, students become familiar with verbs, adjectives, and nouns that combine with certain prepositions like *excel in*. At this level, ELLs learn to use gerunds after prepositions (*excel in fixing cars*), and they study common idioms, special units of meaning that often include prepositions, like *fall in love, be up to,* and *on the other hand.*

At the advanced level, all lessons revolve around reviewing and consolidating the multitude of preposition information that ELLs have been exposed to at that point. At the upper-intermediate and advanced levels, ELLs are learning new vocabulary that often requires certain prepositions. For example, once they learn the word *relevant*, ELLs need to know that it is followed by the preposition *to* if there are additional words after it (e.g., *some relevant information* but *information that is relevant* **to** *our request*).

ELL Grammar Key 7:
Articles

Most English speakers recognize three articles: the indefinite articles **a** and **an** and the definite article **the**, but there is another article usage that occurs as well: the use of no article, as in *I don't like coffee*. Articles are problematic because some languages have no articles (Chinese, Japanese, Malay, Polish, Russian, Thai, Vietnamese), some have only the definite article (Arabic), and others have the same articles as English but their usage does not overlap exactly (French, German, Spanish). For ELLs, these little words can wreak havoc with their English.

7.A. *Typical ELL Errors: Noticing the Gap*

Can you identify and explain these five common ELL errors with this grammar point?

1. *Every family dreams about comfortable and luxurious house. For this goal, some people try to save a sufficient amount of money to buy a great place to live.
2. I like this grammar book because it explains everything so well. *After reading this book, I can understand the nouns and the verbs much better. I still need help with the adjectives.
3. *There are many reasons for being homeless, including the low education, the natural disaster, and the alcoholism.
4. *The light is an important factor in how much people enjoy working in their offices. Offices should have lots of windows to allow as much sunshine in as possible.
5. Thank you so much for the document that you sent me. *I will read it carefully and then send you a feedback about its content as well as its format.

7.B. Grammar Explanation

7.B.1. Indefinite Articles *a* and *an*

We use the indefinite articles **a** and **an** only before singular count nouns. We use **a** and **an** with singular count nouns that are not specific and are being mentioned for the first time.

A penguin is **a** small black and white bird.

A simple computer serves many purposes.

An igloo is **a** dwelling that is made of ice.

Indefinite Articles: *a, an*	
Rule	**Example**
1. Use *a* before a noun or an adjective (+ noun) that begins with a consonant sound.	**a feather, a gray feather**
2. Use *an* before a noun or an adjective (+ noun) that begins with a vowel sound.	**an idea, an absurd idea**
3. Remember that words beginning with the letters *h* or *u* can be problematic. The use of *a* and *an* depends on the beginning sound of the word.	**a hat, an hour** The word *hat* begins with the consonant sound /h/, but *hour* begins with a vowel sound because the letter *h* is silent. **a university, an umbrella** The word *university* begins with the consonant sound /y/, but *umbrella* begins with a vowel sound. The use of *a* or *an* is determined by the next word's initial sound, not its spelling.

A common error for some language groups learning English is to omit all articles because their languages do not have articles. An especially common but serious error is the omission of an article of any kind before **a singular count noun:** **I have cat and two dogs. *If you get pet, you will be happy. *I think the best pet is cat because it can be very affectionate.* This type of error is particularly common among speakers of Chinese, Japanese, and Russian.

A common error for Spanish and French speakers is to omit an indefinite article before a profession: **Mr. Johnson is teacher. *Maria was good student.* This omission error is due to a direct translation from Spanish and French; it is very specific to sentences with professions after the verb **be.**

7.B.2. The Definite Article *the*

There are several different situations in which we use the definite article **the** in English.

Definite Article: *the*	
Rule	**Example**
1. Use *the* when you are talking about something specific.	*general:* All of us have **an** umbrella. *specific:* **The** umbrella next to the door is not mine.
2. Use *the* when the speaker and the listener are talking about the same specific item.	*general:* Every kitchen has **a** refrigerator. *specific:* William, don't forget to close **the** refrigerator!
3. Use *the* for the second and all other references to the same noun.	*first reference:* James and I bought **a** new computer last month. *second reference:* **The** computer lets us access the Internet really quickly.
4. Use *the* with the superlative form of an adjective, which means with the word *most* or with the ending –*est*.	*comparative:* In a jewelry store, gold is more expensive than silver. *superlative:* In a jewelry store, diamonds are **the** most expensive item.
5. Use *the* for the names of countries that look plural, including countries that end in –*s* or have the words *united, union, republic,* or *kingdom.*	**the** Philippines, **the** Netherlands **the** United States, **the** Soviet Union **the** Dominican Republic, **the** Republic of Angola **the** United Kingdom, **the** Kingdom of Saudi Arabia
6. Use *the* for the parts of something. (Exception: In general, we do not use *the* for body parts.)	*general:* In a kitchen, there is **a** stove, **a** refrigerator, and **a** clock. *parts:* I went to Mary's new house last night. Her kitchen is beautiful. **The** refrigerator is silver, **the** stove is black, and **the** clock above **the** door has really big numbers on it.
7. Use *the* with most bodies of water except individual lakes.	**the** Mississippi River **the** Pacific Ocean **the** Mediterranean Sea **the** Great Lakes (but Lake Michigan)
8. Use *the* with geographic parts of the globe and geographic areas, deserts, and peninsulas.	**the** equator **the** Middle East **the** Gobi Desert **the** South

7.B.3. No Article

In English, there are a few situations in which we do not use any article with a noun. In these cases, many other languages require the use of **the**, so a common ELL error is overuse of **the**.

Many ELLs tend to **overuse *the*** when they want to refer to the whole category of something. Common errors include *The basketball is my favorite sport* and *I think the basketball players are the great athletes*. In addition, it is not common to use any article with abstract nouns, so we do not say *People need the patience*, *The absence makes the heart grow fonder*, or *The silence is golden*. We call this usage the **null article** (Ø).

No Article: *(Ø)*	
Rule	**Example**
1. When you want to talk about a category or group in general, use no article.	*general:* Cats can be great pets. *specific:* The cats in the pet store are expensive.
2. Use no article before abstract nouns such as feelings or ideas.	*wrong:* A person's future success depends on the education. *correct:* A person's future success depends on education. *wrong:* The patience is a virtue. *correct:* Patience is a virtue.

Common ELL Mistakes: What Your ELLs Should Know

1. Do not use a singular count noun without an article (or other determiner).

   wrong: job, apple, reason, best choice, delicious sandwich

   correct: a job, an apple, the reason, the best choice, a delicious sandwich

2. Do not use **a** with a noun that begins with a vowel sound.

   wrong: a hour, a heir, a honorable colleague, a hourly rate

   correct: an hour, an heir, an honorable colleague, an hourly rate

3. Do not use **the** with a plural count noun that refers to the whole category.

   wrong: I don't trust the politicians. They are an ornery bunch of people.

   correct: I don't trust politicians. They are an ornery bunch of people.

4. Do not use **the** with abstract nouns or ideas.

   wrong: The education is the most important thing in my life.

   correct: Education is the most important thing in my life.

7.C. Native Language Interference:
Compare English with Other Languages

Language	Notes on *Articles*
Arabic	1. Arabic has a definite article. 2. Unlike English, Arabic requires the definite article with abstract nouns: *The honesty is important.* 3. The definite article is used for specific things as in English, but it is also used in Arabic when referring to the whole group. In Arabic, you must say, *My favorite sport is the tennis* and *I am afraid of the spiders.* 4. Arabic has no indefinite article.
Chinese **Japanese** **Korean** **Russian**	1. These languages have no articles. Some of these languages have a word for *this* and/or *that*, so students may overuse these two words in lieu of articles. 2. ELLs who speak these languages exhibit persistent errors with articles. (Articles and prepositions are two of the last grammatical areas that all ELLs acquire.)
French **Spanish**	1. These languages have indefinite and definite articles. 2. The definite article is used for specific things as in English, but it is also used when referring to the whole group. In these languages, you must say, *My favorite sport is the tennis* and *I am afraid of the spiders.* 3. The definite article must be used with abstract nouns: *The honesty is important for the nice trips.* 4. Indefinite articles are not used when talking about professions: *My mother is teacher.* 5. Unlike English, both French and Spanish have singular and plural forms of their indefinite and definite articles. ELLs of these languages may ask you about the plural of *the* in English, a question that may seem strange until you consider this grammar in these languages.

7.D. Ideas for Teaching

Like prepositions, articles take a great deal of time to be acquired by ELLs. On the surface, the learning load does not appear to be so great with articles. While there are more than 150 prepositions in English, there are only two common kinds of articles in English: indefinite (*a, an*) and definite (*the*). From an ELL point of view, there are times when we use no article, but ELLs are inclined to use something. Thus, even if we count everything here, there are only four articles (*a, an, the, Ø*). Because there are only four, each article has to do many different tasks.

In planning a class on articles, it is important to know how articles are used within the native language of your students. Some languages have no articles at all, including Chinese, Japanese, and Russian. Arabic has a definite article. Some languages have articles that appear to be equivalent to ours, but the usages do not overlap exactly: French, German, Spanish.

At beginning level, ELLs learn (1) a singular count noun must have something in front of it, and this is usually *a* or *an*, (2) *the* for more specific usages, (3) *the* or Ø with geographical terms, and (4) Ø for general meaning. The first point applies mainly to languages that have no articles at all. If your students speak languages that have indefinite articles, like Spanish or French, you do not have to worry about (1). Teach your Chinese, Japanese, or Russian students that every time they learn a new noun, they should write down the noun with *a* or *an* in front. They should write down *a book, a cat,* and *an excuse*. They need to get used to including *a* or *an*. ELLs will never have any reason to write *book, cat,* or *excuse* as bare nouns, so learning them as bare nouns is useless and counterproductive. You should have separate lessons on each of the usages of these articles. One reason that article instruction is difficult for ELLs is that lessons on articles naively present several usages on one or two pages as if they were just one small issue. This would be the equivalent of teaching seven or eight distinct verb tenses all at one time, something that no grammar book would ever advocate.

At the intermediate level, ELLs consolidate information on articles. At this point, *a* or *an* is no longer a problem, but definite articles may still cause some problems. Common errors in intermediate writing include overuse of *the*, as in **I think the honesty is the most important human characteristic.*

At the advanced level, instruction no longer deals with global rules. Instead, teacher instruction on articles, if it occurs, takes place in the form of feedback on individual expressions or idioms, such as *once upon a time*, not *once upon the time*.

ELL Grammar Key 8:
Pronunciation of –s and –ed

Consider these four verbs: *wrapped, begged, kissed, worked.* Can you find the odd verb in terms of pronunciation? Of these four verbs, which one has a different final sound from the other three? (The answer is *begged* because it ends in /d/ while the others end in /t/.)

Now consider these four nouns: *bees, birds, cats, dogs.* Which of these living creatures has a different final pronunciation from the other three? (The answer is *cats* because it ends in /s/, but the others end in /z/.)

Native speakers are not usually consciously aware that we have three pronunciations for –s (/s/, /z/, /əz/) and three pronunciations for –ed /t/, /d/, /əd/). Teachers need to understand the pronunciation variations of these two grammar markers so that they can better understand their ELLs' linguistic needs.

8.A. Typical ELL Errors: Noticing the Gap

Can you identify and explain these five common ELL errors with this grammar point? The pronunciation of three words within each sentence is indicated. Concentrating on the ending of each word, identify which one word in each sentence has been pronounced incorrectly by the ELL.

---

1. *Some cats [cat + /s/] are sleeping by the trees [tree + /s/] that we planted [plant + /əd/] last year.

2. *The police followed [follow + /əd/] the speeding car and proceeded [proceed + /əd/] to interrogate the driver and her passengers [passenger + /z/].

3. *The most popular animals at the zoo are the monkeys [monkey + /s/], giraffes [giraffe + /s/], and elephants [elephant + /s/].

4. *There are many reasons [reason + /z/] why the judges [judge + /əz/] reached [reach + /əd/] their verdict so quickly.

5. *When spring arrived [arrive + /əd/], the seeds [seed + /z/] that she had planted [plant + /əd/] a month earlier began to sprout from the earth.

8.B. Grammar Explanation

8.B.1. The Scope of –s and –ed

You might be wondering—quite logically—why pronunciation is being discussed in a grammar book. Two of the most basic, frequently used grammar markers are –s and –ed. While these markers may appear to be just two little suffixes, each carries in reality quite an important grammar load in English.

The marker –s is used in English for two parts of speech: verbs and nouns. With verbs, –s is used for third person singular (*he/she/it works*). With nouns, –s is the plural marker (*cats*). Therefore, every time you talk about what a person usually does, all the verbs are in third person singular with –s. With nouns, –s is the usual way to form the plural. In fact, all but a handful of the thousands of nouns in English form their plural with –s. With nouns, it is also used to mark possession, for example, *Pat's, Mary's.*

Many people associate the marker –ed with simple past tense (*work-worked-worked*). In addition, –ed is used for past participles (*work-worked-worked*). However, because past participles are used in three tenses—namely, present perfect, past perfect, and future perfect—the –ed is involved in a total of four tenses. Four of twelve tenses may not seem to be a substantial number, but simple past and present perfect are among the most frequently used verb tenses in English. In addition, past participles can also function as adjectives (*The captured prisoner was sent back to jail*), so the –ed form occurs much more widely than just in verbs.

Elsewhere in this book, we have focused exclusively on the grammar of these two markers with little reference to any pronunciation problem. If the pronunciation of these common markers were straightforward as is the case with other markers such as –ing, –ly, or –ness, there would be no need for this discussion.

When I ask native speakers with no ELL training or experience how to pronounce –s, they often think I am posing a trick question. They routinely reply, "Well, –s is /s/, right?" The answer is no. The marker –s has three possible pronunciations, /s/, /z/, /əz/, and the most common one is not /s/ but /z/.

Similarly, when asked about the pronunciation of –ed, native speakers overwhelmingly answer /əd/. For –ed, there are three possible pronunciations—/t/, /d/, /əd/—and the most common one is not /əd/ but rather /d/. In fact, /əd/ is the least common in actual usage.

These pronunciations are not exceptions and are not due to the native speaker's accent, dialect, age, gender, or any other individual factor. The reason that the pronunciation of the marker –s is /s/ in *cats* but /z/ in *dogs* is the same reason that the marker –ed is /t/ in *worked* but /d/ in *begged*: the pronunciation depends completely on the final sound of the word before the marker is added—and this pronunciation depends on a physically different, unconscious action that we refer to as **voicing**.

How do we really pronounce **-s** and **-ed**? The most common way to pronounce -s is /z/, but many natives and all ELLs will hear /s/. The most common pronunciation of -ed is /d/, but many natives and most ELLs expect /əd/. Do not confuse spelling and pronunciation. These pronunciations /z/ and /əd/ are due to the final sound of the word before we add -s or -ed.

8.B.2. Voiced and Voiceless Sounds

When you speak, air passes through your mouth and/or nose to produce sounds. Variations of these sounds are produced by altering the place where the sound is made, by altering the manner in which the sound is made, or by altering voicing.

First, we can alter where the sound is made. The vowel in *beat* is made near the top front of the mouth while the vowel in *but* is made near the middle of the mouth. Say these words together several times, and then say just the two vowel sounds together. You should hear the difference. If not, pay attention to how your jaw drops as you say these words in succession: *beat, bit, bait, bet, bat, baht* (Thai currency; pronounce it just like the *a* in *father*), *boot, boat, bought, but, bit, bout.* Can you pronounce *beat* at the back of your mouth? What about *bout* at the front of your mouth? No, you can't. Each sound has its assigned place of articulation.

Second, we can alter the manner of articulation, which means that we can vary how a sound is produced. Pronounce /f/. Can you feel that you are making the sound of /f/ by the friction created by forcing the air to pass through the gap between your top teeth and your bottom lip? Pronounce /b/. Can you feel that you are actually stopping the air for a split second? With these two sounds, it is the friction or stopping of air that produces the sounds.

The final way to alter the pronunciation of a sound is by vibrating your vocal cords, which are located in your larynx (colloquially, your voice box) in your neck. Put your finger on your Adam's apple. Pronounce /s/ and then pronounce /z/. Can you feel the increased vibration for /z/? Notice that both /s/ and /z/ have the same place and manner of articulation; the lone difference is in voicing. We say that /s/ is **voiceless,** without vibration, and /z/ is **voiced,** with vibration.

Just as with /s/ and /z/, many other consonant sounds occur in pairs, including /p/–/b/ and /t/–/d/. Say /p/. Now say /b/. Both of these sounds are produced in the front of the mouth by stopping air. They have the same place and manner of production. The only difference is in voicing: /p/ is voiceless and /b/ is voiced.

All vowel sounds in English are voiced sounds. In fact, the word *vowel* comes from Latin *vocalis*, which means "voice." Therefore, nouns that end in a vowel sound form their plural by adding /z/: *plays, bees, flies, bows, views*. Likewise, verbs that end in a vowel sound form their past tense by adding /d/: *stayed, keyed, tried, glowed, chewed*.

Some voiced consonants, such as /m/ and /n/, do not have a corresponding voiceless partner. All vowels in English are voiced. This chart shows which sounds are voiced and which are voiceless. (This chart uses modified IPA symbols. Use whatever system of symbols that is meaningful to you.)

A **minimal pair** is two words that differ in only one sound (phoneme). Examples include *cab – cap* and *have – half*. Minimal pairs are useful in practicing the pronunciation of difficult sounds. When common vocabulary items are used, the pair serves to illustrate pronunciation contrasts. However, it is important to note that very few useful minimal pairs exist for less common sounds such as the soft *th* and the hard *th*. For instance, the minimal pair of *thy – thigh* does contrast these sounds well, but how useful are these words in everyday or academic English?

All English Sounds	
Voiced	**Voiceless**
/b/ *cab*	/p/ *cap*
/d/ *grade*	/t/ *grate*
/g/ *bag*	/k/ *back*
/v/ *have*	/f/ *half*
/z/ *rise*	/s/ *rice*
[ǰ] *surge*	[č] *search*
[ʒ] or (zh) *massage*	[š] *cash*
[ð] *bathe*	[θ] *bath*
/l/ *call*	---
/m/ *name*	---
/n/ *can*	---
/ŋ/ *song*	---
/r/ *purr*	---
all vowels *play, see, try, go, buy*, etc.	---

8.B.3. Pronunciation of –s: /s/, /z/, /əz/

In English, we use –s to mark the plural of nouns (e.g., *cat, cats*) and to make third person singular of a verb (e.g., *I need, he needs*). Note that this –s unit is sometimes spelled –es (e.g., *watches, dishes*), but this variation involves spelling, not pronunciation.

This –s unit can be pronounced three ways in English:

Pronunciation of –s		
Ending Sound	**Add This Sound**	**Examples**
Voiced /d/, /v/, /g/, /b/, /ð/, /l/, /m/, /n/, /ŋ/, /r/, all vowels	/z/	*beds, loves, bags, Rob's*
Voiceless /t/, /f/, /k/, /p/, /θ/	/s/	*bets, Jeff's, socks, wraps*
Other /s/, /z/, /č/, /š/, /ǰ/	/əz/	*Bess's, raises, watches*

8.B.4. Pronunciation of –ed: /t/, /d/, /əd/

This *–ed* suffix can be pronounced three ways in English:

Pronunciation of *–ed*		
Ending Sound	**Add This Sound**	**Examples**
Voiced /z/, /v/, /g/, /b/, /ð/, /l/, /m/, /n/, /ŋ/, /r/, all vowels	/d/	*raised, loved, bagged, robbed*
Voiceless /s/, /f/, /k/, /p/, /θ/, /č/, /š/	/t/	*voiced, laughed, backed, dropped*
Other /d/, /t/	/əd/	*needed, wanted*

Source: *The Art of Teaching Speaking: Research and Pedagogy for the ESL/EFL Classroom.* (Folse, 2006), p. 241.

8.B.5. Hearing the Final Sound

Sometimes the best way to help students hear these three differences is to put an example word in a phrase in which the next word begins with a vowel. By doing this, the final ending joins with the beginning vowel sound of the subsequent word as in these examples: *He bagged all of the cans. He backed all my ideas.* In the first example, *bagged all* produces the sounds of the word *doll* while *backed all* produces the sounds of the word *tall*.

doll   *tall*

He bagged all of the cans.   He backed all of my ideas.

For many students (and native speakers), it is much easier to hear the final /d/, /t/, /s/, or /z/ when the next word begins with a vowel sound. It is important to try to say the whole phrase as naturally as possible, which means at normal speed. If you pronounce the words individually, it is much more difficult to hear the sounds because you are not pronouncing them naturally, as you would in an ongoing conversation.

Even native speakers sometimes have trouble **hearing /d/ or /t/** with some verbs. (These native speakers pronounce it 100% correctly, but they don't realize which sound they are adding.) Try adding a phrase that begins with a vowel just after the *–ed* word, and you will be able to hear the /d/ or /t/ ending more clearly. (This technique helps not only the native teacher but also the ELLs hear the /d/ and /t/ endings.)

Common ELL Mistake: What Your ELLs Should Know

1. Do not consider the last written letter of the original word; consider the last *sound.*

   wrong: *baked = bake* + /d/ because it ends in the letter *e*

   correct: *baked = bake* + /t/ because it ends in the sound /k/

   wrong: *laughed = laugh* + /d/ because it ends in the letter *h*

   correct: *laughed = laugh* + /t/ because it ends in the sound /f/

8.C. Native Language Interference: Compare English with Other Languages

Language	Notes on *Pronunciation of –s and –ed*
All Languages	1. Most ELLs expect a one-to-one correspondence between a letter in English and its sound, but English is notorious for allowing multiple pronunciations of letters, as with the six pronunciations for the letters *ough* in *cough, rough, dough, through, bough,* and *bought.* 2. Initially, all ELLs will mispronounce every *–s* as /s/: *goes* */gos/ and *shoes* */shus/.* 3. Initially, all ELLs will mispronounce every *–ed* as a separate syllable /əd/: *slapped* */slap•əd/ and *lived* */liv•əd/.* 4. All ELLs are surprised to find that *–s* can be pronounced /s/, /z/, or /əz/ and that *–ed* can be pronounced /t/, /d/, or /əd/. Beginning students will unconsciously repeat these endings correctly (*robbed* with /d/ and *wrapped* with /t/), but once ELLs see the form of the word on the board, they will say *rob•bed and *wrap•ped with two separate syllables.
Arabic	The phoneme /p/ does not exist, so Arabic speakers have difficulty with the distinction *cab–cap,* which forms the plural with /z/ and /s/, and *rub–wrap,* which forms the past tense with /d/ and /t/.
Chinese	1. Verbs and nouns are not marked for singular and plural, so the concept of word endings may surprise Chinese–speaking ELLs. 2. Consonant clusters, such as *desks* and *clasps,* are especially difficult to pronounce.

French	1. Like most ELLs, French speakers tend to pronounce all –s endings as /s/ instead of including /z/ or /əz/. 2. French does not have either of the *th* sounds in English (*th*is or *th*ink), so French-speaking ELLs find it difficult to pronounce words that end in these sounds, particularly when followed by an additional ending (*bathes* or *Keith's*).
Japanese	1. Verbs and nouns are not marked for singular and plural, so this is a new concept in English. 2. Most Japanese words end in a vowel sound (*sushi, sake, sayonara*), with the lone exception being /n/ (*Nihon* [Japan], *Nissan, gohan* [rice]). Consonant clusters in English are difficult.
Korean	1. Verbs and nouns are not marked for singular and plural, so this is a new concept in English. 2. The phoneme /z/ does not exist in Korean, so Korean ELLs may substitute /s/ instead.
Russian	1. When Russian speakers begin to learn English, they tend to read and pronounce English words the way they are written. 2. Russians have trouble with /θ/, which is rendered as /t/. This problem may impact whether the past tense ending is rendered as /d/ or /t/, the –s is rendered as /z/ or /s/, or the ending is maistakenly rendered as an extra syllable /əd/ or /əz/. 3. /v/ and /w/ are confusing. English does not have final /w/; a final w letter influences the vowel sound. 4. English /r/ is problematic.
Spanish	The phoneme /v/ does not exist, and Spanish speakers often misuse /b/ instead. This may cause pronunciation problems of verb endings after /v/–/b/ (*lives, robs*) as well as past tense endings after /v/–/b/ (*lived, robbed*).

FIND OUT

What is the most common sound to make nouns plural in English? Make a list of 25 animal names at random. (HINT: If you get stuck, pretend that you are walking by the animals at a zoo.) Eliminate any animals that have irregular plurals such as *deer* → *deer* or *mouse* → *mice*. Determine the percentage of your words that end in /s/, /z/, and /əz/.

8.D. Ideas for Teaching

ELLs at all levels will repeat an inflected word such as *monkeys* or *talked* correctly with the /z/ and /t/ endings respectively, but once they see the spelling of the word, they may revert to pronunciations ending in /s/ and /əd/ because of spelling interference. For beginners in particular, the teaching point is that spelling and pronunciation of these endings are not related, but you should anticipate this kind of interference.

For beginners, it is helpful to present the words grouped according to sounds instead of the usual alphabetical listing.

Method 1: Alphabetically		
cats	horses	rats
dogs	lions	snakes
giraffes	monkeys	turkeys

Method 2: By Sounds		
/s/	/z/	/əz/
cats	dogs	horses
giraffes	lions	
rats	monkeys	
snakes	turkeys	

For beginning learners, it is not necessary to go into depth as to why *cats* ends in /s/ and *dogs* in /z/, but if you present the words in groups according to the final sound and emphasize these final sounds even indirectly, students can benefit from this pronunciation foundation. An especially helpful way to focus attention on these endings is to practice the words in phrases where the next word begins with a vowel sound. In this way, it is much easier to hear the actual sound. For example, put the animal names in a sentence where the next word is *are: The cats are here. The dogs are there. The giraffes are here. The lions are there.* In these four sentences, you can hear the alternating /s/–/z/ sounds: *cats are* /s/, *dogs are* /z/, *giraffes are* /s/, and *lions are* /z/.

For very young learners, you could choose a song that has a preponderance of –s endings pronounced as /z/. In reality, a song is nothing more than a drill set to music. Learners repeat the words to the song without realizing that they are actually assimilating a very important language pattern. Another good point is that songs produce no student papers and, therefore, require no teacher grading time.

ELL Grammar Key 9:
Adjective Clauses and Reductions

Consider: The sentence that you are reading right now contains an **adjective clause.** Do you know which words make up the adjective clause? The answer is *that you are reading right now.* This clause describes the word *sentence.* Though most ELLs can understand the gist of this sentence, the grammar of it can be a bit perplexing. They may ask you, *Why are there two verbs?* or *What is the purpose of the word* that?

To express the same idea of this sentence, we could also omit the word *that* and say, *The sentence you are reading right now contains an adjective clause.* In fact, in spoken English, this second sentence may be more common. (Both are correct English.) Can you always omit the word *that* from adjective clauses? Consider: The sentence that has twelve words seems hard to understand. No, we cannot say, **The sentence has twelve words seems hard to understand.* Why? (The answer is in Key 9.)

If your students are reading English texts or listening to English, they are being exposed to adjective clauses a great deal because adjective clauses—whether "full" or "reduced"—are very common in English. Even frequent exposure to this particular structure is usually not enough to learn it well. Your ELLs need a teacher with knowledge of this grammar point to help them figure out this important structure.

> **A clause** is a group of words with both a subject and a verb. The two kinds of clauses are independent and dependent. There are three kinds of dependent clauses: adjective, adverb, and noun.

9.A. Typical ELL Errors: Noticing the Gap

Can you identify and explain these five common ELL errors with this grammar point?

1. **The lawyer informed all of us that the document was signed in 1991 ceased to be valid in 2001.*

2. **Where did you put the letter that I wrote it yesterday?*

3. **To check out a book from the downtown public library, patrons need a special card who has their current address at the top.*

4. **Marvin Brown's best-selling book that written in 2007 caused many problems in the business community.*

5. **Congress wants to know the names of the banks what are willing to invest in our economy now.*

9.B. Grammar Explanation

9.B.1. What Is an Adjective Clause?

Another term for *adjective clause* is **relative clause.** In your teaching, you should use the term used in your students' textbook. The two are interchangeable.

An adjective clause is a clause that describes or gives more information about a noun. An adjective clause usually begins with *who, that, which, whom,* or *whose,* and these initial words are called **relative pronouns.** As you will see, *that, which,* and *whom* are sometimes omitted from adjective clauses.

Adjectives are usually single words that describe a noun. A typical position in a sentence is immediately *before* the noun. In contrast, adjective clauses go *after* the noun.

Simple Sentence: *I rented a house.*	
(additional idea: *big*) →	ADJECTIVE + NOUN I rented a |big| |house|.
(additional idea: *the house had six bedrooms*) →	NOUN + ADJECTIVE CLAUSE I rented a |house| |that had six bedrooms|.

9.B.2. Use of Relative Pronouns

A **relative pronoun** is a pronoun in an adjective clause. The most common relative pronouns are *who, whom, that,* and *which.* In general, *who, whom,* and *that* can be used for people, and *that* and *which* can be used for things.

Other relative pronouns include *whose* (*The girl whose arm is broken loves sports*), *where* (*We saw the place where the accident occurred*), and *when* (*I don't remember the date when they got married*).

In formal language, a distinction is always made between *who* **(for subjects) and** *whom* **(for objects).** In everyday informal language, *who* is used as either a subject or an object.

People	who, whom	1. A person |who builds houses| is a carpenter. 2. I hope to meet the person |whom you hired|.
Things	which	3. This book is the type of literature |which Matt likes|.
People or Things	that	4. A person |that builds houses| is a carpenter. 5. This book is the type of literature |that Matt likes|.

9.B.3. Relative Pronouns as Subjects and Objects in Adjective Clauses

The relative pronoun in an adjective clause can function as the subject or as an object in the clause. It is much easier for ELLs to work with adjective clauses where the relative pronoun is the subject, so it is important for you to understand the difference between the two well before you begin teaching this grammar point. At some point, ELLs need to learn both positions, but in terms of instruction, it may be more prudent to work first with the subject types and then the object types. At the very least, knowing this distinction can help teachers predict ELLs' difficulties and thereby plan their instruction accordingly.

who	SUBJ	SUBJ + VERB 1. A person **who** builds houses is a carpenter.
	OBJ	Ø (who *is only a subject in formal language*)
whom	SUBJ	Ø (whom *is only an object*)
	OBJ	OBJ + SUBJ + VERB 2. I hope to meet the person **whom** you hired.
that	SUBJ	SUBJ + VERB 3. This book is the type of literature **that** is interesting to me.
	OBJ	OBJ + SUBJ + VERB 4. This book is the type of literature **that** Matthew likes.
which	SUBJ	SUBJ + VERB 5. This book is the type of literature **which** is interesting to me.
	OBJ	OBJ + SUBJ+ VERB 6. This book is the type of literature **which** Matthew likes.

Both **that** and **which** can be used for adjective clauses that refer to a thing. However, some grammar books make a distinction between *that* (for clauses with necessary information, known as **restrictive clauses**) and *which* (for clauses with extra information, known as **non-restrictive clauses**). Consider: *One incredible country that I visited in 2007 was Peru.* vs. *Peru, which I visited in 2007, was incredible.* When ELLs first learn about adjective clauses, the *that/which* distinction is not taught. Instead, ELLs are taught that either word is okay to refer to things.

9.B.5. Reduction of Adjective Clauses

What is the function of *–ing* words in sentences such as *On domestic flights **lasting** at least three hours, a meal is served* or *Students **needing** extra help can go to the writing center*? It can't be the main verb—because the sentences already have a main verb. It can't be an adjective—because adjectives come before nouns, not after them. If this *–ing* word in the middle of the sentence seems strange to you, you can now empathize with the plight of your ELLs.

In this section, you will see that these *–ing–words* are **reduced adjective clauses**. The good news is that ELLs generally have little to no difficulty understanding the content of sentences containing adjective clauses. The bad news, however, is that English also allows adjective clauses to be reduced, and these reductions are not only common but also tricky to produce. In fact, even young native readers have some difficulty with texts that contain adjective clause reductions. There are two common ways to reduce adjective clauses:

> **Reduced adjective clauses** can contain present participles (*People needing help can call at noon*), past participles (*People chosen for that award win cash*), or prepositional phrases (*People in our office work from 8 AM to 6 PM*).

Omitting SUBJ + *be:* When an adjective clause has **who/which/that** as the subject and any form of **be**, these two parts may be omitted without changing the meaning of the sentence. This reduction affects prepositional phrases, present participles, and past participles. **who/which/that** + **be** → ∅	*Prepositional Phrases* 1a. The magazines [that are] on the table belong to me. 1b. The magazines ***on the table*** belong to me.
	Present Participles 2a. People [who are] living in the dorm now will get a refund. 2b. People ***living*** in the dorm now will get a refund.
	Past Participles 3a. The students [that had been] chosen for the contest were very happy. 3b. The students ***chosen*** for the contest were very happy.
Reducing SUBJ + VERB: When an adjective clause has **who/which/that** as the SUBJ + VERB, these two parts may be changed to the *–ing* form (present participle) without changing the meaning of the sentence. **who/which/that** + VERB → VERB + *–ing*	*Present Participles* 4a. On domestic flights [that last] at least three hours, a meal is served. 4b. On domestic flights ***lasting*** at least three hours, a meal is served.

Common ELL Mistakes: What Your ELLs Should Know

1. Do not forget to use a relative pronoun (**who, that, which**).

   wrong: The book has 250 pages is on the table.

   correct: The book that has 250 pages is on the table.

   correct: The book which has 250 pages is on the table.

2. Do not use the wrong word to begin a relative clause. Do not use **which** for people or **who** for things in relative clauses.

   wrong: The student which made 100 on the test is from China.

   correct: The student who made 100 on the test is from China.

   correct: The student that made 100 on the test is from China.

3. Do not include a pronoun after the verb of a relative clause.

   wrong: The man that we spoke to h~~im~~ is Mr. O'Leary.

   correct: The man that we spoke to is Mr. O'Leary.

4. Don't forget to omit both the subject and the verb **be**. You can't omit just one of them.

   wrong: The book that written in 1991 caused many problems.

   wrong: The book was written in 1991 caused many problems.

   correct: The book written in 1991 caused many problems.

   correct: The book that was written in 1991 caused many problems.

   correct: The book which was written in 1991 caused many problems.

9.C. Native Language Interference: Compare English with Other Languages

Language	Notes on *Adjective Clauses*
Arabic	1. As in English, relative clauses come after the noun. 2. The relative pronoun in Arabic does not make a distinction between human (*who, whom*) and non-human (*that, which*), so Arabic speakers may produce *This is the book who I bought. 3. The object pronoun in a relative clause is included in Arabic, so Arabic speakers will say *Mrs. Wilson is the teacher that we like h~~er~~. 4. Clause reductions are not possible.

Chinese	1. Adjective clauses appear before the noun, not after as in English.
	2. No reductions of adjective clauses are possible.
	3. Chinese learners have great difficulty with relative clauses, often avoiding this construction in favor of using several smaller sentences.
French	1. As in English, relative clauses come after the noun.
	2. No reductions of adjective clauses are possible.
	3. The relative pronoun in French is different for subjects (*qui*) and for objects (*que*). Thus, French speakers frequently make errors such as, **The book who is on the table belongs to me* (because *who* is the subject of *is on the table* and in French must be rendered by *qui*, which usually means *who*) and **The book what we read is on the table* (because *what* is the object of *we read about* and in French must be rendered by *que*, which may mean *what, that,* or *which*).
Japanese Korean	1. Adjective clauses appear before the noun, not after as in English.
	2. There is no relative pronoun, so there is no distinction between *who/whom/that/which*. Word order and placement of the clause before the noun indicate an adjective clause.
	3. No reductions of adjective clauses are possible.
Russian	1. As in English, relative clauses come after the noun.
	2. The same relative pronoun is used for humans and things, so *who/whom* may be interchanged with *which/that*. Russian ELLs may write **The person which you met lives in this apartment.*
	3. Russian sets off dependent clauses with a comma, so a frequent punctuation error in English is **Here is the book, that you bought.*
Spanish	1. As in English, relative clauses come after the noun.
	2. No reductions of adjective clauses are possible.
	3. The relative pronoun in Spanish is *que*, a polysemous word that can mean *what, which, that,* or *than* depending on the context. Thus, Spanish speakers frequently make errors such as **This is the dictionary what we use in our class* and **The leader which we studied about fought for civil rights.*

4. Spanish allows for subject-verb inversion in adjective clauses, so common mistakes include *This happened at the time when explored the New World Christopher Columbus* and *The first play that wrote Shakespeare was Henry VI.* Notice how the subjects *Christopher Columbus* and *play* come after their respective verbs *explored* and *wrote.*

9.D. Ideas for Teaching

The term *adjective clause* may sound like a very exotic and rare grammar component, but even beginning-level materials contain adjective clauses. Before teaching this grammar point, check your own knowledge first. As the teacher, you should understand three things about adjective clauses well. First, you should know the most common adjective clause markers (*who, whom,* etc.) and thereby be able to identify an adjective clause instantly. Second, you should know when the marker may be omitted, thereby "tricking" the student into thinking that he or she has come upon a new sentence instead of part of the same sentence. Third, you should understand adjective clause reductions well.

Demonstrate how you can embed one sentence inside the other:

> **FIND OUT**
>
> Examine a content book (a science book or a business website) written by native speakers. Identify all adjective clauses (both full and reduced forms). For those that describe a person, how many use *who/whom* and how many use *that*? What percentage of clauses are full and what percentage are reduced?

1.	2.	3.
The book has 200 pages.	→ *that* ~~the book~~ is on the table	The book that is on the table has 200 pages.
The book is on the table.		

After you have demonstrated this, then let students work with three or four pairs of sentences to create new sentences with adjective clauses.

Armed with this information, choose a paragraph from reading material that is appropriate for your students' proficiency level. The paragraph ideally would come from another of your students' books, their reading or composition book, for example.

With beginning students, you could ask them to underline adjective clauses inside a reading passage. It is imperative that you give them a "cleaned up" version of the reading, which means that you have made sure that there are no reductions, no clauses with *whose* (not beginning level) and preferably none with *whom.* You want only *who/that* + VERB + *–s.* Examples include *The book that is on the table has 200 pages* and *The man who is standing by the door drives a red sports car.*

With intermediate students, ask them to identify the adjective clauses, but also ask them to come up with the two original sentences.

Combining two sentences to practice adjective clauses can sometimes produce multiple answers. In addition to *The book that is on the table has 200 pages,* the answer could have been *The book that has 200 pages is on the table.* Therefore, it is important that you discuss all possible answers as a class. I think that teaching adjective clauses can be similar to teaching in a math class where the math teacher checks homework by asking if anyone else got a different answer and then asking that person how he or she arrived at that answer. In isolation, both of these answers are correct. Within a larger piece of writing, one would be preferred due to the purpose of the sentence: to tell the number of pages or to tell the location of the book. This type of grammatical comparison is useful for intermediate and higher-proficiency ELLs.

Intermediate students will practice not only *who/that* in the subject position but also *whom/that* in the object position. Intermediate ELLs will also practice omitting the relative pronouns in the object position. At this level, students need to be told to include more adjective clauses in their writing. Make it a specific part of the assignment, such as *Write a paragraph about the causes of the Vietnam War. Use and underline our four new vocabulary words in your paragraph: presume, liable, logical, detrimental. Use and put a box around at least two adjective clauses in your paper.*

Advanced students are expected to be able to understand full and reduced adjective clauses in their reading and listening material. In addition, they should be able to use both full and reduced forms in writing and speaking.

ELL Grammar Key 10:
Infinitives and Gerunds

My doctor asked me trying avoiding to eat greasy foods. What? Most people have to read that sentence several times before they have any idea of what it means. The actual sentence is supposed to be *My doctor asked me to try to avoid eating greasy foods.* This sentence has four verb expressions in it. In this sentence, how do we know when to use an infinitive (*to try*) and when to use a gerund (*eating*)?

10.A. Typical ELL Errors: Noticing the Gap

Can you identify and explain these five common ELL errors with this grammar point?

1. *Write letters in English is not so difficult for me now, but I used to have a lot of problems.
2. *I am so sorry for not to inform you about what has happened to me in the past few days, but I have been extremely busy.
3. *We were tired, so we stopped to drive. After taking a rest, we then drove all the way home.
4. *Thanks for wrote an email to me. I can't tell you how happy I was to receive your news.
5. *I want that you eat dinner with me tonight.

10.B. Grammar Explanation

10.B.1. Form and Function of Infinitives and Gerunds

An **infinitive** consists of **to** plus the simple or base form of a verb. An infinitive can function as a noun, adjective, or adverb. A **gerund** consists of a VERB and *–ing*. A gerund is always used as a noun. It is important to remember that infinitives and gerunds are verb forms, not verbs.

Infinitive = *to* + VERB	Gerund = VERB + *–ing*
1. *To be* or *not to be*—that is the question.	4. *Getting* a good job is my top priority.
2. The decision *to quit* my job was tough.	5. Are you interested in *going* to the store?
3. She wants *to eat* lunch with our family.	6. She enjoys *eating* lunch with our family.

10.B.2. Subject of the Sentence

When you want to use a verb as the subject of a sentence, use a gerund. Yes, it is theoretically possible to use an infinitive as the subject, but this happens only in very formal language. In daily speaking, we almost never use an infinitive as the subject. As a subject, a gerund or an infinitive is singular and takes a singular verb.

Gerund as Subject	Infinitive as Subject
1. **Speaking** three languages is hard. 2. **Arriving** on time is important. 3. **Running** burns up a lot of calories.	4. **To speak** three languages is hard. 5. **To arrive** on time is important. 6. *__To run__ burns up a lot of calories.
NOTE: These three examples represent natural, correct English. These sentences could occur in either writing or speaking and in either formal or informal situations. They sound better.	NOTE: Examples 4 and 5 sound much more formal than their gerund counterparts, Examples 1 and 2. No native speaker would ever say Example 6. Until they have a much higher English proficiency level and can appreciate the potential nuance of using an infinitive as subject, ELLs should avoid infinitives as subjects. For lower-level ELLs, I sometimes tell a "grammar lie" and say that infinitives are never the subject of a sentence.

10.B.3. Infinitive to Show Purpose or Reason

Infinitives can be a reduction of the phrase *in order to*, which shows a purpose for doing something. Ask students to notice the comma after this introductory phrase. This comma is a sure indication of an infinitive of purpose.

                    PURPOSE   RESULT

<u>To achieve</u> their goals, the <u>**officials**</u> quickly <u>**hired**</u> a new manager.
infinitive   (comma) subject   verb

10.B.4. Infinitives or Gerunds Following Certain Verbs

Consider these two example sentences:

> She wants **to eat** lunch with our family.
>
> She enjoys **eating** lunch with our family.

Why is *to eat*—and not *eating*—correct in the first example? Why is *eating*—and not *to eat*—correct in the second example? Whether to use an infinitive or a gerund here is determined by the first verb. In English, we use an infinitive after *want, need, promise,* and other verbs. We use a gerund after *enjoy, avoid, consider,* and other verbs. There is no obvious rhyme or reason to account for which verbs must be followed by an infinitive and which must be followed by a gerund.

For ELLs, there is no difficult concept to understand here. It is simply a matter of good old-fashioned memorizing which verbs are followed by infinitives and which verbs by gerunds as seen in Group 4a and 4b.

Group 4a. Verbs Followed by Infinitives					
afford	demand	hope	need	promise	
agree	deserve	intend	offer	refuse	
ask	expect	know (how)	plan	want	
decide	hesitate	learn	pretend	would like	

Example:

I *intended* **to study** last night, but I *decided* **to watch** TV instead.

Group 4b. Verbs Followed by Gerunds			
appreciate	dislike	keep on	recommend
avoid	dread	look forward to	risk
can't help	enjoy	miss	suggest
consider	finish	postpone	think about
delay	get through	practice	be tired of
detest	go (shopping)	put off	be used to
discuss	insist on	quit	

> A **gerund often follows *go*** when it is a sport or a fun activity: *go swimming, go bowling, go shopping, go fishing, go running.*

Example:

We may *dread* **visiting** the dentist's ofice, but we cannot *avoid* **going** there.

Some verbs can be followed by either an infinitive or a gerund with no difference in meaning, as seen in Group 4c.

Group 4c. Verbs Followed by Gerunds or Infinitives: Same Meaning			
begin can't stand	continue hate	like love	prefer start

Examples:

If you ***begin* to cook** now, dinner will be ready by 7:30.

If you ***begin* cooking** now, dinner will be ready by 7:30.

There are a few verbs that can be followed by either an infinitive or a gerund, but the meaning of the sentence is different. This group includes *remember, stop, forget,* and *try,* as seen in Group 4d.

Group 4d. Verbs Followed by Gerunds or Infinitives: Different Meaning			
remember	stop	forget	try

Examples:

remember

1. *Susan:* Here are the tomatoes that you asked me to buy.
   Sam: Thanks. I'm happy that you ***remembered* to buy** them.
   (*remember* + **infinitive** means she remembered first and then she acted.)

2. *Chuck:* I found this old book with your name in it. Is it yours?
   Chris: Well, I don't ***remember* buying** it, but it must be mine if it has my name in it.
   (*remember* + **gerund** means she acted first and then she remembered.)

stop

1. *Allie:* Why are you late?
   Peter: My car was almost on empty, so I ***stopped* to get** some gas.
   (*stop* + **infinitive** tells why. **To** is the same as **in order to.**)

2. *Robert:* Does Stan still smoke?
   Cindy: No, he doesn't. He ***stopped* smoking** last May.
   (*stop* + **gerund** tells what he stopped.)

Group 4e. Verbs Followed by Noun/Pronoun Followed by Infinitive						
advise	cause	forbid	invite	permit	teach	want
allow	convince	force	need	persuade	tell	warn
ask	expect	get	order	remind	urge	would like

The verbs in group 4e behave differently from those in 4a–4d. These verbs usually require a noun or pronoun and then an infinitive. Notice that many of the verbs in this group are words that mean "to ask or tell someone to do something."

This group is important because some of these verbs are used very frequently. Interference from ELLs' native language is often problematic here. Many languages use a different pattern with these verbs, and a very common ELL error is *I want that you call me* instead of *I want you to call me*.

Examples:

wrong: I would like that you help me tonight.

correct: I would like you to help me tonight.

wrong: She asked that Kevin lends her some money.

correct: She asked Kevin to lend her some money.

wrong: The president told that the soldiers do their best.

correct: The president told the soldiers to do their best.

wrong: The boss persuaded that we attend next week's meeting.

correct: The boss persuaded us to attend next week's meeting.

One of the most common ELL errors (especially in ELLs who speak French or Spanish) is putting a **that-clause after verbs** that express a command or a strong desire such as *want, tell, ask, need,* and *would like*. **I want that you call me* should be *I want you to call me*. **The boss needs that we are here at 8 AM* should be *The boss needs us to be here at 8 AM*. **The captain told that the soldiers stand up* should be *The captain told the soldiers to stand up*. Example sentences with these key verbs should be on the classroom walls.

Group 4f. Four Special Verbs: *make, let, have, help*	
make:	She *made* the children **eat** their vegetables.
let:	She *let* the children **play** outside.
have:	She *had* the children **do** their homework first.
help:	Can you *help* me **carry** these boxes to the basement?
NOTE: The verb *help* also allows an infinitive (with no change in meaning). Can you *help* me **to carry** these boxes to the basement?	

To **have someone do something** means that someone else does the work for you because you paid the person, because you have power (e.g., mother – daughter), or because you asked the person to do the work. ELLs are confused by this structure because it is yet another meaning of **have** and is followed by some rather complex grammar.

Group 4f includes *make, let, have,* and *help*. These verbs are different in that they are usually followed by a noun or pronoun and then the base form of the verb. These four verbs are extremely common in spoken English, so they deserve extra attention in your lessons.

10.B.5. Gerunds Following Prepositions

Prepositions are followed by nouns (or pronouns). If the object of a preposition is an action (verb), then you must use a gerund, which is the noun form of a verb. The use of preposition + gerund is a very common structure in English. (See Key 6.) Study these examples:

Group 5. Gerunds after Prepositions
Thank you **for doing** this favor for me.
They always argue **about spending** too much money.
The president is not in favor **of traveling** to that area now.
The children kept **on talking**.

Common ELL Mistakes: What Your ELLs Should Know

1. Do not use infinitives after verbs that take gerunds (and vice versa).

    wrong: Many parents avoid to give sweets to their kids.

    correct: Many parents avoid giving sweets to their kids.

2. The most common verb form for the subject of a sentence is a gerund.

    wrong: Drive to Boston is more dangerous than fly there.

    uncommon: To drive to Boston is more dangerous than to fly there.

    correct: Driving to Boston is more dangerous than flying there.

3. Don't use a plural verb form with a gerund or infinitive as subject. Don't be tricked by a plural object after the gerund. The object of a gerund does not affect the verb.

    wrong: Eating green vegetables are good for your health.

    correct: Eating green vegetables is good for your health.

10.C. Native Language Interference:
Compare English with Other Languages

Language	Notes on *Infinitives and Gerunds*
All Languages	1. In English, some verbs are followed by infinitives (*want* **to read** *it,* *need* **to read** *it,* *refuse* **to read** *it*), and others are followed by gerunds (*enjoy* **reading** *it, finish* **reading** *it, postpone* **reading** *it*). No other language requires this grammatical distinction. 2. With this grammar point, ELLs of all first language backgrounds are at an equal disadvantage because there is no possibility of positive transfer from their native language to English. Common errors include **I want reading it* or **I enjoy to read it* or even **I like read it.* 3. In English, modals are followed by simple forms of the verb (*can read it, will read it, must read it*). Especially after studying gerunds and infinitives, ELLs are likely to experience interference and produce utterances such as **I can to read it* or **I can reading it.*
Arabic Chinese Japanese Korean Russian	These languages generally allow verbs to occur back to back without any special marking. In some of these languages, an English sentence with three verbs where the second one is an infinitive and the third is a gerund (*I want to enjoy sitting on the beach*) may be rendered as series of unmarked verb forms **I want enjoy sit on the beach.*
French Spanish	1. In these two languages, the most common verb form for the second and third verbs in a sequence is the infinitive, so errors may include overuse of the infinitive **I want to enjoy to sit on the beach* and the more universal series of unmarked verb forms **I want enjoy sit on the beach.* 2. ELLs of these languages overuse *that*-clauses instead of infinitives when the first verb expresses a command or strong desire. Common errors include **I want that you help me* or **She told that I arrive at noon.*

10.D. Ideas for Teaching

The basic teaching objective here is to train ELLs to know when a verb is followed by an infinitive and when it is followed by a gerund. To be sure, there are other points, but this is the main question, so most of your instruction will revolve around this single issue.

Early in their English study, ELLs use *–ing* verb forms in present progressive tense: *I am eating; he is sleeping.* This is not a gerund, but rather a present participle. In this case, the *–ing* is used as part of the verb. A gerund is an *–ing* form used as a noun: *I like swimming; swimming is fun.* The label is not important (to me), but you need to be aware that your students may think they know what a gerund is when you first present it, but they do not. They are mistakenly assuming that this is previous knowledge.

ELLs have learned VERB + infinitive as their default setting: *I want to go, I need to go, I plan to go.* This is so ingrained that it explains why when ELLs are introduced to modals such as *can* and *will,* they default to **I can to go* and **I will to go.* Thus, between VERB + infinitive and VERB + gerund, the harder one will be the second one. ELLs already default to the infinitive. In fact, the most common ELL beginning-level error is to put only the base form of a verb: **I want go, *I enjoy go,* and a common intermediate error is to opt for the infinitive, which is correct in some cases, *I want to go, *I enjoy to go.*

When I teach a new word to beginners that I know is followed by gerunds, I teach them that the new verb is followed immediately by VERB + *–ing.* For example, when I teach the word *enjoy* to beginners, I explain the word and then I write on the board *enjoy* + VERB + *–ing* and give a short example, *I enjoy watching TV.* I tell students to memorize that formula. I make them write it in their notebooks.

At the intermediate level, ELLs are introduced to the concept that some verbs are followed by infinitives and others by gerunds. You will need to teach the lists, which can be a rather monotonous task for the students and for you. For the initial teaching at this level, I like to create a "need to know" moment by starting with a pre-test. On the board, I write six examples and ask the students to complete the sentence with either *do, to do,* or *doing.* (I include *do*—not because it will be correct but rather because I want students to see that we do not use their default of a base form of a verb here.)

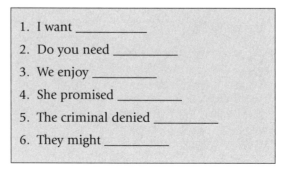

1. I want _____
2. Do you need _____
3. We enjoy _____
4. She promised _____
5. The criminal denied _____
6. They might _____

Most students at this level will get two to four correct. This tells them that they do not know this material and need to pay attention to the rest of your lesson. You have piqued their curiosity. This general teaching technique of issuing a challenge can be used in teaching any grammar point. (See Teaching Technique 21.)

At this point, I would review the group of verbs (in your ELL grammar book) that take infinitives. Ask students how many of the verbs are new to them. There will be only a few that are unfamiliar to the students (because many high-frequency verbs are in this group and are therefore known vocabulary items). Do the practice activities in the book.

Problems will rarely occur until you teach the second group of verbs, those that take gerunds. Ask students about unfamiliar verbs. There should be a pretty good number, including *avoid, deny, dread,* etc. Do the practice activities in the book.

When you practice the two groups together, this is the first real problem for many ELLs because they now have to make a choice between an infinitive or a gerund. In other words, you have moved away from the "safety" provided by simple controlled exercises. A good practice activity for this discrimination involves flash cards. In essence, it is a drill.

You could also do a language drill by saying, *I* and a verb, and then letting the students add *doing* or *to do.* The fourth example is more complicated, so you may wish to use only the simpler first three with some classes. (See Teaching Technique 4.)

T: I enjoy	C: I enjoy doing
T: I want	C: I want to do
T: I need	C: I need to do
T: I dread / need	C: I dread needing to do

At the advanced level, ELLs consolidate their knowledge of all the aspects of this grammar point. At this level, ELLs should be required to show sentence variety in their writing by including gerunds as subjects as well as VERB + gerund constructions in their sentences. To reduce your work load, have students underline these assigned constructions in their papers. This requirement helps ELLs identify their target structures and lightens your search for them as you read your students' papers.

ELL Grammar Key 11:
Phrasal Verbs

At some point around the eighth grade, native English speakers are taught—incorrectly—that the word *up* in the sentence *Luke came up with the correct answer* is an adverb. This is wrong. To be sure, *up* can be an adverb, as in *Luke put his hands up.* However, in the phrase *come up with,* meaning "to provide," the correct way to analyze this sentence is to acknowledge that we do not have three separate words *come* and *up* and *with.* Instead, we have one phrase, *come up with.* This combination is called a **phrasal verb**. Native speakers have no problem using *come up with,* but phrasal verbs are one of a non-native speaker's biggest challenges. In fact, after more than three decades of language study and teaching, I consider phrasal verb and present perfect tense to be the two most difficult areas of English for ELLs.

Phrasal verbs are also called **two-word verbs** or **three-word verbs**. The more generic term *phrasal verb* may be less daunting to ELLs.

Consider the example, *Luke put his hands up.* Word order in English is usually pretty rigid, so you cannot say *book read yesterday I the* instead of *I read the book yesterday.* Here, however, you can say *put your hands up* or *put up your hands,* but why is this flexibility in word order possible? If you use the pronoun *them* for *your hands,* then by extension, you should be able to say *put them up* or *put up them,* but only the first is possible. Can you figure out why? (Note that this last sentence also contains the phrasal verb *figure out.*) The answer is in Key 11.

11.A. Typical ELL Errors: Noticing the Gap

Can you identify and explain these five common ELL errors with this grammar point?

1. *When you finish with the sugar, please put back in the cabinet next to the refrigerator.*
2. *When they ran out money, Jill and Ann could not play the video game any more.*
3. *In yesterday's race, Joseph got off to a very bad start, and he had to work extra hard to catch up the other runners.*
4. *If you make a mistake in filling the application out, just cross out it and write the correct information above.*
5. *My little sister told my mom, "Mom, make José decrease the volume of the TV!"*

11.B. Grammar Explanation

11.B.1. The Form of Phrasal Verbs: VERB + Particle

A **phrasal verb** consists of a verb followed by a **particle** (or a preposition or an adverb) such as *after, away, back, over, in, into, out, on, off, up,* or *down.*

> *Example*: He didn't *turn off* the light.

In this sentence, the word *turn* is not enough to express the meaning of the sentence. It is necessary to have both *turn* and *off*. In addition, the meaning of *turn off* is not equal to the meaning of *turn* plus the meaning of *off*. *Turn off* is a phrasal verb. Other common examples of phrasal verbs are *call up, put on, call on,* and *look after.*

ELLs avoid using phrasal verbs first because they do not know about their existence and then because they appear to be more difficult. For every phrasal verb, there is almost always a single-word equivalent in a dictionary. These single-word equivalents are often of Latin origin and tend to be used in modern English in more technical or formal situations while phrasal verbs are often of Anglo–Saxon origin (meaning they are from the original English before Latin and French words were introduced) and are very common in spoken English. For example, you might ask someone, *Could you **put out** that cigarette?* but in the days when smoking was allowed on flights, the safety card said, *In the event that oxygen masks appear, please **extinguish** all smoking materials.* If a child is sick, the doctor will ask, *Did you **throw up**?* but the bottle of medicine will say, *Children: This medicine may cause young children to **vomit**.*

Consider the two sentences *She ran up the hill* and *She ran up the bill*:

Sentence	Meaningful Parts
(1) *She ran up the hill.*	She + ran + up the hill. SUBJ VERB PREP. PHRASE
(2) *She ran up the bill.*	She + ran up + the bill. SUBJ VERB DIR. OBJ

Can you understand why only the second sentence has a phrasal verb? In the first sentence, the sentence can be divided into three parts: *She* (subject) + *ran* (verb) + *up the hill* (prepositional phrase telling where she ran). The three parts of the second sentence are: *She* (subject) + *ran up* (phrasal verb meaning "to increase"), and *the bill* (direct object).

> There is no compelling reason to use the term **particle**—or any grammar label for that matter. Instead, simply make reference to phrasal verbs or verbs and prepositions or use no label if you wish. No one knows your students better than you do, so you decide which terminology to use or not to use. (See Teaching Technique 5 in Chapter 5.)

If you have ELLs who speak Spanish, French, Portuguese, or Italian—which are languages from Latin—these ELLs are more likely to use a Latin-based word than a phrasal verb. Not using phrasal verbs makes an ELL's English sound strange. A native speaker might say, *I need to look into the price of a hotel room,* but an ELL would most likely say, *I need to investigate the price of a hotel room.*

Phrasal Verbs and Single-Word Equivalents	
Phrasal Verb (Anglo–Saxon, informal to neutral tone)	*Single-Word Equivalent* (Latin, more formal tone)
put out	extinguish
throw up	vomit
look into	investigate
put off	postpone
take off	remove
show up	appear
put in	install
think over	consider
find out	discover

11.B.2. The Difficulty of Phrasal Verbs

For ELLs, phrasal verbs cause special problems in both grammar and vocabulary. To begin with, phrasal verbs are extremely common. They are used in both speaking and writing, and because they are verbs and verbs are so important, phrasal verbs often determine the meaning of an entire sentence or utterance. Consider the sentence *He should put _____ the lamp.* Notice how the meaning changes dramatically by adding *in, out, on, off, up, down, away,* or *back.* If he puts the lamp **on,** we have light, but if he puts **out** the lamp, there is no light. The phrasal verb controls the meaning of the sentence.

ELLs are surprised by the mere existence of phrasal verbs because very few other languages have phrasal verbs. ELLs need to understand that sometimes multiple words are needed to express the idea of one action. ELLs are probably accustomed to the idea that a noun can have several components, such as *the downtown bus station,* but the notion that a verb might have multiple parts is bizarre to say the least. In English, we don't usually say, *What time did you* **wake** *today?* but rather *What time did you* **wake up** *today?* We need a phrasal verb here, not just a single-word verb. Native speakers would never use just *wake* here; instead, they would use *wake up* (or *get up*). We don't say, **They ran of money* or **They ran out money* but rather *They ran out of money.* Here the phrasal verb *run out of* requires three words.

Another confusing aspect is that phrasal verbs come in two types: **separable** and **non–separable.** For separable phrasal verbs, the second part (i.e., the particle) can "float" when the object is a noun: *write down a number* OR *write a number down.* There is no difference in meaning or accuracy of these two interchangeable forms. However, when we change *a number* to the pronoun *it,* we do not have the same two options. We can say *write it down* but not **write down it.*

With the second type of phrasal verbs, which are called non–separable phrasal verbs, the phrasal verb can never be separated: *look after the baby* but not **look the baby after, look after her* but never **look her after.*

Although phrasal verbs do present grammatical challenges, by far the most common ELL errors with phrasal verbs are semantic (i.e., vocabulary) mistakes, which indicates that ELLs need to focus more on the meaning of phrasal verbs. Phrasal verbs are usually idiomatic, which means that the meanings of the individual words do not add up to the meaning of the whole phrasal verb. How could an ELL know that *take up* means to begin a new activity, as in the sentence *I took up tennis in college?* The meanings of *take* and *up* in no way equal or even hint at this meaning of *take up.* Further complicating the situation for ELLs is the fact that phrasal verbs are often **polysemous,** that is, they have multiple meanings. The phrasal verb *take up* has at least seven different meanings:

> Words have **multiple meanings.** *Take* can mean "grab" (*take a pen*), "use" (*take a bus*), "consume" (*take an aspirin*), etc. **Polysemous** words cause problems for ELLs because of the multiple meanings.

Polysemy of *Take Up*	
Meanings	*Examples*
1. reduce in size; alter	*Please **take up** these pants.*
2. begin again	*We'll **take up** where we left off.*
3. consume	*Buying a car **took up** all my savings.*
4. develop an interest in something new	*I **took up** tennis in college.*
5. absorb, internalize	*A sponge **takes up** water.*
6. accept a challenge or offer	*We **took up** his offer in 2008.*
7. deal with, work with	*Let's **take up** these issues one at a time.*

A much more thorough discussion of these and other problems that phrasal verbs pose for ELLs can be found in *Vocabulary Myths: Applying Second Language Research to Classroom Teaching* (Folse, 2004, pp. 5–8, 101–6).

11.B.3. Separable Phrasal Verbs

The phrasal verbs in this group can be separated when there is a noun object. For example, you can say, *call up Mike* or *call Mike up*. If there is a pronoun object, the phrasal verb *must* be separated. You have to say, *call him up*, never **call up him*.

Note that many of these expressions have multiple meanings. In the chart that follows, only the most common meanings are included for the purposes of this grammar lesson. You should provide your ELLs with relevant examples to help them remember the meanings. Be sure they pay close attention to the separation patterns for noun objects and pronoun objects.

Separable Phrasal Verbs				
Phrasal Verb	**No. 1 VERB + NOUN**	**No. 2 Separated by NOUN**	**No. 3 VERB + PRONOUN**	**No. 4 Separated by PRONOUN**
call back (return a call)	*call back John*	*call John back*	~~*call back him*~~	*call him back*
call off (cancel)	*call off the game*	*call the game off*	~~*call off it*~~	*call it off*
call up (telephone)	*call up the teacher*	*call the teacher up*	~~*call up her*~~	*call her up*
cross out (draw a line through)	*cross out the mistake*	*cross the mistake out*	~~*cross out it*~~	*cross it out*
figure out (find the answer to a problem)	*figure out the answer*	*figure the answer out*	~~*figure out it*~~	*figure it out*
fill in (write information)	*fill in the blank*	*fill the blank in*	~~*fill in it*~~	*fill it in*
fill out (complete a paper)	*fill out the form*	*fill the form out*	~~*fill out it*~~	*fill it out*
find out (get information)	*find out the price*	*find the price out*	~~*find out it*~~	*find it out*

give away (give something to someone)	*give away the prize*	*give the prize away*	~~*give away it*~~	*give it away*
give back (return something to someone)	*give back the reward*	*give the reward back*	~~*give back it*~~	*give it back*
hand in (submit)	*hand in my paper*	*hand my paper in*	~~*hand in it*~~	*hand it in*
hand out (give one to everyone)	*hand out the papers*	*hand the papers out*	~~*hand out them*~~	*hand them out*
leave out (omit)	*leave out the sentence*	*leave the sentence out*	~~*leave out it*~~	*leave it out*
look up (look for information)	*look up this word*	*look this word up*	~~*look up it*~~	*look it up*
make up (invent a story)	*make up a story*	*make a story up*	~~*make up one*~~	*make one up*
pick up (1. lift; 2. go get someone)	*pick up my son*	*pick my son up*	~~*pick up him*~~	*pick him up*
put away (return to the correct place)	*put away the clothes*	*put the clothes away*	~~*put away them*~~	*put them away*
put back (return to the original place)	*put back the boxes*	*put the boxes back*	~~*put back them*~~	*put them back*
put off (postpone)	*put off the test*	*put the test off*	~~*put off it*~~	*put it off*
put on (wear)	*put on your coat*	*put your coat on*	~~*put on it*~~	*put it on*
put out (extinguish)	*put out the fire*	*put the fire out*	~~*put out it*~~	*put it out*

take off (remove)	*take off your shoes*	*take your shoes off*	~~take off them~~	*take them off*
tear up (rip into small pieces)	*tear up the bill*	*tear the bill up*	~~tear up it~~	*tear it up*
throw away (discard, put in the trash)	*throw away the bag*	*throw the bag away*	~~throw away it~~	*throw it away*
try on (check to see if clothing fits)	*try on those shoes*	*try those shoes on*	~~try on them~~	*try them on*
turn down (decrease)	*turn down the radio*	*turn the radio down*	~~turn down it~~	*turn it down*
turn on (start)	*turn on the lights*	*turn the lights on*	~~turn them on~~	*turn them on*
turn off (stop)	*turn off the TV*	*turn the TV off*	~~turn off it~~	*turn it off*
turn up (increase)	*turn up the volume*	*turn the volume up*	~~turn up it~~	*turn it up*
wake up (stop sleeping)	*wake up the baby*	*wake the baby up*	~~wake up him~~	*wake him up*
write down (make a note of something)	*write down the name*	*write the name down*	~~write down it~~	*write it down*

REMEMBER: The phrasal verbs in the separable group have three possible grammatical forms:

- phrasal verb + noun object (No. 1.), *I called up John.*
- phrasal verb separated by noun object (No. 2), *I called John up.*
- phrasal verb separated by pronoun object (No. 4), *I called him up.*

A common ELL error is to assume that you can follow these verbs by a pronoun object (No. 3). They produce sentences such as **I called up him* and **The teacher put off it.*

11.B.4. Non–Separable Phrasal Verbs

In this group, the verb and the particle are always together, with the verb first and then the noun (or pronoun) object afterward. Some students find this group much easier than the separable ones because the word order is the regular English word order of subject-verb-object. In other words, nothing moves.

Non–separable phrasal verbs have only two patterns: verb plus noun object (No. 1) and verb plus pronoun object (No. 3). Some of the verbs in this group have three words. Three-word phrasal verbs are always non–separable. For example, *The car ran out of gas* is correct, but *The car ran out gas of* is wrong.

Non–Separable Phrasal Verbs				
Phrasal Verb	**No. 1 VERB + NOUN**	**No. 2 Separated by NOUN**	**No. 3 VERB + PRONOUN**	**No. 4 Separated by PRONOUN**
call on (ask a question in class)	*call on the student*	~~*call the student on*~~	*call on him*	~~*call him on*~~
catch up (with) (reach the same level or position as)	*catch up with the others*	~~*catch with the others up*~~	*catch up with them*	~~*catch with them up*~~
check into (1. register at a hotel; 2. investigate)	*check into the hotel*	~~*check the hotel into*~~	*check into it*	~~*check it into*~~
come across (find by chance)	*come across a wallet*	~~*come a wallet across*~~	*come across it*	~~*come it across*~~
count on (depend on)	*count on your help*	~~*count your help on*~~	*count on it*	~~*count it on*~~
get along (with) (be friends with)	*get along with some-one*	~~*get with someone along*~~	*get along with her*	~~*get with him along*~~
get in (enter)	*get in a car*	~~*get a car in*~~	*get in it*	~~*get it in*~~
get off (exit)	*get off a bus*	~~*get a bus off*~~	*get off it*	~~*get it off*~~
get on (enter)	*get on a plane*	~~*get a plane on*~~	*get on it*	~~*get it on*~~

get out of (exit)	*get out of a taxi*	~~*get of a taxi out*~~	get out of it	~~*get of it out*~~
get over (recover from an illness or a problem)	*get over a cold*	~~*get a cold over*~~	get over it	~~*get it over*~~
get through (complete)	*get through the exam*	~~*get the exam through*~~	get through it	~~*get it through*~~
go over (review or check carefully)	*go over the test*	~~*go the test over*~~	go over it	~~*get it over*~~
look after (take care of)	*look after the baby*	~~*look the baby after*~~	look after him	~~*look him after*~~
look out (for) (be careful)	*look out for that car*	~~*look for that car out*~~	look out for it	~~*look for it out*~~
put up with (tolerate, stand)	*put up with that noise*	~~*put with that noise up*~~	put up with it	~~*put with it up*~~
run into (meet by chance)	*run into an old friend*	~~*run an old friend into*~~	run into her	~~*run her into*~~
run out (of) (not have any more)	*run out of gas*	~~*run of gas out*~~	run out of it	~~*run of it out*~~
watch out (for) (be careful)	*watch out for that dog*	~~*watch for that dog out*~~	watch out for it	~~*watch for it out*~~

REMEMBER: The phrasal verbs in the non–separable group have only two possible grammatical forms:

- phrasal verb + noun object (No. 1)   *The teacher went over the notes.*
- phrasal verb + pronoun object (No. 3)   *The teacher went over them.*

A common ELL error is to assume that you need to separate the phrasal verb (based on what we saw in the previous group—the separable phrasal verbs). ELLs may produce sentences such as *The teacher went the notes over* (No. 2) and *The teacher went them over* (No. 4).

11.B.5. Phrasal Verbs without Objects (Intransitive)

Some phrasal verbs are intransitive, which means that they never have an object. These intransitive verbs consist of just a verb and a particle. An example is *pass away,* meaning "to die." It is possible to say, *Mrs. Riley passed away,* but it is not possible to say, *Mrs. Riley passed away her* or **Mrs. Riley passed her away.*

This chart demonstrates that no object comes after these intransitive phrasal verbs. Of course, an adverb of time (*yesterday*) or a prepositional phrase *(in her house)* is possible with any kind of verb: *She passed away in her house yesterday.* However, there is no noun or pronoun object that serves as a direct object of the verb.

Intransitive Phrasal Verbs with Examples		
Phrasal Verb		**VERB + No Object**
break down	(stop functioning)	My car *broke down.*
break up	(end a relationship)	Susan and Jack *broke up.*
catch on	(begin to understand)	It took me a long time to *catch on.*
come on	(go faster)	*Come on!* We're going to be late.
eat out	(eat at a restaurant)	It's expensive to *eat out* every day.
get up	(leave bed)	What time do you usually *get up?*
give up	(stop trying)	I was learning French, but I *gave up.*
go off	(make a noise)	My alarm *went off* at 6:30.
grow up	(become an adult)	I *grew up* in Canada.
hold on	(wait)	*Hold on* a minute.
hurry up	(go faster)	*Hurry up* or we'll be late.
keep on	(continue)	Mike *kept on* talking.
show up	(arrive, appear at a place)	Not many people *showed up.*
slow down	(go more slowly)	Please *slow down.*
take off	(leave the ground)	The plane didn't *take off* on time.
wake up	(stop sleeping)	I *woke up* when I heard the noise.

Common ELL Mistakes: What Your ELLs Should Know

1. Do not avoid using phrasal verbs. The single-word alternatives found in a dictionary often sound more technical or formal than the equivalent phrasal verb.

    too formal: Excuse me. How can I ascertain which bus goes to Jensen Stadium?

    correct: Excuse me. How can I find out which bus goes to Jensen Stadium?

2. Do not confuse the meanings of phrasal verbs.

    wrong: The coach put down the game because of the bad weather.

    correct: The coach called off the game because of the bad weather.

3. Do not forget to use the whole phrasal verb, not just the verb.

    wrong: My husband picked me at the airport last night.

    correct: My husband picked me up at the airport last night.

4. Do not forget to separate separable phrasal verbs when there is a pronoun object.

    wrong: If you make a mistake on the application, just cross out it and write the correct information above.

    correct: If you make a mistake on the application, just cross it out and write the correct information above.

11.C. Native Language Interference: Compare English with Other Languages

Language	Notes on *Phrasal Verbs*
Arabic **Chinese** **French** **Japanese** **Korean** **Russian** **Spanish**	None of these languages has phrasal verbs, so the whole concept of phrasal verbs is new to most ELLs. Phrasal verbs are very difficult for all ELLs, and many ELLs avoid phrasal verbs completely. (Speakers of Germanic languages such as German, Swedish, Danish, Norwegian, and Icelandic may have fewer difficulties since these languages have phrasal verbs. However, verbs that are phrasal verbs in English may not be phrasal verbs in these languages.)

11.D. Ideas for Teaching

Some teachers wonder why phrasal verbs are in ELL grammar books. In fact, some grammar series do not deal much with phrasal verbs because phrasal verbs are more of a vocabulary learning task than a grammar issue for ELLs.

The grammar component to phrasal verbs involves separability. In my opinion, this is not a serious error, and I would spend much more time practicing the phrasal verbs in sentences so that learners can get a better sense of both meaning and the word order than focusing on separability options.

Phrasal verbs are used from the very beginning of instruction in the English class. Five common examples that ELLs can understand when they hear them are *sit down, take out (a sheet of paper), fill in (the blank), pass out (the papers),* and *hand in (your homework).* If you ask an ELL who has not been instructed in these five examples to verbalize them on his or her own, the ELL would probably say *sit, take, fill, pass,* and *hand* (or *give).* If you told the student that we usually put a second word there, you might hear all sorts of guesses such as *sit up, take from, fill down, pass to,* and *hand to.* **My point is that passive understanding does not equal active production, so being able to comprehend a phrasal verb does not mean that ELLs "know" it.**

Passive understanding is a good first step, so one way to begin teaching or focusing student attention on phrasal verbs is by presenting a set of eight sentences on one topic that contain phrasal verbs. If your topic is sports, you could begin with these four sentences:

> 1. The coach called off the game due to lightning.
> 2. To join a gym, you have to fill out a membership form.
> 3. Many people take up a sport when they are in high school.
> 4. At 6 AM every morning, I wake up my son so we can go running together.

Ask the students some questions about your sentences: What is the overall topic? What does *fill out* mean? How many people have joined a gym? What time do you usually wake up? At this point, I ask the class to help me analyze the grammar of these sentences. I always tell students to find the verb of a sentence first. The verb is usually the easiest part to identify correctly, so everyone will be successful in this task, which in turn encourages more interaction. In addition, you want to train your students to identify and be able to avoid fragments, and identification of fragments depends heavily on being able to find the verb—if there is one (as there should be). Underline the main verbs in your sentences.

FIND OUT

Examine a 1,000-word excerpt of text written by a native speaker (e.g., from a newspaper or the Internet). Underline all phrasal verbs. Which phrasal verb is the most common? Is there a particle that is used more often? Predict which phrasal verbs are problematic for ELLs and which ones are not. Explain your predictions.

In Sentence 1, ELLs will identify *call*. Then put a box around the word *off*. Ask students if they think *off* goes more with *call* (as a unit) or with *the game*. After some discussion, most ELLs will say *call*, which is correct. Say, "Yes, that's right. *Call off* expresses one idea, but we write it with two words. It means *cancel—The coach canceled the game.*" Do Sentences 2 and 3 with the class helping you in the same manner. Maintain interaction. Then ask the class to do the rest of the sentences without your input.

Make a separate list (one column) at the end of the sentences. When you have finished, write the term **phrasal verb** at the top. You have now introduced your students to phrasal verbs.

	Phrasal Verb
1. The coach <u>called</u> off the game due to the lightning.	*call off*
2. To join a gym, you <u>fill</u> out a membership form.	*fill out*
3. Many people <u>take</u> up a sport when they are in high school.	*take up*
4. At 6 AM every morning, I <u>wake</u> up my son for our morning run.	*wake up*

At this point, you should do some simple practice exercises and then follow up with a more detailed explanation of phrasal verbs, including which verbs and which particles are commonly used. Students need a list of common phrasal verbs.

Once you have explained what a phrasal verb looks like and what it does—its form and its function—then it is time to tackle the issue of separability. You can either explain this directly, or if you have enough class time, you can ask students to make an attempt at deducing the rule on their own. For the former, use your textbook explanation. For the latter, give students 15–20 examples of phrasal verbs used correctly or incorrectly. These examples can be on a single worksheet, but if you want to turn this into a speaking task, put each example on a strip of paper. (You will need copies of the sentences for each pair or group of students.) The examples are marked with a check for correct and an X for incorrect.

> ✓ 1. Mary called up her best friend around midnight.
>
> X 2. Susan called up me last night.
>
> ✓ 3. He said the address, but I didn't write it down.
>
> X 4. "Class, here are the test dates. Please write down them."

In essence, you are giving your students **positive** and **negative evidence** of phrasal verb usage and you are asking them to try to figure out what the rules are. In the process, students may be practicing English, too, so it is a win-win situation. They are speaking English, and they are focusing on grammar.

ELL Grammar Key 12:
Modals

Modals are small but important words or phrases that allow the speaker or writer to include nuances of meaning for verbs. Consider the subtle but profound differences in meaning in these four statements: *I might go, I can go, I must go,* and *I should go.* Consider why it is that a parent can tell a child, *It's getting late, so you'd better finish your homework now,* but a child cannot in turn respond, *Well, it's almost dinner time, so you'd better get in the kitchen and cook something good.* (The answer is that *had better* is used only by persons of power or authority to subordinates.)

The grammar of all modals is fairly straightforward, but not all modals are acquired by ELLs quickly. The modal *can* is acquired correctly very early. The modal *will* is also learned early, but this modal is overused. ELLs tend to use *will* incorrectly for all future sentences (instead of *be going to*). For example, an ELL might ask, **What will you do tomorrow?* and another ELL may reply, **I will stay home.* Finally, some modals that have equally simple grammar such as *might* are hardly ever used by an ELL—correctly or incorrectly—even though these modals are just as easy to learn, grammatically speaking, as the others.

12.A. Typical ELL Errors: Noticing the Gap

Can you identify and explain these five common ELL errors with this grammar point?

1. It's noon. *I must meet Jack for lunch now. *Then I must go to the bank.
2. *Paul was happy because he could find his keys.
3. *A student wrote on the test paper, "Dear Teacher, you'd better give me an A."
4. The price tag on this radio says one dollar. *The price should be wrong.
5. *The government will to announce a new economic stimulus plan tomorrow.

12.B. Grammar Explanation

12.B.1. What Are Modals?

A modal verb is an auxiliary or helping verb that alters the meaning of the sentence by adding shades of meaning, or mood, to the main verb that it modifies. One way to explain modals to ELLs is to teach that modals add "flavor" to verbs to change the meaning. The ten most common modals in order of frequency are *would, will, can, could, may, must, should, might, ought to,* and *had better*. In the General Service List (West, 1953), *would, will,* and *can* are in the top 40 most common words in English.

In addition to single-word modals such as *will* and *can*, there are also modal phrases such as *be going to* for *will* (*He is going to arrive at noon; He will arrive at noon*) and *be able to* for *can* (*She is able to speak six languages; She can speak six languages*).

12.B.2. Why Are Modals Difficult for ELLs?

Modals present both vocabulary and grammar problems for ELLs. In terms of vocabulary, each of these modals is a completely different word. For some ELLs, their native language will have an equivalent word for the modal, but in other cases, it will not. For example, in Spanish, there is no word for *will* or *would*. Instead, these meanings are communicated through the use of verb **inflections**, which are changes in the endings of words *(he need<u>ed</u>, he need<u>s</u>)*.

A second vocabulary problem is that any modal can have multiple meanings that overlap with another modal. For example, *may* means possibility (e.g., *it may rain*), but it also means permission (e.g., *May I sit here?*). *Could* also means possibility (*it could rain*), but it also means polite request (*Could you help me?*) and past ability (*I couldn't find my keys*).

Grammatically speaking, modals present three problems. First, ELLs try to conjugate modals: *I can go; you can go; *he cans go*. For example, ELLs may say, *My brother cans help you* because *my brother* is third person singular, and its verb needs *–s* (*my brother helps, my brother goes, my brother takes*). Second, a modal is followed directly by a verb (*I can go, she might believe, they should stay*). In contrast, when a verb is followed by another verb, the second verb is often in the infinitive form (*I want to go, she needs to believe, they plan to stay*). Therefore, ELLs try to mimic this pattern and produce errors such as *I can to go, *she might to believe*, and **they should to stay*. A third but less common error occurs when negating and in questions when ELLs attempt to use the auxiliary *do*, as in *I don't should use Susan's cell phone* or *Do you can help me?*

> **The General Service List** (GSL) consists of 2,000 frequently used words that provide the greatest general service to ELLs. Published in its final form in 1953, this list has been influential because it was used to produce graded readers for many years. Though it was obviously not developed using modern corpus data or computers, the list is still fairly accurate today, with only a handful of its original 2,000 words not being useful in current language usage.

12.B.3. Two Ways that ELL Grammar Books Usually Present Modals

Textbooks generally take one of two approaches in presenting modals. One approach is to teach the modals one by one. Thus, the textbook will teach *can*, then *will*, etc. This approach is very clear for students and also later serves as a good reference source since ELLs can find information about any one modal very easily. The disadvantage to this approach is that modals usually share meanings. For example, after students study that *might* is for possibility, they will then see a few pages later that *may* and *can* are also used for possibility. In other words, a modal rarely has just one meaning, and rarely is one meaning expressed by only one modal. We can see this approach in this chart:

Organizing by Modal: Modals and Multiple Meanings		
Modal	**Meanings**	**Examples**
might	possibility	*A one-way ticket might cost more than $400.*
may	(1) possibility	*A one-way ticket may cost more than $400.*
	(2) permission	*May I sit here?*
can	(1) ability	*She can speak several languages fluently.*
	(2) permission	*Can I sit here? (informal)*
could	(1) polite request	*Could you tell me where the bank is?*
	(2) past ability	*When I was a child, I could run much faster.*
	(3) suggestion	*You could fly to New York. It's not so expensive now.*
	(4) conditional	*If I had a million dollars, I could travel anywhere.*
	(5) possibility	*Mark could be at work now, but I'm not sure.*

will	(1) future	*According to the report, the rain will be heavy.*
	(2) polite request	*Will you explain this grammar point to me again?*
would	(1) offering, inviting	*Would you like some tea?*
	(2) polite request	*Would you read this letter and give me your opinion?*
	(3) conditional	*If you received a hundred dollars from your father, what would you do?*
should / ought to	(1) advising, suggesting	*I like both shirts, but I think you should get the red one.*
	(2) expectation	*We ought to have 52 cards, but there are only 50.*
must	(1) obligation, necessity	*The rule book says that applicants must be at least 16 years old to apply for a license.*
	(2) conclusion	*The new library is huge. There must be thousands of books in it.*
had better	strong advice or warning	*You'd better leave now, or you'll miss the bus.*

Another approach is to group modals by meanings. Thus, the textbook will teach "modals that mean request," and "modals that mean permission." I favor the first approach for lower-proficiency students who are initially learning about modals and the second approach for more advanced students who are trying to consolidate knowledge. Lower-proficiency students are learning the modals as new words, for example, *might* = possibility. They need time to absorb this type of information. Higher-proficiency students, on the other hand, who are already familiar with *might, may,* and *could* are able to appreciate a lesson that starts out with *ways to express possibility* and then reviews and even ranks *might, may,* and *could* in terms of **degrees of possibility**. We can see this second approach on the chart on page 228.

Organizing by Meaning: Modals and Multiple Meanings		
Meanings	**Modals**	**Examples**
request	**can**	*Can you tell me where the bank is?*
	could	*Could you tell me where the bank is?*
	would	*Would you read this letter and give me your opinion?*
	may	*May I have your full name?*
	might	*Might I offer you some tea?*
permission	**can**	*Can I sit here? (informal)*
	could	*Could I sit here?*
	would	*Would you mind if I sit here?*
	may	*May I sit here?*
necessity	**must, have to**	*The rule book says that applicants must be at least 16 years old to apply for a license.*
possibility	**may, might, could**	*A one-way ticket may cost more than $400. (50% chance)*
	should, ought to	*A one-way ticket should cost more than $400. (better chance)*
	must	*A one-way ticket must cost more than $400. (almost certain)*
	will	*A one-way ticket will cost more than $400. (definite)*
advisability	**should, ought to**	*I like both shirts, but I think you should get the red one.*
	had better	*You'd better leave now, or you'll miss the bus.*
expectation	**should, ought to**	*We should have 52 cards, but there are only 50.*
conclusion	**must**	*The new library is huge. There must be thousands of books in it.*

Common ELL Mistakes: What Your ELLs Should Know

1. Do not use **to** after single-word modals.

   wrong: Andrea should to study more.

   correct: Andrea should study more.

2. Do not add any endings (**–s**, **–ed**, or **–ing**) to verbs after modals.

   wrong: Shawn will helps Jim with the work.

   correct: Shawn will help Jim with the work.

3. Do not use **don't, doesn't**, or **didn't** to make negative forms of modals. Most modals form the negative by adding **not** after the modal. (This is just like with **be** and other auxiliary verbs.)

   wrong: Kathy doesn't can speak Japanese well.

   correct: Kathy can't speak Japanese well.

4. Do not use **do, does**, or **did** in a question with a modal. Most modals form the question by inverting the subject and the modal. (This is just like with **be** and other auxiliary verbs.)

   wrong: Do you could help me with this homework?

   correct: Could you help me with this homework?

5. Do not use **could** for past ability if it is a single past action in an affirmative sentence. In this case, we use **was able to** or **were able to**. In a negative sentence, **couldn't** and **wasn't** or **weren't able to** are okay. We only use **could** for the past of **can** when the action was over a period of time.

   wrong: *Ann:* Did you find your wallet?

             Sue: Yes, I could find it.

   correct: *Sue:* Yes, I **was able to** find it. It was under the bed!

             OR Yes, I **found** it. It was under the bed!

   For a negative answer, both are possible:

             Sue: No, I **wasn't able to** find it.

             OR No, I **couldn't** find it.

12.C. Native Language Interference: Compare English with Other Languages

Language	Notes on *Modals*
Arabic **Chinese** **French** **Japanese** **Korean** **Russian** **Spanish**	1. All languages are able to express the ideas associated with modals such as possibility (*may, might, could*), ability (*can, could*), advisability (*should*), obligation (*must*), and intention (*will*). Some languages have words for some of these concepts while other languages use a combination of separate words and some word endings. 2. Modals present a very complex vocabulary problem for ELLs. Even with languages that have words that appear to have similar meanings for certain English modals, there is rarely a one-to-one correspondence between these words. For example, *must* in English has at least two separate meanings: *conclusion* and *obligation*. Other languages may require two (or more) different words or word endings to express these meanings.

FIND OUT

How common are modals? Many people mistakenly believe that modals are relatively rare and are used for only certain kinds of writing. Look up any animal in an encyclopedia such as an online source. How many and which modals do you find in the article? What are the meanings of the modals that you find? Keep an inventory.

12.D. Ideas for Teaching

How you teach modals will depend on whether your students are beginning, intermediate, or advanced learners.

A beginning lesson would focus on only one modal per lesson. Modals taught early usually include *can, will,* and *should*. Each modal would be taught separately from the others. For these, you would cover typical ELL grammatical mistakes such as adding *–s (I can, you can, *it cans)* or adding *to (*I can to go, *you will to do)*.

At the intermediate level, ELLs are familiar with some of the modals and some of their meanings. Your syllabus might include some of the more difficult modals, such as *might, must,* and *could*, as well as the finer details about modals, such as: *must* has two meanings and the most important one is conclusion, not necessity; *could* is not used for single affirmative accomplishments; and *could* means more than the past of *can* (e.g., it can mean probability).

At the advanced level, you should introduce the past modals: *could have gone, should have written,* etc. Teaching the present modals is easy. In some ways, it is like teaching new vocabulary, which sometimes has multiple meanings, where you define the words, give examples, and provide students with practice. With the past modals, setting up contexts for examples and then providing meaningful student practice is more difficult and more time-consuming.

Most ELL textbooks offer straightforward information on teaching modals. There is usually so much to cover that teachers have little time to do anything else. However, I would spend time drilling the patterns because modals are a very important part of English. Modals are important to our ELLs because modals help "soften" a person's speech. Sometimes native speakers perceive the tone of our ELLs as rude or overly aggressive, and this is often because our ELLs don't use modals. Instead of saying the more usual *You might talk to the other teacher* as a suggestion, an ELL might say, *You need to talk to other teacher,* which sounds more like a demand and maybe even reprimand, which was not the ELL's intention. (Remember that they do not realize that it sounds that way to native speakers.)

Why should we do language drills? Our students make mistakes such as, *I am take the bus to school every day* because they have internalized *I am* from all the practice that they have had with this is in their beginning-level classes. You should aim for the same goal with *I can, I should,* and *I might.* Students need to retrieve and use these as chunks instead of having to think to themselves "Which modal means ability? *Can? Could? May?"* Here are three examples of drills that increase in difficulty:

> For some unknown reason, ELLs rarely use the model **might,** but natives use it a lot. Instead, ELLs tend to overuse *maybe,* with an occasional *perhaps.* As you read your ELLs' essays or listen to their conversations, notice how rarely the modal *might* is used.

Drill 1: Subject Change	
T: I should go.	*C:* I should go
T: she	*C:* she should go
T: Larry and Joe	*C:* Larry and Joe should go

Drill 2: Modal Change	
T: I should go.	*C:* I should go
T: can	*C:* I can go
T: will	*C:* I will go

Drill 3: Substitution (students make a change to previous sentence)	
T: I should go.	*C:* I should go
T: she	*C:* she should go
T: take	*C:* she should take
T: can	*C:* she can take
T: we	*C:* we can take
T: not	*C:* we cannot take
T: stay	*C:* we cannot stay

ELL Grammar Key 13:
Word Forms

In English, there are dozens of word endings, or **suffixes,** that can change one part of speech into another, as *–ize* changes an adjective into a verb (*legal* → *legalize*) and *–ment* transforms a verb into a noun (*enjoy* → *enjoyment*). For ELLs (and for native speaking children), word endings are not so straightforward and thus require effort to be learned.

One reason for this difficulty is that there are dozens of such suffixes that ELLs must learn. Nouns can end in *–tion*, verbs can end in *–ize*, adverbs can end in *–ly*, and adjectives can end in *–ful*.

A much more daunting challenge for ELLs is that there is never one way to change a given part of speech into another. Consider, for instance, how we form adjectives. Yes, we can use *–ful* to change a noun into an adjective (*beauty* → *beautiful*), but we also have as many as nine other endings to make adjectives from nouns, including *–ous* (*danger*→*dangerous*), *–ic* (*hero*→*heroic*), *–an* (*Italy*→*Italian*), *–y* (*rain*→*rainy*), *–al* (*season*→*seasonal*), and *–ive* (*expense*→*expensive*).

There is no way for ELLs to predict that *danger* becomes *dangerous* any more than they can predict that we do not say **dangerful*, **dangeric*, or **dangerive*. A good initial learning goal is that ELLs will be able to recognize the part of speech of a word by using its suffix. A later goal is that ELLs will be able to produce correct forms of a given word by adding the correct suffix. Thus, at least initially, knowledge of word endings can only be used one way: to decipher an already existing word by using its base and any word parts (but not to know which suffix to add to a base word to create a correct English word). Word form knowledge helps with decoding words, but it has limited value in forming new words.

13.A. Typical ELL Errors: Noticing the Gap

Can you identify and explain these five common ELL errors with this grammar point?

1. *Members of the book club automatically receive preferentially prices.
2. *Siberia has a substantial number of nature resources.
3. *Second language readers' very limited vocabulary knowledge hinders their ability to make fully use of context clues as well.
4. *Politics debates are part of the democratic process.
5. *Olympic clocks must be very accuracy to be useful.

13.B. Grammar Explanation

13.B.1. The Importance of Word Endings

Certain word endings, or suffixes, can be used to create new grammatical forms of a word. Thus, these new words have a meaning similar to the original word, but the function, or part of speech, will change. For example, the adjective *final* becomes a verb by adding **–ize:** *finalize.*

ADJECTIVE
|

By the *final* week of school, we were ready for a vacation.

VERB
|

Please call Global Travel so we can *finalize* our vacation plans.

Suffixes can be used to create four of the eight parts of speech, namely verbs, adjectives, adverbs, and nouns.

Verb	Adjective	Adverb	Noun
finalize	*final*	*finally*	*finalization*

13.B.2. Verb Endings

Word Endings for Verbs		
Ending	**Meaning**	**Example**
–ate	to cause, to become, to supply with	*motivate, oxygenate*
–en	to make something have a certain quality	*darken, lighten*
–ify	to cause or make into something	*identify, solidify, unify*
–ize	to become	*generalize, finalize*

It is important to check for spelling changes when adding word endings.

vowel dropped: clear + *–ify* = **clar**ify
vowel added: different + *–ate* = differen**tia**te

13.B.3. Adjective Endings

Word Endings for Adjectives		
Ending	**Meaning**	**Examples**
–able, –ible	having a particular quality	*comfortable, reversible*
–al	of or relating to something	*musical, occasional*
–an, –ian	relating to someone or something from a place; relating to someone who has certain knowledge or belief	*American, vegetarian*
–ant, –ent	having the quality of	*defiant, persistent*
–ary	belonging to	*planetary*
–ate	having, containing, or having to do with something	*compassionate*
–ative, –itive	having the quality of	*talkative, primitive*
–ed	past participle	*confused*
–en	past participle	*stolen, written*
–en	made of	*wooden*
–ese	of a country	*Chinese*
–ful	full of	*beautiful*
–ic	of or relating to a particular thing	*periodic*
–ing	present participle	*confusing*
–ish	having qualities of, or tending to be	*childish*
–ive	having a particular quality	*expensive*
–less	without something	*useless*
–like	similar to	*childlike*
–ly	having qualities of	*manly*
–ory	relating to	*obligatory*
–ous, –ious	having qualities of	*dangerous, delicious*
–proof	protected from	*waterproof*
–y	having the character of	*curly, funny*

13.B.4. Adverb Endings

Word Endings for Adverbs		
Ending	**Meaning**	**Examples**
–ly	in a particular way or at times	*easily, occasionally*

NOTE: Not all words that end in **–ly** are adverbs.

early	adjective	Gary is in his *early* twenties.
	adverb	Carlos has to wake up *early*.
daily	adjective	Our library subscribes to four *daily* newspapers.
	adverb	Kumiko exercises *daily*.
oily	adjective	Irma doesn't like *oily* foods.
lonely	adjective	Ronald was a very *lonely* child.
friendly	adjective	She is such a *friendly* person.

In addition, not all adverbs end in **–ly**: *fast, well, soon, always, here.*

13.B.5. Noun Endings

Word Endings for Nouns		
Ending	**Meaning**	**Example**
–al	the act of doing something	*rehearsal, denial*
–ence, –ance, –cy	action or process; quality	*confidence, performance, lunacy*
–ent, –ant	someone or something that does something	*president, resident*
–er, –or, –ar, –r	someone or something that does something	*teacher, elevator, registrar, writer*
–hood	having a quality or state	*brotherhood, childhood*
–ity, –ty	having a quality	*equality, specialty*
–tion, –ion	act or result of doing something	*attention, impression*
–ism	a belief or set of ideas	*capitalism*
–ist	a person who performs a specific action; a person with certain beliefs	*typist, capitalist*
–ment	a result of doing something; a place of action	*development, department*
–ness	state or condition	*happiness*
–ure	an act or process	*failure, pressure*
–ship	a state or quality; an art or skill	*friendship, sportsmanship*

13.B.6. Lack of Word Endings to Indicate Part of Speech

The lack of consistency for the use of word endings in English to indicate the part of speech of a word is a serious problem for ELLs. For instance, *-ous* indicates an adjective, but not all adjectives end in *-ous*. While *-tion* indicates a noun, not all nouns end in *-tion*. Thus, we should not be surprised when ELLs create words such as **naturous* for *natural* or **employation* for *employment*.

For ELLs, a more serious inconsistency in English is that a word can often be more than one part of speech without any change in endings. A word can be a noun or a verb (*a photograph* vs. *I photograph*), a noun or an adjective (*I speak English* vs. *an English word*), or all three—a noun, a verb, and an adjective (*a survey* vs. *to survey a group* vs. *a survey question*). In many languages, this is simply impossible because parts of speech are more marked in those languages.

Unfortunately, there is no way to predict which ending—or even if any ending—must be added to a base word to change its part of speech. Consider how these words change for different parts of speech. Note also the variations in meaning.

Noun	Verb	Adjective	Adverb
sadness	to sadden	a sad story	sadly
decision deciding	to decide	a decisive ending	decisively
a talk talking	to talk	a talk show a talkative person a talking dog	– – – talkatively – – –
an explanation	to explain	an explanatory note	– – –
a struggle	to struggle	a struggling actor	– – –
a nation	– – –	a national problem	nationally
a city	– – –	a city problem	citywide
wood woodenness	– – –	wooden	woodenly
love lovability	to love	a love story a loving cat a loved story loveable	– – – lovingly – – – lovably

Consider the nouns *city* and *nation*. The adjective form for *city* is *city;* the adjective form for *nation* is *national.* By default, we use the noun form as an adjective when a separate adjective form does not exist. Thus, we say *a city* and *a city problem.* We say *a nation,* but we cannot say **a nation problem.* Instead, we have to say *a national problem* because we have an adjective form for this noun. ELLs have to learn (and remember) not only that we can use a noun as an adjective but also when a given adjective form does not exist and therefore requires the use of the noun form instead.

Given these difficulties for ELLs, I repeat my initial advice: Knowledge of word endings can only be used one way—that is, to decipher an already existing word by using its base and any word parts (but not to put a base word with an ending to create a correct English word). Except in controlled exercises where we tell ELLs to add a specific suffix to a certain word—for example, add *–or* to *act*—we cannot reasonably expect ELLs to know to add *–or* to a verb to make a noun instead of adding *–er* or *–ist* or *–ian.* All four of these suffixes indicate **one who does an action,** but there is no way for an ELL to predict which ending is correct. However, when ELLs encounter the word *actor,* they can reasonably conclude that it means "a person who acts."

Common ELL Mistakes: What Your ELLs Should Know

1. Creating new words with word endings is very difficult. Check a dictionary when you are trying to create a new word.

    wrong:　The spectators were very impressed with the runner's quickation.

    correct:　The spectators were very impressed with the runner's quickness.

2. Not all words that end in **–ly** are adverbs. (examples: *early, daily, oily, lonely, friendly*).

    wrong:　How much does a day newspaper cost?

    correct:　How much does a daily newspaper cost?

3. Not all adverbs end in **–ly.** (examples: *fast, well, soon, always, here, hard*)

    wrong:　A bullet train can go fastly, but an airplane goes more quickly.

    correct:　A bullet train can go fast, but an airplane goes more quickly.

13.C. Native Language Interference: Compare English with Other Languages

Language	Notes on *Word Forms*
Arabic **Chinese** **French** **Japanese** **Korean** **Russian** **Spanish**	No two languages have the same set of prefixes and suffixes, so transferability will vary considerably based on the ELL's native language. Of these seven languages, word forms in French and Spanish have the most in common with word forms in English.
Arabic	1. Arabic uses a word root system that is based on a combination of three consonants, which is the basis for much of Arabic word formation. There are at least ten patterns to produce new words by either adding prefixes to this three-consonant root or infixing vowel sounds between the three consonants. For example, *d-r-s* is the root for "to study." Adding the prefix *y–* produces *yidrus*, "He studies." Adding the suffix *–t* produces past tense *darast*, "He studied." Adding the prefix *ma–* and altering internal vowel sounds gives us *madrasa*, "school" (place of study). 2. Arabic–speaking ELLs appreciate explicit, detailed instruction and practice in the use of prefixes and suffixes for word formation in English. (Many books give a rather cursory list of common prefixes and suffixes, but this superficial treatment is in no way sufficient for Arabic speakers. A good source of step-by–step instruction and practice is *Intermediate Reading Practices, 3rd Ed.* [Folse, 2004].)
Chinese **Japanese** **Korean**	1. Chinese does not use affixes in the way English does, but Chinese makes extensive use of compounding to build words. Hong Kong means "fragrant harbor." Beijing means "north capital." Shanghai means "on [the] sea." The word *lu-kuo*, which consists of *road* and *mouth*, means "intersection." The word *xiong-mao*, which consists of *bear* and *cat*, means "panda." 2. Japanese and Korean make use of this kind of compounding, but they also use word endings.

13.D. Ideas for Teaching

From an ELL point of view, knowing a word part can be helpful in figuring out the meaning of a word, but it is not so useful when lower-proficiency ELLs are trying to create a word. Passive recognition is possible, but active production is difficult because ELLs have to know which ending is not only grammatically appropriate but also the correct one for that word. In other words, ELLs practically have to know the word first to be able to create it, which is illogical.

Suppose we have the word *create,* and we know that it is a verb. We want to produce the noun form for this verb, but we have several suffixes to convert verbs into nouns, including *–tion, –ment,* or *–ance.* How do we know that we should say *creation* but not **createment* or **creatance?* Because of this ambiguity, I prefer to concentrate initially on recognition skills. If you opt to do production practices, you need to provide a controlled practice—that is, one in which all the words are formed the same way. For example, don't give students a list of 20 verbs and tell them to add *–tion, –ment,* or *–ance* as appropriate because there is no way for them to know which is appropriate. Even young native speakers make errors and say *‡mountainy* instead of *mountainous* and **discolorment* instead of *discoloration.* In contrast, an acceptable exercise is to give students ten verbs that you know combine with *–tion* and then ask students to write these ten new nouns. This may seem extremely easy to you, but that is because you already know these ten nouns. These ten nouns are not new to you, but they are to the ELLs.

With any grammar point, you should always look for and teach any aspects of the grammar that are similar to what is happening in your ELLs' native languages—if there are similarities—and the ones that are the most frequently used in English. The purpose of using **cognates** is that ELLs will benefit more from structures that may already be familiar to them in their native languages and that they will encounter more often as they interact in English. Many ELLs in the United States speak Spanish, and one of the most common suffixes in Spanish is *–ción,* which is the same as our English *–tion,* which changes a verb to a noun. Even if your ELLs are not Spanish (or French, Portuguese, or Italian) speakers, starting with *–tion* first makes sense because it is one of the most common suffixes, especially in academic writing.

Write three examples on the board one at a time. Get the students involved in writing the second and third words. After you have written *celebrate* and the suffix *–tion* on the board, hesitate. Then ask your students, "Ok, what is my noun form? How about **the celebrate?* What

FIND OUT

How good are ELLs at knowing the correct word forms of words in English? Prepare a quiz for an ELL by providing a list of words and then asking the ELL to change the part of speech. For example: *What is the adjective for the noun color?* Prepare ten questions. Before you give your questions to five ELLs to complete, predict which three questions you think will be the most difficult and which three questions will be the easiest? Try to use words that the ELLs will not have seen already so that this task really examines ELLs' ability to predict the use of word endings to form new words.

about *celebratement?" Students will tell you the correct form, *celebration*, and you should write it. To maintain teacher-class interaction, after someone says *celebration*, ask, "How do you spell that?" and write the word on the board as students spell the word.

act	+ –tion →	action
select	+ –tion →	selection
celebrate	+ –tion →	celebration

Consider these two controlled practice exercises. Students are not asked to choose the correct suffix; instead, they are asked to combine a specific word with a specific suffix to produce a new word. In essence, errors are virtually impossible.

–less	
Noun	**Adjective**
1. color	2. *colorless*
3. job	4.
5. end	6.
7. stress	8.
9. life	10.

Source: *Intermediate Reading Practices: Building Reading and Vocabulary Skills, 3rd Ed.* (Folse, 2004), p. 57.

–ment	
Verb	**Noun**
1. agree	2. *agreement*
3. enjoy	4.
5. state	6.
7. move	8.
9. argue	10.

Source: *Intermediate Reading Practices: Building Reading and Vocabulary Skills, 3rd Ed.* (Folse, 2004), p. 140.

After students have studied and practiced various word forms, teachers can then increase the difficulty of practice exercises by asking students to select the correct form among several potential forms (*Joseph signed the [agreetion, agreement, agreeness] yesterday*) or to produce the correct form (*AGREE: Joseph signed the _____ yesterday*). Now write three more verbs on the board and ask students to list the new nouns on their paper. Give a time limit of 30 seconds. Then ask students to tell you the answers, which you will write on the board (or let students write their words on the board).

After students have studied several suffixes, give them a paragraph or a mini-essay at the ELLs' reading level. Ask them to go through it to underline words with word forms that they have studied. If you really want students to focus on what you have taught, give specific instructions, such as *Underline nine words as follows: three words with –tion, two with –er meaning comparison, one with –er meaning a profession, two with -est meaning very (superlative), and one with –ness meaning a noun.*

Let students work alone (possibly as homework), and then ask them to work in class in pairs or threes to check their answers. When you review the answers, do not just announce the answers. Be interactive with your ELLs. If someone underlined *–ness* as a noun, ask the student what part of speech the word is without *–ness*. Ask which word is the easiest to produce and which is the most difficult. Ask why. Don't just give answers. Probe. Make sure they are noticing things about English that will help them. Make your ELLs talk about the language.

ELL Grammar Key 14:
Passive Voice

In grammar, we talk about **active voice** and **passive voice.** In active voice, the sentence structure is SUBJECT + VERB + DIRECT OBJECT, where the subject is doing something and the direct object is the receiver of the action: *Mary wrote six detailed emails.* In passive voice, the sentence structure is SUBJECT + a form of *be* + PAST PARTICIPLE, where the subject is the receiver of the action: *Six detailed emails were written by Mary.*

Native speakers have been told—incorrectly—to avoid the passive voice. This was usually taught in school as something that would make our writing weak. There is nothing wrong with passive voice, but it is a problem when people overuse passive voice or even active voice. There are specific times when the passive is appropriate, but it depends on what the writer or speaker wants to accomplish with any given sentence and how that sentence fits into the paragraph.

14.A. Typical ELL Errors: Noticing the Gap

Can you identify and explain these five common ELL errors with this grammar point?

1. *Thousands of people went to California in the 1840s because gold discovered there.
2. *Where were you when the accident was happened?
3. *More than one hundred people killed in that plane crash.
4. *The Japanese language can write from left to right or from top to bottom.
5. *If you find a wallet, it should be returning to the owner immediately.

14.B. Grammar Explanation

14.B.1. What Does a Verb in the Passive Voice Look Like?

The passive voice is composed of the verb *be* and the **past participle**. The verb *be* should be in the correct tense to indicate the time of the action. In addition, it should also be singular or plural according to the number of the subject.

be + PAST PARTICIPLE		
The residence of the President of the United States	*is called*	the White House.
The current White House	*was built*	in 1818.
By 1815, the original White House	*had been destroyed*	in a fire.

14.B.2. How Is Active Voice Different from Passive Voice?

Active Voice. A common sentence pattern in English is SUBJECT + VERB + DIRECT OBJECT. In these sentences, the most important topic is the person or thing that is doing the action (the "doer" of the action). In these sentences, the subject is the agent of the action. This is called the **active voice.** Can you identify the three parts (subject, verb, and direct object) in these example sentences?

1. The people of France gave the Statue of Liberty to the United States.
2. Leonardo da Vinci painted the famous *Mona Lisa.*
3. We will make a decision about our trip soon.
4. The people reelected George Washington for a second term in 1792.

In these four sentences with active voice, the emphasis is on *the people of France, Leonardo da Vinci, we,* and *the people.*

Passive Voice. Sentences in passive voice also begin with a subject and have a verb, but the subject here is not the agent of the action. In passive voice, the subject is the person or thing that "receives" the action of the verb. The same four examples are repeated, but now in passive voice. Can you see the differences?

5. The Statue of Liberty was given to the United States by the people of France.
6. The famous *Mona Lisa* was painted by Leonardo da Vinci.
7. A decision about our trip will be made soon.
8. George Washington was reelected for a second term in 1792.

In Sentences 5 through 8 with passive voice, the emphasis is *on the Statue of Liberty, the famous Mona Lisa, a decision about our trip,* and *George Washington.*

Compare the differences between active voice and passive voice of the verbs in these sentences:

Verb Tense	Active Voice VERB	Passive Voice *be* + PAST PARTICIPLE
Present	I *wash* my car every Saturday.	My car *is washed* every Saturday.
Past	Shakespeare *wrote* that play.	That play *was written* by Shakespeare.
Present Progressive	They *are making* a special plan.	A special plan *is being made*.
be + going to	They're *going to build* a house here.	A house *is going to be built* here.
Present Perfect	People *have* officially *celebrated* Mother's Day since 1914.	Mother's Day *has* officially *been celebrated* since 1914.
Modals	The government *should prohibit* the sale of cigarettes.	The sale of cigarettes *should be prohibited* by the government.

14.B.3. Intransitive Verbs

Some verbs can never be used in the passive voice. These verbs are called **intransitive verbs.** Intransitive verbs are never followed by a direct object, so they cannot be changed to passive voice. Examples of verbs that are never used in passive voice are *happen, die, arrive, depart* (and many other verbs of motion). However, many ELLs incorrectly use these intransitive verbs in constructions that look like passive voice such as **The accident was happened late last night* or **Ten people were died in the accident.*

14.B.4. When Is Passive Voice Used?

In general, we use passive voice when the agent of the action is not the most important thing. In passive voice, the subject of the sentence is the receiver of the action. The subject can be either a person or a thing.

If you want to name the agent in a passive voice sentence, you can use a *by* + agent phrase. However, sometimes it sounds strange to name the agent. You should not name the agent when it is not new information or when the agent is not important. For example, in Sentence 8 on

Are we supposed to **avoid passive voice?** Many native speakers were incorrectly taught that passive voice is bad in writing. Our teachers were trying to help us avoid wordy writing, so telling us to limit our use of passive voice made sense. The task for ELLs is to learn how to form passive voice of verb tenses and when to use it so that a student's essay is more effective in accurately and efficiently conveying the writer's intended message. The bottom line is that there is nothing wrong with using passive voice. In some cases, it is actually preferred to active voice. For example, the first two sentences of this message use passive voice.

page 243, we know that every president is elected *by the people,* so it is unconventional to say, *President Washington was reelected by the people for a second term in 1792.* The phrase *by the people* does not tell us any new or important information and can be omitted.

Passive voice is common in both written and spoken language as well as in formal, planned language and informal, ordinary conversations. It can occur in all of these situations.

14.B.5. Passive Voice with *get*

The passive for the verb *get* consists of a form of the verb *get* followed by a past participle. The *get* passive indicates a sudden change; the *be* passive indicates a result. Thus, *We were lost* describes our situation at a certain point, but *We got lost* indicates that we were traveling and suddenly did not know our location. The past participle functions here as an adjective that describes the subject.

The use of *get* is considered informal language and is therefore much more common in spoken language than written language. Formal writing generally avoids the use of *get.* Instead, use *become* as a synonym.

14.B.6. Passive Forms Used as Adjectives (*closed*)

In some instances, it is possible to use a passive verb form as an adjective to describe a condition or state instead of an action. In this case, we use a past participle after a form of the verb *be.*

Sentence	Notes
The window **is closed**.	This sentence describes the condition of the window now.
All of the checks **are gone**.	This sentence describes the condition of the checks now.

14.B.7. *–ing* vs. *–ed* Adjectives (Participial Adjectives) (*interesting* vs. *interested*)

A past participle of a verb can function as an adjective.

> *Example:* When I heard the news yesterday, I was **surprised**.

A present participle of a verb can also function as an adjective.

> *Example:* The news was **surprising**.

ELLs have a particularly difficult time figuring out when to use the past participle and the present participle forms as adjectives. They confuse pairs such as *interested* → *interesting, confused* → *confusing,* and *surprised* → *surprising.*

ELLs need to remember that the **–ing** form is for the person or thing that makes (causes) the action and the **–ed** form (or any past participle ending) is for the person or thing that receives the action.

–ing	–ed (OR –en)
Present Participles Used as Adjectives	**Past Participles Used as Adjectives**
• are active • refer to the cause of the experience • describe what the effect is • often describe inanimate (non-living) nouns	• are passive • refer to the person or thing that feels or has the experience • describe how the person or thing is affected • often describe animate (living) nouns

Consider these examples:

Example Sentences	*The news surprised me.*	*Joe disappointed us.*
action	surprise	disappoint
the person or thing that causes the action	*the news =* *The news was surprising.*	*Joe =* *Joe was disappointing.*
the person or thing that receives the action	*me =* *I was surprised.*	*us =* *We were disappointed.*

Common *–ing/–ed* (or Participial) Adjectives

annoying—annoyed amazing—amazed amusing—amused astonishing—astonished boring—bored confusing—confused convincing—convinced depressing—depressed disappointing—disappointed disgusting—disgusted embarrassing—embarrassed entertaining—entertained	exciting—excited exhausting—exhausted fascinating—fascinated frightening—frightened horrifying—horrified interesting—interested puzzling—puzzled satisfying—satisfied shocking—shocked startling—startled terrifying—terrified tiring—tired

14.B.8. Past Participle + Preposition Combinations as Adjectives

With passive voice, the past participle can be followed by a *by* + agent construction, as in *They were* <u>married by</u> *an old minister*. However, when past participles are used as adjectives, they are followed by different prepositions depending on the past participle. For example, we say *I am* <u>accustomed to</u> *something* but *I am* <u>interested in</u> *something*. There is no way to predict which preposition is used with which adjective, so ELLs need to memorize the correct adjective + preposition combinations.

> Three common uses of **past participles** in English include: (1) perfect tenses (*I have needed, she had chosen*); (2) passive voice (*I was needed, she had been chosen*); and (3) adjectives (*a much needed change, a carefully chosen gift*).

be accustomed to	be divorced from	be married to
be acquainted with	be done with	be opposed to
be ashamed of	be dressed in	be related to
be bored with/by	be excited about	be satisfied with
be committed to	be exhausted from	be scared of
be composed of	be finished with	be surprised at/by
be confused about	be fed up with	be terrified of
be convinced of	be impressed by/with	be tired of
be dedicated to	be interested in	be tired from
be devoted to	be known for	be used to
be disappointed in/with	be made of/from	be worried about

Common ELL Mistakes: What Your ELLs Should Know

1. Do not use active voice when you should use passive voice.

   wrong: The man bit the snake. (grammatically possible but not probable!)

   correct: The man was bitten by the snake.

2. Do not forget to use a form of **be** in the passive voice.

   wrong: This letter sent to the wrong address.

   correct: This letter was sent to the wrong address.

3. Do not use the **by** + agent phrase if the information is not new or important.

   unusual: President Clinton was elected by the people in 1992.

   usual: President Clinton was elected in 1992.

4. Do not mix up when to use **–ing** (present participle) and when to use **–ed** (past participle). They are completely different.

   wrong: I'm boring in that class. (possible but not likely)

   correct: I'm bored in that class.

5. Do not forget to use an appropriate ending. Do not use just the simple verb form as an adjective.

wrong: The surprise results were on the front page of the paper.

correct: The surprising results were on the front page of the paper.

14.C. Native Language Interference: Compare English with Other Languages

Language	Notes on *Passive Voice*
Arabic	1. Arabic has a passive form for all verb tenses, but passive voice is rare. Active voice dominates. 2. Passive is formed by a slight change of a vowel sound in the middle of the verb. In Arabic, vowels are written only in very formal writing such as in the Koran, so active and passive forms look similar though they sound different. (Perhaps the best analogy in English is with the word *read,* which can be pronounced two ways depending on the context, but native speakers never confuse the two.) There is a tendency for Arabic–speaking ELLs to rely on the similarity of the two forms in Arabic and thereby confuse active and passive in English: **The house built last year by my uncle.* 3. In Arabic, *by* + agent is usually absent. When it does occur, it is expressed by the preposition *b-,* which coincidentally mirrors *by* in English. (Unfortunately, this similarity leads to overuse of *by,* as in **The letter was written by ink.*) In passive constructions in Arabic, the agent is usually a thing, not a person. 4. In general, Arabic–speaking ELLs tend to avoid using passive voice in their writing or speaking because passive voice is rare in Arabic.
Chinese	1. Passive voice exists, but it is not formed with the verb *to be* and past participle as in English. 2. The agent is marked by *bei,* which can facilitate the use of the *by* + agent structure.

French	French has three ways to express passive voice.
	1. French has a passive voice construction that is very similar to *be* + past participle in English. In French, however, the past participle must agree with the subject in number and gender. Therefore, French ELLs may write **The plants were watereds all night* or **Every semester letters are sents to students' parents.*
	2. French also uses reflexive verbs to express passive voice. A common example is in telling someone your name, as in *Je m'appelle Keith*, which translates literally as "I call myself Keith." A more natural translation would be "I am called Keith," which is passive voice, or simply, "My name is Keith."
	3. Another common way to express passivity is through the use of the pronoun *on*, which translates as "one." You may have seen a sign in a store window that said *on parle français ici*, which translates literally as "one speaks French here." A more natural translation would be "French is spoken here," which is passive voice.
Japanese	1. Japanese has a special verb form for passive voice, which consists of one word that has an infix to signal passive voice. It does not involve *to be* or a past participle as in English, so Japanese ELLs often omit *be* and write **Naoko chosen the winner in the essay contest.*
	2. The subject in a passive voice construction is usually animate.
	3. The *by* + agent is expressed by *ni*, which usually means "in."
Korean	1. Korean has a special verb form for passive voice, which consists of one word. It does not involve *to be* or a past participle as in English. Thus, Korean ELLs often omit *be* and write **Naoko chosen the winner in the essay contest.*
	2. The *by* + agent is often rendered in English by the word *from*, producing an error such as **This book was written from Maria.*
Russian	1. Russian has a special verb form for passive voice. Russian ELLs often omit *be* and write **Katya given the award for best essay.*
	2. Passive voice of verbs in progressive and perfect tenses may be problematic because these are not indicated by separate tenses but rather modifications to the verb.

Spanish	Spanish has two principle ways to express passive voice.
	1. Spanish uses reflexive verbs to express passive voice. A common example is in telling someone your name, as in *Yo me llamo Keith*, which translates literally as "I call myself Keith." A more natural translation would be "I am called Keith," which is passive voice, or simply, "My name is Keith." In addition, you may have seen a sign in a store window that said *Aqui se habla español*, which translates literally as "[it] speaks Spanish to itself here." A more natural translation would be "Spanish is spoken here," which is passive voice.
	2. Spanish has a passive voice construction that is very similar to the *be* + past participle in English, but there are two differences that may influence Spanish–speaking ELLs' English. In Spanish, there are two verbs for *to be*, so ELLs may be confused about which one matches the use of passive voice in English. In addition, the past participle in this construction must agree with the subject in number and gender. Therefore, Spanish ELLs may write *The plants were watereds all night* or *Every semester letters are sents to students' parents*.
	3. In English, the sentence *The teacher gave the students a test* can produce two equally correct passive sentences: *The students were given a test by the teacher* or *A test was given to the students by the teacher*. In Spanish, however, only the second is possible because the students were not really "given" by anyone. (The subject of a passive voice sentence has to be the direct object of the verb in active voice, not the indirect object.) Spanish–speaking ELLs may find the first passive sentence somewhat difficult to comprehend and certainly to produce, causing learners to avoid this structure in their English altogether.

14.D. Ideas for Teaching

Passive voice is not for beginners. In fact, if a beginning-level ELL asks you in class about a verb that is in passive voice, deflect the question. Just say that it is a difficult grammar area and that the student will learn about this in the next course or level. If the student persists, you can explain it briefly or better yet, explain it to the one student after class.

Tell the ELL that passive voice will be covered in much greater detail in a higher-level course. Explaining passive voice in front of a whole class of beginners can truly create more questions than solutions.

Beginning ELL materials are often written in active voice, even if it sounds weird, to avoid exposing ELLs to passive voice. This is especially true when the past participle is irregular *(grind–ground–ground)*, but it is somewhat less likely with regular verbs *(produce–produced–produced)* or "less irregular" verbs *(take–took–taken)* where the past participle looks similar to the base form of the verb.

Passive voice is often taught in intermediate classes. The traditional way to teach passive voice is to start with a clearly active voice verb example, one where there is a clear actor, a clear action, and a clear receiver of the action. The most traditional sentence is one like *John built the house.* This active voice sentence changes in passive voice to *The house was built by John.* I recommend doing several examples like this one on the board. No doubt, your ELL grammar textbook will have several examples of this transformation. See Teaching Technique 20.

A fun activity to practice passive voice is Auction, which is described on pp. 137–40 in *The Art of Teaching Speaking: Research and Pedagogy for the ESL/EFL Classroom* (Folse, 2006). A simplified version requires you to create a worksheet with 15 statements in passive voice. Make eight statements correct and seven with passive voice errors of various kinds. Students must identify the eight correct sentences. In Auction, students work in groups to decide which sentences they are most confident about, and then use money to buy as many correct sentences as possible at the auction.

Upper-intermediate and advanced students can be pushed to increase their vocabulary by learning as many *–ing* and *–ed* participial adjectives as possible. Although there are hundreds of *–ing* and *–ed* adjectives, most ELLs rarely move beyond the typical comfort zone of *interesting* and *surprised*. You can encourage students to take a chance by telling them that in their next piece of writing—whether it is a paragraph, an essay, or ten single sentences—they must use two *–ing* adjectives and one *–ed* adjective and circle them. By requiring students to circle these three words (or similar), you put the burden on them to help you grade their papers by making it easier for you to see whether they have or have not completed the assignment accurately.

Alternatively, you could have students identify participial adjectives in a selection from *Time, Newsweek,* or other publication. In these non-ELL texts, ELLs are likely to find participial adjectives such as *endangered* (species), *policing* (forces), *bewildered* (customers), and *surrounding* (areas) instead of the mundane, overused examples found in ELL textbooks (*interesting, surprised,* or *boring*).

FIND OUT

Give ELLs a list of five participle pairs such as *interested and interesting* or *annoyed and annoying*. Ask ELLs to explain the difference in the pairs and then write examples for both words. Can they write correct example sentences that clearly differentiate the meanings of the each pair of adjectives?

ELL Grammar Key 15:
Conditionals (If *Clauses*) *and* Wish

A commonly heard English sentence is, *If I had a million dollars, I'd* (*pay off my house, take a trip around the world, immediately quit my job*). I had never thought that this was a complicated sentence until an ELL asked me one day, *Why do you say* **had** *and not* **have**? *Do you think this is a past tense sentence?*

Native speakers frequently use conditional sentences or *wish* sentences (*I wish I had a million dollars now*), but we usually have no idea why we use past tense for an obviously present time action. It is easy to see how an ELL who hears, *If you'd told me you needed help, I would've helped you* delivered at native–speaker speed has difficulty catching the words and may not understand that this sentence really means "You did not tell me that you had a problem and therefore I did not help you, but I was ready to help you."

In natural spoken English, the actual verb forms used (*'d told* and *would've helped*) are reduced and unstressed, so it is practically impossible for an ELL to hear the endings, let alone pick them up through natural exposure. This grammar point is one that ELL teachers should know well and anticipate needing to explain to their students. Passive comprehension will not lead to active knowledge or ability to use this grammar point. Instead, ELLs need explicit instruction in this rather difficult grammar point.

15.A. Typical ELL Errors: Noticing the Gap

Can you identify and explain these five common ELL errors with this grammar point?

> 1. *If I suddenly have a million dollars, the first thing that I would do is to quit my job today.
>
> 2. *We wish we can go to the concert tomorrow, but we already have something else that we have to do.
>
> 3. *If you had studied this chapter more thoroughly, you won't be so confused by this sentence.
>
> 4. *If we would have bought them online, we could have gotten our concert tickets for half-price
>
> 5. I'm confused about this grammar. *I wish I have understood the rules for making sentences with wish.

15.B. Grammar Explanation

15.B.1. What Is a Conditional Sentence?

A **conditional sentence** expresses the idea that the action in the main clause (the result clause) can only happen if a certain condition (the clause that begins with *if*) is fulfilled. The *if* clause states the condition, and the main clause states the result.

Condition	Result
If I were you,	*I wouldn't buy that car.*

It is possible to reverse the order of the clauses of a conditional sentence without changing its meaning.

Result	Condition
I wouldn't buy that car	*if I were you.*

In actual communication, the *if* clause is often understood or implied and is not stated.

Result	Unstated Condition
I wouldn't buy that car	*(if I were you).*

Note that we must use a comma after an introductory *if* clause.

Condition, result.	*If you study more, you will pass the test.*
Result condition.	*You will pass the test if you study more.*

15.B.2. Four Types of Conditional Sentences

There are four types of conditional sentences: zero, one, two, and three. Zero conditional is not a true conditional, but it is included here because it uses the word *if*.

Type of Conditional Sentence	Example	Notes on Usage
Zero	*If it rains, I stay home.*	used for facts or situations that are always true; *when* or *whenever* can be used instead of *if*
	If it rained, I stayed home.	used for situations that were always true in the past; *when* or *whenever* can be used instead of *if*
First	*If it rains, I will stay home.*	used for an action that is likely to happen
Second	*If it rained, I would stay home.*	used for an action that is not true or that the speaker thinks is not very possible
Third	*If it had rained, I would have stayed home.*	used for an action that did not happen

15.B.3. Zero Conditional

Condition	Result
If + simple present tense *If it rains,*	simple present tense *I stay home.*
If + simple past tense *If I had any questions about Arabic while I was living in Saudi Arabia,*	simple past tense *I called my good friend Ahmed in Washington, DC.*

Zero conditionals express facts or situations that are always true in the present or were always true in the past. In zero conditionals talking about the present, we use the simple present tense form of the verb in both the *if* clause (i.e., the condition) and the result. In zero conditionals talking about the past, we use the simple past tense form of the verb in both the *if* clause (i.e., the condition) and the result, as in *If I had any questions about Arabic while I was living in Saudi Arabia, I called my good friend Ahmed in Washington, DC.*

With zero conditionals, we can substitute *when* or *whenever* for *if* and not change the meaning of the sentence.

Whenever it rains, I stay home.

When I had any questions about Arabic while I was living in Saudi Arabia, I called my good friend Ahmed in Washington, DC.

15.B.4. First Conditional

Condition (Future Time)	Result (Future Time)
If + simple present tense, *If it rains,*	future tense. *I will stay home.*
If + present progressive tense, *If it is raining,*	
If + present perfect tense, *If it has rained,*	
If + present perfect progressive tense, *If it has been raining,*	

First conditionals express an action that is likely to happen. In first conditionals, we use a present form of the verb in the *if* clause, including simple present tense (*rains*), present progressive (*is raining*), present perfect (*has rained*), or present perfect tense *(has been raining)*. We use a future verb form in the result clause, including future (*will stay*), *be going to* (*am going to stay*), or another modal (*might stay*).

15.B.5. Second Conditional: Unreal (not true or not possible)

Condition (Present or Future Time)	Result (Present or Future Time)
If + simple past tense *If it rained*	*would* + VERB. *I would stay home.*
If + past progressive tense *If it were raining*	

Second conditionals express something that is not true or not possible. In second conditionals, we use a past form of the verb in the *if* clause, including simple past tense (*rained*) or past progressive (*were raining*). We use *would* in the result clause as well as *could* or *might*. Note that with the *if* clause, we use *were*, not *was*, for all persons with the verb *to be* (*if I were, if you were, if he were, if she were, if it were, if we were, if they were*).

If I were you,	I wouldn't buy that car.
If today were her birthday,	she would organize a party.

Although the verb form used with second conditionals looks like simple past tense, it is actually **subjunctive mood.** The subjective mood is especially common after *if* or *wish*: *If I were a doctor, I would work in a small clinic.* You can call this verb form by its real name of subjunctive mood or you can tell ELLs that it is the simple past tense. How much terminology you use or do not use is your decision based on your ELLs' language goals.

15.B.6. Third Conditional

Condition (Past Time)	Result (Past Time)
If + past perfect tense *If it had rained,*	*would have* + PAST PARTICIPLE. *I would have stayed home.*
If + past perfect progressive tense *If it had been raining*	

Third conditionals express an action that did not happen. In third conditionals, we use the past perfect tense or past perfect progressive tense of the verb in the *if* clause. In the result clause, we use *would have, could have,* or *might have* followed by the past participle.

15.B.7. Mixed Conditional Sentences

The four patterns for forming conditional sentences are straightforward when the condition and the result occur at the same time. In the real world, however, we often talk about conditions from the past that affect a result in the present or future, and we sometimes talk about conditions of the present (facts) that would have affected a certain result in the past time. These mixed sentences are quite common in real communication. In these mixed cases, the verb follows the rules for the time of the condition and the time of the result.

Condition	Result
If he were rich, (present time)	*he would have bought that BMW yesterday.* (past time)
If he had become a citizen, (past time)	*he would vote in tomorrow's election.* (future time)
If I weren't taking my car to the shop tomorrow, (future time)	*I would have lent you my car.* (past time)
If you were giving a big speech tomorrow, (future time)	*you'd be busy planning it right now.* (present time)

15.B.8. Omission of *if*

With conditional clauses that contain *were, had,* or *should,* we can omit the word *if* and then invert the subject and verb.

If he **were** here, **Were** he here,	he **would lead** the discussion skillfully.
If they **had** known about the fundraiser, **Had** they known about the fundraiser,	they **would have made** a donation.
If you **should** find an electronic dictionary, **Should** you find an electronic dictionary,	please let me know. I've lost mine.

15.B.9. Contractions

Note that *'d* can be substituted for *would* or for *had*. In spoken English, ELLs can hardly hear this sound, so they are not likely to acquire this grammar feature unless the teacher helps them notice it through direct instruction. In written English, ELLs have a difficult time figuring out whether *'d* refers to *would* or *had*. What appears to be a simple contraction can be very difficult for ELLs.

> If *you'd* told me, I could have helped you.
> (*you'd = you had*)
>
> If the course were easier, *you'd* be able to make a better grade. (*you'd = you would*)

15.B.10. *Wish*

The verb *wish* has a special grammar that is similar to verbs in the *if* clause. Sentences with *wish* are similar in meaning to unreal conditions in the present, future, or past. The situation is not true, does not exist, is unlikely to happen, or did not happen.

Wish expresses the fact that you want the opposite of the real situation to be true. While the meaning of *wish* is easy for ELLs, the grammar of *wish* is not. The difficult part about *wish* sentences is that the verb tense is never the same as the time of the action. For example, to wish about a past action, we use past perfect tense (instead of simple past). To wish about a present situation, we use past tense (instead of present tense). To wish about a future event, *will* changes to *would*. The verb after the word *wish* is usually in a tense that is **one time earlier than the actual time of the action.**

Situation	Change	Sentence
I **didn't study** last night.	past time → past perfect tense	I wish I **had studied** last night.
I **don't study** much.	present time → past tense	My dad wishes I **studied** more.
I **won't study** tonight.	*will → would*	My dad wishes I **would study** tonight.
I **can't go** tomorrow.	*can → could*	I wish I **could go** tomorrow.

Common ELL Mistakes: What Your ELL Should Know

1. Don't use past tense to talk about past conditions.

   wrong: If I studied more last week, I would have passed yesterday's test.

   correct: If I had studied more last week, I would have passed yesterday's test.

2. Don't use present tense to talk about present conditions.

   wrong: If I know Spanish, I would translate this letter for you right now.

   correct: If I knew Spanish, I would translate this letter for you right now.

3. When the verb **to be** is used in unreal conditions for actions in the present (or future), use **were** instead of **was** for all persons, singular and plural. (This error is also common with native speakers in informal language.) See Hot Seat Question 5.

   wrong: If I was you, I would memorize this rule about unreal conditions.

   correct: If I were you, I would memorize this rule about unreal conditions.

4. Don't get confused by the contracted forms used with conditionals.

   If I'd had more time last month, I'd have finished reading that novel.

   (I had had)   *(I would have finished)*

5. Remember that verbs in sentences with *wish* follow similar patterns to those for *if.* Wishing in the present time requires past tense, and wishing in the past time requires past perfect tense.

   wrong: Who is that girl? I wish I know her name.

   correct: Who is that girl? I wish I knew her name.

15.C. Native Language Interference:
Compare English with Other Languages

Language	Notes on *Conditionals and* Wish *Sentences*
Arabic	1. Arabic has two words for *if*, reflecting classical/ formal and colloquial variations of the language. 2. Past tense is used for hypothetical situations, so Arabic–speaking ELLs might say, **If I studied last night, I passed the test this morning* instead of *If I had studied last night, I would have passed the test this morning.*
Chinese	1. There is a word that means *if*. 2. An *if* structure in Chinese requires two markers: *if* and *then*, as in *If you study, then you (will) pass the exam.* This requirement exists in Chinese and explains why Chinese ELLs often write incorrect sentences with two other incompatible markers: **Although I studied hard, but I did not pass the exam.*
French	1. French has a word for *if*. 2. French verb tenses in conditional sentences are similar to those in English. 3. There is no separate word for *would*. Instead, endings indicate conditional verbs. French–speaking ELLs may produce **If I had studied, I passed the test* or **If I had studied, I had passed the test.* 4. For future conditionals, the use of future tense is required in the *if* clause: **If I <u>will make</u> a good grade on the final, my parents will be so happy.* 5. The lack of progressive tenses in French may cause French–speaking ELLs to encounter problems producing structures such as *If I were living here, I'd complain to the landlord.* 6. French uses **subjunctive mood** in unreal clauses. Knowledge of this verb form may cause some interference for French–speaking ELLs.

Japanese Korean	1. These languages have a word for *if*. However, the word *if* is not obligatory because the verb endings signal a conditional sentence. 2. In Japanese and Korean, the *if* clause must always come before the main verb. English allows inversion: *If you study, you will pass* or *You will pass if you study*. These ELLs seldom write sentences with the *if* clause after the main verb. Though not an error, Japanese and Korean ELL writers may appear to lack sentence variety when in fact they are merely translating from their mother tongue. 3. Japanese and Korean ELLs fail to differentiate real and unreal situations, writing sentences such as **If I had won the lottery, I will buy a new house* or **I will help you with your homework if I were good at math.* 4. These languages use a different verb ending when expressing *provided that* or *if and only if* instead of just *if*. In other words, there is a verb form for conditional and another for strong conditional.
Russian	1. Russian has a word for *if*. 2. As in English, the word *if* can be omitted. In English, this is possible but rare and requires inverted word order: <u>*Were I*</u> *the president, I would raise taxes* and <u>*Had you told*</u> *me, I would have helped you.* In Russian, however, omitting *if* is common and does not make a sentence sound as formal as is the case in English. 3. The use of future tense is possible in the *if* clause: **If I <u>will make</u> a good grade on the final, my parents will be so happy.*
Spanish	1. Spanish has a word for *if*. 2. Spanish verb tenses in conditional sentences are similar to those in English. 3. There is no separate word for *would*. Instead, endings indicate conditional verbs. 4. Spanish–speaking ELLs may be confused by the English verb form used in present contrary-to-fact sentences (*If you spoke good French, you could translate this letter for me now*) because the form *spoke* looks like English past tense. This verb form in Spanish, which is called **subjunctive mood**, is very different from its past tense counterpart.

All Languages	All ELLs have trouble with the myriad of verb forms used in *if* clauses and main clauses in the various tenses. This grammar point appears complicated, but it is systematic and can be mastered after sufficient practice.

15.D. Ideas for Teaching Conditionals *and* Wish *Sentences*

As you have seen, conditional sentences can be divided into four different types of conditionals. Depending on the class, you might teach all four of these in one class meeting or you might separate them. In an intensive program, perhaps giving an overview of all four and then teaching each type one at a time makes the most sense.

In an EFL setting, students are not exposed to English much outside of class, and more class time is spent providing opportunities for recycling of previous material and for English practice. This allocation of class time means that there is less class time for introducing a great deal of material. For classes that meet only once a week, I would recommend covering these one at a time and contrasting the new type with any previously learned types as you go along. Students will have no problem with whichever type you present first, but as they see subsequent types, their brains will work to sort out the contrast in forms and the contrast in usages.

It is common in teaching grammar that the initial presentation and practice of one item goes very well. The problem occurs when a second, competing grammar option is raised. With *if*, when you present zero conditional, you can expect very few problems. When you present conditional one, you can also expect few problems. However, when you present conditional two, get ready for the questions. Conditional two requires ELLs (and teachers) to really think about what conditional sentences are. In addition, the verb changes in conditional two are sharper than they are with conditional zero or one.

The key to teaching conditionals is to make sure that all students understand the word *if*. If 100 percent of your students do not understand the word *if*, then you have no lesson. *If* is a hard word to explain clearly, but good examples, a translation or two from a classmate, and letting students use their dictionaries in class all add to making your teaching task much easier.

To teach any of these conditionals, put the pattern on the board. Start with some easy examples. Choose meaningful topics, but for most cultures, winning the lottery and changing your life are two concepts that seem to transcend geographic and linguistic boundaries.

> **FIND OUT**
>
> Examine a 500-word excerpt of a transcript of spoken English. Identify all of the conditional structures. How many of the structures have the main clause (i.e., the result clause with a form of *will* or *would*) but lack a directly stated *if* clause, such as *I would never have done that.* When both clauses are stated, which clause comes first? Is there any pattern to this usage?

The grammar of *wish* functions similar to that of the *if* clauses in conditional sentences. The verb after *wish* or after *if* is usually one tense earlier than the actual action of the verb. If your neighbor's cat died, you state a wish by saying, *I wish my neighbor's pet hadn't died.* We use *hadn't died* because of the verb in the original sentence was *died,* which is past tense. The verb after *wish* or *if* is usually one time earlier, so simple past tense changes to past perfect.

4

Being on the Hot Seat: Grammar Questions from ELLs

- Why does *opening* have one *n* but *beginning* has two? Does the rule change if we add *–ed* instead of *–ing: opened* or *openned?*

- How come we say *want to go, need to go,* and *promise to go* but *enjoy going, dread going,* and *keep going?*

- Why is the word *rain* in present tense in the question, *Did it rain yesterday?* when the word *yesterday* clearly means past tense—and why doesn't *rain* end in *–s* if the subject is *it?*

In education, we often hear about the "teachable moment," a time when a student is most likely to benefit from instruction. For many language teachers, the ultimate teachable moment occurs when a student raises his or her hand to ask a question—such as those posed here—but what happens when the teacher has absolutely NO idea of how to answer the question? What can teachers do when they suddenly find themselves on the proverbial hot seat?

Students who raise their hands in class and present a question want to know the answer at that moment, so that moment is THE teachable moment. What you are able to do with that special moment is crucial to student learning, and how you handle that question says something very important about your teaching ability, not only to that particular student but also to the entire class of students.

This chapter presents 20 grammar Hot Seat Questions involving ELL grammar problems that ELLs frequently ask about. Each of these questions is followed by a detailed answer with examples. Some responses are very straightforward and go right to the grammar solution. Other answers actually demonstrate useful dialogue between the teacher and the student(s) with the goal of not only providing the answer to the grammar query but also training you as the teacher to learn to guide the ELL into discovering the answer from several example sentences. Thus, the Hot Seat Questions here serve both the student and the teacher.

At some point in our teaching careers, all of us are asked questions that we cannot answer. Sometimes the answer has to do with data that we simply cannot recall at that moment, but with ESL grammar, it might involve a question that we have never even considered, let alone answered. While it is not necessary that the teacher know the answer to every student question, teacher credibility is damaged by replying too often with, "I don't know. I'll check on that and get back with you tomorrow." To be sure, this reply does have its place in good teaching, but no teacher should need to play this card too often.

So what are good teaching strategies for those moments when you are at the board on the proverbial hot seat and a learner asks you a grammar question that is not part of your prepared lesson and that you cannot answer at that particular time? Grammar is by definition a pattern, and your job is to figure out—with the students in tow—what the pattern is. It is recommended that you walk the students through a discovery process regarding their question. Such guided learning is at the heart of excellence in teaching, especially during a student-generated teachable moment.

When a student asks me a grammar question that I don't know the answer to—*and even one that I do know the answer to*—I try to set up a scenario on the board that will ultimately allow the students themselves to figure out the grammatical pattern that will answer the question. If you know the answer to the student's question, then you simply need to develop the teaching techniques that will set up the discovery process. If you do not know the answer but are a good teacher, oftentimes students are so absorbed by the discovery process you are orchestrating on the board that they are not even aware that you do not really know the answer.

Either way—whether you actually know the answer or are trying to figure it out right there in front of your students—there are some specific teaching techniques that you can use to facilitate student learning:

1. If you do not know the answer, buy time. Yes, stall for time. Ask the student to repeat the question. Ask other students to help with the question. Can they explain the question better or with other examples? The other students can be a valuable source of information in answering the original question.

2. ELL grammar questions are often about the correctness of specific phrases or sentences that they have heard or seen, such as, *Is it correct English to say, "She don't love me now?"*

   In this case, write the student's phrase on the board. Ask the student to repeat the question again. Ask the student where he or she heard or saw this language. This information is important because many times students are asking about vocabulary or grammar in a song or a TV show, which probably features informal language. With the *she don't love me now* example, my first reaction would be to say no (because it is *not* correct grammar). However, if the student says it is in a current song, then that tells me that the singer was trying to sound "cool" or informal or perhaps trying to make something rhyme, so that language is acceptable for that song—but it is still incorrect grammar when I consider my students' real-world need to write a good paragraph, fill out an application, or impress a job interviewer.

3. If you know the grammatical answer that underpins the question, then you can proceed to guide the student through other carefully selected examples. If the rule does have exceptions, you don't want to accidentally bring up one of the exceptions to a rule—at least initially. However, if you don't know the answer to the grammar question, then keep eliciting more examples.

   For example, if a student asks, "How do you pronounce the ending sound of the word *missed*? What about *sneezed*? What about *needed*?" and you don't know the answer and therefore don't know how to tailor your instruction, YOU must be the language detective. You need to figure this out while looking calm and still running the class.

   What do all three of these words have in common? What exactly is the student's question? If you can see that all three end in *–ed*, then ask the student—and the whole class—to generate more examples. This is almost always a very good technique because it involves everyone and because it is quite likely that someone else in the class knows the answer and may be able to explain it in a learner-to-learner way that you cannot, so use this great resource presented by fellow classmates.

4. As examples are given, try to help students figure out the answer by grouping the new examples on the board to represent the answer. The *–ed* suffix is pronounced one of three ways (/d/, /t/, /əd/), so when someone says *coughed*, write it near *missed* because they both share the /t/ pronunciation.

   If you don't know about the three pronunciations, then keep eliciting examples from the students. When you have 15 examples—pieces of data—then ask your class, "Okay, what is going on here? Can anyone see a pattern?" In language, there is almost always a pattern; your student may have coincidentally asked you about an exception, but this is rarely the case. If someone knows the pattern, then the student's question has been answered.

5. If no one can figure out the answer, then offer more examples. However, as you offer an example, say, "Okay, what about the verb *persuade*? What is the past tense?" When someone says, *persuaded*, then ask, "Where should I write this word—with *missed*, *sneezed*, or *needed*?"

   After five or six more examples from you, if no one is able to figure out the rule, then tell them. If you don't know the rule and you have exhausted all of your detective potential, then you should say that you want your students to keep working on this tonight and you want to see who can figure this out by the next class. Say that you are confident that someone can do this. Depending on your grading system, you may even offer extra points for the first student to tell you the answer. By doing this, you have just bought yourself time if you still need it, without losing face.

Our students in ESL settings are exposed to English all day. With the massive amount of English material on the Internet, even EFL students have access to English input that was not possible just ten years ago. Whether from you, the Internet, or another source, your students are hearing these grammatical structures in natural speech or seeing them in print. Though your students may in fact have understood the content of this language, this comprehensible input is not sufficient for learning to take place. If it were, your students would not be asking these grammar questions. In their quest to improve their English proficiency, most adult learners are not satisfied with comprehensible input; they also want to know why the language in the input is arranged the way it is. Why is there an *–ing* ending? Why does *needed* have two syllables but *called* and *robbed* don't? As you read the 20 questions and answers in this chapter, your goal is to learn to recognize these patterns yourself so that you can help your ELLs as they tackle English.

One final point worth noting is that a good teacher also knows when NOT to answer a question. Sometimes an ELL asks a question that is a valid question about a good language point (such as conditionals) but you as the teacher know that that particular moment is not the right time to explain that answer to the whole class. You know that explaining that grammar point right then would be opening up the proverbial can of worms and would cause more confusion than comprehension. The bottom line is that no one knows your students better than you do, so use your judgment about what to explain at what point and to what degree.

Hot Seat Question 1: Adjective Word Order

Which is correct: *a big house* or *a house big*? Why?

Your Answer

In both examples, *big* is an adjective and *house* is a noun. In English, adjectives come before nouns, so only the first example is correct: *a big house*. Following this pattern of ADJECTIVE + NOUN, we can also say *a green book, a Colombian girl, a world map, four tired students,* and *seven yellow pencils*.

Extra Information for the Teacher

This question is probably from a beginning or low-intermediate ELL whose native language allows adjectives to go after the noun, as in Spanish *una persona importante* and *un estudiante inteligente*. Put a list of singular nouns on the board, and then ask students to choose an appropriate adjective to go with each noun. Before writing the adjective in front of each noun, ask students where to place the adjective. For example, if your noun on the board is *girl* and a student says *tall* for the adjective, ask the class, "Which is correct: *a tall girl* or *a girl tall*?" Make your students practice saying the combination of ARTICLE + ADJECTIVE + SINGULAR COUNT NOUN. To keep vocabulary simple (and thereby facilitate attention on the grammatical pattern without vocabulary distractions), teachers should use things that are visible in the classroom. Even better, the teacher should let the student give the examples, and no new vocabulary will be introduced.

Hot Seat Question 2: Inverted Word Order with Negative Expressions

Never has the weather been so cold! I understand all the words in this sentence and the meaning, but the grammar looks strange to me. Why does the word *has* come before the subject *the weather*? Actually, this sentence looks more like a question than a statement: *Has the weather been so cold?* Why don't you say, **Never the weather has been so cold!*

Your Answer

You're right that this sentence looks more like a question than a statement because in a question, we would certainly ask, *Has the weather ever been this cold?* Sometimes when you find a sentence where the grammar looks strange to you, it is a good idea to see if there is a pattern. Can you generate some more sentences that look like this one to check if there is indeed a general pattern?

Look at this sentence again. What is strange or unique about this sentence? How many times have you seen a sentence begin with *never*? (I know, almost never!) The word *never* is usually in the middle of a sentence, not at the beginning. We would say, *The weather has never been so cold.*

If we make other sentences with *never* in the usual middle position and then move *never* to the beginning, look what happens:

A. *It never rains here in January.* ➔ *Never <u>does it rain here in January</u>.*
B. *My bank is never open on Sunday.* ➔ *Never <u>is my bank open on Sunday</u>.*

If you look at the part underlined, what do you see? Yes, the underlined portion by itself is set up as a question.

Now we have a potential rule (or pattern) that when you begin a sentence with *never*, you have to use the same word order as in a yes-no question. However, we need to see if there are other words that do this, too, or does this pattern only happen with *never*?

What makes the word *never* special or unique in meaning? It is a negative word that shows frequency. Let's try out our new pattern with similar words: *seldom, rarely, not once,* or *not even one time.* Let's also try a sentence with a positive adverb of frequency, *sometimes,* to test out our hypothesis:

C. We seldom pay by credit card. → Seldom <u>do we pay by credit card</u>.

D. Movie tickets are rarely over $10. → Rarely <u>are movie tickets over $10</u>.

E. Movie tickets are sometimes over $10. → *Sometimes <u>are movie tickets over $10</u>.

Because E did not work out, we can conclude that this pattern of inverted word order, which looks like the grammar of a question, is connected to sentences that begin with a negative adverb of frequency (or similar word).

A writer or speaker begins a sentence with a negative word to emphasize the negative meaning of that sentence. In this case, English grammar requires you to invert the subject and verb and use appropriate auxiliary verbs such as *do, does,* and *did.*

Extra Information for the Teacher

This question probably came from a high-intermediate or advanced student.

Hot Seat Question 3: Spelling Words with Double Consonants

When you add *–ing* or *–ed* to a word, how do you know how to spell the word? I mean, how do you know when to double the final consonant? Which is correct: *happening* or *happenning? opened* or *openned? prefered* or *preferred?*

Your Answer

The correct spellings are *happening, opened,* and *preferred.* The spelling of the original word is important. If a one–syllable word ends in consonant-vowel-consonant (C-V-C), then we double the last consonant before adding not only *–ed* and *–ing* but other endings that start with a vowel such as *–er* (for comparison and for a doer), *–est* (for superlative), and *–en* (to make a verb from an adjective, e.g., *red* → *redden*).

If a word ending in C-V-C has two syllables, we double the last consonant only if the (pronunciation) stress is on the second syllable.

Not Ending in C-V-C	Ending in C-V-C		
	1 Syllable	**2 Syllables, 1ˢᵗ Stressed**	**2 Syllables, 2ⁿᵈ Stressed**
		1 2 → 1 letter	1 **2** → 2 letters
act → acted	wrap → wrapped	<u>en</u>ter → entered	com<u>mit</u> → committed
react → reacted	plan → planned	<u>lis</u>ten → listened	pre<u>fer</u> → preferred
clean → cleaned	stop → stopped	<u>tra</u>vel → traveled	oc<u>cur</u> → occurred
take → taking	clap → clapped	<u>hap</u>pen → happened	re<u>fer</u> → referred
read → reading	get → getting	<u>o</u>pen → opening	be<u>gin</u> → beginning
look → looking	run → running	<u>of</u>fer → offering	ad<u>mit</u> → admitting
sing → singing	cut → cutting	<u>o</u>pen → opened	in<u>fer</u> → inferring
push → pushed	beg → begging	<u>hap</u>pen → happening	com<u>pel</u> → compelling

Extra Information for the Teacher

We never double any words that end in these letters: *w (saw → sawing), x (fix → fixing),* or *y (say → saying).* Verbs that end in the letter *c* (without *k*) usually add *–k: panic → panicked.*

An engaging way to teach this is using a discovery approach. Put the *–ing* forms of ten to fifteen of these verbs on the board. Ask students to work in small groups and figure out the spelling patterns here. These spelling patterns can be taught to high-beginners and up. Intermediate and even advanced ELLs appreciate reviewing these spelling patterns. (See Teaching Technique 9.)

Hot Seat Question 4: used to

When do you use *used to?* I think it's for past tense, so what's the difference between simple past tense and *used to?* Does *I went to that school* mean the same as *I used to go to that school?* If they mean the same thing, is one form preferred? Is one slang?

Your Answer

We use *used to* to talk about past actions that were true at one time but are now no longer true. In addition, the speaker is indirectly saying that the action will probably not happen again. Consider these examples:

    A. When I was in kindergarten, I remember that we used to take naps every day.
    B. When Kelly lived in Michigan, she used to hate winters because of all the snow.
    C. I used to play tennis almost every day, but now my job doesn't let me.
    D. Before computers, kids used to play outside more.
    E. My grandmother didn't use to wear a hearing aid, but now she does.

Simple past tense is often for an event that happened once at a specific time in the past. *Used to* lets the speaker or writer give a subtle "flavor" about the action that simple past does not.

Notice the correct negative form in Example E is *didn't use to*. (For more information on past tense usages of *used to* and *would*, see pages 127–28.)

Extra Information for the Teacher

This kind of question is probably from an intermediate or higher-proficiency ELL.

In addition, ELLs may confuse *used to* and *be used to*. The expression *be used to* has the same meaning as *be accustomed to*. This expression can be used in any tense, so we have *are used to* and *was used to*. A noun usually follows this expression, *I am used to this job*. If the name of an action follows, it must be a **gerund**, *I am used to waking up early*.

Hot Seat Question 5: Present Unreal Conditional Sentences

If I had a million dollars right now, I would buy a new house. This sentence is talking about the present. That's what *right now* means. I don't understand how you can use *had* here because *had* is past tense, and this sentence is talking about the present.

Your Answer

Verbs after *if* use a special grammar aspect called **subjunctive mood** when the action after *if* is unreal or imaginary. (You don't have a million dollars right now, do you? That makes the situation unreal or imaginary.) By coincidence, the subjunctive mood in English looks just like the simple past tense. NOTE: If you think that using a term such as *subjunctive* will confuse your students, then just label this form *past*. I have never found using the label *subjunctive* very helpful, so I usually avoid it as excessive grammar labeling. However, upper-intermediate or advanced ELLs may appreciate knowing this term.

Subjunctive Mood				
Need	*Use*	*Be*	*Know*	*Have*
if I needed	if I used	if I were	if I knew	if I had
if you needed	if you used	if you were	if you knew	if you had
if he needed	if he used	if he were	if he knew	if he had
if she needed	if she used	if she were	if she knew	if she had
if it needed	if it used	if it were	if it knew	if it had
if we needed	if we used	if we were	if we knew	if we had
if they needed	if they used	if they were	if they knew	if they had

In an *if* sentence to talk about the present, we use what looks like past tense for that *if* verb, but it really is subjunctive. The other verb, called the conditional verb, will usually have the form: *would* + VERB. Consider these examples:

Present Unreal Situation	Conditional Sentence about Present Time
A. I want to buy a house. I don't have a million dollars.	D. If I **had** a million dollars, I would buy a house.
B. I want to call Sue. I don't know her number.	E. If I **knew** Sue's number, I would call her.
C. I want to change many things. I am not the president.	F. If I **were** the president, I would change many things.

Extra Information for the Teacher

This question probably came from an upper-intermediate or advanced ELL. Note that the subjunctive of *be* is *were* for all pronouns, including *I*, *he*, *she*, and *it*, which use *was* in simple past tense. You may hear some native speakers say, *If I was you*, but this is considered informal spoken language. However, the standard written form is *If I were you*.

Hot Seat Question 6: had had

I saw a sentence with the word *had* two times in a row: *Before Lucas bought his classic 1973 Ford Mustang, he had had many other cars. However, not one of them was as nice as his Ford Mustang.* Is this really possible? What does *had had* mean?

Your Answer

Yes, *had had* is possible. Let's look at your sentence and figure out what the pattern (rule) might be:

A. *Before Lucas bought . . . ,*   *he had had. . . .*

B. *Before I came here,*   *I had studied English for many years.*

C. *When we got married,*   *we had known each other for a long time.*

D. *By the time she graduated,*   *she had been in college six years.*

Look at the verbs that are in the same slot, or place, where we see *had had* in your original sentence. Do you see a pattern? Yes, all the other verbs consist of *had* + PAST PARTICIPLE. This tense is called past perfect. In B, the main verb is *study*, and the past participle is *studied*. In C, the main verb is *know*, and the past participle is *known*. In D, the main verb is *be*, and the past participle is *been*.

In your example A, the main verb is *have*, and the past participle is *had*. Your verb might look a little strange, but *had had* is correct. The first *had* is the auxiliary, or helping verb, that we always find in past perfect, and the second *had* is the past participle of the main verb *have*. Therefore, *had had* is 100 percent correct here.

Extra Information for the Teacher

This question probably came from an upper-intermediate or advanced ELL.

Hot Seat Question 7: Adverbs of Frequency Word Order

I play usually tennis on Saturday morning with my doubles partner. Is this sentence okay? Why or why not? My roommate is a native speaker, and she understands me when I say this, but my teacher says that this sentence is not right.

Your Answer

The grammar in your sentence is not 100 percent correct, but if you have good pronunciation, most native speakers will have no problem understanding your sentence. The grammatical error involves the placement of the word *usually*. You have probably already studied a group of words called **adverbs of frequency** (*always, usually, often, sometimes, rarely, never*). I'm going to rewrite your sentence with the correct word order and give you several other examples. Let's see if you can figure out what the pattern is.

A.	I	usually	play		tennis on Saturday morning....
B.	My uncle		is	always	late for everything.
C.	Soldiers	never	needed		chemical protection suits before.
D.	Children	usually	love		to drink juice for a snack.
E.	Stores		were	rarely	open on weekends when I....
F.	My two cats		are	usually	extra friendly when they want....
.G.	Schools here		are	never	open during Christmas holidays.
H.	Most cars	usually	get		more than 30 mpg these days.

What do you think the rule is so far? Yes, we use adverbs of frequency before all verbs except *am, is, are, was, were*. Adverbs of frequency come after these five forms of *be*. Let's look at six other examples now:

I.	Drivers	should	always	wear	a seatbelt.
J.	My dad	has	never	had	a car accident.
K.	I	have	often	wondered	what it would be like to....
L.	If you	don't	ever	try	something new, how can you....
M.	Beetles	can	sometimes	bite	so badly that your skin will....
N.	Mark	has	always	taught	in this small school.

Now you can see the second part of the rule: When a verb has an auxiliary, or helping verb, the adverb of frequency goes after the first part of the verb.

You can simplify this rule as follows: When a verb (except *am, is, are, was, were*) is a single word, the adverb of frequency goes before it. When a verb has more than one word (an auxiliary plus main verb), the adverb of frequency goes after the first word.

Extra Information for the Teacher

Adverbs of frequency are covered in many beginning classes. Placement of these adverbs in a sentence is a common question for even beginning ELLs. A single pronunciation error or a single grammar error hardly ever impedes communication between an ELL and a native speaker. Communication usually breaks down completely, however, when an ELL makes both a pronunciation error and a grammatical error simultaneously. Consider the ELL, Felipe, who says, **My cousin is our teast*. Did he mean to say *teeth*? (Some languages don't have the *th* sound in the word *teeth*.) Did he mean *teacher*? Actually, this student meant to say, *My cousin is an artist*. Some languages do not use an indefinite article with professions after the verb *to be*, so this ELL dropped the word *an* completely. At the same time, he mispronounced the word *artist* by stressing the second syllable ar•tíst instead of the first syllable ár•tist and by changing the second vowel from schwa /ə/ to long *e*. Even if he had had the same pronunciation errors but had included the word *an*, I believe that a native speaker could have understood him. While a misplaced adverb of frequency is not so serious, this error can block communication completely if one or two words in the same utterance are mispronounced. Correct word order, or syntax, can help compensate for less than perfect pronunciation.

Hot Seat Question 8: will *in* if *Clauses*

I learned that I can't use *will* in an *if* clause, so I can't say, **If I will study harder, my grades will improve*. I'm supposed to use present tense and say, *If I study harder, my grades will improve*. The other day I heard a native speaker say, *If you will lend me $100, I will pay you back in a few days*. Is this sentence okay? Why? Or why not?

Key 15

Your Answer

You are right that we don't usually use any future tense in an *if* clause even if the action is clearly going to take place in the future, as in your example. It is clear that both the studying and the better grades are in the future.

The new sentence that you heard is indeed correct. It is possible to use future in an *if* clause when the meaning is "if you agree to do this." Thus, when the speaker said, *If you will lend me $100, I will pay you back*, he or she is saying that if the listener agrees to lend the money, then he or she will pay her back. The meaning is similar to "if you promise to lend me $100."

Here are some more possible examples:

A. If you will clean the kitchen, I will clean the bathroom.
B. If the hotel manager will reduce the price, we can stay there.

Here are some examples where it is NOT possible:

C. *If it will rain tomorrow, we will stay home. (The rain can't make a promise.)
D. *If your plane will be late, I will pick you up at the airport. (The plane can't agree.)

Extra Information for the Teacher

A clause is any subject-verb relationship. *I will call you* has one clause. The sentence *If I study harder, my grades will improve* consists of two clauses; *my grades will improve* is the main clause and *If I study harder* is an *if* clause. This question probably came from an upper-intermediate or advanced ELL.

Hot Seat Question 9: Contractions

For the words *you are not*, I can say *you're not*, and I can also say *you aren't*. Is there any difference in these two? Are they both okay?

Your Answer

There is no difference in meaning between these two contractions. With the negative forms of *is, are, have, has, had, will,* and *would,* there are always two contractions possible: *she isn't, she's not; they aren't, they're not; we haven't, we've not; it hasn't, it's not; you hadn't, you'd not; I won't, I'll not;* and *she wouldn't, she'd not.* Using either one is fine.

Extra Information for the Teacher

Questions about contractions can come from all proficiency levels. Beginners need help with the concept of contracting since not all languages have written contractions. Higher-proficiency ELLs need help with confusing contractions such as **it's** for *it is* or *it has* or **they'd** for *they would* or *they had.*

Another question that many ELLs ask about contractions is whether or not it is considered acceptable to use contractions. Contractions are normal in speech, and informal writing such as emails and text messages; in fact, we even make contractions in speech with nouns, not just pronouns: *Kevin's not here, those *cats're not mine, that bus'll take you downtown.* (These last two examples occur in spoken English only.) However, these "contractions" represent informal, relaxed spoken language. Writing is quite different from speaking in that it is usually more formal. Contractions should be avoided in academic writing.

Hot Seat Question 10: Verb Forms in Past Tense Questions

Did you ever work there? When you ask a question about the past, why do you use the present form of a verb?

Your Answer

This is a good question that many students ask. Your sentence looks confusing, but actually it is not. The word *work* looks like present tense, but it is not. It is really the base or simple form of the verb. In English, we do not use *–s* or *–ed* for main verbs in questions or negative statements. Study these two examples:

Question	*wrong:*	*Where does she works?
	correct:	Where does she work?
Negative	*wrong:*	*The manager of the bank does not works on Saturdays.
	correct:	The manager of the bank does not work on Saturdays.

For past tense, we can use only one past tense marker (indicator) for each verb. If you already have *–ed*, you can't have *did*, and if you have *did*, you can't have *–ed*.

What are the past tense markers in these sentences? Look at the markers and the number in each sentence.

Affirmative Sentences	Past Tense Marker	No.
A. Frank work**ed** for BMW for eleven years.	*–ed* (regular verb)	1
B. Our aunt live**d** in Dallas for her whole life.	*–d* (regular verb)	1
C. My co-workers **went** to a small café for lunch.	*went* (irregular verb)	1
D. Earlier today, James **did** something important.	*did* (irregular verb)	1

When we make questions for these sentences, we still have only one past tense marker, as seen in these four questions in past tense:

Questions	Past Tense Marker	No.
E. *Did* Frank work for BMW for eleven years?	*did* (auxiliary verb)	1
F. *Did* our aunt live in Dallas for her whole life?	*did* (auxiliary verb)	1
G. *Did* my co-workers go to a small café for lunch?	*did* (auxiliary verb)	1
H. Earlier today, ***did*** James do something important?	*did* (auxiliary verb)	1

The pattern that we use for a past tense question is *did* + SUBJECT + VERB. I think your confusion is that the base verb looks just like the simple present tense. However, in simple present tense, we add –*s* for *he/she/it*. To ask a question about Example E, we cannot ask, **Did Frank works for BMW?* If we could use *works* with an –*s*, then yes, we would be using present tense, but for all subjects, we use *did* + SUBJECT + VERB.

You may think that it looks strange to use the base or simple form of the verb here, but if we also put the main verb in past tense, we have a serious problem because then we have two past tense markers instead of just one. The rule in English is that you can have only one past tense marker for each verb.

Study Examples I–L carefully. These sentences represent typical ELL errors. Can you understand why all four questions are incorrect?

Yes-No Questions	Past Tense Marker	No.
I. ***Did** Frank work**ed** for BMW for eleven years?	*did* (auxiliary verb) + –*ed*	2
J. ***Did** our aunt liv**ed** in Dallas for her whole life?	*did* (auxiliary verb) + –*ed*	2
K. ***Did** my co-workers **went** to a small café for lunch?	*did* (auxiliary verb) + *went*	2
L. ***Earlier today, **did** James **did** something important?	*did* (auxiliary verb) + *did*	2

Extra Information for the Teacher

This is a common question from beginning ELLs. The same grammar (pattern) is also true for negatives, as seen in the same four sentences:

Negative Sentence	Past Tense Marker	No.
M. Frank **did** not **work** for BMW for eleven years.	*did* (auxiliary verb)	1
N. Our aunt **did** not **live** in Dallas for her whole life.	*did* (auxiliary verb)	1
O. My co-workers **did** not **go** to a small café for lunch.	*did* (auxiliary verb)	1
P. Earlier today, James **did** not **do** something important.	*did* (auxiliary verb)	1

Hot Seat Question 11: since *versus* for

I have lived here _____ two years. Should I use *since* or *for* to fill in the blank?

Your Answer

The answer is *for: I have lived here for two years.* We use *for* with quantity of time, and we use *since* with the name of a time. *For* tells the duration of something, and *since* indicates when something began. (See p. 170 for more information on the use of *since* and *for.*)

for	since
for two years for a decade for six hours for at least half an hour for my entire life	since 1999 since the last century since the war began since last summer since July 1st
For can be used with many verb tenses: • I have lived here for two years. • I lived there for two years. • I will live there for two years.	*Since* is usually used with perfect tenses: • I have lived here since 1999. • I have been living here since 1999. • I had lived there since I was born.

Extra Information for the Teacher

The distinction between *since* and *for* is usually mentioned in high-beginner or lower-intermediate books.

Hot Seat Question 12: Noun Clauses as Embedded Questions

*Can you tell me where does Karen live? My roommate told me that this sentence is wrong because I'm supposed to ask, *Can you tell me where Karen lives?* I thought that I needed to use *do/does/did* with questions.

Your Answer

Your roommate is correct. Your sentence has two clauses. The independent clause is *Can you tell me* (something)? This sentence would usually have a simple noun as the direct object: *Can you tell me Karen's address?* In your example, the direct object is actually a noun clause that asks for information. The normal word order in a noun clause is QUESTION WORD + SUBJ + VERB. However, the word order is NOT like that in a question, so we do not use *do/does/did* as auxiliary verbs here.

Typical ELL Error	Correct Sentence
*The report didn't say *where did he go.*	The report didn't say *where he went.*
*I don't know *what time is it.*	I don't know *what time it is.*

Whether the sentence is a statement or a question does not matter:

Statement: You know <u>where Jonathan works</u>.
Question: Do you know <u>where Jonathan works</u>?

Extra Information for the Teacher

Noun clauses as embedded questions are usually addressed at the upper-intermediate level. Most ELLs have never noticed this grammatical pattern, and first language interference can be a problem here, too.

Hot Seat Question 13: another, other, *and* others

I have a hard time with the word *other*. *Other* means "one more," so can I say, **I need other book now?* *Other* looks singular, but my teacher said you can use it with plural nouns like *other books*. What about *others?* I thought *others* is the plural form of *other*. *Others* looks plural, so why can't I say **others books?* When do I use *other* and when do I use *others?*

Your Answer

To answer this question, we need to look at not just two words but rather three words: *another, other,* and *others*.

Yes, you are correct in that the meaning of *another, other,* and *others* is "additional." All three words have the same basic meaning, but they do not have the same grammar.

If you want to talk about one thing, you must use *another*. Your sentence *I need other book* is not correct. *Book* is a singular count noun, and there is a rule in English that a singular count noun must have the articles *a, an,* or *the* in front of it. You can also put another singular marker word like *this* or *that*. You can also use possessive adjectives such as *my* or *her*, but you cannot have the word *other* all by itself.

If you want to check your sentence, take out the word *other* and what do you have: *I need book*. I think you can see that this is not good English, right? You have to say *I need a book*. Now, if you take this new sentence *I need a book* and put in the word *other*, you get *I need other book*, which we know is not right because we need the article *a*. However, if we add *a*, look what we get: *I need a other book*. Do you see the problem? Yes, *other* begins with a vowel, so we need *an*, not *a*, so now we have *I need an other book*. This used to be correct, but over time, English has come to write *an* + *other* in one word: *another*. Your correct sentence should be: *I need another book*.

Your second question is about *other* and *others*. *Others* is always a plural pronoun, and remember that you cannot use two plural words together. This means that you cannot say *I need others books* but rather *I need other books*. The word *others* cannot be an adjective because adjectives in English are never plural. The word *others* is only a pronoun. If you give your classmate some books and ask that person, *Okay, how are those books? Are those enough or do you need some others?* then your classmate might answer, *I don't think these are enough, so please give me some others if you can.*

another, other, others	
Singular	**Plural**
A. Please give me **another**. B. Please give me **another** book.	E. Please give me some **others**. F. Please give me some **other** books.
C. NO: *Please give me **other**. D. NO: *Please give me **other** book. Reason: You need an article or similar word.	G. NO: *Please give me some **others** books. Reason: You can't use two plurals together.

Extra Information for the Teacher

All ELLs at all levels have persistent problems with the forms of *other*. The patterns of usage for *the other* and *the others* are similar to those presented here for *other* and *others*.

As stated, adjectives in English are never plural. However, demonstrative adjectives have both singular forms (*this, that*) and plural forms (*these, those*).

Hot Seat Question 14: good *versus* well

I feel good or *I feel well*. Which one should I say when everyone asks me, *How are you doing?*

Your Answer

Both are grammatically correct. When talking about your health, you can use both. Some people consider *I feel well* to sound a little more formal than *I feel good*, but both are correct.

When talking about your demeanor or your spirits, you should use only *I feel good*. If you just found out that you made 100 on your grammar test, you would answer *I feel good*. If you are playing a tennis match today and someone wants to know about your mental or emotional condition before this important match, you would also answer *I feel good*, which means *I feel good about my chances of playing well today and maybe even winning today.*

Extra Information for the Teacher

This question was probably asked by an intermediate ELL. When asked *How are you doing?* the typical response is *Fine.* This quick question and answer is a polite exchange that acknowledges the other person. It opens the door to further communication if either person appears to want to pursue it. It is not usually a question about the person's health. If something is wrong, the person is free to comment on this, but in general, speakers do not expect an explanation of what ails the person.

Hot Seat Question 15: gonna *(Informal and Formal Language)*

Is *gonna* okay? If so, when can I use it?

Your Answer

Here is the short answer: in writing, **no**; in speaking, **sometimes**. In writing, there are certain contractions that are permitted. You can write *I've* for *I have* or *she'd* for *she had* or *she would*, but contractions are not common in academic writing. If you are writing an essay for a class or filling out an application for a job, then no, you should definitely not use any contractions at all. However, in emails, letters, notes, and fiction, it is acceptable to write contractions.

Gonna is a reduction for *going to* that naturally occurs in spoken English. The more relaxed and informal the setting or the better you know the person that you are speaking to, the more likely a native speaker is to use a reduced form such as *gonna*. However, *gonna* is never acceptable in formal writing. If you have seen *gonna* written somewhere, you probably saw it in some song lyrics. Song lyrics are written language, but the language in a song is trying to sound like spoken language, so the songwriter tries to write on paper the way the words should sound when you sing (or say) them. To make the words match the beat of the song, the songwriter often writes in "speech language."

In English, we use *going to* for two different reasons, but *going to* can be reduced to *gonna* in only one of these two cases. Read these ten sentences with *going to* and decide which ones you think *gonna* is possible for.

1. I am going to love you forever.
2. Careful! The baby is going to fall off the chair.
3. Tomorrow I am going to the bank.
4. Nobody really knew when the rain was going to stop.
5. When I get home tonight, I am going to watch that movie on TV.
6. Many people are going to Florida for spring break.
7. The president and his wife are going to travel to China.
8. I hope the exam is not going to be hard.
9. If you are going to the store, can you buy some butter for me?
10. Kelly was going to go to Orlando, but her plans changed.

After looking through these examples, you should have said that *gonna* is possible for all of these except Numbers 3, 6, and 9. We can say *gonna* only when a verb follows *going to* and never when a place follows. When native speakers hear *gonna*, they know that a verb will come next.

Extra Information for the Teacher

This question is commonly asked by ELLs at all proficiency levels. They hear *gonna* all the time, and they want to know about it. Many ELLs, however, do not realize that *be* *going to* can be followed by two different grammar patterns, namely an action or a place, and when trying to sound more advanced, they say, *"I'm gonna the bank" or *"we're gonna New York tomorrow." In addition, many ELLs initially make the mistake of saying *gonna* followed by *to*, so instead of saying, "I'm *gonna* eat dinner now," they say, *"I'm *gonna* to eat dinner now."

Only a high-intermediate or advanced proficiency ELL should really put forth much effort in trying to use *gonna*. Beginning and lower-intermediate ELLs would benefit more if they spent their study time learning new vocabulary or practicing fluency.

Hot Seat Question 16: Present Perfect Tense

Why do people ask me, *Have you ever eaten sushi?* with present perfect tense *(have eaten)* when they are asking about the past? Why do you use a tense named *present* to talk about the past? If you mean present time, then the person has to answer no about the sushi because I can see that he's not eating sushi now, and if he is eating sushi now, I think it would be stupid to ask someone if they are eating sushi. Do you see my point?

Your Answer

Yes, I see your point. Your question is a very good one. We call this verb tense **present perfect,** but that is because present perfect is used to describe situations that connect the past and the present. Most languages do not have one verb tense that is used like present perfect in English. The reality is that present perfect is probably the single most difficult verb tense in English because this one verb tense can be used for at least three different times. In fact, it can be used for the past and for the present, which is what makes it so difficult for ELLs to grasp.

Verb tenses have one or two uses, and those uses are usually very closely connected to the time of the action. Simple past tense, for example, is for the past, and simple future tense is for the future. Present perfect is different. Consider these three common usages:

Present Perfect	
Meaning	**Example**
1. an action that began in the past but still continues now (continuing past)	I **have lived** here since 2003.
2. an action that took place in the past but the time is not mentioned (indefinite past)	I **have lived** in three foreign countries.
3. an action that took place in the past (the time is not mentioned) that is relevant to the current situation (past-present connection)	*Bob:* I'm selling my house and moving to an apartment. It's expensive to maintain a house. *Tim:* Well, I **have lived** in an apartment, and I think you're right. Houses are expensive to keep up.

Extra Information for the Teacher

This question probably came from an intermediate ELL. Present perfect is one of the most difficult things in English grammar. Most languages do not have a tense that works like present perfect in English. For example, Spanish has a tense that looks like present perfect, but it can be used with a definite past time marker that is not possible in English: *Ha llovido fuerte anoche* = **It has rained hard last night.* French, too, has a tense that looks like our present perfect, but there is no simple past tense in French, so this tense doubles up as our simple past and present perfect: *Il a plû* = *It has rained* or *it rained.* Since present perfect has different usages in English, many languages use different verb tenses or different expressions for each of these different usages, resulting in very little overlap of real usage for what would appear to be similar verb tenses. In the most common English usage of present perfect, which is a past action that continues, as in *I have worked here for five years,* many languages—unlike English—use some type of present tense.

The bottom line: Any ELL who can use these three kinds of present perfect with ease is probably reaching advanced proficiency in English. (See pp. 104–5 and 119–24 for more information about present perfect.) When I have to do a quick interview to check a new ELL's general proficiency, I try to ask questions that would normally elicit answers in the present perfect tense.

Hot Seat Question 17: Possessive Forms

Which is correct: *boys'* or *boy's*?

Your Answer

Both are correct, depending on the situation where it is used, but the meaning is very different. The first one, *boys',* means that something belongs to several boys. The second one, *boy's,* means that something belongs to one boy. Part of the confusion of these two items comes from the fact that both are pronounced exactly the same way.

An easy trick to figure this out is to omit the apostrophe and anything to the right. The remaining word should tell you who the owner is. Look at these examples:

Shortcut for the Possessive in English		
Possessive Word	**Omit the Apostrophe and Anything to the Right**	*Real Owner*
the student's books	— 's	the student
the students' books	— '	the students
the Smiths' books	— '	the Smiths

If two children have a kitten, the correct possessive is *the children's kitten.* Let's suppose you are confused about the rule for possessive and don't know if the correct form is *children's* or *childrens'*. Look what happens if we test this here:

two children's	— 's	✓ two children NOTE: Yes, *children* is a word in English.
two childrens'	— '	✗ two childrens NOTE: No, *childrens* is not a word in English.

Possessive in English is a little difficult, but with practice, you can get it right. You add *'s* to a word to make its possessive form. If the word already ends in *–s,* add just the apostrophe. If it is a proper noun—a person's name—it is possible to add either just apostrophe or *'s: Bess'* or *Bess's;* however, the word is pronounced exactly the same—two syllables /bes əz/. If you want to check to see if your form is written correctly, remember to use the technique that we just considered.

Extra Information for the Teacher

ELLs of all proficiency levels need to use possessive forms, so this type of question could be from any proficiency level. Be prepared to tailor your answer, giving only the basics to beginners but more details to higher-proficiency levels.

Hot Seat Question 18: Comparison of Adjectives

How do I know when to add *–er* for comparison and when to use the word *more? Taller* or *more tall? Rapider* or *more rapid?* What's the secret trick?

Your Answer

We use the comparative forms (*–er* or *more*) to compare two things. There is no secret trick, but there is a relatively easy rule. There are a few exceptions, but in general, add *–er* for one-syllable adjectives (*tall* → *taller*) and for two-syllable adjectives that end in *–y*: (*lazy* → *lazier*). All others use *more* before: *expensive* → *more expensive*. The same rule applies for adding *the* before the adjective and *-est* after or using the words *the most* before the adjective.

One Syllable	Two Syllable, End in *–y*	Others
tall— *taller—* *the tallest*	*lazy—* *lazier—* *the laziest*	*modern—* *more modern—* *the most modern*
new— *newer—* *the newest*	*heavy—* *heavier—* *the heaviest*	*serious—* *more serious—* *the most serious*
wide— *wider—* *the widest*	*busy—* *busier—* *the busiest*	*expensive—* *more expensive—* *the most expensive—*
fast— *faster—* *the fastest*	*cozy—* *cozier—* *the coziest*	*rapid—* *more rapid—* *the most rapid*

Some common irregular forms are *good* → *better* → *the best* and *bad* → *worse* → *the worst*. In addition, some adjectives in everyday usage may vary: *common, quiet, simple*. Therefore, you will hear *simpler* and *more simple, the quietest* and *the most quiet*.

Extra Information for the Teacher

This question was probably asked by an intermediate ELL. For whether or not to double the final consonant: *hot* → *hotter* (not *hoter*) and *cold* → *colder* (not *coldder*), see Hot Seat Question 3.

Hot Seat Question 19: do *versus* make

What is the difference between *do* and *make*? You say *I do the dishes* but *I make the beds*. Can I use one for the other?

Your Answer

You use *do* or *make* depending on the other words that they are used with. For example, *we do the dishes*, but *we make the bed*. Why? There is no special reason; these are idiomatic usages.

In general, we use *do* with different kinds of work. We say *do a job, do work,* and *do homework.* In general, we use *make* to indicate creating or producing something new.

The problem is that English has many special expressions with *do* or *make.* These expressions are idiomatic and must therefore be memorized. There is no other solution. Here are some common expressions using *do* and *make:*

Special Expressions with *Do*		Special Expressions with *Make*	
How are you doing?	do business	make the bed	make food
What do you do?	do badly	make dinner	make coffee
How do you do?	do well	make money	make a plan
do work	do housework	make a living	make
do the laundry	do the ironing	make a mistake	arrangements
do homework	do the dishes	make a promise	make a call
do something over	do an exercise	make a difference	make noise
do a favor	do exercise	make an	make an effort
do a job	do an assignment	agreement	make a speech
		make a decision	make sense
		make a suggestion	make progress
		make an excuse	make up your mind

Extra Information for the Teacher

The words *do* and *make* perplex all proficiency levels of ELLs. For beginners, use common examples such as *do homework* and *make a sandwich.* More proficient ELLs can tackle *do business* and *make sense.* Longer lists of examples of *do* and *make* can be found in almost any grammar book for ELLs or even on the Internet, but long lists can be overwhelming to ELLs. When you go over a list with ELLs, a good technique is to ask students to go through the list to see how many of the items they already know. This helps them see that the list is not all new information, and this reduces learner anxiety.

Another useful teaching technique is to teach ELLs that a good strategy is for them to look at the list of items and select the ten items that they think they will need to use in their English. In this list, for example, a person who is studying business or who will use English for business purposes might need expressions such as *make a plan, do business, make progress,* and *make an agreement.*

Many ELLs confuse *do* and *make* because many languages have only one word that means *do* or *make.* For example, Spanish has only *hacer,* and French has only *faire.*

Hot Seat Question 20: Adverbs of Degree Word Order

Which of these two sentences is correct? *I like very much tennis* or *I like tennis very much.* Is there any difference in meaning between these two sentences?

Your Answer

Only the second sentence is correct: *I like tennis very much.* In this sentence, *very much* is an adverb phrase. It tells how much you like tennis.

Sentences in English follow a subject-verb-object (S-V-O) order. It is not common to put an adverb between the verb and the object. In this sentence, the subject is *I*, the verb is *like,* and the object is *tennis*. It is not possible to put an adverb between the verb *like* and the object *tennis*.

The adverb *well* is also difficult for some students. Which do you think is correct? *She sang well the song* or *she sang the song well.*

In some languages, both of these word orders are possible, but in English, only the second sentence is possible. The word *well* is an adverb, and we cannot place an adverb between the verb *sang* and the object *the song*. Therefore, the correct sentence is *She sang the song well.*

Extra Information for the Teacher

A word order question is usually a high-beginner to low-intermediate issue. Word order errors usually reflect direct translations from the ELLs' native languages. Some languages allow much more freedom with word order than English does. For the most part, English sticks to a word order of S-V-O. If there is an adverb, it usually comes after the object.

In French, adverbs can come between the verb and the object, so a French-speaking ELL might write *I like well the coffee*. In Spanish, verbs can come before subjects at times, so a Spanish–speaking ELL may write *Suddenly entered in the room a stranger*. In Japanese, sentences with adverbs of degree follow a S-O-ADV-V word order so a beginning Japanese ELL might write *American people Japanese language very fluently don't speak.*

5

Specific Techniques
for Teaching ELL Grammar

Armed with adequate knowledge about ELL grammar as well as a mindset toward teaching grammar, you are ready to prepare your lesson and teach your class. However, there is always a gap between what any book says about teaching and what actually happens in the classroom. This gap is not surprising given that in a typical class of 20 ELLs, there are 21 human beings (including the teacher) who bring to the learning table 21 different sets of life experiences, world and subject knowledge, and teaching and learning ability.

With this interactive chemistry, it is almost impossible to plan a lesson and carry it out to the letter. Unexpected things not only **can** but **will** happen. For instance, imagine that you have planned your first grammar activity on count nouns. For your lesson, students need their books and their homework, but some students may not have their books, and some may not have completed their homework. You have also planned a second short Internet activity, but when you attempt to access the website in class, it is not working for some reason.

These problems involve human beings and technology, but grammar problems can also happen. Imagine that you have planned a lesson on the past tense of regular verbs and come to class fully prepared with great visuals, examples, and worksheets to practice the form of this tense in affirmative (*wanted*), negative (*did not want*), and interrogative (*did you want?*) forms. However, in the middle of your great teaching presentation, a student asks you about the pronunciation of the *–ed* in *wanted*, *missed*, and *robbed*. "I write *–ed* for these three words, so why is the pronunciation different?" Unmistakably, this Hot Seat Question is a teachable moment, but you have no idea about this pronunciation difference. It was not part of your plan to teach this today.

In all of these cases, you will learn to improvise—as all experienced teachers have. There is no book that can prepare you 100 percent for the real world of teaching grammar. Over the years, many things have happened in my classes that I could not have predicted, but each of these had the potential to become a learning event for both the students and me. For teachers who want to improve their grammar classes, there are two things that I can wholeheartedly recommend: a solid base of grammar knowledge and an extensive repertoire of techniques for teaching grammar.

My first suggestion deals with ELL grammar knowledge. You need to learn as much about ELL grammar as possible. The information in Chapter 3 and the Hot Seat Questions in Chapter 4 will help you tremendously. Teachers often ask me how I learned so much about ELL grammar. The answer is *experience.* It has taken me many years to reach a point where I not only know most of the students' grammar questions, but I can also pretty much predict what the questions will be when an ELL opens his or her mouth to pose the question.

My second suggestion has to do with teaching techniques. As teachers, we have our own individual repertoires of teaching tidbits, techniques, games, and activities that we have developed over time. To increase our repertoires, teachers can read activity books and attend teacher conferences and presentations where practical activities are shared. In this final chapter, I offer 25 different techniques for presenting, explaining, practicing, and assessing grammar that I have learned over the years as a language student and a language teacher.

Teaching Technique 1
You don't need a grammar book to start your lesson.

Many teachers, especially novice teachers, begin lessons with, "Please open your books to page . . . . " The textbook is a tool, not your lesson plan. It is not necessary to begin every lesson with the book. There are other more interesting and more engaging ways to start your grammar lesson.

Why not open the lesson with a sentence and ask students to analyze a grammar point? In other words, start the lesson with a question, not with an answer (or explanation). One effective approach is to set up a comparison between two grammar options. With articles, it could be *a/an* versus *the*, as in this example, which is followed by three teaching options:

Thomas Jefferson was <u>an</u> important person in U.S. history. He was <u>the</u> third president.

Option 1: Write these sentences on the board with the words underlined and ask "Why do we use *an* here but *the* here?" Seek a group explanation.

Option 2: Write the sentences on the board but leave two blanks. Ask students to put *an* and *the* in the blanks. Explain that their choices are *an* and *an, an* and *the, the* and *an,* or *the* and *the.* Seek a group explanation.

Option 3: Write *an* and *the* on the board. Then ask if anyone can come up with a sentence that has both *an* and *the* in it.

Next Step: Ask the class to come up with more examples. In content classes, ask students to find examples of the grammar point in their textbooks. In each case, have ELLs talk about why the writer used *an* or *the* in a particular place in a sentence.

This same teaching technique contrasting two (or more) options can work with most ELL grammar points. Two other examples include *many/much* and verb tenses:

many/much: Sue has <u>many</u> great ideas for the project, but she doesn't have <u>much</u> time to do them.

verb tenses: My cat <u>is losing</u> her hair. Every June she <u>loses</u> a lot of it.

Teaching Technique 2
In example sentences, use content that is relevant and meaningful to your students.

Your students may pay more attention if the content of your teaching examples is interesting and meaningful to them. If you are teaching adults who want to get a job, then your examples might talk about working in an office or applying for a job. If you teach in a university-prep program, your sentences should use topics relevant to being a college student. If your students are more interested in pop culture, use examples that are related to that topic. Teachers should always remember their students' primary reasons for studying English.

In Japan, I once taught English conversation to a group of very talented junior tennis players. At first, I tried to use the traditional kinds of materials for my classes with them, but they tuned me out. These tennis players were not interested in sentences about jobs, school, or international politics. They were, however, extremely interested in tennis. I figured out that they were interested in learning more information about their favorite tennis players, so I went out of my way to use sentences about tennis and tennis players when I was trying to emphasize a particular grammar point.

Here are three examples of how students' interests and ultimate goals in learning English can influence the content of class material, including example sentences:

Students' Interest or Goal	Example Sentences for *is/are*
Tennis	1. Rafael Nadal is a Wimbledon champion. 2. The Williams sisters are from the United States. 3. Maria Sharapova is a great player. 4. Roger Federer is in England now.
Getting a job	1. The night shift is from 11 PM to 7 AM. 2. The applications are available online. 3. The salary is about $15 an hour. 4. The benefits are good at that company.
In a classroom	1. Our grammar class is from 7 to 7:45 PM. 2. The teacher for this class is Mrs. Jenkins. 3. The students in our class are from six countries. 4. Four students in our class are from Korea.

Teaching Technique 3
Find a real task that is suitable for low-proficiency adult ELLs.

If you are teaching adults, it is essential to remember that adults are not children. They do not want to be treated as children, and we need tasks that are not childish. For teachers of low-proficiency ELLs, it can be challenging to find tasks that actually practice the ELL grammar point at hand and are appropriate for adult learners.

An example of such a quandary is how to practice *a* and *an*. Of course the teacher can do drills where the teacher says a noun and students repeat the noun with *a* or *an* (e.g., "cat." "A cat." "book." "A book."), but even low-proficiency students need to go beyond this type of drill. Students need to come up with the word on their own, but it should be for a real communicative purpose.

One activity is to ask students to write the letters of the alphabet along the side of their paper, with one letter for every line. Give students no more than ten minutes to write anything that they can see at that time (in class) that begins with that letter. Answers can have only a noun or an adjective that starts with that letter followed by any noun that they see (that can begin with any letter). Thus, for the letter *c*, they can say "a cat" or "a cute baby"—provided that both of these are visible at the time. True beginners should work only with nouns, but slightly more proficient students can be challenged by working with not only nouns but also **adjective** + **noun** combinations.

Students then take turns saying their answers. When they say their answers, such as *I see a book*, everyone else should be listening for the use of *a* or *an* since that is the ELL grammar point being practiced. See Key 7.

Teaching Technique 4
Use a rapid language drill for practice, assessment, or both.

As a teacher, you know that there is a step (or series of steps) between seeing the form of a new grammar point and being able to actively produce this structure at the right time. One of the early missing steps is just being able to say (or write) the structure. ELLs need a chance to practice using this structure in a safe environment—with the teacher—and teachers can get some feedback as to whether ELLs understand the grammar of the new structure.

A very efficient practice technique is to use a language drill, especially with pairs or small groups of language points that ELLs confuse. For example, many ELLs confuse the use of *since* and *for*, so some rapid, guided practice can be very helpful. In this drill, the teacher will say a time word or phrase such as *yesterday* or *six weeks*, and students (either individually and/or chorally) should say the whole phrase using either *since* or *for*. (Teachers should monitor choral response as carefully as possible because individual student problems may be less obvious.)

A drill is a good technique here because (1) the distinction in English is relatively clear, (2) this grammar point does not require elaborate or multi–sentence examples, and (3) ELLs need to encounter this structure many times.

In this drill, the teacher should explain that he (or she) will say a time word or phrase. Students should then say either *since* or *for* followed by the teacher's utterance. In other words, saying just *for* or only *since* is not acceptable. The whole idea of a drill is to become accustomed to the combination of *for* with a duration and *since* with a name of a time. Requiring this target chunk of language in a rapid-fire manner that simulates ELLs' need to produce these utterances quickly in the real world is what differentiates a good drill from a traditional paper assessment.

After each correct student response, the teacher should repeat the correct response. The teacher's goal is to maintain a brisk pace that keeps students motivated but is still within their reach.

> *Teacher:* yesterday
> *Class:*   since yesterday
> *Teacher:* since yesterday
> *Teacher:* six weeks
> *Class:*   for six weeks
> *Teacher:* for six weeks

Alternatively, the teacher may call on (or gesture to) individual students or divide a larger class into smaller groups. If no response is given, which frequently happens early in the drill, pause and then after a few extra seconds, ask another student. Then go back to the original student. Say the correct answer. Then repeat the prompt and coax students to say the correct phrase this time.

> *Teacher:* Monday . . . Susan
> *Susan:*   (silence)
> *Teacher:* Martha
> *Martha:* since Monday
> *Class:*   Susan
> *Susan:*   since Monday
> *Teacher:* Good . . . three days . . . Jose
> *Jose:*   for three days

Doing a drill well requires a great deal of skill. For example, a drill on a topic such as *for* versus *since* should probably last between 30 and 60 seconds. To accomplish this, the teacher needs to be able to produce a series of time phrases such as *yesterday* and *six weeks,* one after the other. If the teacher hesitates too much, the activity loses its momentum and can very quickly become monotonous.

A drill only works if students are engaged. "Drills are boring" was a common complaint about the audio-lingual method (ALM) used in language learning a few decades ago, but the problem with ALM was not necessarily the drill but rather that ALM used only one technique for the entire class period. Regardless of the teaching method, I can't imagine any class being interesting when it consists of one activity that is carried out day after day. Drills should be used judiciously, and they should be used frequently but in small spurts.

For practice, try to think of a language point studied in this book and come up with a simple drill. Remember that depending on the grammar point, you may need to come up with as many as 20 items in a drill that lasts 30 to 60 seconds. Doing a "live" drill well in class requires skill on the teacher's part, and it is definitely a skill that can be practiced and perfected. Some teachers prefer to plan their drills by making a list of 15–20 drill items on a small notecard. Here is an example of such a crib sheet:

1. yesterday	6. last year
2. six weeks	7. September
3. Monday	8. last September
4. three days	9. 1999
5. a long time	10. a minute

Teaching Technique 5
Limit grammar terminology as much as possible.

I remember visiting a class once where a teacher insisted on making students identify the particles in phrasal verbs (see Key 11). He had them write the word *particle* by the particles. I could not see any useful purpose in having the students use the term *particle*. I wonder how those students liked having to use this grammar label.

Imagine that you have given up one year of your life to enroll in a Bulgarian intensive language program in Sofia, Bulgaria. You have left your family in your country, and you are surrounded by signs in a foreign alphabet that you cannot decipher. You need a great deal of vocabulary to be able to order food in a restaurant or open a bank account. You need language that can help you function in your foreign language setting.

In your Bulgarian class, however, your teacher makes you learn words such as *subject*, *predicate*, and *particle* in Bulgarian. How will these words serve your real-world language needs?

To be certain, we do need some meta-language to discuss grammar. We need words such as *noun* and *verb* fairly early on in the process, but how much more do your students need? No one knows your students better than you do, so you are the best person to answer this question. I would like to recommend, however, erring on the side of using less grammar terminology whenever possible, and for ELLs in primarily conversation courses, almost no grammar terminology.

Teaching Technique 6

Help students sort out and then consolidate
new grammar information.

Students need help consolidating new grammar information. Many times students are
not confused until there are two language options competing for the same slot in their
brain. For instance, students can use simple present very well until they run into present progressive. Now there are two "present" forms that are competing for the same
grammatical slot. ELLs begin mixing up *I do* and *I am doing*. Many ELLs begin to produce hybrid forms such as **I am do.*

Students need your help through practice to sort out which is which. Consider
these two tasks:

**Task 1. Verb Tense Discrimination: Simple Present, Simple Past, Present
Progressive, Future. Underline the correct form of the verb.**

1. *The boy (is going to play, is playing, played, plays) tennis last week.*
2. *Mark and Joe (are going to study, are studying, studied, study) vocabulary next week.*
3. *We (are going to be, are being, were, are) on the plane before you were.*

**Task 2. Verb Tense Discrimination: Simple Present, Simple Past, Present
Progressive, Future. Write the correct form of the verb on the line.**

verb: study

1. She _____ grammar now.

2. They _____ vocabulary last night.

3. He always _____ spelling.

4. I _____ grammar tomorrow.

verb: do

5. You _____ the homework last night.

6. I _____ the exercises every day.

7. We _____ Lesson 5 right now.

8. She _____ the questions tomorrow.

Both of these exercises require students to discriminate among several seemingly
logical answer options for the target grammar point, namely verb tenses. In Task 1,
ELLs must choose the correct answer among four options. In Task 2, ELLs must come
up with the correct verb tense on their own. Task 1 requires passive recognition, but
Task 2 requires active production. Both types of exercises are useful in helping ELLs
refine their ability to use grammar correctly. As a teacher, you should recognize that
Task 2 requires more English proficiency than Task 1 does.

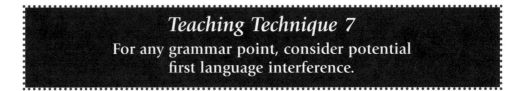

Teaching Technique 7
For any grammar point, consider potential
first language interference.

First language interference causes many but not all ELL grammatical errors. Language errors can come from three sources:

1. First language (L1) interference. Spanish speakers say *I have hungry* because Spanish uses *have* in lieu of *be* in certain expressions that use *be* + adjective in English.
2. Universal problems. All ELLs say *The accident was happen/ed* even though they do not say *was happened* in their own language, and almost all ELLs initially negate with *no* as in *I no like tea* or *I am no like tea* even though they may not negate that way in their L1s.
3. Target language (L2) interference—yes, interference from English itself. Very early in their English studies, ELLs learn *What time is it?* and *Where does Mark live?* so well that they also produce *I don't know what time is it* and *Could you tell me where does Mark live?*

No one expects ELL teachers to know all their ELLs' first languages, but the more foreign languages you know and the more that you know about your students' languages in particular, the better you will be able to understand and predict your students' English errors. This in turn allows you to evaluate student learning and plan your teaching more effectively because you can differentiate between an error that represents L1 interference and one that shows a lack of learning or mastery.

In an ESL setting, your classroom will be multilingual. Based on information provided by the National Clearinghouse for English Language Acquisition and Language Instruction Programs (2002), Florida Department of Education (2007), and California Department of Education (2008), the foreign languages spoken by many ELLs in the United States are (in descending order): Spanish, Vietnamese, Hmong, Chinese, Korean, Haitian French Creole, Arabic, Russian, Tagalog, Portuguese, and Japanese. In contrast, in an EFL setting, all of your students will most likely speak the same native language. In either setting, knowledge of your students' L1 in relation to English impacts your ability to teach ELL grammar.

How can you learn what you need to know about your students' L1 to spot interference? One obvious way is to enroll in a foreign language class. Not only will you learn about the foreign language, you will also experience what it is like to be a language student—to be in your students' shoes—and you will have an opportunity to evaluate how you perceive different teaching techniques used by your language teacher. This can be quite enlightening.

Since enrolling in a class is not a viable option for everyone, a second method to gain the L1 knowledge that you need is to pay close attention to the notes about the potential interference for various L1s that can be found at the end of every ELL grammar point covered in Chapter 3. For novice ELL teachers, there is much to learn, but the more you deal with ELLs, the more you will begin to recognize the specific types of grammatical errors that speakers of Spanish, Chinese, Arabic, or another foreign languages make.

Teaching Technique 8
Simple exercises may not be so simple.

Don't assume that an exercise is "simple" or does not activate learners' minds because it appears shallow. For instance, simple error identification in the form of two answer options with only one being correct requires students to select the correct form and at the same time begin to distance themselves from the error in the other option. This task is very good if the errors are actual errors that your ELLs might make. The type of error may be influenced by ELLs' first languages and their English proficiency levels.

The following task, which requires very little teacher preparation time, is a short example of a simple but successful **comparative** and **superlative** forms exercise:

Directions: Put a check mark (✓) to indicate which of these two forms is possible.			

__A. successfuller
__B. more
    successful
	__A. the most bad
	__B. the worst
		__A. the slowliest
		__B. the most
		    slowly
			__A. more serious
			__B. seriouser

Teaching Technique 9
Use the board to help ELLs visualize a pattern.

When students can *see* the grammar pattern, they are more likely to remember the pattern. To illustrate this, let's look at the problematic grammar issue of when to double the final consonant before adding *–ing* or *–ed*.

The rule is that you double the last consonant if it is a one–syllable word ending in C-V-C (consonant-vowel-consonant). Thus, we double the *t* in hit to *hitting* but not in *act* to **actting*.

As this rule is illustrated on the board, a good teacher would try to make sure that the examples are aligned so that at the end you can clearly see three columns and then write C-V-C above.

For example, notice how the material on the board progresses as you add examples, which you are eliciting from the students rather than your own mental word bank. *Teach actively:* Always keep your students involved in whatever you are doing at the board.

Without actually telling anyone the rule first, ask the students to say verbs and then write them correctly with either one or doubled consonants:

When your board has eight to ten examples, there is probably enough information to help "prove" the generalization.

At this point, ask students if anyone can figure out when you double the consonant and when you do not. Respond positively to all answers. Say something like, "No, that's not exactly right" to wrong guesses. Whether someone says the actual rule or not, draw vertical lines to help students figure out the rule.

CVC	not CVC

cut|t ing   ea|t|ing
grab|b ing   need|ing
put|t ing   reach|ing
brag|g ing   look|ing

Point out that the base form of the verbs on the left end in C-V-C while those on the right do not. Ask students to come up with three more verbs for both columns.

Teaching Technique 10
Use songs to practice ELL grammar.

Just about everyone loves music. Using songs from time to time in class can be not only fun but very educational. Songs tend to repeat certain phrases or lines, so in essence, a song is really a language drill set to music. Be sure to give your students a copy of the lyrics (but be careful to not violate copyright law) so that they can both hear and see the grammar point. Instead of telling students the grammar point that you are emphasizing, ask the students to see if they recognize any grammar points that you have studied. It is imperative that you choose songs that have lyrics that your students can understand fairly well and that are worth learning. One of the worst experiences for an ELL is to work hard to learn some new vocabulary only to find out that it is rarely used outside of the classroom.

Here are four examples of songs connected with particular grammar points:

Song and Artist	Grammar Point
"El Condor Pasa" (Simon and Garfunkel)	verbs and modals in *if* sentences
"Tom's Diner" (Suzanne Vega)	present progressive tense
"In the Ghetto" (Elvis Presley)	simple present tense, 3rd person *-s*
"We've Only Just Begun" (Carpenters)	present perfect tense; infinitives and gerunds

Teaching Technique 11
Choose grammar materials for false beginners carefully.

Many of the students that I taught in Japan who placed into our Level 1 classes had studied English for many years. To be certain, they knew some English words, and some had even memorized complicated grammar points such as *if* clauses, yet these students could not say very much in English. Such ELLs are referred to as **false beginners** because they are not really beginners even though their lack of oral fluency might make a teacher mistakenly misjudge their actual level. In a way, false beginners are trying to retrieve previously studied material, so you can teach them material beyond what you would with true beginners.

Let's imagine a lesson about *is* with **true beginners** and **false beginners**. We know that *is* can be followed by many different structures, including a noun (*is a doctor*), an adjective (*is good*), a present participle (*is eating*), a past participle (*is eaten*), a preposi-tional phrase (*is in the room*).

With true beginners, we should focus on only <u>one</u> of these categories first; in other words, we should not include noun examples and prepositional phrase examples because these are two different grammatical patterns.

With false beginners, however, the situation might be different if you believe that your ELLs can handle this material. For many false beginners, it may be a matter more of re-awakening their previous knowledge or shoring up their courage to use their prior English knowledge. In this case, you can be less concerned about mixing up sub-points of the primary grammar point.

Compare these two sets of examples for true beginners and false beginners. Note that the topic of tennis is the same for both groups.

TOPIC: Famous Tennis Players	
True Beginners	**False Beginners**
1. Rafael Nadal is from Spain.	1. Rafael Nadal is from Spain.
2. Serena Williams is from the U.S.	2. Serena Williams is 27 years old.
3. Maria Sharapova is from Russia.	3. Maria Sharapova is a great player.
4. Roger Federer is from Switzerland.	4. Roger Federer is in England now.
Comments: 1. One pattern: SUBJ + *is* + *from* + country 2. A novice teacher might have mistak-enly used nationalities instead of country names, but nationalities are irregular in English and form a sepa-rate vocabulary lesson. Many people can relate to learning the name of a country and may in fact already know it, but nationalities are much more difficult. Consider how the four countries in our examples change irregularly to *Spanish, Ameri-can, Russian,* and *Swiss,* which would add a new grammar point if includ-ed in the example sentences. 3. Great content for these students, all of whom are serious tennis players.	Comments: 1. These examples would not be good for true beginners because they are four different patterns that express origin, age, occupation, and location. 2. False beginners can be pushed a lit-tle, and such prodding is good as long as material is still within their grasp. While different aspects of *be* are mixed together here (origin, age, occupation, and location), note that only present tense of *be* is on the board. We have no past tense, no conditionals, and no modals.

Teaching Technique 12
Use pantomime when it matches the grammar point.

Teaching present progressive tense is relatively easy. The only problem is that some verbs are rarely used in this tense, but our ELLs attempt to make sentences such as *I am being sick this week.*

How can we help our ELLs remember whether a verb can or cannot be in the present progressive tense? The following verbs do not show action in English and are therefore rarely used in progressive form: *own, possess, like, love, need, want, seem, feel, be, prefer, remember, forget, believe.* What is able to be the "action" can vary from language to language, so I do not recommend belaboring this concept much.

One way to deal with this is to play charades. It is very difficult to illustrate *want* or *prefer* in gestures. Explain to students that verbs that they cannot physically demonstrate well are probably not used in progressive tenses in English.

Teaching Technique 13
Multiple choice questions are useful in teaching, not just testing, grammar.

In language learning, we often hear about comprehensible input, meaning that learners need large amounts of understandable speaking and reading samples so that they can assimilate grammar patterns and develop their English proficiency. All of this input from you that our learners are hearing is real English usage, which can be referred to as positive evidence. In other words, the utterances that our ELLs hear is possible English (hence, positive). Equally valuable and, some might argue, even more valuable is **negative evidence.** That is, our learners also need to know ***what is not possible.***

Native speakers have had years and years of positive input. The combination of a large amount of input, surely thousands of millions of words in both print and speech, with at least 15 to 20 years of cognitive development time, allows native speakers to learn our first language with relatively little negative evidence. For example, you know that the words in this paragraph are in a correct order (or you would not be able to understand these sentences!), but no one ever told you to say *have had* instead of *had have* or *thousands of millions* instead of *millions of thousands.*

In stark contrast, most non-native learners have relatively little input (especially in an EFL setting or even in an ESL setting where the students are not readily exposed to English so much at home or outside of school). In addition, many ESL learners have a very short time frame in which to reach a certain level of English proficiency.

For ELLs who have such tight time constraints along with very limited English input, negative evidence is critical. Very young ELLs may not benefit from negative feedback, but adult learners who are accustomed to being in a classroom setting have the requisite study and classroom skills to ask questions about language points and benefit from feedback about what is and what is not possible in English.

One practice technique for doing this is multiple choice questions. Multiple choice questions force learners to discriminate among various answer options and figure out which ones are not possible and why. Teachers should capitalize on the built-in language discrimination in multiple choice questions, as in these examples:

1. At the store, he bought some _____.
   (A) can of beans   (B) loaf of bread   (C) carrot   (D) rice

2. I'm a tennis fanatic! _____ I'm tired, I usually have enough energy to play.
   (A) Only if   (B) Even if   (C) Since   (D) Now that

The bottom line: You should be able to create a multiple choice question for any language point. In fact, a good teaching technique is to write three or four multiple choice questions on the board and then ask students to work on their answers individually and then in pairs or small groups. In addition to being a good source of negative input and speaking practice, students will develop better test-taking as well as editing skills.

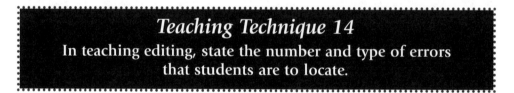

Teaching Technique 14
In teaching editing, state the number and type of errors that students are to locate.

Editing is an important composition skill for ELLs to practice and master because it helps them to function in English independently of the teacher or textbook. Some editing tasks ask students to "locate and repair the errors" in a short piece of writing, but the ELLs are not told which errors to look for. We should focus on *teaching*, not *testing*. We should be teaching our students to be careful with specific kinds of errors—and not testing for just any and all possible errors in English. For better teaching outcomes, I recommend using exercises that tell students specifically what kinds of errors to look for. When teachers do not specify this information, students tend to identify more errors than actually exist in the exercise. Since our goal is to improve ELLs' ability to repair specific errors, such as subject-verb agreement or verb tense, tell your students exactly what they are looking for. By doing so, you are ***teaching***, not testing.

Find the Errors

Directions: *Locate and correct the seven errors in: modals (2), missing subject (1), noun plurals (1), verb form (1), pronouns (1), and negatives (1).*

   If you fall down or got hit in the mouth, one of your tooth might come out. Knowing what to do in this emergency may can allow you to save your tooth. First, you shall try to put the tooth back in its socket, or original hole, and hold it there firmly. You should no wash the tooth, as this can actually harm it. If you are unable to put the tooth back in its socket, then put in the cheek area and hold it there. If this is not possible, should put the tooth in a glass of milk until you can get to the hospital. Of course it is important to meet with your doctor or dentist as soon as possible.

Source: *Intermediate Reading Practices: Building Reading and Vocabulary Skills, 3rd Ed.* (Folse, 2004).

Teaching Technique 15
Help ELLs manage the daunting chunks of grammar information.

Some grammar points are about a general system, such as present progressive tense or modals. In contrast, other grammar points require students to learn information about a long list of items. Examples include irregular past tense forms, verbs that are followed by gerunds, and common non-count nouns.

   One of our jobs as teachers is to help our learners manage what appear to be large, daunting learning tasks such as lists. A good teacher never gives students a list and says, "Now go memorize this list" without any kind of advice. A good teacher helps students figure out strategies that will help with memorization.

   One good strategy is to train students to look for patterns within the list. For example, all ELLs must deal with irregular past tense forms, which are among some of the most frequently used words in English—*took, put,* or *said*. To be certain, an alphabetical list of irregular past tense and past participle forms may initially appear daunting, but some students may benefit from a task that requires learners to group the items by pronunciation or spelling patterns, such as A-A-A for *cut, cut, cut* is A-B-B for *teach, taught, taught* or A-B-C for *go, went, gone.* Many times we grammar teachers rush past the form of a grammar point in order to get to the actual practice. However, grammar points can be difficult because of their form, because of their usage, or for both reasons.

   Ask students to refer to a given list of irregular past tense and past participle forms. Remind students that they may use some verbs twice. Beyond additional work with learning these forms, ELLs may come to realize that the list of, say, 100 items is really not 100 individual items but instead ten groups of items that are similar. In other words, within the seemingly haphazard list of completely irregular forms, there are some patterns that will make the learning load lighter.

Each student should have a pattern sheet. Students should go through their reference list of verbs to find other verbs that match these patterns for forming the present, past, and past participle of these irregular verbs.

Present	Past	Past Participle
long *i*	long *o*	–*en*
drive	_drove_	_driven_
_____	_____	_____
_____	_____	_____
All 3 forms are the same.		
cost	_cost_	_cost_
_____	_____	_____
_____	_____	_____
present	past	present + –*en*
eat	_ate_	_eaten_
_____	_____	_____
_____	_____	_____
long *e*	long *o*	–*en*
speak	_spoke_	_spoken_
_____	_____	_____
_____	_____	_____
short *i*	short *a*	short *u*
begin	_began_	_begun_
_____	_____	_____
_____	_____	_____
present	past	same as present
become	_became_	_become_
_____	_____	_____
_____	_____	_____
present	past	present + –*n*
drive	_drove_	_driven_
_____	_____	_____
_____	_____	_____

Teaching Technique 16
Help ELLs see all the pieces of a grammar puzzle.

Students are accustomed to seeing information, not just hearing it. A good teacher will have some kind of visual that helps ELLs follow the lesson better. The example here is an overhead transparency that helps students consolidate the present and past tense forms of some common verbs. I normally do two or three examples as a class and then let students work individually or in pairs to fill in the other forms. An effective teaching plan is to give this to students as a homework sheet a few days later.

Present Statement	Present Negative	Past Statement	Past Negative	Present Question	Past Question
he goes	he doesn't go	he went	he didn't go	Does he go	Did he go
they catch				Do they catch	
		we had			
			she didn't get		
	I don't wake				

Teaching Technique 17
Break up longer or difficult grammar lessons.

For some strange reason, many teachers feel compelled to follow their grammar book (or other ELL book) rigidly. Just because a lesson in the book is very long, it does not mean that you must teach that entire lesson in one class period to your students. The authors of the textbook may not have had the foresight to split up the material into more manageable chunks, but you can do this. The authors do not know your students' capabilities, but you do.

Consider irregular past tense verbs, for example. In terms of forms to learn, there are about 150 irregular verbs with perhaps 60 to 70 of these being of high frequency. In addition, there are grammatical patterns to learn here, such as the negative is *did* plus the base form, not the irregular form (*I did not go* versus **I did not went.*).

Why not divide this grammar point into two (or three) lessons with some time in between? There is a good rationale for teaching a few irregular verbs first and then teaching all of those plus the others later. Teach high-frequency irregular verbs first. Students are then likely to run into them in their reading or listening and therefore have some time to consolidate meaning. At the very least, students may notice these words more and pay attention to their use.

Teaching Technique 18
Gimmicks help all learners.

The rule for doubling letters of one–syllable words before adding *–ing* or *–ed* has been demonstrated in Teaching Technique 9, but what do you do for two–syllable words? The rule is that for verbs of two syllables that end in C-V-C, you double the last consonant before adding *–ing* or *–ed* if the stress is on the second syllable (*commit* → *committed*) but not if the stress is on the first syllable (*open* → *opened*).

One effective gimmick to practice this point is to have students first circle which syllable is stressed. This number is important because the number they have circled (1 or 2) indicates which syllable is stressed and also indicates how many letters to put before adding the *–ing* or *–ed*. When you write this on the board, you will see the proverbial light bulbs go off in your learners' heads.

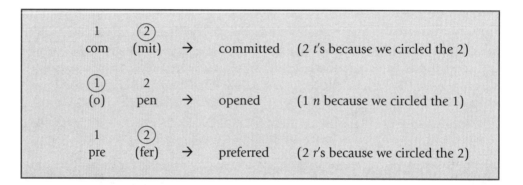

Teaching Technique 19
Use examples that match the target grammar point.

Your example sentences when teaching any grammar point are the key to successful teaching and learning. As you introduce *to be* (and any grammar point) to your students, you will be writing and saying many example sentences. What should you keep in mind as you come up with the example sentences?

Your example sentences should not go much beyond the current grammar point. For example, when you are teaching present tense of *be* (*am, is, are*), you should not use sentences that contain more complex grammar points such as past tense of *be* (*was, were*), other verbs, other tenses, conditionals, or adjective clauses. Your overall goal is to keep the pattern as simple as possible when you are presenting new grammar.

Consider these good and bad examples when you are first introducing ELLs to *am, is, are*:

Good Example	Bad Example	Notes
Kevin is thirsty.	Kevin is thirsty. He was thirsty yesterday, too.	1. Don't introduce *was* with *is*. 2. Students don't know *too*.
Laura is tired.	Laura is tired. She was at the office all day today.	3. Don't introduce *was* with *is*. 4. Students don't know *all day*. *(all day* vs. *every day)*
John is happy.	If John is happy, he will go with us to the beach.	5. Conditional sentences are difficult to comprehend. 6. Students don't know *will, us, beach.*
The books are green.	The books that are on the table are green.	7. Adjective clause *(that are on the table)* is hard/confusing.

Let's move to a later class meeting when the lesson is now focusing on using a form of *be* in sentences that state a person's occupation. The target English pattern is: subject + *am/is/are* + article + occupation. This pattern produces sentences such as *I am a student* and *She is a doctor*. However, a teacher who wants to provide some clear examples of this pattern might inadvertently throw in additional grammar points, resulting in confused ELLs.

Consider these examples from three different teachers:

Initial Presentation Examples of *am/is/are*		
Class A: One Grammar Point	**Class B: Two Grammar Points**	**Class C: Three Grammar Points**
1. I am a student. 2. You are a teacher. 3. He is a lawyer. 4. She is a doctor. 5. It is a tiger.	1. I am a student. 2. You are a teacher. 3. He is an architect. 4. She is an architect. 5. It is a tiger.	1. I am a good student. 2. You are a nice teacher. 3. He is a great architect. 4. She is an excellent lawyer. 5. It is a unique elephant.

In these examples, students in Class A see five good examples because the only part that is changing—the only part that grabs learners' attention—is the variation of *am, is,* and *are*. Therefore, it is logical that this variation, which is the purpose of the lesson, is the focus of the learners' attention.

In Class B, however, the teacher has unwittingly introduced the question of when to use *a* and *an*. In B, students will have no problems with 1, 2, and 5, but when ELLs see 3 and 4, they will want to know why you use *an* instead of *a* here. The teacher has now introduced an additional grammar point: *a/an*. For some groups, this additional grammar point may be all right; for other groups, it may be a problem. In either case, the teacher should be aware of the *actual* grammar points being illustrated.

In Class C, students may have problems with all five examples because many ELLs want to put adjectives after nouns (due to L1 interference). Some ELLs will want to know why we say *a good student*, not **a student good*. Therefore, in C, the teacher should <u>not</u> include adjectives in any of the initial examples. Furthermore, the teacher in C has also included the *a/an* grammar point. ELLs will want to know why we say *an* before *excellent* but not before *unique* in the next sentence. This is precisely the kind of question that ELLs will ask—because the teacher has not chosen examples carefully. If you think the reason for the use of *an* in #3 is that *excellent* begins with a vowel, then why don't we say *an* in #5 as well? The difference is that *unique* begins with a vowel letter but not a vowel sound.

Teaching Technique 20
Teach mnemonic devices to help ELLs remember grammar.

When you change a verb from active voice to passive voice, a helpful hint is to count the number of verb parts in the active sentence and then add one. The number of verb parts in the passive sentence is usually one more than the number of verb parts in the active sentence because we add a form of the verb *be* to the passive sentence.

Pay attention to the number of verb parts in these active and passive sentences.

Active	Passive
1 People *write* Arabic from right to left.	2 Arabic *is written* from right to left.
2 The vice president *will lead* the meeting.	3 The meeting *will be led* by the vice president.
4 Local artists *are going to do* the paintings.	5 The paintings *are going to be done* by local artists.

As your ELLs are exposed to more verb tenses, it is essential to guide your students to compare verb forms from one tense to the next. When dealing with passive voice, for example, too many books and teachers use only examples from simple past tense. Include different tenses as well as modals and *be*.

	Active Voice	**Passive Voice**
simple present tense	People do X.	X _____ *is done.* _____
present progressive tense	People are doing X.	X _____
simple past tense	People did X.	X _____
modal	People might do X.	X _____
have to	People have to do X.	X _____
be going to	People are going to do X.	X _____
past progressive tense	People were doing X.	X _____
present perfect tense	People have done X.	X _____

Teaching Technique 21
Motivate your ELLs with a challenge.

I learned this trick from my high school French teacher, Mrs. de Montluzin, who told us one day in French class, "The sound of /ɾ/ in French is very difficult, and I don't know if any of you will be able to pronounce this sound yet. I'm going to pronounce some words, and you see if you can say them after me." For some reason, being told that I might not be able to learn something actually motivated me. This challenge made me even more determined to try to pronounce the French /ɾ/.

Issuing this kind of challenge takes no teacher preparation time or special effort, but its effect on your class can be dramatic. I find it especially effective when I am going to present a grammar point that is somewhat difficult. If students are able to learn the grammar point well right away, they feel especially good. At the same time, students who have difficulties do not feel so bad because I acknowledged that this grammar point was a little difficult before starting the lesson. Thus, you can see that this challenge benefits not only the best but all students in a class.

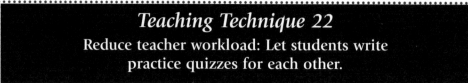

Teaching Technique 22
Reduce teacher workload: Let students write
practice quizzes for each other.

We teachers are overworked. We recognize the value of frequent small assessments of our ELLs' progress—for both our and their benefit—but we cannot manage all of the paperwork that frequent quizzes entail.

The solution: Let students quiz each other. Have students write simple quizzes for each other. This works best with grammar rules that are relatively straightforward and/or require memorization of many items. It is not recommended for activities that require actual usage since non-native speakers, many of whom have limited proficiency, will be grading the usage of other similarly limited proficiency ELLs. Student-written quizzes work particularly well, however, with any grammar point that comes in a list, including irregular past tense and past participles (pp. 336–40), verbs followed by gerunds or infinitives (pp. 201–7), and separable versus non–separable phrasal verbs (pp. 214–18).

By making one simple quiz of 20 items, students have at least four different encounters with the grammar material: (1) when students create an original quiz, (2) when students exchange papers and take a classmate's quiz, (3) when students return quizzes to the original writer who then checks the answers, and finally (4) when students have an opportunity to look over their corrected quizzes. This activity is probably unfamiliar to most ELLs, so you need to make a sample quiz so that all students can follow the same formatting in your model.

This great activity requires minimum work on the teacher's part, but it provides maximum student practice with the grammar material. The bottom line: no teacher grading required!

Quiz Writer: _____

Quiz Taker: _____ Date: _____

	Present	Past	Past Participle
1.	be	_____	_____
2.	make	_____	_____
3.	break	_____	_____

(Continue until 20 items are in place.)

Teaching Technique 23
Find grammar points in non-ELL materials.

It is very empowering for ELLs to be able to recognize recently studied grammar points in non-ELL materials. Our ELLs can tell the difference between materials that have been modified for their limited English proficiency and original, non-modified materials. Choose material that is not too far beyond your ELLs' reading ability.

A simple grammar point is that all singular count nouns must have an article (*a, an, the*) or some other determiner before them. Ask your students to find every noun in a paragraph from the textbook or newspaper or other source. Students should underline the singular noun, and then circle the determiner that comes before it, remembering that sometimes there may be one or two words in between: *a cat* versus *a very young cat*.

Teaching Technique 24
Use guided grammar writing activities to help ELLs see the connection between grammar and writing.

One way to move beyond the traditional fill-in-the-blank activities in so many grammar books and practice limited composition at the same time is with what I call Guided Grammar Writing. For this activity, choose a paragraph that you would like your students to focus on. For example, if you are studying descriptive writing, choose a paragraph that has many descriptive adjectives or that has words that evoke strong feelings of emotion. Conversely, you could choose a short narrative for narrative writing or a paragraph from the letter to the editor column in a newspaper for argumentative writing.

Keeping in mind your grammar points related to your writing objective, identify five to eight areas of interest in the paragraph. These might include verbs, descriptive adjectives, clauses, or longer sentences.

What you are going to do is remove certain features from the paragraph and then provide directions to put these pieces back in. Be sure that when you remove these items, the resulting language is still grammatically correct and logical. In this exercise, ELLs are not correcting errors. They are editing to make improvements.

Guided Grammar Writing   Name: _____

Read the paragraph below. Rewrite it by making the six changes listed.
<u>Careful</u>: You may have to make other changes, including adding prepositions and changing verb forms.

1. Change *many* in Line 1 to *a wide variety*.
2. In Line 4, use a pronoun for *these magazines*.
3. In Line 7, add a word that means "most important" to describe focus.
4. Combine the sentence *A few are older* with the sentence just before it.
5. Add *lately* to the sentence that begins *This magazine has . . .*
6. Change the last question to one that begins with *Should*. In this question, present the two possibilities. (For example, *Should we leave now or go later?*)

At our school office, we subscribe to many magazines. We make these magazines available to our students, much as magazines are available in the waiting rooms of doctors' offices. These magazines are not used in classes, and students are free to read them or ignore them. These magazines are for extra English practice. Some of these magazines are about science. Others are about business, and others are general interest. The fact is that we have a wide variety of types of magazines for our students. The focus of one of these magazines is on pop culture. It deals with celebrities and topics that appeal to college-age students. (Most of our students are college-age students. None is younger. A few are older.) This magazine has been coming with semi-nude models on the cover. Certain parts of the body are always strategically covered, but there is no doubt that the models are unclothed. My question is: What should we do?

Source: *First Discussion Starters: Speaking Fluency Activities for Lower-Level ESL/EFL Students* (Folse & Ivone, 2002).

Now let's look at a copy of the original paragraph, which is our answer key for this guided grammar activity. For changes that have only one option, such as substituting one word for another, there is only one correct answer. However, for this to be a good activity, you want to go beyond mere copying and substituting. You want changes that allow for more leeway and creativity on the ELL's part. For example, Change 5 asks students to add the word *lately*, but this word can go in several different places, not just one. The teacher's goal is to design an activity that requires students to apply the grammar rule in a real world situation.

At our school office, we subscribe to **a wide variety of** magazines. We make these magazines available to our students, much as magazines are available in the waiting rooms of doctors' offices. These magazines are not used in classes, and students are free to read them or ignore them. **They** are for extra English practice. Some of these magazines are about science. Others are about business, and others are general interest. The fact is that we have a wide variety of types of magazines for our students. The **main** focus of one of these magazines is on pop culture. It deals with celebrities and topics that appeal to college-age students. (Most of our students are college-age students. **None is younger, but a few are older.**) **Lately** this magazine has been coming with semi-nude models on the cover. Certain parts of the body are always strategically covered, but there is no doubt that the models are unclothed. My question is: **Should we remove this magazine from circulation in our program?**

This activity can be displayed on an overhead transparency or similar available technology. A real advantage for teachers is that this writing activity does not generate stacks of papers that you have to grade. Many writing activities contain original writing that you do need to look at; however, this activity should be shared in pairs or small groups first and then can be checked easily as a whole class.

I find that this activity works best when it is intentionally kept short, as more is not necessarily better here.

Teaching Technique 25
Develop your own system for correcting grammar errors.

Teachers often ask when and how they should correct grammar errors. The answer is, "It depends."

In speaking, I would not correct any errors directly. If you interrupt the students when they are talking, they might lose their train of thought or suddenly become quiet, which is not what you want. You want your ELLs to speak in English as much as possible. In addition, when you correct someone who is speaking, the speaker may not realize that you are making a correction. If the speaker does realize that you have made a correction, he or she may not actually use your correction in a reformulation. In other words, at best your correction will not be noticed by the ELL; at worst, your correction will stop communication.

In writing, the answer depends on the purpose of the writing. If this is a student journal, you should not make corrections. Some students, however, may request that you correct their writing. In this case, I recommend that you choose one, two, or three main errors and point only those out.

In a paragraph or essay, you should mark the errors. This brings up the question of how errors should be marked. I have not seen any conclusive research finding that strongly indicates that any one method of marking a written paper produces better learning than any other method. Research has looked at numerous marking options including not marking errors, marking only certain errors, circling the error but not indicating the nature of the mistake, and using error codes such as S-V for subject-verb agreement errors or ART for article errors. I recommend marking your ELLs' papers in a way that you are comfortable with and that you have explained completely to your ELLs. Find out what works best with your ELLs.

Remember that error correction should be helpful and lead to better learning, not become a huge burden on you or the students. Try to view error correction as a necessary and important part of student learning, not just testing.

APPENDIX 1
Common Grammar Errors
Made by Native Speakers

Errors that Occur in Writing and Speaking	Errors that Occur Predominantly in Writing
1. unnecessary prepositions (e.g., *Where do you live at?*‡)	12. *have, of*
2. *I, me*	13. *it's, its, its'*‡
3. *myself* (reflexive pronouns)	14. *your, you're*
4. past participles and past tense (e.g., *gone, went*)	15. *'s*
5. *lie, lay*	16. *who's, whose*
6. *whoever, whomever* (or *who–whom*)	17. *to, too, two*
7. *he/she/it don't*‡	18. *affect, effect*
8. *if I would have known*‡	19. *lose, loose*
9. double negatives	20. *they're, there, their*
10. *bad, badly*	
11. *them, those*	

This appendix consists of twenty errors made by native English speakers. The selection of these errors is based on my years of teaching experience and interviews with college composition instructors. In addition, I collected examples of errors in native speaker writing in the form of letters, emails, and essays for three years as I prepared to write this book. The twenty errors are divided into two groups, namely those made in both writing and speaking and those made primarily in writing. Errors 1–11 are errors made in both writing and speaking. Errors 12–20 occur in writing.

In the first group of errors, native speakers often misuse one word for another, so they might say (or write) ‡*I feel badly* instead of *I feel bad*, or they might say (or write) ‡*We went should have there* instead of *We should have gone there*. A native speaker who consistently says, ‡*We should have went* is likely to write that same error as well.

The second group of errors occurs in writing. With these errors, the correct form and the incorrect form have the same or very similar pronunciations. For example, Error 12 involves the mistaken use of the word *of* for the auxiliary *have* in past modal constructions such as ‡*must of gone* instead of *must have gone*. In natural spoken English, the auxiliary *have* is not stressed and is reduced to the sound of schwa /ə/, which makes is sound just like the preposition *of*, which is also not stressed in natural spoken English and is reduced to the sound of schwa.

Native and non-native English speakers need to proofread their written work carefully to edit for these errors but especially for this second group of errors. Students cannot rely on the spellchecker on their computers with these errors. For example, the combination ‡*must of gone* is not possible, but all three words are in fact correct English words, so this combination may not be marked in any way.

Errors that Occur in Writing and Speaking

Error 1: Unnecessary Prepositions	
• in writing • in speaking	‡Where do you live at?

Many of us were told that we should never end a sentence with a preposition. Unfortunately, this "rule" is not true. There are in fact many times when it is absolutely necessary to do so.

Possible with Final Preposition	Not Possible without Final Preposition
1. What are you looking at?	‡What are you looking? ?At what are you looking?
2. What are you waiting for?	‡What are you waiting? ?For what are you waiting?
3. Lying is one thing she won't put up with.	‡Lying is one thing she won't put up. ?Lying is one thing up with which she won't put.
4. I know which song he's listening to.	‡I know which song he's listening. I know to which song he's listening. *(possible but much more formal than the left column)*

NOTE: ‡before a sentence indicates an ungrammatical sentence. ? before a sentence indicates an awkward sentence. *before a sentence indicates an ELL error.

If some sentences have to end in a preposition to maintain their intended meaning, why did our teachers tell us, "Never end a sentence with a preposition"? Their intention was to stop people from ending sentences with **unnecessary** prepositions. The most common example of this involves the question word *where* and the prepositions *at* or *to*, as in ‡*Where do you live at?* More examples follow.

Incorrect	Correct
‡Where do you live at?	Where do you live?
‡Where are you going to?	Where are you going?
‡That is where she works at.	That is where she works.
‡Brown bears inhabit places where it's difficult for humans to live in.	Brown bears inhabit places where it's difficult for humans to live.
‡It's essential to get the message out to parents that they have to know who their loved ones associate with and where they are at.	It's essential to get the message out to parents that they have to know who their loved ones associate with and where they are.

Error 2: *I, me*	
• in writing • in speaking	‡Between you and I, this situation is going to have a very unhappy ending.

I or *me?* When do we use *I*, and when do we use *me?* *I* is a subject pronoun, and *me* is an object pronoun. The word *I* almost always functions as the subject of a sentence (*I am here*). It occurs less commonly after the verb *to be* and sounds very formal (*The mystery donor is I*).

The word *me* is usually an object after a verb. It can be a direct object (*The judges selected me as the winner*) or indirect object (*The judges gave me the prize*). It can also function as the object of a preposition (*The judges listened to me when I sang*).

Confusion of *I* and *me* occurs for several reasons. First, people generally think that *I* sounds more correct (or somehow better) than *me*, so they tend to overuse *I* as a hyper correction. This idea is totally without merit; the use of *I* or *me* depends on the function of the word within a given sentence. Second, people mistakenly believe that *you* should always use *I* somewhere before a verb and *me* somewhere after a verb, which means that *I* is used near the beginning of a sentence and *me* toward the end. This misconception has a good basis in that subjects usually come before the verb, and *I* functions as a subject. However, a problem occurs with prepositional phrases because they may occur either before or after the verb. Thus, people think that they should open their sentence with *Between you and I* because this phrase is occurring before the verb.

When there are multiple objects, people often make a mistake with *I* and *me*. The sentence ‡*The teacher gave the award to Justin, Kim, and I because we sang so well* is incorrect because you should use an object form since the three people here are functioning as objects of the preposition *to*. This usage error is actually quite common. It is extremely easy, however, to figure out whether to use *I* or *me* in this case. Omit all of the other names so that you have only one slot left and then fill it with *I* or *me*. Although many native speakers might commit the grammatical faux pas in this example, almost no native speaker would ever say **The teacher gave the award to I*. In this case, it is now obvious to any native speaker that *to me* sounds much better than *to I*.

Incorrect	Correct
‡*Between you and I, this situation is going to have a very unhappy ending.	Between you and me, this situation is going to have a very unhappy ending.
‡Laura has been frank from day one and explained to Donna, Carlos, and I what she is going through.	Laura has been frank from day one and explained to Donna, Carlos, and me what she is going through.
‡Your place was terrific, but I want to say that your warm hospitality and great facilities are what we enjoyed the most and what made the trip so special to Mary and I.	Your place was terrific, but I want to say that your warm hospitality and great facilities are what we enjoyed the most and what made the trip so special to Mary and me.
‡Listen, if the manager wants to give more responsibility to you and I, well, I think that's a wonderful thing.	Listen, if the manager wants to give more responsibility to you and me, well, I think that's a wonderful thing.
‡I am currently working on my master's degree in teaching. My ultimate goal is for my wife and I to teach overseas together.	I am currently working on my master's degree in teaching. My ultimate goal is for my wife and me to teach overseas together.

Error 3: *Myself* (Reflexive Pronouns)

• in writing • in speaking	‡My wife and I look forward to working more with the Matthew Community Program. Founded a decade ago by Theodore Jabil and myself, this organization serves children and families in the Brooklyn area.

Currently, we are seeing a surge in the overuse of reflexive pronouns, especially *myself* and *yourself*. Reflexive pronouns can be used only when the subject of the sentence also refers to the same person. Thus, I can say *I sometimes talk to myself*, but I can never say *I sometimes talk to yourself*.

Be careful with the NOUN + *such as* + PERSON structure, as in *People such as me need to wear glasses at all times*. A common error is to use a reflexive pronoun here, but you cannot say *People such as myself . . .* because *people* and *myself* do not refer to the same person. (Yes, you are part of people, but not all people are you.) We need *me* here (not *I*) because *as* is a preposition, so we need an object form. A reflexive pronoun can be used only when it refers to the same person that is being mentioned.

Incorrect	Correct
My wife and I look forward to working more with the Matthew Community Program. ‡Founded a decade ago by Theodore Jabil and myself, this organization serves children and families in the Brooklyn area.	My wife and I look forward to working more with the Matthew Community Program. Founded a decade ago by Theodore Jabil and me, this organization serves children and families in the Brooklyn area.
Please read the attached sheet of instructions. ‡If any of you has any questions, please contact Harry or myself at once.	Please read the attached sheet of instructions. If any of you has any questions, please contact Harry or me at once.
‡People such as myself tend to believe that there is no true political solution to the problem in Yugoslavia, but this concept is untenable to others.	People such as me tend to believe that there is no true political solution to the problem in Yugoslavia, but this concept is untenable to others.
‡That's one of the many differences between you and myself. You are a night owl, but I just can't function like that.	That's one of the many differences between you and me. You are a night owl, but I just can't function like that.
Here is a list of the schedule changes that need to be implemented. ‡Please advise Anne and myself when these changes have been made to the master schedule.	Here is a list of the schedule changes that need to be implemented. Please advise Anne and me when these changes have been made to the master schedule.

Error 4: Past Participles and Past Tense (e.g., *gone, went*)	
• in writing • in speaking	‡I had went to different tax services, but TaxPlus was the best ever.

Verbs in English have four principal parts: base, past, past participle, and present participle. For the vast majority of verbs, the past participle is formed the same as the past tense by adding –*ed*. For irregular verbs, the past participle has many endings, including –*en* and –*ne*, but some verbs (especially short one–syllable verbs) have the same form in present, past, and past participle. (A longer list of these forms can be found in Appendix 2.) The present participle of a verb is formed by adding –*ing*. Examples follow.

Present	Past	Past Participle	Present Participle
work	worked	worked	working
live	lived	lived	living
choose	chose	chosen	choosing
go	went	gone	going
put	put	put	putting

The phrase **be broken** means that something is not functioning, but the phrase **be broke** means have no money. Thus, *He was a broken man* and *He was a broke man* are both grammatically possible but do not mean the same thing at all. In the first example, he has lost his spirit or will to do something; in the second, he has no money.

An unfortunately common (and serious) error is misuse of the past participle. Some speakers use the wrong form in the past participle slot, as in ‡*I have sang this tune many times*, while others use the past participle form for the past tense, as in ‡*I seen the tornado*. While these sentences may be considered acceptable in certain dialects of American English, both are wrong in Standard American English.

Incorrect	Correct
‡I had went to different tax services, but TaxPlus was the best ever.	I had gone to different tax services, but TaxPlus was the best ever.
‡We seen the tornado when it hit our neighbor's house.	We saw the tornado when it hit our neighbor's house.
‡I have sang this tune many times.	I have sung this tune many times.
‡Unfortunately, that computer is broke, so you'll have to use another one.	Unfortunately, that computer is broken, so you'll have to use another one.
‡As soon as the girls seen the accident, they called the police. Chaos ensued.	As soon as the girls saw the accident, they called the police. Chaos ensued.

Error 5: *lie, lay*	
• in writing • in speaking	‡The DC-10 jet cracked into two pieces and came to rest with the front section laying on its side

The confusion here involves the verbs *lie* and *lay*. This confusion is actually understandable because the words do look alike (e.g., both are short words that begin with the letter *l*) and because the past tense of *lie* is *lay*. Furthermore, *lie* can be an irregular verb meaning "to recline" as well as a regular verb meaning "to tell a falsehood."

Native speakers have no problem with the use of *lie* as a regular verb as in *He lied about his whereabouts,* so let's concentrate on the two irregular usages, which are in fact the source of the error here. When *lie* means "recline," it is an intransitive verb, which means that it cannot have a direct object. Thus, you cannot say, ‡*Lie the tree on its side* but rather *Lay the tree on its side. Lay* is a transitive verb, which means that it must have a direct object in all cases. You cannot say, ‡*I'm going to lay out by the pool* because there is no direct object after *lay*. Correct usage here would be *I'm going to lie out by the pool.*

Meaning	Present	Past	Past Participle	Present Participle
not tell the truth (regular intrasitive verb)	lie *I never lie.*	lied *You lied to me.*	lied *Have you ever lied to me?*	lying *Are you lying about this?*
recline (irregular intrasitive verb)	lie *Please lie down.*	lay *The wolf lay down and died.*	lain *Why have you lain on the sofa so long?*	lying *Was the cat lying on this sheet?*
put, deposit (regular transitive verb)	lay *Please lay the boxes there.*	laid *They laid the tree on its side.*	laid *This hen has laid two eggs this week.*	laying *The dealer was laying the cards on the table.*

Incorrect	Correct
‡The DC-10 jet cracked in two pieces and came to rest with the front section laying on its side.	The DC-10 jet cracked in two pieces and came to rest with the front section lying on its side.
‡Why don't you lay down for a while?	Why don't you lie down for a while?
‡Are you going to lay there all day? Are you going to lie there all day? Most teenagers in our neighborhood are lazy. ‡They just lay out by the pool	day after day, wondering what life is about.
Most teenagers in our neighborhood are lazy. They just lie out by the pool	day after day, wondering what life is about.

Error 6: *whoever, whomever* (or: *who, whom*)	
• in writing • in speaking	‡Team captains are receiving this article because they might want to pass it on to whomever would benefit from it the most.

The forms *who* and *whoever* are subjects, and the forms *whom* and *whomever* are objects. The most common mistake here is using the subject pronouns in an object slot. This error occurs because people mistakenly assume that *who* and *whoever* are always used toward the beginning of a sentence (since subjects usually occur near the beginning of a sentence) and that *whom* and *whomever* toward the end of a sentence (since objects usually occur after the verb and, therefore, toward the end of a sentence). In the sample error, *would benefit* is the verb for its clause. Every verb needs a subject, so *would benefit* needs a subject. Thus, we have to use *whoever* in this case. It does not matter that the clause *whoever would benefit* comes after a preposition since *whoever* is not the object of this preposition; instead, the whole clause is the object of the preposition.

When in doubt as to which form to use, circle the verbs. Make sure that each verb has a subject. If every verb already has a subject, the slot is likely an object and you should use *whom* or *whomever*.

The bottom line: A verb needs a subject, and the *–m* forms cannot be used in the subject slot.

Incorrect	Correct
‡Team captains are receiving this article because they might want to pass it on to whomever would benefit from it the most.	Team captains are receiving this article because they might want to pass it on to whoever would benefit from it the most.
‡Whomever has the most points by the last week of the course will receive a prize.	Whoever has the most points by the last week of the course will receive a prize.
‡Editorial writers often endorse a certain candidate because they hope to convince their readers to vote for the candidates whom the writers think will do the best job.	Editorial writers often endorse a certain candidate because they hope to convince their readers to vote for the candidates who the writers think will do the best job.
‡I thought you might like to scan this article and pass it on to whomever would benefit from it the most.	I thought you might like to scan this article and pass it on to whoever would benefit from it the most.
‡My main goal is allowing the students to take pride in whom they are. I think it's an important goal for all teachers.	My main goal is allowing the students to take pride in who they are. I think it's an important goal for all teachers.

Error 7: *he/she/it don't*‡	
• in writing • in speaking	‡What the boss don't know won't matter in the end.

Present tense verbs for the third person singular (*he, she, it*) need an –s ending for both affirmative and negative utterances. The most common error occurs in the negative when speakers say or write ‡*it don't matter* or ‡*this problem don't have anything to do with your situation.* Using double negatives is considered a serious error in standard English and so might well mark you to many people as an uneducated person of lower socioeconomic status. Using double negatives is common in some regional varieties of English.

At times, you will hear educated speakers use this construction, but they know that they are using incorrect language and are doing this to attract attention, to sound very informal, or to joke. Everyone agrees, however, that this is non–standard English. Many of our native–speaking students make this particular error. To fit in with their peers, they need to continue using the non–standard form, but to sound professional and educated and get a good job, they need to know the difference between what is standard English and what is not standard English. In particular, they need to be able to turn one form off and the other on at the appropriate time.

This chart shows the correct conjugation of the verb *need* in both affirmative and negative in simple present tense. Note the use of –s for third person singular.

Verb: *Need*	Affirmative	Negative
Singular	I need	I don't need
	you need	you don't need
	he needs	he doesn't need
	she needs	she doesn't need
	it needs	it doesn't need
Plural	we need	we don't need
	you need	you don't need
	they need	they don't need

Incorrect	Correct
‡What the boss don't know won't matter in the end.	What the boss doesn't know won't matter in the end.
‡She don't even treat you like I do.	She doesn't even treat you like I do.
‡It don't seem fair that you lost the contest.	It doesn't seem fair that you lost the contest.
‡LeToya Luckett sang a song called "She Don't."	NOTE: We cannot change the title of someone else's song, but the correct title should be "She Doesn't." (Songs often have grammatical errors that reflect the current language usage of the song's intended audience or for poetic purposes.)
‡The first single taken from the Human Nature 2005 album was called "He Don't Love You." The lyrics include "He don't love you, no, but he don't want anyone else to have you. He don't want to let go."	NOTE: Again, we can't change the title of an existing work, but the correct title should be "He Doesn't Love You," and the correct lyrics should say "He doesn't love you, no, but he doesn't want anyone else to have you. He doesn't want to let go."

Error 8: *If I would have known*‡	
• in writing • in speaking	‡If I would have known about the free movie tickets, I would have gone to see the movie with you.

A sentence that begins with *if* has two parts or clauses: the *if* clause (which states the condition) and the main clause (which states the result or effect of the condition). The correct verb form in the *if* clause to describe a past action is *if* + SUBJECT + *had* + PAST PARTICIPLE (e.g., *if I had known*). The construction *would* + *have* + PAST PARTICIPLE is used only in the main clause, which is also called the result or effect clause.

The use of *would have* in the *if* clause is very common in American English—even among educated speakers, but it is not correct. All languages evolve, and this grammar point appears to be moving toward acceptance into standard English. However, only time will tell if the descriptive use of this grammar item will eventually become accepted into standard English by the prescriptive grammarians.

Incorrect	**Correct**
‡If I would have known about the free movie tickets, I would have gone to see the movie with you.	If I had known about the free movie tickets, I would have gone to see the movie with you.
‡On the band's 1986 album called *Chicago 18*, the group Chicago sang the song "If She Would Have Been Faithful." A song from this album reached #17 on the Billboard Hot 100 chart.	NOTE: We cannot change the title of someone else's song, but the correct title should be "If She Had Been Faithful." (Songs often have grammatical errors that reflect the current language usage of the song's intended audience for poetic purposes.)
‡If he would have taken his medicine, he wouldn't have had that heart attack.	If he had taken his medicine, he wouldn't have had that heart attack.
‡If John would have been here, he would have solved the problem without a doubt.	If John had been here, he would have solved the problem without a doubt.
‡If it wouldn't have been raining, the kids could have played in the backyard.	If it hadn't been raining, the kids could have played in the backyard.

Error 9: Double Negatives	
• in writing • in speaking	‡We think the airline made a mistake. We couldn't find none of our luggage when we arrived.

A double negative is the use of two negatives in the same clause. A double negative is considered non–standard English. Examples of negative words include *not, none, never, no, hardly, rarely, scarcely, barely, nothing, nobody, no one, neither,* and *seldom.* It is possible to have two negatives in a sentence if they are in different clauses: (*Most people do not have a passport*) (*because they have never traveled abroad*).

The bottom line: Use only one negative word per clause.

Incorrect	Correct
‡We think the airline made a mistake. We couldn't find none of our luggage when we arrived.	We think the airline made a mistake. We couldn't find any of our luggage when we arrived. (OR more formal: We think the airline made a mistake. We could find none of our luggage when we arrived.)
‡The school board's new plan will not hardly affect the students at this elementary school.	The school board's new plan will hardly affect the students at this elementary school.
‡Those people don't know nothing about what happened in the '80s.	Those people don't know anything about what happened in the '80s.
No, he's gone. ‡He doesn't live here no more.	No, he's gone. He doesn't live here any more.
‡They barely did not arrive at the airport in time to catch their return flight.	They barely arrived at the airport in time to catch their return flight.

Error 10: *bad, badly*	
• in writing • in speaking	‡Aunt Mildred is okay but probably won't get around much again. The operation was complicated. I feel so badly for her.

What is the grammatical difference between *bad* and *badly?* The answer is easy: *bad* is an adjective and *badly* is an adverb. Thus, we say, *His timing was bad today* and *He played badly today. Feel* can be a transitive verb that means "to touch something," but it is also an intransitive linking verb that means to "perceive a certain condition of the body or mind." People almost always use the second meaning because they want to tell about their health. However, after the verb *to be* and linking verbs such as *feel, look, seem,* and *appear,* we use adjectives. (See p. 48 for a review of this material.) Using this rule, we say, *He was bad, He felt bad, He looked bad, He seemed bad,"* and *He appeared bad.*

The most common mistake that native speakers make is to use the phrase *feel badly,* which is incorrect (unless your job happens to be to feel things, in which case you might feel things well or feel things badly). In the slot just after a verb, we would usually use an adverb of manner ending in *–ly,* but feel here is an intransitive linking verb and needs an adjective form. Thus, the combination *feel badly* is a hypercorrection.

Incorrect	Correct
Aunt Mildred is okay but probably won't get around much again. The operation was complicated. ‡I feel so badly for her.	Aunt Mildred is okay but probably won't get around much again. The operation was complicated. I feel so bad for her.
‡The thin blonde model on the cover of a magazine makes all women feel badly about their own bodies despite the size, shape, height, or age of the magazine's readership.	The thin blonde model on the cover of a magazine makes all women feel bad about their own bodies despite the size, shape, height, or age of the magazine's readership.
According to the author, when people feel stressed, angry, or ashamed, we give off negative energy. ‡This is why viewing negative events causes us to feel badly. Similarly, witnessing acts of kindness causes us to feel good.	According to the author, when people feel stressed, angry, or ashamed, we give off negative energy. This is why viewing negative events causes us to feel bad. Similarly, witnessing acts of kindness causes us to feel good.
‡I could tell that Mr. Frompton felt badly, and I left thinking how difficult it can be to pick up the pieces and go on, especially when you are already trying hard and feel uncertain about what your next step should be.	I could tell that Mr. Frompton felt bad, and I left thinking how difficult it can be to pick up the pieces and go on, especially when you are already trying hard and feel uncertain about what your next step should be.
We should have been free and given the same opportunities others had. ‡We always felt badly because our people were not treated fairly.	We should have been free and given the same opportunities others had. We always felt bad because our people were not treated fairly.

Error 11: *them, those*	
• in writing • in speaking	‡We can't let them people vote. If we let them vote, they're not going to make the right decision.

What is the grammatical difference between *them* and *those?* The confusion here occurs because *them* is a pronoun (*Who are those boys? I don't know them*), and *those* is an adjective (*I know those boys*) or a pronoun (*Those are the boys that I know*). Because *them* is a pronoun, it can never modify (i.e., describe) a noun. It is never correct to say *them people* or *them reasons.*

Incorrect	Correct
‡We can't let them people vote. If we let them vote, they're not going to make the right decision.	We can't let those people vote. If we let them vote, they're not going to make the right decision.
‡If Fred had known how fast people were going to buy them horses, he would have brought more horses to sell at the auction.	If Fred had known how fast people were going to buy those horses, he would have brought more horses to sell at the auction.
‡Well, how do you like them apples?	Well, how do you like those apples?
‡Why are all them people cheering? What happened? Does anyone know?	Why are all those people cheering? What happened? Does anyone know?
‡They said that change was coming, but them politicians were lying to us once again.	They said that change was coming, but those politicians were lying to us once again.

Error 12: *have, of*	
• in writing	‡My opinion is that the manager should of fired those employees on the spot.

A modal phrase expressing past time always consists of three parts: the modal, auxiliary *have,* and the past participle of a verb. Examples include *must have gone, might have taken,* and *couldn't have been.* In normal speech, the auxiliary verb *have* is often reduced and sounds similar to the pronunciation of the word *of.* (Note that *of* ends in a /v/ pronunciation; there is no /f/ in *of.*) Due to the similarity in sound, people mistakenly substitute *of* for *have* in past modal phrases. **The bottom line:** It is never acceptable to substitute *of* for *have* after a modal.

Incorrect	Correct
‡My opinion is that the manager should of fired those employees on the spot.	My opinion is that the manager should have fired those employees on the spot.
‡I think the survivors of the Titanic must of felt guilty for surviving the sinking.	I think the survivors of the Titanic must have felt guilty for surviving the sinking.
‡What a great speech you gave! I couldn't of said it any better.	What a great speech you gave! I couldn't have said it any better.
‡If NASA had launched the rocket a day later, perhaps the accident could of been avoided.	If NASA had launched the rocket a day later, perhaps the accident could have been avoided.
‡I guess I should of thought something was up when you kept on calling me Rick instead of Rich.	I guess I should have thought something was up when you kept on calling me Rick instead of Rich.

Error 13: *it's, its, its'*‡	
• in writing	‡If you apply enough liquid, the tick will come out on it's own.

What is the possessive adjective for the pronoun *it*? *I* changes to *my*, *you* changes to *your*, and *she* changes to *her*, but what about *it*? The possessive form of *it* is *its*. There is no apostrophe.

The two most common mistakes are substituting *its'* or *it's*. Avoiding this error is easy. In the case of *its'*, remember this unequivocal statement: *its'* **is not a word in the English language.** You can never use *its'* under any circumstances. As for the second substitution—*it's*, this word does exist in English but only as a contraction for *it is*.

If you are not sure whether to write *its* or *it's*, try using the full form *it is* in the slot. If you can use *it is*, then the correct form is *it's*. If you cannot use *it is*, then the correct form is *its*. Again, *its'* is not a word and is never correct.

Incorrect	Correct
Cover the tick with the liquid for a few seconds. ‡If you apply enough liquid, the tick will let go on it's own.	Cover the tick with the liquid for a few seconds. If you apply enough liquid, the tick will let go on its own.
‡Queen School of English (UAE) is looking for two English speakers to join it's team of English teachers. A competitive, tax-free, salary is offered, as well as furnished accommodation, a travel allowance, and utility bills allowance. Abu Dhabi is a beautiful city and the capital of the UAE. (NOTE: Yes, this is an actual job ad for an English teaching position.)	Queen School of English (UAE) is looking for two English speakers to join its team of English teachers. A competitive, tax-free, salary is offered, as well as furnished accommodation, a travel allowance, and utility bills allowance. Abu Dhabi is a beautiful city and the capital of the UAE.
‡As part of this methodology, Huron has manufactured its' own books for a decade.	As part of this methodology, Huron has manufactured its own books for a decade.
UMB is moving ahead. "I do believe we've finally got it! ‡Teamwork at its' best!"	UMB is moving ahead. "I do believe we've finally got it! Teamwork at its best!"
‡South Carolina was the first southern state to hold it's primary, and it brought out a complex but straightforward debate.	South Carolina was the first southern state to hold its primary, and it brought out a complex but straightforward debate.
The campus police department is proud to announce the publication of the long awaited and revised "Student Safety Guide." ‡Note that the name has been changed to the "Annual Report & Safety Guide" to reflect it's content more appropriately.	The campus police department is proud to announce the publication of the long awaited and revised "Student Safety Guide." Note that the name has been changed to the "Annual Report & Safety Guide" to reflect its content more appropriately.

Error 14: *your, you're*	
• in writing	‡If you want to play on the team, please send me an email letting me know that your interested. I need your response no later than Saturday.

Although *your* and *you're* are pronounced exactly the same way, they have different meanings and different grammatical functions. *Your* is a possessive adjective meaning that something that belongs to you: *your book, your cat, your answer*. *You're* is the contraction for *you are*: *you're late, you're thinking, you're on the list*.

If you are not sure whether to write *your* or *you're*, try using the full form *you are* in the slot. If you can use *you are*, then the contracted form *you're* is correct. If you cannot use *you are*, then the correct form is *your*.

Incorrect	Correct
‡If you want to play on the team, please send me an email letting me know that your interested. I need your response no later than Saturday.	If you want to play on the team, please send me an email letting me know that you're interested. I need your response no later than Saturday.
You don't need to thank me. It was my pleasure to help you with your work today. ‡Your welcome.	You don't need to thank me. It was my pleasure to help you with your work today. You're welcome.
Pay attention! ‡Your not listening to me.	Pay attention! You're not listening to me.
‡What was you're reaction when you heard the news about the government's new economic plan?	What was your reaction when you heard the news about the government's new economic plan?
I've encountered a problem when I'm trying to insert a record. ‡Sometimes while your trying to build a menu list, you'll get an error message telling you something about too much recursion. What does this mean?	I've encountered a problem when I'm trying to insert a record. Sometimes while you're trying to build a menu list, you'll get an error message telling you something about too much recursion. What does this mean?

Error 15: 's

• in writing	‡The period of the data is somewhat restricted, but the results are nonetheless fascinating. The fact's presented here challenge some present-day assumptions about where the tornado threat is highest.

Errors with apostrophes have gotten out of control. We have to use an apostrophe to indicate contractions (*it's, you're, they're*), but a more common error occurs when indicating possession.

The rule is quite simple. (1) If a noun is singular, add *'s*: a boy → a boy's. (2) If a singular noun ends in *–s*, you can add just *'* or *'s*: Bess → Bess' or Bess's. (3) If a noun is plural, just add *'*: the boys → the boys'. (4) If a noun is plural but does not end in *–s*, add *'s*: the children → the children's.

For no apparent reason, native speakers are adding apostrophes on nouns when there is no possession. I remember seeing a sign that said "2 Kitten's for sale." What did the kitten own? Even more bizarre are examples of apostrophes being used with verbs: "Oxygen require's more time in this experiment."

The bottom line: Only use an apostrophe to indicate a contraction or possession.

Incorrect	Correct
The period of the data is somewhat restricted, but the results are nonetheless fascinating. ‡The fact's presented here challenge some present-day assumptions about where the tornado threat is highest.	The period of the data is somewhat restricted, but the results are nonetheless fascinating. The facts presented here challenge some present-day assumptions about where the tornado threat is highest.
‡Krashen came up with the concept of *i + 1* to help describe the distance between a persons language proficiency and the level of the language in the material.	Krashen came up with the concept of *i + 1* to help describe the distance between a person's language proficiency and the level of the language in the material.
‡Maybe we will be able to see you guy's in the near future.	Maybe we will be able to see you guys in the near future.
‡You can borrow a shovel from the Smith's.	You can borrow a shovel from the Smiths.
I can schedule all the interviews for two-hour time frames. ‡Let me know if this works for you, and I will confirm the dates on everyones calendar.	I can schedule all the interviews for two-hour time frames. Let me know if this works for you, and I will confirm the dates on everyone's calendar.

Error 16: *who's, whose*	
• in writing	‡If you are an employee who's contract expires annually and a renewal is done at the beginning of a semester, you may not be entered into the data system yet.

Both *who's* and *whose* are correct words in English, but their uses are completely different. People often confuse the contraction *who's* with the possessive word *whose* because these two words are pronounced exactly the same. Though these words sound alike, this error is not just about spelling. It shows a lack of grammatical knowledge and gives the reader a poor impression of your writing.

If you are not sure whether to write *who's* or *whose*, try using the full form *who is* in the slot. If you can use *who is*, then the correct form is *who's*. If you cannot use *who is*, then the correct form is *whose*. Remember that *whose* can come immediately before a noun as an adjective (e.g., *Whose wallet is this?*), or it can be a pronoun (e.g., *Whose is this?*).

Incorrect	Correct
‡If you are an employee who's contract expires annually and a renewal is done at the beginning of a semester, you may not be entered into the data system yet.	If you are an employee whose contract expires annually and a renewal is done at the beginning of a semester, you may not be entered into the data system yet.
‡Would you think differently of someone who's husband or wife was in jail?	Would you think differently of someone whose husband or wife was in jail?
‡Currently, there are two children in my classroom who's primary language is something other than English.	Currently, there are two children in my classroom whose primary language is something other than English.
‡Our office computer is experiencing a problem when we attempt to delete files who's names include numbers instead of just letters.	Our office computer is experiencing a problem when we attempt to delete files whose names include numbers instead of just letters.
‡The federal court who's jurisdiction includes seven heavily populated metropolitan areas lacks judges to hear all its assigned cases.	The federal court whose jurisdiction includes seven heavily populated metropolitan areas lacks judges to hear all its assigned cases.

Error 17: *to, too, two*	
• in writing	‡Yes, I'm looking for something that is more stable than my current job, but I haven't been going to job interviews to much.

Why do people confuse these three words? The easiest (and least problematic) is the number *two*. If you can insert an actual numeral in the sentence, use *two*, not *to* or *too*. In the sentence *I have (to, too, two) books*, the missing word is *two* because you could also write *I have 2 books.*

The most common mistake is misusing *to* for *too*. The word *to* is either a preposition (e.g., *to the bank*) or part of an infinitive (e.g., *to go, to be, to do*). (The infinitive form of a verb consists of *to* and the simple form of the verb.) In the sentence "If the officials would like to decide to postpone the trip, they must vote to do so at tomorrow's meeting," there are three infinitives (i.e., *to decide, to postpone, to do*). The word *too* is an intensifier adverb meaning very or extremely (e.g., *too good, too difficult, too much*) or an adverb meaning also (e.g., *Chile has a large maritime industry, too*).

There is a "question test" that can help you remember when to use *too*. Ask yourself if you can use *very* or *also* in the slot. If so, then the correct form is *too*. Here are two slots where *too* is the only possible choice: (1) The test was _____ difficult. (2) The homework was tough, _____. In the first sentence, *too* means "very or extremely," and in the second sentence, *too* means "also."

Incorrect	Correct
‡Yes, I'm looking for something that is more stable than my current job, but I haven't been going to job interviews to much.	Yes, I'm looking for something that is more stable than my current job, but I haven't been going to job interviews too much.
‡I don't forward a lot of emails to people, but this one was to good not to pass along.	I don't forward a lot of emails to people, but this one was too good not to pass along.
‡Having so much to do on a Saturday makes the weekend go by to fast.	Having so much to do on a Saturday makes the weekend go by too fast.
‡Most people will not buy that kind of vehicle these days because it uses to much fuel.	Most people will not buy that kind of vehicle these days because it uses too much fuel.
‡Did you want to go, to?	Did you want to go, too?

Error 18: *affect, effect*	
• in writing	Applicants may submit their paperwork either in person or via email. ‡Note that the submission method will not effect the committee's decision regarding your application.

In general usage, *affect* is a verb and *effect* is a noun. In normal conversation, stressed syllables of words are enunciated more strongly than unstressed syllables. In the words *affect* and *effect,* the stress is on the second syllable –*fect,* which means that we reduce the first syllable to the schwa /ə/ sound. Thus, in normal conversation, these two words sound very similar, so it is not surprising that there is some confusion regarding the spelling.

SPECIAL NOTE: In specialized academic and medical language, there are two other uses of these words. These specialized meanings have different pronunciations (but the same spelling).

When *affect* is used as a noun, it means a feeling associated with an idea or action. In this case, the first syllable is stressed and the vowel is pronounced as short *a* as in *cat.*

Effect can be used as a verb in the idiomatic expression *to effect change,* which means to cause or bring about change. In this case, the vowel is pronounced as a long *e* as in *need.* Note that *effect* is used as a verb only in the infrequent expression *to effect change,* which means that the spelling *effect* is almost always a noun in English.

The bottom line: In general usage, *affect* is a verb and *effect* is a noun.

Incorrect	Correct
‡Applicants may submit their paperwork either in person or via email. Note that the submission method will not effect the committee's decision regarding your application.	Applicants may submit their paperwork either in person or via email. Note that the submission method will not affect the committee's decision regarding your application.
‡Carolyn Chan reports on the strong wintry weather pattern that could effect much of the Great Plains in the coming week.	Carolyn Chan reports on the strong wintry weather pattern that could affect much of the Great Plains in the coming week.
A new study confirms that Florida beaches are in trouble. ‡This study looked at the affects of growing numbers of people living close to the seashore.	A new study confirms that Florida beaches are in trouble. This study looked at the effects of growing numbers of people living close to the seashore.
‡We hear a great deal today about global warming and its potential impact on the earth, but do we ever stop to think how this warming might effect us?	We hear a great deal today about global warming and its potential impact on the earth, but do we ever stop to think how this warming might affect us?
‡Without a doubt, the government's decision will effect everyone by the middle of the year.	Without a doubt, the government's decision will affect everyone by the middle of the year.

Error 19: *lose, loose*	
• in writing	‡My goal for the wedding was to loose 15 to 20 pounds. I also decided that my future husband could stand to loose a few pounds, too.

Native speakers know how to spell both of these words, but many people mix them up. The word *lose* is a verb; the letter *s* here is pronounced as /z/. The word *loose* is an adjective meaning "not tight"; the letter *s* here is pronounced as /s/.

Incorrect	Correct
‡My goal for the wedding was to loose 15 to 20 pounds. I also decided that my future husband could stand to loose a few pounds, too.	My goal for the wedding was to lose 15 to 20 pounds. I also decided that my future husband could stand to lose a few pounds, too.
‡This plant can withstand temperatures to 5 degrees Fahrenheit, which is the point at which the plant may loose some or all of its leaves (but still not kill the plant).	This plant can withstand temperatures to 5 degrees Fahrenheit, which is the point at which the plant may lose some or all of its leaves (but still not kill the plant).
I also began to change my lifestyle. ‡I must loose weight.	I also began to change my lifestyle. I must lose weight.
‡Those pants are so lose on you. You really do have to buy new clothes soon.	Those pants are so loose on you. You really do have to buy new clothes soon.
‡I have set a goal of being down to my ideal weight range by March 1st of 2000, so I need to loose about 25 pounds.	I have set a goal of being down to my ideal weight range by March 1st of 2000, so I need to lose about 25 pounds.

Error 20: *they're, there, their*	
• in writing	‡In a recent ruling by five of the Supreme Court justices, there conclusion was that police should have more authority in some cases.

Native speakers know the meanings of these three words, but some people mix them up because they are all pronounced the same. The word *they're* is a contraction for *they are*. The word *their* is a possessive adjective, so *their* is always in front of a noun. *There* usually refers to a place, as in *She lives there*. You can remember *there* easily because you can see the word *here* inside *there*, and both of them are places.

Incorrect	Correct
‡In a recent ruling by five of the Supreme Court justices, there conclusion was that police should have more authority in some cases.	In a recent ruling by five of the Supreme Court justices, their conclusion was that police should have more authority in some cases.
‡In her article "High School Writing Programs and There Effect on College Composition Grades," Professor Maritza Hernandez explores a very timely topic.	In her article "High School Writing Programs and Their Effect on College Composition Grades," Professor Maritza Hernandez explores a very timely topic.
‡No one wants to visit my cousins' place because they're cat has fleas.	No one wants to visit my cousins' place because their cat has fleas.
‡To all employees: Be sure to put international stickers on all correspondence from this office. If you need stickers, there in the top drawer of the filing cabinet.	To all employees: Be sure to put international stickers on all correspondence from this office. If you need stickers, they're in the top drawer of the filing cabinet.
‡Clothing items that will be on sale tomorrow need to have they're original price tags removed.	Clothing items that will be on sale tomorrow need to have their original price tags removed.

APPENDIX 2
Irregular Past and Past Participles of Verbs

Present	Past	Past Participle
add	added	added
call	called	called
like	liked	liked
map	mapped	mapped
rob	robbed	robbed

The vast majority of verbs in English are regular verbs, which means that their past tense and their past participles end in *–ed.*

Other verbs, however, are irregular, which means that their past tense and past participles are formed in some other way, including internal vowel changes (*sing–sang–sung*), internal vowel changes and *–en* or *–ne* (*choose, chose, chosen* or *go-went-gone*), and no change at all *(cut-cut-cut)*. (Note that the present participle has not been included here because it always ends in *–ing.*)

Though some sources claim to have more than 350 irregular verbs, these lists often include rare words such as *forego (forego-forwent-forgone)*, *hew (hew-hewed-hewn/hewed)*, and *unspin (unspin-unspun-unspun)*. The following chart lists 155 of the most frequently used irregular verbs. A list of 155 items may seem daunting to ELLs, but these verbs should be introduced in much smaller groups. For example, beginning students are often given a list of 25 of the most common verbs, and this list is increased as ELLs attain intermediate proficiency. (See Teaching Technique 15 for specific ideas for teaching these verb forms.)

Present	Past	Past Participle
arise	arose	arisen
awake	awoke	awoken
be	was / were	been
bear	bore	born / borne
beat	beat	beaten / beat
become	became	become
begin	began	begun
bend	bent	bent
bet	bet	bet
bid	bid	bid
bind	bound	bound
bite	bit	bitten
bleed	bled	bled
blow	blew	blown
break	broke	broken
bring	brought	brought
broadcast	broadcast	broadcast
build	built	built
burst	burst	burst
buy	bought	bought
cast	cast	cast
catch	caught	caught
choose	chose	chosen
come	came	come
cost	cost	cost
creep	crept	crept
cut	cut	cut
deal	dealt	dealt
dig	dug	dug
dive	dove	dived
do	did	done
draw	drew	drawn
dream	dreamed / dreamt	dreamed / dreamt
drink	drank	drunk
drive	drove	driven
eat	ate	eaten
fall	fell	fallen
feed	fed	fed
feel	felt	felt
fight	fought	fought
find	found	found
fit	fit	fit
flee	fled	fled

fly	flew	flown
forbid	forbade	forbidden
forecast	forecast	forecast
foresee	foresaw	foreseen
forget	forgot	forgotten
forgive	forgave	forgiven
forsake	forsook	forsaken
freeze	froze	frozen
get	got	gotten
give	gave	given
go	went	gone
grind	ground	ground
grow	grew	grown
hang	hung	hung
have	had	had
hear	heard	heard
hide	hid	hidden
hit	hit	hit
hold	held	hold
hurt	hurt	hurt
input	input	input
keep	kept	kept
kneel	knelt	knelt
know	knew	known
lay	laid	laid
lead	led	led
leave	left	left
lend	lent	lent
let	let	let
lie	lay	lain
light	lit / lighted	lit / lighted
lose	lost	lost
make	made	made
mean	meant	meant
meet	met	met
mislead	misled	misled
mistake	mistook	mistaken
misunderstand	misunderstood	misunderstood
overcome	overcame	overcome
overdo	overdid	overdone
override	overrode	overridden
oversee	oversaw	overseen
oversleep	overslept	overslept
overtake	overtook	overtaken
overthrow	overthrew	overthrown

pay	paid	paid
prove	proved	proven / proved
put	put	put
quit	quit	quit
read	read	read
ride	rode	ridden
ring	rang	rung
rise	rose	risen
run	ran	run
say	said	said
see	saw	seen
seek	sought	sought
sell	sold	sold
send	sent	sent
set	set	set
sew	sewed	sewn / sewed
shake	shook	shaken
shed	shed	shed
shoot	shot	shot
show	showed	shown / showed
shrink	shrank	shrunk
shut	shut	shut
sing	sang	sung
sit	sat	sat
sleep	slept	slept
slide	slid	slid
sling	slung	slung
slit	slit	slit
speak	spoke	spoken
speed	sped	sped
spend	spent	spent
spin	spun	spun
split	split	split
spread	spread	spread
stand	stood	stood
steal	stole	stolen
stick	stuck	stuck
stink	stank / stunk	stunk
strike	struck	struck / stricken
string	strung	strung
swear	swore	sworn
sweep	swept	swept
swell	swelled	swollen
swim	swam	swum
swing	swung	swung

take	took	taken
teach	taught	taught
tear	tore	torn
tell	told	told
think	thought	thought
throw	threw	thrown
thrust	thrust	thrust
understand	understood	understood
undertake	undertook	undertaken
undo	undid	undone
uphold	upheld	upheld
upset	upset	upset
wake	woke	woken
wear	wore	worn
weave	wove	woven
weep	wept	wept
wet	wet	wet
win	won	won
wind	wound	wound
withdraw	withdrew	withdrawn
write	wrote	written

APPENDIX 3
Glossary of Grammar Terms

abstract noun: a noun that names an emotion, idea, or quality; an abstract noun cannot be perceived with any of the five senses (*honesty*) (see also concrete nouns)

action research: a small–scale research project that investigates a specific question that a teacher has about something important to his or her class

active voice: verb form used when the subject is acting upon an object—that is, the receiver of the action (*Mary <u>wrote</u> the letter.*) (see also passive voice)

adjective: a word that describes or limits a noun or pronoun

adjective clause: a dependent clause that functions as an adjective

adverb: a word that modifies a verb, an adjective, or another adverb

adverb clause: a dependent clause that functions as an adverb

affix: a prefix or a suffix

antecedent: the noun for which a pronoun stands

appositive: a word or a group of words, usually set off by commas, that renames or defines a noun (*Seafood gumbo, <u>a popular Cajun dish in Louisiana</u>, is made with onions and green peppers.*)

article: an adjective that makes a noun definite or indefinite

auxiliary verb: a helping verb (see also *to be*; *have, has, had*; *do, does, did*; modals)

avoidance: term applied to situations in which ELLs avoid using certain grammatical structures because of perceived difficulty or fear of making an error

base form of a verb: a verb form without *to* or any endings (also called simple form or dictionary form)

***to be*:** a main verb in English that indicates existence or describes the subject and an auxiliary verb that forms the progressive tenses and the passive voice; the most irregular verb in English with eight forms (*be, am, is, are, was, were, being, been*)

***by* + agent:** phrase used in passive voice constructions to indicate who performed the action (*The house was built <u>by my two uncles</u>.*)

causative verbs: a verb that expresses the idea of somebody causing something to occur (*get, have, let, make: She <u>had</u> the man change the tire.*)

clause: a group of words with both a subject and a verb

cognate: a word in one language that looks or sounds like a word in another language; cognates share a common origin

341

comma splice: an incorrect sentence with two clauses that have been connected with a comma in without any connector word

common noun: the name of any person, place, or thing (see proper noun)

comparative: adjective or adverb form used for comparing two or more people, things, or actions; formed with *more* (*more quickly*) or *–er* (*taller*)

complement: the part of a sentence that comes after a verb and is needed to make the sentence complete

complex sentence: a sentence consisting of one independent clause and at least one dependent clause

compound-complex sentence: a sentence consisting two independent clauses and at least one dependent clause

compound sentence: a sentence consisting of two independent clauses

concrete noun: a noun that you can perceive with your five senses *(newspaper)* (see abstract noun)

conditional sentence: a sentence with a hypothetical situation and its consequence or result

conjunction: a word that connects parts of a sentence together, including words, phrases, and clauses

conjunctive adverb: transitional devices between two main ideas; the adverb appears with the second of the two ideas (*consequently, however, therefore*)

content teachers: K–12 teachers of non-ELL subjects such as mathematics and science who today have ELLs in their classes, which means that these teachers are a primary source of English input for the ELLs (in addition to the content subject matter)

contraction: a reduced form of a noun or pronoun and a verb (*it's*) made by substituting an apostrophe for the missing letters

coordinating conjunction: a word that connects two independent clauses in a compound sentence (*and, but, or*)

correlative conjunctions: pairs of words that connect equivalent sentence parts (*both . . . and, neither . . . nor, not only . . . but also*)

count nouns: nouns that can be counted and therefore have both a singular and a plural form (*one book, two books; a child, many children; a fish, five fish*) (see also non-count nouns)

dangling modifier: a phrase that modifies a word that it was not logically intended to modify (*Running across the street, the driver hit her brakes but hit the cat anyway.* NOTE: The driver was not running, so the phrase *running across the street* cannot be next to *the driver.*)

declarative sentence: a statement

definite article: article that indicates a specific noun (*the*)

demonstrative adjective: an adjective that points out a specific noun (*these books*)

demonstrative pronoun: a pronoun that substitutes for a specific noun that can be understood from context (*those books are mine, but these are yours*)

dependent clause: a clause that cannot stand alone as a complete sentence

descriptive grammar: a view of grammar that considers actual usage of language rather than relying on prescribed rules

dictionary form of a verb: See base form of a verb

direct object: a noun or pronoun that receives the action of the verb

double negative: the incorrect use of two negative structures within one clause

drill: a practice technique that includes multiple encounters with the target language structure in a relatively short period

−ed participial adjective: a participial adjective ending in *−ed, −en, −ne,* or other irregular form that implies that the noun in question is receiving or being affected by the action (*an amazed viewer*)

EFL: English as a Foreign Language; English learning setting in which English is not spoken widely outside the classroom, such as Japan (see also ESL)

embedded question: a question in the form of a noun clause that is embedded in an independent clause (*No one knows <u>where she lives</u>.*)

emphatic: a form used for expressing emphasis (*I <u>do understand</u>.*)

ESL: English as a Second Language; English learning setting in which English is widely spoken outside the classroom, such as the U.S., Canada, the U.K., Australia, New Zealand (see also EFL)

ESP: English for Specific Purposes; ESL or EFL course or curriculum that meets the unique needs of students who are learning English for one specific reason (English for tourism, English for pilots, English for business)

essential relative clause: an adjective clause that follows a general noun and is therefore essential to the reader's understanding of the sentence; never punctuated with a comma: *We want to visit a city <u>that enjoys a warm climate</u>.* (see also non-essential relative clause)

exclamation: a sentence that expresses strong emotion and is followed by an exclamation point (*Help!*)

first conditional: a structure used for talking about possibilities in the present or future that consists of a condition clause and a result clause (also called conditional type 1)

first person: subject pronouns *I* (singular) and *we* (plural)

fragment: an incomplete sentence frequently consisting of a phrase or a dependent clause that is not properly connected to the main clause

fused sentence: an incorrect sentence with two clauses that have been put together without a proper conjunction or punctuation (also called run-on sentence)

gender: the restriction of a noun, pronoun, or possessive adjective to a specific gender (*he, him, his* for males)

Generation 1.5: term referring to the growing number of ELLs who graduate from U.S. high schools but enter college without sufficient English language skills; the term refers to the fact that these ELLs resemble both first- and second-generation immigrants

gerund: an *−ing* form that functions as a noun

idiom: a multi-word expression in which the meanings of the individual words do not equal the meaning of the complete expression (*The test was a piece of cake.*)

imperative sentence: a sentence that expresses a request or a command

indefinite article: articles that do not indicate a specific noun (*a, an*)

indefinite pronoun: pronouns that do not refer to any specific person or thing (*anyone, something*)

independent clause: a clause that can stand alone as a complete sentence

indirect object: an object (person or thing) for whom or to whom or for which or to which something is done; an indirect object occurs before a direct object

infinitive: *to* plus base form a verb (*to go, to be, to take*)

infix: a letter or letters inverted in a word; English does not have infixes.

–*ing* participial adjective: a participial adjective ending in –*ing* that implies that the noun in question is actually doing or causing the action (*an amazing movie*)

interjection: a word that expresses strong feeling or emotion

interrogative pronoun: a pronoun that is used to form a question (*who, what, whose*)

interrogative sentence: a question

intransitive verb: a verb that is never followed by a direct object (*happen*)

irregular verb: a verb whose past tense and past participle forms are not formed by adding –*d* or –*ed*

K–12: term applied to regular subjects taught from kindergarten to twelfth grades in U.S. and Canadian schools

linking verb: a verb that connects the subject and a complement (*be, seem, look*)

main clause: the central independent clause of a sentence

mass nouns: See non-count nouns

mixed conditional: a conditional sentence in which the verb in one clause expresses an action in the present or future and the other verb expresses an action in the past

modals: an auxiliary verb that expresses feelings, attitudes, or opinions in a verb phrase (*can, might, should*)

modify: describe or limit; often used is discussing the role of adverbs

negative: the "no" form of an utterance; negative grammatical words include *no, not, never, hardly,* and *rarely*

negative evidence: information to ELLs about what is not possible in the target language; conduits include explicit teaching, error correction, or communication breakdown

non-count nouns: nouns that cannot be counted and therefore have only one form (*air, homework, machinery*): also called mass nouns (see count nouns)

non-essential relative clause: an adjective clause that follows a specific, known noun and therefore provides information that is non-essential to the reader's understanding of the sentence; always punctuated with a comma: *Miami, which enjoys a warm climate, is the largest city in Florida.* (also called non-restrictive clause) (see also essential relative clause)

non-restrictive clause: See non-essential relative clause

non–separable: term used to describe a phrasal verb in which an object cannot separate the verb and its particle (*takes after her aunt, *takes her aunt after*)

non–standard: language that does not conform to the rules of standard usage

noun: the name of a person, place, thing, or quality

noun clause: a dependent clause that functions as a noun

null article: the absence of any article before a noun

number: singular or plural in reference to a noun or pronoun

object of preposition: a noun or pronoun after a preposition

object pronoun: a pronoun form that can function as a direct object, indirect object, or object of a preposition (*me, him, her*) (see also subject pronoun)

order of adjectives: sequence of adjectives deemed grammatical in current English usage, namely articles, opinion, size, shape, condition, age, color, and origin (*a magnificent, small, oval, shin, antique, silver, French spoon*)

participle: a verb form ending in *–ing, –ed* or *–en* that functions as an adjective or part of a verb

particle: second part of a phrasal verb

part of speech: one of the traditional eight categories of words, including noun, pronoun, adjective, adverb, verb, preposition, conjunction, interjection

passive voice: verb form used when the subject is being acted upon an object—that is, the agent of the action (*The letter was written by Mary.*) (see also active voice)

past participle: a participle formed with *–d* or *–ed* for regular verbs and with *–en, –ne,* or other ways for irregular verbs that is used in the perfect tenses, passive voice, or as an adjective

perfect tenses: present perfect tense, present perfect progressive tense, past perfect tense, past perfect progressive tense, future perfect tense, future perfect progressive tense; verb tenses consisting of a form of the auxiliary verb *have* and a past participle

person: three categories of subject pronouns (see first person, second person, third person)

phrasal verb: a verb and its particle (or preposition) (*take after, look over, call off*)

phrase: a group of words that functions as a single part of speech

plural: the form that represents more than one person, place, or thing

polysemous: having multiple meanings

positive evidence: correct input or models that language learners receive about the target language

possessive adjective: an adjective that indicates ownership (*my, your, our*)

possessive pronoun: a pronoun that takes the place of a possessive word and its object (*mine, yours, ours*)

predicate: part of a sentence excluding the subject; the verb and anything that modifies it

predicate nominative: a noun or pronoun after the verb *to be* or a linking verb that renames the subject (*She is a doctor*).

prefix: a group of letters placed before a base word that changes the meaning of the word (*happy, unhappy*)

preposition: a word that shows the relationship between a noun (or pronoun) and the rest of the sentence

prepositional phrase: combination of a preposition and its object (and any modifiers or describing words)

prescriptive grammar: a view of grammar that prescribes, or dictates, exactly what we should or should not say without any consideration of actual usage

present participle: a participle formed with *–ing* that is used in the progressive tenses or as an adjective

principal parts of a verb: the four forms of a verb from which all tenses of the verb can be made—namely base form, past tense, past participle, present participle (*go, went, gone, going*). Some sources do not count the present participle as a principal part of a verb.

progressive tenses: present progressive tense, present perfect progressive tense, past progressive tense, past perfect progressive tense, future progressive tense, future perfect progressive tense; verb tenses that contain a form of the verb *to be* and a present participle

pronoun: a word that can take the place of a noun

proper noun: the name of a specific person, place, or thing (see also common noun)

quantifiers: numbers and words such as *many, much, a few, a little* that function as adjectives (also called quantity adjectives)

reflexive pronoun: a pronoun ending in *–self* that is preceded by the noun or pronoun to which it refers inside the same clause

regular verb: a verb whose past tense and past participle forms end in *–d or –ed*

relative clause: an adjective clause

relative pronoun: a pronoun that connects a relative clause to the rest of the sentence (*who, that, which, whom*)

run-on sentence: an incorrect sentence with two clauses that have been put together without a proper conjunction or punctuation (also called fused sentence)

schwa: vowel sound that occurs in unstressed syllables (sof*a*, lem*o*n, grad*e*d)

second conditional: a structure used for talking about unreal or contrary-to-fact situations in the present or future which consists of a condition clause and a result clause (also called conditional type 2)

second person: subject pronouns *you* (singular) and *you* (plural)

sentence: a group of words that expresses a complete thought

separable: term used to describe a phrasal verb in which an object can separate the verb and its particle (*pick up the papers, pick the papers up*)

simple form of a verb: see base form of a verb

simple sentence: a sentence with one independent clause

singular: the form that represents one person, place, or thing

slot and filler: a system of grammatical analysis that uses sentence patterns containing slots for the target grammar item

split infinitive: a nonstandard form in which an adverb has been placed between *to* and the verb (*to never repeat*)

stranding: a structure in which a preposition does not occur next to its object (*The woman <u>whom</u> he is talking <u>to</u> is my aunt.*) (also called preposition stranding)

subject: part of a sentence excluding the predicate; the noun (or pronoun) and anything that modifies it that performs the action of the verb (*Where is <u>she</u>? Rarely is <u>she</u> late.*)

subject-auxiliary inversion: placement of the auxiliary verb before the subject that usually occurs in questions

subject pronoun: a pronoun that can function as the subject of a sentence (*I, he, she*) (see also object pronouns)

subject-verb agreement: condition in which the subject and the verb agree in number—that is, singular subjects accompany singular verbs and plural subjects accompany plural verbs

subjunctive: the mood of a verb that shows hopes, doubts, or wishes (*I recommend that you <u>be</u> given this job.*)

subordinate clause: a dependent clause

subordinating conjunction: a word that introduces an adverb clause and explains its relationship to the main part of the sentence (*after, because, while*)

suffix: a word ending that changes the meaning of the word (*sad, sadder*) or its part of speech (*sad, sadness*)

superlative: the highest level of an adjective or adverb; formed with *the most* (*the most quickly*) or *–est* (*the tallest*)

syntax: the rules that show how the words of a language can be arranged to make a phrase or sentence

tag question: a short question attached to the end of a statement to elicit confirmation from the speaker (*Apples grow on trees, <u>don't they</u>?*)

third conditional: a structure used for talking about unreal situations in the past that consists of a condition clause and a result clause (also called conditional type 3)

third person: subject pronouns *he, she, it* (singular) and *they* (plural)

transitive verb: a verb that requires a direct object (*put*)

understood subject: the subject *you* is rarely stated and is therefore said to be *understood* in imperatives (*Please open the door*).

verb: a word that shows action or state of being

verbal: a participle, infinitive, or gerund

verb tense: simply put, the time of the action or state conveyed by the verb

voiced sounds: sounds produced by moving or vibrating the vocal cords (/b/, /g/, /v/)

voiceless sounds: sounds produced without moving or vibrating the vocal cords (/p/, /k/, /f/)

wh- question: an information question that begins with a *wh-* word such as *who, what,* or *where* (compare with yes-no question)

word part: a prefix, a root (base), or a suffix of a word

yes-no question: an information question for which the answer is either *yes* or *no*

zero article: the use of no article before certain classes of words, including plural nouns for general reference, non-count nouns, abstract nouns, and names of countries

zero conditional: a structure consisting of a condition clause and a result clause that is used for talking about things that always happen or happened under certain conditions

REFERENCES

Florida Comprehensive Assessment Test (FCAT) 2007. Retrieved August 1, 2008, from: http://fcat.fldoe.org/pdf/releasepdf/07/FL07_G5M_TB-Rel_WT_C002.pdf

Folse, K. (2004a). *Intermediate reading practices: Building reading and vocabulary skills, 3rd ed.* Ann Arbor: University of Michigan Press.

_____. (2004b). *Vocabulary myths: Applying second language research to classroom teaching.* Ann Arbor: University of Michigan Press.

_____. (2006). *The art of teaching speaking: Research and pedagogy for the ESL/EFL classroom.* Ann Arbor: University of Michigan Press.

Folse, K., & Ivone, J. (1997). *First discussion starters: Speaking fluency activities for lower-level ESL/EFL students.* Ann Arbor: University of Michigan Press.

Folse, K., Mitchell, D., Smith-Palinkas, B., & Tortorella, D. (2004). *Clear grammar 4: Activities for spoken and written communication.* Ann Arbor: University of Michigan Press.

Liu, D. (2003). The most frequently used spoken American English idioms: A corpus analysis and its implications. *TESOL Quarterly, 37,* 671–700.

Selinker, L. (1972). Interlanguage. *IRAL, 10,* 209–231.

West, M. (1953). *A general service list of English words.* London: Longman.

INDEX